# Multi-Cloud Architecture and Governance

Leverage Azure, AWS, GCP, and VMware vSphere to build effective multi-cloud solutions

**Jeroen Mulder**

BIRMINGHAM—MUMBAI

# Multi-Cloud Architecture and Governance



**Commissioning Editor**: Vijin Boricha

**Acquisition Editor**: Yogesh Deokar

**Senior Editor**: Arun Nadar

**Content Development Editor**: Romy Dias

**Technical Editor**: Sarvesh Jaywant

**Copy Editor**: Safis Editing

**Project Coordinator**: Neil Dmello

**Proofreader**: Safis Editing

**Indexer**: Manju Arasan

**Production Designer**: Alishon Mendonca

First published: November 2020

Production reference: 2111220

Published by Packt Publishing Ltd.

Livery Place

35 Livery Street

Birmingham

B3 2PB, UK.

ISBN 978-1-80020-319-8

www.packt.com

*To the doctors, nurses, public health officials, and first responders who are protecting us from COVID-19.*

Packt.com

Subscribe to our online digital library for full access to over 7,000 books and videos, as well as industry leading tools to help you plan your personal development and advance your career. For more information, please visit our website.

## Why subscribe?

- Spend less time learning and more time coding with practical eBooks and Videos from over 4,000 industry professionals
- Improve your learning with Skill Plans built especially for you
- Get a free eBook or video every month
- Fully searchable for easy access to vital information
- Copy and paste, print, and bookmark content

Did you know that Packt offers eBook versions of every book published, with PDF and ePub files available? You can upgrade to the eBook version at packt.com and, as a print book customer, you are entitled to a discount on the eBook copy. Get in touch with us at customercare@packtpub.com for more details.

At www.packt.com, you can also read a collection of free technical articles, sign up for a range of free newsletters, and receive exclusive discounts and offers on Packt books and eBooks.

# Contributors

## About the author

After studying journalism, **Jeroen Mulder** (born 1970) started his career as an editor for Dutch newspapers. In 2000, he joined the IT company Origin as a communication specialist in cross-media platforms. At (Atos) Origin and Atos, he fulfilled a variety of roles, most recently as a principal architect. Since 2017, he has been working for Fujitsu, where he boarded as senior lead architect. In 2020, he was promoted to the position of head of applications and multi-cloud services for Fujitsu in the Netherlands.

Jeroen is a certified enterprise and security architect, concentrating on cloud technology. This includes the architecture for cloud infrastructure, serverless and container technology, application development, and digital transformation using various DevOps methodologies and tools.

*I want to thank my wonderful wife, Judith, for giving me the space and support I've needed to write this book, even while the COVID-19 global pandemic was raging around us. I'd also like to thank Fujitsu for granting me the opportunity and time to complete this journey. The whole Packt editing team has helped this first-time book author immensely, but I'd like to give special thanks to Romy Dias, who edited most of my work.*

# About the reviewers

**Duane Morgan** is a multi-cloud technical solutions architect with 15+ year's experience in infrastructure and has a passion for innovative next-gen, cloud-native architectures and emerging tech, such as blockchain, ML, and AI. He lives in the United States and has worked for multiple industries and tech consulting firms, including Accenture and Deloitte.

Duane began his career as a Linux administrator, and further incorporated networking, security, virtualization, and cloud computing infrastructure tech along the way, earning certification as a VMware advanced professional, AWS solutions architect, GCP professional architect, Cisco design professional, and checkpoint expert, as well as gaining blockchain certifications. Technologists in the cloud, digital, and emerging tech domains are welcome to connect with him on LinkedIn.

**Chris Rasco** has worked in nearly every facet of IT over his 20+ years in the field. He currently works for a leading global financial services firm, where he serves as one of the chief cloud architects. He also leads the technology team for the Atlanta-based vehicle history reporting start-up, VINwiki. Chris is passionate about all things technology and spends his free time working on various projects, advising other start-ups, and doing the occasional home renovation.

*I would like to thank my wife, Lauren, and my children, Ethan and Evie, for their support.*

# Packt is searching for authors like you

If you're interested in becoming an author for Packt, please visit `authors.packtpub.com` and apply today. We have worked with thousands of developers and tech professionals, just like you, to help them share their insight with the global tech community. You can make a general application, apply for a specific hot topic that we are recruiting an author for, or submit your own idea.

# Table of Contents

# 3

## Getting Connected – Designing Connectivity



# 4

## Service Designs for Multi-Cloud

# 5

# Managing the Enterprise Cloud Architecture

# Section 2 - Getting the Basics Right with BaseOps

## 6

## Designing, Implementing, and Managing the Landing Zone



## 7

## Designing Resilience and Performance

# 8

## Defining Automation Tools and Processes



# 9

## Defining and Using Monitoring and Management Tools

# Section 3 – Cost Control in Multi-Cloud with FinOps

## 10
## Managing Licenses



## 11
## Defining Principles for Resource Provisioning and Consumption

# 12

## Defining Naming Conventions and Tagging



# 13

## Validating and Managing Bills



# Section 4 – Security Control in Multi-Cloud with SecOps

# 14

## Defining Security Policies

# 15
# Implementing Identity and Access Management



# 16
# Defining Security Policies for Data



# 17
# Implementing and Integrating Security Monitoring

# Section 5 – Structured Development on Multi-Cloud Environments with DevOps

## 18
## Designing and Implementing CI/CD Pipelines



## 19
## Introducing AIOps in Multi-Cloud

# 20
# Introducing Site Reliability Engineering in Multi-Cloud



# Assessments



# Other Books You May Enjoy

# Index

# Preface

Enterprises move environments to the cloud. Applications and systems are not migrated to just one cloud platform: enterprises will use a mix of **Software as a Service** (**SaaS**), **Platform as a Service** (**PaaS**), and **Infrastructure as a Service** (**IaaS**), hosted on different platforms such as AWS, Azure, Google Cloud, and on-premises private clouds. Enterprises are adopting a multi-cloud strategy, leaving the architects and lead engineers with the challenge of how to integrate architectures and manage the enterprise cloud. Architects and engineers will learn how to design, implement, and integrate cloud solutions and set up controls for governance.

After the introduction of the concept of multi-cloud, this book covers all of the topics that architects should consider when designing systems for multi-cloud platforms. That starts with designing connectivity to and between the various platforms and creating the landing zones in Azure, AWS, and GCP.

The book is divided into four main sections, covering the following:

- Operations, including setting up and managing the landing zones that provide the infrastructure for cloud environments
- Financial operations including cost control and license management
- Security operations, covering identity and access management, securing data, security information, and event management
- Continuous delivery and deployment using DevOps, CI/CD pipelines, and new concepts such as AIOps and Site Reliability Engineering

The book contains best practices for the major providers, discusses common pitfalls and how to avoid them, and gives recommendations for methodologies and tools. Of course, a book about multi-cloud could never be complete, but this book will provide you with good guidelines to get started with architecting for multi-cloud.

## Who this book is for

This book targets architects and lead engineers who are involved in architecting multi-cloud environments. A basic understanding of cloud platforms such as AWS, Azure, and Google Cloud Platform and overall Cloud Adoption Frameworks is required.

## What this book covers

*Chapter 1, Introduction to Multi-Cloud*, provides the definition of multi-cloud and why companies have a multi-cloud strategy.

*Chapter 2, Business Acceleration Using a Multi-Cloud Strategy*, discusses how enterprises could accelerate business results by implementing a multi-cloud strategy.

*Chapter 3, Getting Connected – Designing Connectivity*, explains how to design connectivity to the platforms. All major public cloud platforms have their own connectivity technology such as Azure ExpressRoute, AWS Direct Connect, Google Dedicated Interconnect, VMware NSX, and more. The chapter provides an overview of the connectivity options.

*Chapter 4, Service Design for Multi-Cloud*, discusses governance in multi-cloud, using the Cloud Adoption Frameworks of cloud providers.

*Chapter 5, Managing the Enterprise Cloud Architecture*, covers the architecture principles of various domains, such as security, data, and applications. You will learn how to create an enterprise architecture for multi-cloud using The Open Group Architecture Framework (TOGAF).

*Chapter 6, Designing, Implementing, and Managing the Landing Zone*, describes how to design the landing zones for Azure, AWS, and Google Cloud Platform. You will learn how to define policies to manage the landing zone and get a deeper understanding of handling accounts in landing zones.

*Chapter 7, Designing Resilience and Performance*, covers solutions for backup, business continuity, and disaster recovery. How do companies increase availability and ensure that data is not lost when an outage occurs and how do they arrange disaster recovery?

*Chapter 8, Defining Automation Tools and Processes*, covers the principles of automation. You will learn how to design an automation process, starting with storing our source code in a single repository and applying version control to that code.

*Chapter 9, Defining and Using Monitoring and Management Tools*, discusses monitoring processes and tools, including the native tools that providers offer. The single pane of glass view is introduced.

*Chapter 10, Managing Licenses*, provides an introduction to financial operations in the cloud by looking at managing licenses, agreements, and the various contract options that cloud providers offer.

*Chapter 11, Defining Principles for Resource Provisioning and Consumption*, describes how enterprises can plan and deploy resources in Azure, AWS, and Google Cloud. Cost control by setting alerts and thresholds is also discussed.

*Chapter 12, Defining Naming Conventions and Tagging*, demonstrates how to create consistent naming and tagging conventions. Cost control starts with enabling the clear identification of resources and accountability for those resources.

*Chapter 13, Validating and Managing Bills*, covers methods to view and analyze costs in the consoles of Azure, AWS, and Google Cloud.

*Chapter 14, Defining Security Policies*, introduces the security frameworks of cloud providers and overall frameworks such as the **Center for Internet Security** (**CIS**) controls. You will learn how to define policies using these frameworks.

*Chapter 15, Implementing Identity and Access Management*, covers authenticating and authorizing identities. It also provides a good understanding of how to deal with least privileged accounts and the use of eligible accounts. Lastly, federation with Active Directory is discussed.

*Chapter 16, Defining Security Policies for Data*, describes how to protect data in rest and in transit. All cloud platforms have technologies to encrypt data but differ in the ways they apply encryption and store and handle keys. The chapter covers various technologies.

*Chapter 17, Implementing and Integrating Security Monitoring*, discusses the function and the need for integrated security monitoring, using SIEM (Security Information and Event Management) and SOAR (Security Orchestration, Automation, and Response).

*Chapter 18, Designing and Implementing CI/CD Pipelines*, demonstrates how CI/CD pipelines work with push and pull mechanisms and how architects can design pipelines for multi-cloud. Many enterprises have adopted DevOps as a way of working and speeding up the development of applications. In this chapter, we study the principles of DevOps with Continuous Integration and Continuous Deployment.

*Chapter 19, Introducing AIOps in Multi-Cloud,* introduces the concept of **Artificial Intelligence Operations** (**AIOps**) and how enterprises can optimize their cloud environments using AIOps.

*Chapter 20, Introducing Site Reliability Engineering in Multi-Cloud*, covers the principles of **Site Reliability Engineering** (**SRE**), Google's way of doing DevOps. SRE is about the stability of systems and keeping them available to users, even when developers apply changes at high velocity.

# To get the most out of this book

It's recommended to have a basic understanding of IT architecture and more specific cloud architecture. Architects are advised to study the foundation of enterprise architecture, using **TOGAF – The Open Group Architecture Framework**.

Since this book also covers aspects of service management as part of governance, it's also recommended to have knowledge about IT service management (ITSM). Common basic knowledge about cloud patterns in public and private clouds is assumed.

All chapters contain a *Further reading* section that provides information on more in-depth literature about topics discussed in the chapters.

# Download the color images

We also provide a PDF file that has color images of the screenshots/diagrams used in this book. You can download it here: `http://www.packtpub.com/sites/default/files/downloads/9781800203198_ColorImages.pdf`.

# Conventions used

There are a number of text conventions used throughout this book.

`Code in text`: Indicates code words in text, database table names, folder names, filenames, file extensions, pathnames, dummy URLs, user input, and Twitter handles. Here is an example: "We can simply start a project with the command `gcloud config set project` followed by the name or ID of the project itself: `gcloud config set project [Project ID]`."

A block of code is set as follows:

```
{
 "labels": {
    "environment": "development",
  … }
}
```

Any command-line input or output is written as follows:

```
gcloud organizations get-iam-policy ORGANIZATION_ID
gcloud resource-manager folders get-iam-policy FOLDER_ID
gcloud projects get-iam-policy PROJECT_ID
```

**Bold**: Indicates a new term, an important word, or words that you see onscreen. For example, words in menus or dialog boxes appear in the text like this. Here is an example: "By clicking the button **Enable Security Hub**, we will be enrolling the mentioned baselines with the named integrations."

> **Tips or important notes**
> Appear like this.

# Get in touch

Feedback from our readers is always welcome.

**General feedback**: If you have questions about any aspect of this book, mention the book title in the subject of your message and email us at `customercare@packtpub.com`.

**Errata**: Although we have taken every care to ensure the accuracy of our content, mistakes do happen. If you have found a mistake in this book, we would be grateful if you would report this to us. Please visit `www.packtpub.com/support/errata`, selecting your book, clicking on the Errata Submission Form link, and entering the details.

**Piracy**: If you come across any illegal copies of our works in any form on the Internet, we would be grateful if you would provide us with the location address or website name. Please contact us at `copyright@packt.com` with a link to the material.

**If you are interested in becoming an author**: If there is a topic that you have expertise in and you are interested in either writing or contributing to a book, please visit `authors.packtpub.com`.

# Reviews

Please leave a review. Once you have read and used this book, why not leave a review on the site that you purchased it from? Potential readers can then see and use your unbiased opinion to make purchase decisions, we at Packt can understand what you think about our products, and our authors can see your feedback on their book. Thank you!

For more information about Packt, please visit `packt.com`.

# Section 1 – Introduction to Architecture and Governance for Multi-Cloud Environments

In this section, you will understand how building and maintaining an environment using different cloud providers, concepts, and technologies requires architecture and clearly defined governance on the multi-cloud estate.

The following chapters will be covered in this section:

- *Chapter 1, Introduction to Multi-Cloud*
- *Chapter 2, Business Acceleration Using a Multi-Cloud Strategy*
- *Chapter 3, Getting Connected – Designing Connectivity*
- *Chapter 4, Service Design for Multi-Cloud*
- *Chapter 5, Managing the Enterprise Cloud Architecture*

# 1
# Introduction to Multi-Cloud

The main goal of this chapter is to develop a foundational understanding of what multi-cloud is and why companies have a multi-cloud strategy. We will focus on the main public cloud platforms of Microsoft Azure, **Amazon Web Services** (**AWS**), and **Google Cloud Platform** (**GCP**), next to the different on-premises variants of these platforms such as Azure Stack, AWS Outposts, Google Anthos, and the VMware propositions such as VMConAWS. We will also look at the benefits, how to develop to a strategy using one or more of these platforms, and what should be the very first starting point for multi-cloud.

In this chapter, we're going to cover the following main topics:

- Understanding what a true multi-cloud concept is
- A basic understanding of translating business requirements to a multi-cloud strategy
- An introduction to the main technology providers

## Understanding multi-cloud concepts

This book aims to take you on a journey along the different major cloud platforms and will try to answer one crucial question: *if my organization deploys IT systems on various cloud platforms, how do I keep control?* We want to avoid cases where costs in multi-cloud environments grow over our heads, where we don't have a clear overview of who's managing the systems, and, most importantly, where system sprawl introduces severe security risks. But before we start our deep dive, we need to agree on a common understanding of *multi-cloud* and multi-cloud concepts.

There are multiple definitions of multi-cloud, but we're using the one stated on `https://www.techopedia.com/definition/33511/multi-cloud-strategy`:

> *Multi-cloud refers to the use of two or more cloud computing systems at the same time. The deployment might use public clouds, private clouds, or some combination of the two. Multi-cloud deployments aim to offer redundancy in case of hardware/software failures and avoid vendor lock-in.*

Let's focus on some topics in that definition. First of all, we need to realize where most organizations come from: traditional data centers with physical and virtual systems, hosting a variety of functions and business applications. If you want to call this *legacy*, that's OK. But do realize that the cutting edge of today is the legacy of tomorrow. Hence, in this book, we will refer to "traditional" IT when we're discussing the traditional systems, typically hosted in physical, privately owned data centers. And with that, we've already introduced the first problem in the definition that we just gave for multi-cloud.

A lot of enterprises call their virtualized environments private clouds, whether these are hosted in external data centers or in self-owned, on-premises data centers. What they usually mean is that these environments host several business units that get billed for consumption on a centrally managed platform. You can have long debates on whether this is really using the cloud, but the fact is that there is a broad description that sort of fits the concept of private clouds.

Of course, when talking about the cloud, most of us will think of the major public cloud offerings that we have today: AWS, Microsoft Azure, and GCP. By another definition, multi-cloud is a best-of-breed solution from these different platforms, creating added value for the business in combination with this solution and/or service. So, using the *cloud* can mean either a combination of solutions and services in the public cloud, or combined with private cloud solutions.

But the simple feature of combining solutions and services from different cloud providers and/or private clouds does not make up the multi-cloud concept alone. There's more to it.

Maybe the best way to explain this is by using the analogy of the smartphone. Let's assume you are buying a new phone. You take it out of the box and switch it on. Now, what can you do with that phone? First of all, if there's no subscription with a telecom provider attached to the phone, the user will discover that the functionality of the device is probably very limited. There will be no connection from the phone to the outside world, at least not on a mobile network. An option would be to connect it through a Wi-Fi device, if Wi-Fi is available. In short, one of the first actions, in order to actually use the phone, would be making sure that it has connectivity.

Now we have a brand new smartphone set to its factory defaults and we have it connected to the outside world. Ready to go? Probably not. The user probably wants to have all sorts of services delivered to their phone, usually through the use of apps, delivered through online catalogs such as an app store. The apps themselves come from different providers and companies including banks and retailers, and might even be coded in different languages. Yet, by compiling the apps – transforming the code in such a way that it can be read and understood by different devices – they will work on different phones with different versions of mobile operating systems such as iOS or Android.

The user will also very likely want to configure these apps to their personal needs and wishes. Lastly, the user needs to be able to access the data on their phone. All in all, the phone has turned into a landing platform for all sorts of personalized services and data.

The best part is that in principle, the user of the phone doesn't have to worry about updates. Every now and then the operating system will automatically be updated and most of the installed apps will still work perfectly. It might take a day or two for some apps to adapt to the new settings, but in the end, they will work. And the data that is stored on the phone or accessed via some cloud directory will also still be available. The whole ecosystem around that smartphone is designed in such a way that from the end user's perspective, the technology is completely transparent:

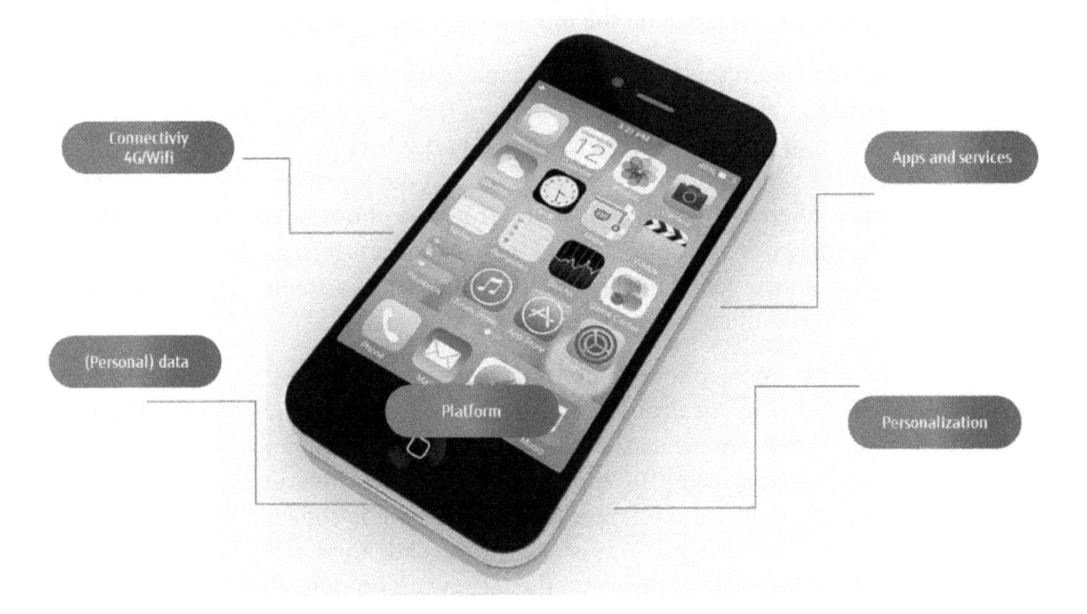


Figure 1.1 – Analogy of the smartphone—a true multi-cloud concept

Well, this is the cloud concept, where the smartphone in our analogy is the actual integrated landing zone, where literally everything comes together, providing a seamless user experience.

# Multi-cloud – more than just public and private

There's a difference between hybrid IT and multi-cloud, and there are different opinions on the definitions. One is that hybrid platforms are homogenous and multi-cloud platforms are heterogenous. *Homogenous* here means that the cloud solutions belong to one stack, for instance, the Azure public cloud with Azure Stack on premises. *Heterogenous*, then, would mean combining Azure and AWS, for instance.

For now, we will keep it very simple: a hybrid environment is combining an on-premises stack – a private cloud – with a public cloud. It is a very common deployment model within enterprises. There have been numerous reports that stated some years ago that most enterprises would transform their IT to the public cloud by 2020. It was the magic year, 2020, and a lot of organizations developed a *Cloud Strategy 2020*. It certainly did have a nice ring to it, but magical? Not really. These same organizations soon discovered that it was not that easy to migrate all of their systems to a public cloud. Some systems would have to remain on premises, for various reasons.

Two obvious reasons were security and latency. To start with the first one: this is all about sensitive data and privacy, especially concerning data that may not be hosted outside a country, or outside certain regional borders, such as the EU. Data may not be accessible in whatever way to – as an example – US-based companies, which in itself is already quite a challenge in the cloud domain. Regulations, laws, guidelines, and compliance rules often prevent companies from moving their data off premises, even though public clouds offer frameworks and technologies to protect data at the very highest level. We will discuss this later on in this book, since security and data privacy are of utmost importance in the cloud.

Latency is the second reason to keep systems on premises. One example that probably everyone can relate to is that of print servers. Print servers in the public cloud might not be a good idea. The problem with print servers is the spooling process. The spooling software accepts the print jobs and controls the printer to which the print assignment has to be sent. It then schedules the order in which print jobs are actually sent to that printer. Although print spoolers have been improved massively over the last years, it still takes some time to execute the process. Print servers in the public cloud might cause delays in that process. Fair enough: it can be done, and it will work if configured in the right way, in a cloud region close to the sending PC and receiving printer device, plus accessed through a proper connection.

You get the idea, in any case: there are functions and applications that are highly sensitive to latency. One more example: retail companies have warehouses where they store their goods. When items are purchased, the process of order picking starts. Items are labeled in a supply system so that the company can track how many of a specific item are still in stock, where the items originate from, and where they have to be sent. For this functionality, items have a barcode or QR code that can be scanned with RFID or the like. These systems have to be close to the production floor in the warehouse or – if you do host them in the cloud – accessible through really high-speed, dedicated connections on fast, responsive systems.

These are pretty simple and easy-to-understand examples, but the issue really comes to life if you start thinking about the medical systems used in operating theatres, or the systems controlling power plants. It is not that useful to have an all-public cloud, cloud-first, or cloud-only strategy for quite a number of companies and institutions. That goes for hospitals, utility companies, and also for companies in less critical environments.

Yet, all of these companies discovered that the development of applications was way more agile in the public cloud. Usually, that's where cloud adoption starts: with developers creating environments and apps in public clouds. It's where hybrid IT is born: the use of private systems in private data centers for critical production systems that host applications with sensitive data that need to be on premises for latency reasons, while the public cloud is used to enable the fast, agile development of new applications.

## Multi-cloud as a true mixed zone

From the analogy with the smartphone, it should be clear that with multi-cloud we're also talking about services, much more than just hosting systems in a private data center and a public cloud. This would mainly be **Infrastructure as a Service** (**IaaS**), where organizations run virtualized and non-virtualized physical machines in that private cloud and virtual machines in the public cloud.

In multi-cloud setups, we are also talking about **Platform as a Service** (**PaaS**) and **Software as a Service** (**SaaS**). In multi-cloud setups, it can become much more of a mixed mode, just as on our smartphone that holds data on the device itself stores and retrieves data from other sources, connecting remotely to apps or hosting the apps on the phone, making use of services through APIs in that app.

In multi-cloud, we can do exactly the same, leveraging functions and applications running on virtual machines on a private system with SaaS functionality connecting over the internet from a third-party provider, for example, to execute specific data analytics. The data may still reside in a private environment, where the runtime environment is executed from a public cloud source, or the other way around in the case of running models against data lakes that are fed with data streams from different sources, where the results of these models are delivered to private systems.

That is what multi-cloud is all about. Leveraging applications, data, and services from different cloud platforms and using different delivery models such as PaaS and SaaS. It might include hybrid IT, but it is more of a mixed mode in order to create more added value for the business by combining and optimizing cloud solutions. The next question is: how can organizations create that optimum combination of services, and by doing so, create that added value for their business?

Let's dive into the definition of a real cloud strategy.

# Setting out a real strategy for multi-cloud

The most common reason for organizations to adopt a multi-cloud strategy is a classic one: to avoid lock-in. Organizations simply do not want to be locked into one platform or a single service. However, that isn't really a strategy. It would be more the outcome of a strategy.

A strategy emerges from the business and the business goals. Business goals, for example, could include the following:

- Creating more brand awareness
- Releasing products to the market faster
- Improving profit margins

Business strategies often start with increasing revenue as a business goal. In all honesty: that should indeed be a goal, otherwise you'll be out of business before you know it. The strategy should focus on *how* to generate and increase revenue. We will explore more on this in the next chapter.

How do you get from business goals to defining an IT strategy? That is where enterprise architecture comes into play. The most used framework for enterprise architecture is **TOGAF, The Open Group Architecture Framework**. The core of TOGAF is the **ADM** cycle, short for **Architecture Development Method**. Also, in architecting multi-cloud environments, ADM is applicable. The ground principle of ADM is **B-D-A-T**: the cycle of **business, data, applications, technology**. This perfectly matches the principle of multi-cloud, where the technology should be transparent. Businesses have to look at their needs, define what data is related to those needs, and how this data is processed in applications. This is translated into technological requirements and finally drives the choice of technology, integrated into the architecture vision as follows:

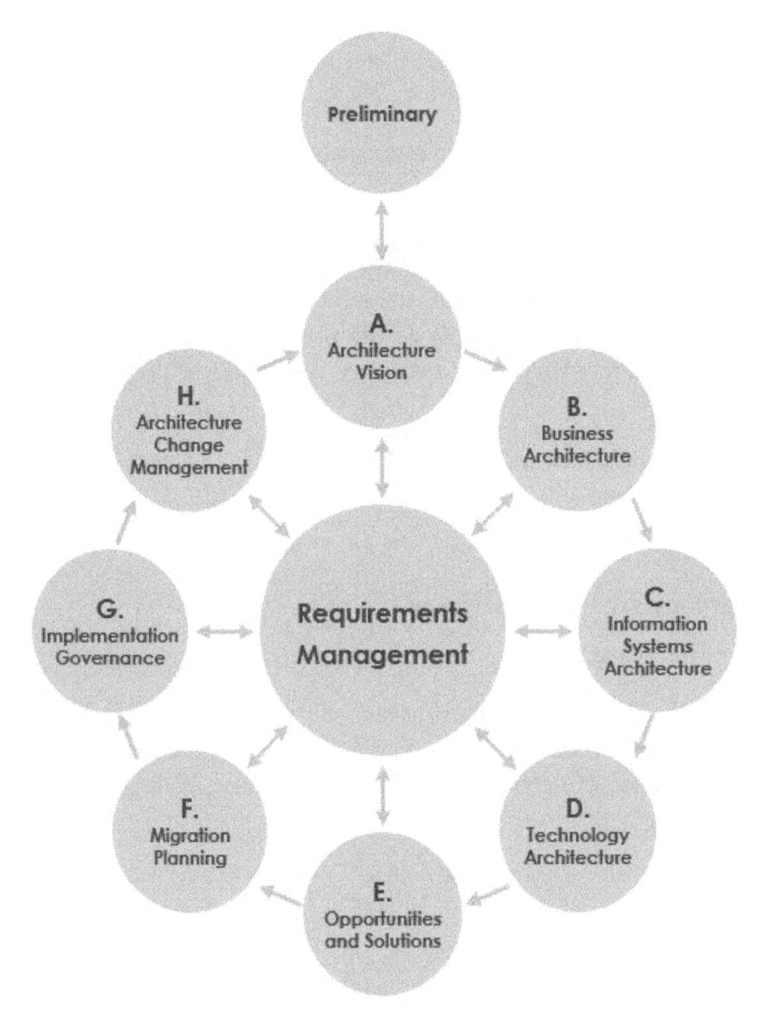


Figure 1.2 – The ADM cycle in the TOGAF enterprise architecture framework

> **Note**
>
> This book is not about TOGAF, but it does make sense to have knowledge of enterprise architecture and, for that matter, TOGAF is the leading framework for that. TOGAF is published and maintained by The Open Group. More information can be found at `https://www.opengroup.org/togaf`.

The good news is that multi-cloud offers organizations flexibility and freedom of choice. That also brings a risk: lack of focus. Therefore, we need a strategy. Most companies adopt cloud and multi-cloud strategies since they are going through a process of transformation from a more-or-less traditional environment to a digital future. Is that relevant for all businesses? The answer is yes. In fact, more and more businesses are coming to the conclusion that IT is a core activity.

Times have changed over the last few years in that respect. At the end of the nineties and even at the beginning of the new millennium, a lot of companies outsourced their IT since it was not considered to be a core activity. That has changed dramatically over the last 10 years or so. Every company is a software company – a message that was rightfully quoted by Microsoft CEO Satya Nadella, following an earlier statement by the father of software quality, Watts S. Humphrey, who already claimed at the beginning of the millennium that every business is a software business.

Both Humprey and Nadella are right. Take banks as an example: they have been transforming to become more and more like IT companies. They deal with a lot of data streams, execute data analytics, and develop apps for their clients. A single provider might not be able to deliver all of the required services, hence these companies look for a multi-cloud, best-of-breed solutions to fulfill these requirements.

These best-of-breed solutions might contain traditional workloads with a classic server-application topology, but will more and more shift to the use of PaaS, SaaS, container, and serverless solutions in an architecture that is more focused on microservices and cloud native. This has to be considered when defining a multi-cloud strategy: a good strategy would not be "cloud first" but "cloud fit."

## What would be the best solution for my business requirements?

Of course, businesses evolve and so does technology. This is translated into a roadmap, driven by the business but including the technical possibilities and opportunities over a certain period of time. Such a roadmap will typically have a number of stages, beginning with a current state of the environment, shifting to industry-standard solutions that are immediately available, to a future state with cutting-edge technology. In the next chapter, we will have a closer look at the definition of such a roadmap and how it helps accelerate the business.

We have to make one final remark when it comes to setting out a multi-cloud strategy. It concerns security: that should always be a key topic in every strategy and in every derived roadmap. All of the public clouds and leading cloud technology providers have adopted security-by-design principles and offer a wide variety of very good solutions for information security. It's fair to say that, for example, Azure, AWS, and GCP are likely the best-secured platforms in the world. But it doesn't take away your responsibility to control security standards, frameworks, principles, and rules that specifically apply for your type of business. Using multi-cloud for hosting businesses might lower the risk of attacks taking down the whole environment, but it does also add complexity. *Section 4, Security Control in Multi-Cloud with SecOps*, of this book is all about **SecOps—security operations**.

# Introducing the main players in the field

We have been talking about public and private clouds. Although it's probably clear what we commonly understand by these terms, it's probably a good idea to have a very clear definition of both. We adhere to the definition as presented on the Microsoft website: the public cloud is defined as *computing services offered by third-party providers over the public internet, making them available to anyone who wants to use or purchase them*. The private cloud is defined as *computing services offered either over the internet or a private internal network and only to select users instead of the general public*. There are many more definitions, but these serve our purpose very well.

## Public clouds

In the public cloud, the best-known providers are AWS, Microsoft Azure, GCP, and public clouds that have OpenStack as their technological foundation. An example of the latter one is Rackspace. These are all public clouds that fit the definition that we just gave, but there are also some major differences.

AWS and Azure have a common starting ground, however – both platforms evolved from making storage publicly available over the internet. At AWS, it started with a storage service called the **Simple Storage Solution**, or **S3**. Azure also started off with storage.

AWS, Azure, and GCP all offer a wide variety of managed services to build environments, but they all differ very much in the way you apply the technology. In short: the concepts are more or less alike, but under the hood, these are completely different beasts. It's exactly this that makes managing multi-cloud solutions complex.

There are many more public cloud offerings, but these are usually not fit for all purposes. Major software manufacturers including Oracle and SAP also have public cloud offerings available, but these are really tailored to hosting the specific software solutions of these companies. Nonetheless, they are part of the multi-cloud landscape, since a lot of enterprises use, for instance, enterprise resource planning software from SAP and/or data solutions from Oracle. These companies are also shifting their solutions more and more to fully scalable cloud environments, where they need to be integrated with systems that reside on premises or in other clouds. In some cases, these propositions have evolved to full clouds, such as OCI by Oracle. Over the course of this book, we will address these specific propositions, since they do require some special attention. Just think of license management, as an example.

In this book, we will mainly focus on the major players in the multi-cloud portfolio, as represented in the following diagram:

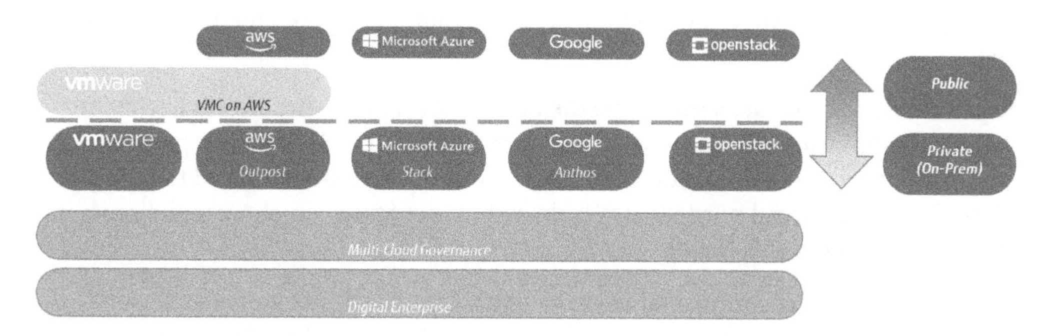


Figure 1.3 – An example multi-cloud portfolio: the main players

> **Note**
>
> We have been discussing Microsoft Azure, AWS, GCP, and OpenStack as the main public cloud platforms. As said, there are more platforms, but in this book, we are limiting our discussions to the main players in the field and adhering to the platforms that have been identified as leaders by Gartner and Forrester.

So far, we've looked at the differences between private and public clouds and the main players in the public cloud domain. In the next section, we will focus on the leading private propositions for enterprises.

## Private clouds

Most companies are planning to move, or are actually in the midst of moving, their workloads to the cloud. In general, they have a selected number of major platforms that they choose to host the workloads: Azure, AWS, GCP, and that's about it. Fair enough, there are more platforms, but the three mentioned are the most dominant ones, and will continue to be so throughout the forthcoming decades, if we look at analysts' reports.

As we already found out in the previous paragraphs, in planning for and migrating workloads to these platforms, organizations also discover that it does get complex. Even more important, there are more and more regulations in terms of compliance, security, and privacy that force these companies to think twice before they bring our data onto these platforms. And it's all about the data, in the end. It's the most valuable asset in any company – next to people.

The solution: instead of bringing data to the cloud, we're taking the cloud to the data – again. Over the last few years, we've seen a new movement where the major cloud providers have started stepping into domains where other companies were still traditionally dominant; companies such as storage providers and system integrators. The new reality is that public cloud providers are shifting more and more into the on-premises domain.

In the private cloud, VMware seems to be the dominant platform, next to environments that have Microsoft with Hyper-V technology as their basis. Yet, Microsoft is pushing customers more and more to consumption in Azure and where systems need to be kept on premises, they have a broad portfolio available with Azure Stack, which we will discuss in a bit more detail later in this chapter.

Especially in European governmental environments, OpenStack still seems to do very well, to avoid having data controlled or even viewed by American-based companies. However, the adoption and usage of OpenStack seems to be declining.

In this chapter, we will look briefly at both VMware and OpenStack as private stack foundations. After that, we'll have a deeper look at AWS Outposts and Google Anthos. Basically, both propositions extend the public clouds of AWS and GCP into the privately owned data center. Outposts is an appliance that comes as a preconfigured rack with compute, storage, and network facilities. Anthos by Google is more a set of components that can be utilized to specifically host container platforms in on-premises environments using the **Google Kubernetes Engine** (**GKE**). Finally, in this chapter, we will have a look at the Azure Stack portfolio.

## VMware

In essence, VMware is still a virtualization technology. It started off with the virtualization of x86-based physical servers, enabling multiple virtual machines on one physical host. Later, VMware introduced the same concept to storage with **vSAN** (**virtualized SAN**) and **NSX** (**network virtualization and security**) that virtualizes the network, making it possible to adopt micro-segmentation in private clouds. The company has been able to constantly find ways to move along with the shift to the cloud – as an example, by developing a proposition together with AWS where VMware private clouds can be seamlessly extended to the public cloud.

Today, VMware is also a strong player in the field of containerization with **Pivotal Kubernetes Services** (**PKS**) and container orchestration with Tanzu Mission Control. Over the last few years, the company has strengthened its position in the security domain, again targeting the multi-cloud stack. Basically, VMware is trying to become the spider in the multi-cloud web by leveraging solutions on top of the native public cloud players.

## OpenStack

There are absolutely benefits to OpenStack. It's a free and open source software platform for cloud computing, mostly used as IaaS. OpenStack uses KVM as its main hypervisor, although there were more hypervisors available for OpenStack. It was—and still is, with a group of companies and institutions—popular since it offered a stable, scalable solution while avoiding vendor lock-in on the major cloud and technology providers. Major integrators and system providers such as IBM and Fujitsu adopted OpenStack in their respective cloud platforms, Bluemix and K5 (decommissioned internationally in 2018).

However, although OpenStack is open source and can be completely tweaked and tuned to specific business needs, it is also complex, and companies find it cumbersome to manage. Most of these platforms do not have the richness of solutions that, for example, Azure, AWS, and GCP offer to their clients. Over the last few years, OpenStack seems to have lost its foothold in the enterprise world, yet it still has a somewhat relevant position and certain aspects are therefore considered in this book.

## AWS Outposts

Everything you run on the AWS public cloud, you can now run on an appliance, including **Elastic Compute Cloud** (EC2), **Elastic Block Store** (**EBS**), databases, and even Kubernetes clusters with **Elastic Kubernetes Services** (**EKS**). It all seamlessly integrates with the **virtual private cloud** (**VPC**) that you would have deployed in the public cloud, using the same APIs and controls. That is, in a nutshell, AWS Outposts: the AWS public cloud on premises.

One question might be what this means for the **VMC** (**VMware on Cloud**) on AWS proposition that both VMware and AWS have in their portfolio.

> **Note**
>
> You can buy VMConAWS through VMware or through AWS.

VMConAWS actually extends the private cloud to the public cloud, based on HCX by VMware. VMware uses bare metal instances in AWS to which it deploys vSphere, vSAN storage, and NSX for software-defined networking.

You can also use AWS services on top of the configuration of VMConAWS through integration with AWS. Outposts works exactly the other way around: bringing AWS to the private cloud.

## Google Anthos

Anthos brings Google Cloud – or more accurately, the Google Kubernetes Engine – to the on-premises data center, just as Azure Stack does for Azure and Outposts for AWS, but it focuses on the use of Kubernetes as a landing platform, moving and converting workloads directly into containers using GKE. It's not a standalone box, such as Azure Stack or Outposts. The solution runs on top of virtualized machines using vSphere, and is more a PaaS solution. Anthos really accelerates the transformation of applications to more cloud-native environments, using open source technology including Istio for microservices and Knative for the scaling and deployment of cloud-native apps on Kubernetes.

> **Tip**
>
> More information on the specifics of Anthos can be found at `https://cloud.google.com/anthos/gke/docs/on-prem/how-to/vsphere-requirements-basic`.

## Azure Stack

And then there is the Azure Stack portfolio with Stack HCI, Hub, and Edge.

The most important feature of Azure Stack **Hyperconverged Infrastructure** (**HCI**) is that it can run "disconnected" from Azure. To put it very simply: HCI works like the commonly known branch office server. Basically, HCI is a box that contains compute power, storage, and network connections. The box holds Hyper-V-based virtualized workloads that you can manage with Windows Admin Center. So, why would you want to run this as Azure Stack then? Well, Azure Stack HCI also has the option to connect to Azure services, such as Azure Site Recovery, Azure Backup, and Azure Monitoring.

It's a very simple solution that only requires Microsoft-validated hardware, the installation of Windows Server 2019 Datacenter Edition, plus Windows Admin Center and optionally an Azure account to connect to specific Azure cloud services.

Pre-warning: it might get a bit complicated from this point onward: Azure Stack HCI is also the foundation underneath Azure Stack Hub (side note: all Azure products are based on Windows Server 2019). Yet, Hub is a different solution. Whereas you can run Stack HCI *standalone*, Hub as a solution is integrated with the Azure public cloud – and that's really a different ballgame. It's the reason why you can't upgrade HCI to Hub.

Azure Stack Hub is really the on-premises extension of the Azure public cloud. Almost everything you can do in the public cloud of Microsoft, you could also deploy on Hub: from VMs to apps, all managed through the Azure portal or even PowerShell. It all really works like Azure, including things such as configuring and updating fault domains. Hub also supports having an availability set with a maximum of three fault domains to be consistent with Azure. This way you can create high availability on Hub just as you would in Azure.

The perfect use case for Hub and the Azure public cloud would be to do development on the public cloud and move production to Hub, should apps or VMs need to be hosted on premises for compliance reasons. The good news is that you can configure your pipeline in such a manner that development and testing can be executed on the public cloud and run deployment of the validated production systems, including desired state configuration, on Hub. This will work fine since both *entities* of the Azure platform use the Azure resource providers in a consistent way.

There are a few things to be aware of, though. The compute resource provider will create its own VMs on Hub. In other words: it does not *copy* the VM from the public cloud to Hub. The same applies to network resources. Hub will create its own network features such as load balancers, vNets, and **network security groups** (**NSGs**). As for storage, Hub allows you to deploy all storage forms that you would have available on the Azure public cloud, such as blob, queue, and tables. Obviously, we will discuss all of this in much more detail in this book, so don't worry if a number of terms don't sound familiar at this time.

One last Stack product is Stack Edge. Previously, Microsoft sold Azure Stack Edge as **Data Box**: it's still part of the Data Box family. Edge makes it easy to send data to Azure. As Microsoft puts it on their website: *Azure Stack Edge acts as a network storage gateway and performs high-speed transfers to Azure*. The best part? You can manage Edge from the Azure portal. Sounds easy, right?

Hold on. There's more to it. It's—again—called Kubernetes. Edge runs containers to enable data analyses, perform queries, and filter data at edge locations. Therefore, Edge supports Azure VMs and **Azure Kubernetes Services** (**AKS**) clusters that you can run containers on. Edge, for that matter, is quite a sophisticated solution since it also integrates with **Azure Machine Learning** (**AML**). You can build and train machine learning models in Azure, run them in Azure Stack Edge, and send the datasets back to Azure. For this, the Edge solution is equipped with the **FPGAs** (**Field Programmable Gate Arrays**) and **GPUs** (**Graphics Processing Units**) required to speed up building and (re)training the models.

Having said this, the obvious use case comes with the implementation of data analytics and machine learning where you don't want raw data to be uploaded to the public cloud straight away.

## Azure Arc

There's one more feature that needs to be discussed at this point and that's Azure Arc, launched at Ignite 2019. Arc allows you to connect non-Azure machines to Azure and manage these non-Azure workloads as if they were fully deployed on Azure itself.

If you want to connect a machine to Arc, you need to install an agent on that machine. It will then get a resource ID and become part of a resource group in your Azure tenant. However, this won't happen until you've configured some settings on the network side of things and registered the appropriate resource providers (`Microsoft.HybridCompute` and `Microsoft.GuestConfiguration`). Yes, this does require proficient PowerShell skills. If you perform the actions successfully, then you can have non-Azure machines managed through Azure. In practice, this means that you can add tagging and policies to these workloads. That sort of defines the use case: managing the non-Azure machines in line with the same policies as the Azure machines. These do not necessarily have to be on premises. That's likely the best part of Arc: it also works on VMs that are deployed in AWS.

With that last remark on Arc, we've come to the core of the multi-cloud discussion, and that's integration. All of the platforms that we studied in this chapter have advantages, disadvantages, dependencies, and even specific use cases. Hence, we see enterprises experimenting with and deploying workloads in more than one cloud. That's not just to avoid cloud vendor lock-in: it's mainly because there's not a "one size fits all" solution.

In short, it should be clear that it's really not about *cloud first*. It's about getting *cloud fit*, that is, getting the best out of an ever-increasing variety of cloud solutions. This book will hopefully help you to master working with the mix of these solutions.

# Summary

In this chapter, we've learned what a true multi-cloud concept is. It's more than a hybrid platform, comprising different cloud solutions such as IaaS, PaaS, SaaS, containers, and serverless in a platform that we can consider to be a best-of-breed mixed zone. You are able to match a solution to the given business strategy. Here, enterprise architecture comes into play: business requirements are leading at all times and enabled by the use of data, applications, and lastly by the technology. Enterprise architecture methodologies such as TOGAF are good frameworks for translating a business strategy into an IT strategy, including roadmaps.

In the last section, we looked at the various main players in the field of private and public clouds. Over the course of this book, we will further explore the portfolios of these providers and discuss how we can integrate solutions, really mastering the multi-cloud domain.

In the next chapter, we will further explore the enterprise strategy and see how we can accelerate business innovation using multi-cloud concepts.

# Questions

1. Although we see a major move to public clouds, companies may have good reasons to keep systems on premises. Compliance is one of them. Please name another argument for keeping systems on premises.
2. The market for public clouds is dominated by a couple of major players, with AWS and Azure being recognized as leaders. They share a common history. How did these platforms start?
3. Google Anthos is described as an on-premises solution, but it differs very much from other on-premises solutions such as Azure Stack or AWS Outposts. What are the two main differences compared to the other propositions?

# Further reading

- The article entitled *Every business is a software business* by João Paulo Carvalho, available at `https://quidgest.com/en/articles/every-business-software-business/`
- *Multi-Cloud for Architects*, by Florian Klaffenbach and Markus Klein from Packt

# 2
# Business Acceleration Using a Multi-Cloud Strategy

This chapter discusses how enterprises could accelerate business results by implementing a multi-cloud strategy. Every cloud platform/technology has its own benefits and by analyzing business strategies and defining what cloud technology fits best, enterprises can really take advantage of multi-cloud. A strategy should not be "cloud first" but "cloud fit." But before we get into the technical strategy and the actual cloud planning, all the way up to even developing and implementing Twelve-Factor Apps, we have to explore the business or enterprise strategy and the financial aspects that drive this strategy. In this chapter, we're going to cover the following main topics:

- Analyzing the enterprise strategy for the cloud
- Mapping the enterprise or business strategy to a technology roadmap
- Keeping track of technology changes in multi-cloud environments
- Exploring the different cloud strategies and how they help accelerate the business

Let's get started!

# Analyzing the enterprise strategy for the cloud

Before we get into a cloud strategy, we need to understand what an enterprise strategy is and how businesses define such a strategy. As we learned in the previous chapter, every business should have the goal of generating revenue and earning money. That's not really a strategy. The strategy is defined by how they generate money with the products the business makes or the services that they deliver.

A good strategy comprises a well-thought-out balance between timing, access to and use of data, and something that has to do with braveness – daring to make decisions at a certain point of time. That decision has to be based on – you guessed it – proper timing, planning, and the right interpretation of data that you have access to. If a business does this well, they will be able to accelerate growth and, indeed, increase revenue. The overall strategy should be translated into use cases.

> **Important Note**
>
> The success of a business is obviously not only measured in terms of revenue. There are a lot of parameters that define success as a whole and for that matter, these are not limited to just financial indicators. Nowadays, companies rightfully also have social indicators to report on. Think of sustainability and social return. However, a company that does not earn money, one way or the other, will likely not last long.

Let's start with time and timing. At the time of writing (March 2020), the world is holding its breath because of the breakout of the COVID-19 virus, better known as coronavirus. Governments are trying to contain the virus by closing schools, universities, forbidding businesses to organize meetings and big events, and even locking down whole regions and entire countries. A lot of people are being confronted by travel restrictions. The breakout is severely impacting the global economy and a number of companies are struggling to survive because of a steep decline in orders. Needless to say, Spring 2020 wasn't a good time to launch new products, unless the product was related to containing the virus or curing people that were contaminated.

That's exactly what happened. Companies that produced, for example, protective face masks started skyrocketing, but companies relying on production and services in locked-down regions saw their markets plummeting at breathtaking speed. In other words, time is one of the most important factors to consider when planning for business acceleration. Having said that, it's also one of the most difficult things to grasp. No-one plans for a virus outbreak. However, it was a reason for businesses not to push for growth at that time. The strategy for a lot of companies probably changed from pushing for growth to staying in business by, indeed, trying to drive the costs down. Here, we have our first parameter in defining a cloud strategy: cost control and, even more so, cost agility.

The second one is access to and use of data. It looks like use of data in business is something completely new, but of course nothing could be further from the truth. Every business in every era can only exist by the use of data. We might not always consider something to be data since it isn't always easy to identify, especially when it's not stored in a central place. This is an odd example, but let's look at Mozart. We're talking mid to late 18th century, ages before the concept of computing was invented. In his era, Mozart was already acknowledged as a great musician since he studied all the major streams of music in his era, from piano pieces to Italian opera. He combined this with a highly creative gift of translating this into original music. All this existing music was data; the gift to translate and transform the data to new music could be perceived as a form of analytics.

Data is the key. It's not only about raw data that a business (can) have access to, but also in analyzing that data. Where are my clients? What are their demands? Under what circumstances are these demands valid and what makes these demands change? How can I respond to these changes? How much time would I have to fulfill the initial demands and apply these changes if required? This all comes from data. Nowadays, we have a lot of data sources. The big trick is how we can make these sources available to a business – in a secured way, with respect to confidentiality, privacy, and other compliance regulations.

Finally, business decisions do take braveness. With a given time and all the data of the world, you need to be bold enough to make a decision at a certain point. Choose a direction and go for it. To quote the famous Canadian ice hockey player Wayne Gretzky:

*"You miss 100 percent of the shots you don't take."*

The million-dollar question is: how can multi-cloud help you in making decisions and fulfilling the enterprise strategy? At the enterprise level, there are four domains that define the strategy at the highest level (source: *University of Virginia, Strategic Thinking and Action, April 2018*):

- Industry position
- Enterprise core competence
- Long-term planning
- Financial structure

In the following sections, we will address these four domains.

## Industry position

The first thing a company should do is analyze what its position is in the industry in which it is operating. Or, if it's entering the market, what position it could initially gain and hold. Analysts often use Michael Porter's five forces model, which comprises competitive rivalry, threat of new entrants, threat of substitutes, bargaining power of suppliers, and the bargaining power of customers. To execute this model, obviously, a lot of data needs to be investigated. This is not a one-time thing. It's a constant analysis of the industry's position. Outcomes will lead to change in the enterprise's strategy. Here's the big thing: in this era of digitalization, these changes occur at an ever-increasing speed and that requires the business to be agile. This model can be depicted with the following diagram:

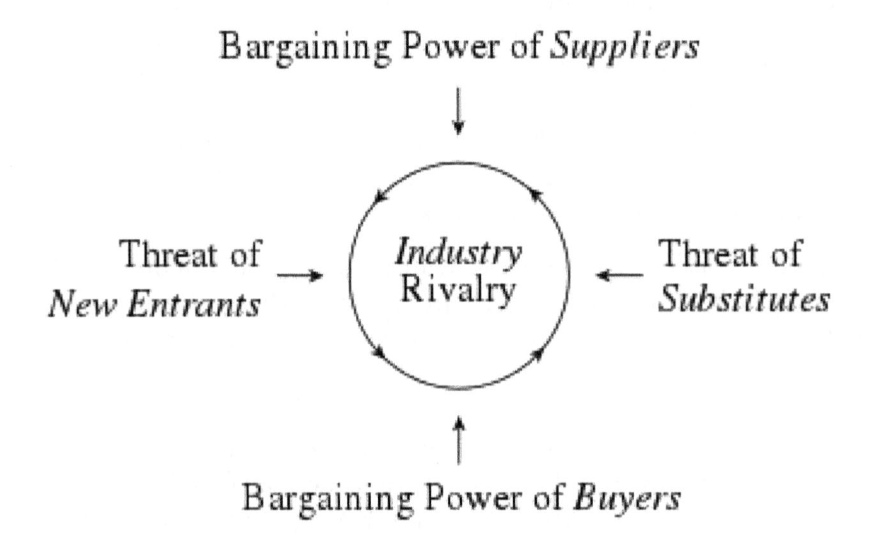


Figure 2.1 – Porter's five forces model

Let's, for example, look at one the model's parameters: the threat of substitutes. Today, customers can easily switch products or services. What's cool today is completely out tomorrow. Plus, as an outcome of globalization of markets and the fact that we are literally globally connected through the internet, customers can easily find cheaper products or services. They're no longer bound to a specific location to purchase products or services. They can get it from all around the world. Therefore, the threat of a substitute is more than substantial and requires a constant drive to adapt the strategy to mitigate this threat. It's all about the time to market. Businesses need platforms that enable that level of agility.

## Enterprise core competence

With the behavior of markets and businesses themselves constantly changing, it's not easy to define the core competency. Businesses have become more and more T-shaped over the last few decades. We've already looked at banks. It's not that long ago that the core activity of a bank was to keep the money of consumers and companies safe on a deposit, issue loans, and invest and enable payments. For that, banks needed financial experts. That has all changed. Their core business still employs the aforementioned factors, but now, delivering these services is done in a completely digitized way with internet sites – even more so with mobile apps. Banks need software developers and IT engineers to execute their core activities. The bank has become T-shaped.

## Long-term planning

When a business is clear on their position and their core competencies, they need to set out a plan. Where does the company want to be in 5 years from now? This is the most difficult part. Based on data and data analytics, it has to determine how the market will develop and how the company can anticipate change. Again, data is the absolute key, but also the swiftness in which companies can change course since market demands do change extremely rapidly.

## Financial structure

Finally, any business needs a clear financial structure. How is the company financed and how are costs related to different business domains, company divisions, and its assets? As we will find out as part of financial operations, the cloud can be of great help in creating fine-grained insight into financial flows throughout a business. With correct and consistent naming and tagging, you can precisely pinpoint how much cost a business generates in terms of IT consumption. The best part of cloud models is that the foundation of cloud computing is *pay for what you use*. Cloud systems can *breathe* at the same frequency as the business itself. When business increases, IT consumption can increase. When business drops, cloud systems can be scaled down and with that, they generate lower costs, whereas traditional IT is way more static.

So, nothing is holding us back from getting our business into the cloud. It does take quite some preparation in terms of (enterprise) architecture. In the following section, we will explore this further.

# Fitting cloud technology to business requirements

We are moving business into the cloud because of the required agility and, of course, to control our costs.

The next two questions will be: with what and how? Before we explore the how and basically the roadmap, we will discuss the first question: with what? A cloud migration plan starts with business planning, which covers business processes, operations, finance, and lastly the technical requirements. We will have to evaluate the business demands and the IT fulfillment of these requirements.

When outsourcing contracts, the company that takes over the services performs a so-called due diligence. As per its definition, due diligence is *"a comprehensive appraisal of a business undertaken by a prospective buyer, especially to establish its assets and liabilities and evaluate its commercial potential"* (source: `https://www.lexico.com/en/definition/due_diligence`). This may sound way too heavy of a process to get a cloud migration asset started, yet it is strongly recommended as a business planning methodology. Just replace the words *prospective buyer* with the words *cloud provider* and you'll immediately get the idea behind this.

## Business planning

Business planning involves the following items:

- Discovery of the entire IT landscape, including applications, servers, network connectivity, storage, APIs, and services from third-party providers.
- Mapping IT landscape components to business-critical or business-important services.
- Identification of commodity and shared services and components in the IT landscape.
- Evaluation of IT support processes with regards to commodity services and critical and important business services. This includes the levels of automation in the delivery of these services.

One really important step in the discovery phase that's crucial to creating a good mapping to cloud services is evaluating the service levels and performance indicators of applications and IT systems. Service levels and **key performance indicators** (**KPIs**) will be applicable to applications and underlying IT infrastructure based on specific business requirements. Think of indicators like metrics of availability, durability, and levels of backup including RTO/RPO specifications, requirements for **business continuity** (**BC**), and **disaster recovery** (**DR**). Are systems monitored 24/7 and what are the support windows? These all need to be considered. As we will find out, service levels and derived service-level agreements might be completely different in cloud deployments, especially when looking at PaaS and SaaS, where the responsibility of platforms (PaaS) and even application (SaaS) management is largely transferred to the solution provider.

If you ask a CFO what the core system is, he/she will probably answer that financial reporting is absolutely critical. It's the role of the enterprise architect to challenge that. If the company is a meat factory, then the financial reporting system is not the most critical system. The company doesn't come to a halt when financial reporting can't be executed. The company does, however, come to a halt when the meat processing systems stop; that immediately impacts the business. What would that mean in planning the migration to cloud systems? Can these processing applications be hosted from cloud systems? And if so, how? Or maybe, when?

## Financial planning

We're not there yet. After the business planning phase, we also need to perform financial analyses. After all, one of the main rationales to move to cloud platforms is cost control. Be aware: moving to the cloud is not at all times a matter of lowering costs. It's about making your costs *responsive* to actual business activity. Setting up a business case to decide whether cloud solutions are an option from a financial perspective is, therefore, not an easy task. Public cloud platforms offer **Total Cost of Ownership** (**TCO**) calculators.

TCO is indeed the total cost of owning a platform and it should include all direct and indirect costs. What do we mean by that? When calculating the TCO, we have to include the costs that are directly related to systems that we run: costs for storage, network components, compute, licenses for software, and so on. But we also need to consider the costs of the labor that is involved in managing systems for engineers, service managers, or even the accountant that evaluates the costs related to the systems. These are all costs; however, these indirect costs are often not taken into the full scope. Especially in the cloud, these should be taken into account. Think of this: what costs can be avoided by, for example, automating service management and financial reporting?

So, there's a lot to cover when evaluating costs and the financial planning driving architecture. Think of the following:

- All direct costs related to IT infrastructure and applications. This also includes hosting and housing costs; for example, (rental of) floor space and power.
- Costs associated with all staff working on IT infrastructure and applications. This includes contractors and staff from third-party vendors working on these systems.
- All licenses and costs associated with vendor or third-party support for systems.
- Ideally, these costs can be allocated to a specific business process, division, or even (groups of) users so that it's evident where IT operations costs come from.

Why is this all important in drafting the architecture? A key financial driver to start a cloud journey is the shift from CapEx to OpEx. In essence, **CapEx – capital expenditure** – concerns upfront investments; for example, in buying physical machines or software licenses. These are often one-off investments, of which the value is depreciated over an economic life cycle. **OpEx – operational expenditure** – is all about costs related to day-to-day operations and for that reason is much more granular. Usually, OpEx is divided into smaller budgets that teams need to have to perform their daily tasks. In most cloud deployments, the client really only pays for what they're using. If resources sit idle, these can be shut down and costs will stop. A single developer could – if mandated for this – decide to spin up an extra resource if required.

That's true for a **pay-as-you-go** (**PAYG**) deployment, but we will discover that a lot of enterprises have environments for which it's not feasible to run in full PAYG. You simply don't shut down instances of large, critical ERP systems. So, for these systems, businesses will probably use more stateful resources, such as reserved instances that are fixed for a longer period. For cloud providers, this means a steady source of income for a longer time and therefore they offer reserved instances against lower tariffs or to apply discounts. The downside is that companies can be obliged to pay for these reserved resources upfront. Indeed, that's CapEx. Cutting a long story short: the cloud is not OpEx by default.

In *Chapter 11*, *Defining Principles for Resource Provisioning and Consumption*, on FinOps, we will explore this in much more detail, including the pitfalls.

## Technical planning

Finally, we've gotten to technical planning, which starts with a foundation architecture. You can plan to build an extra room on top of your house, but you'll need to build the house first – assuming that it doesn't exist. The house needs a firm foundation that can hold the house in the first place, but can also *carry* the extra room in the future. The room needs to be integrated with the house – for one, since it would really be completely useless to have it *standalone* from the rest of the house. It all takes good planning. Good planning requires information – data, if you like.

In the world of multi-cloud, you don't have to figure it out all by yourself. The major cloud providers all have reference architectures, best practices, and use cases that will help you plan and build the foundation, making sure that you can fit in new components and solutions almost all the time.

That's exactly what we are going to do in this book: plan, design, and manage a future-proof multi-cloud environment. In the next section, we will take our first look at the foundation architecture.

## IT4IT

The problem that many organizations face is controlling the architecture from the business perspective. IT4IT is a framework that helps organizations with that. It's complementary to TOGAF and, for this reason, also issued as a standard by The Open Group. IT4IT is also complementary to ITIL, where ITIL provides best practices for IT service management. IT4IT provides the foundation to enable IT service management processes with ITIL. It is meant to align and manage the digital enterprise. It deals with the challenges that these enterprises have, such as the ever-speeding push for embracing and adopting new technology. The base concept of IT4IT consists of four value streams:

- **Strategy to portfolio**: The portfolio contains technology standards, plans, and policies. It deals with the IT demands from the business and mapping these demands to IT delivery. An important aspect of the portfolio is project management, to align business and IT.
- **Requirements to deploy**: This stream focuses on creating and implementing new services or adapting existing services, in order to reach a higher standard of quality or to obtain a lower cost level. According to the documentation of The Open Group, this is complementary to methods such as Agile Scrum and DevOps.

- **Request to fulfill**: To put it very simply, this value stream is all about making life easy for the end customers of the deployed services. As companies and their IT adopt structures such as IaaS, PaaS, and SaaS, this stream enables service brokering by offering and managing a catalog and with that, speeds up fulfilling new requests being made by end users.
- **Detect to correct**: Services will change. This stream enables monitoring, management, remediation, and other operational aspects that drive these changes.

The following diagram shows the four streams of IT4IT:

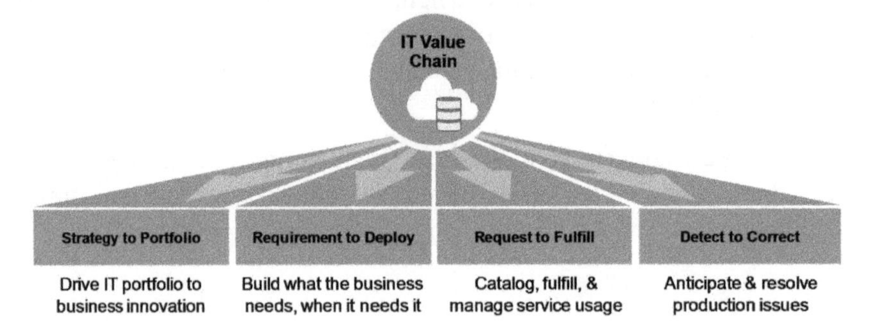


Figure 2.2 – IT4IT value streams (The Open Group)

In this section, we learned how to map business requirements and plans to an IT strategy. Frameworks such as IT4IT are very valuable in successfully executing this mapping. In the next section, we will focus on how cloud technology fits into the business strategy.

# Keeping track of cloud developments – focusing on the business strategy

Any cloud architect or engineer will tell you that it's hard to keep up with developments. Just for reference, AWS and Azure issue over 2,000 features in their respective cloud platforms over just 1 year. These can be big releases or just some minor tweaks.

What would be major releases of features? Think about Azure Arc, Bastion, or Lighthouse in Azure, the absolutely stunning quantum computing engine Braket, and the open source operating system for container hosts known as Bottlerocket, in AWS. In GCP, we got Cloud Run in 2019, which combines serverless technology with containerized application development and a dozen open source integrations for data management and analytics. In March 2020, VMware released vSphere 7, including a lot of cool cloud integration features such as VMware Cloud Foundation 4 with Pacific, as well as Tanzu Kubernetes Grid, a catalog powered by Bitnami and Pivotal Labs to deploy and manage containers in multi-cloud environments.

It is a constant stream of innovations: big, medium, and small. There is, however, two overall movements: from software to service and from virtual machine to container. We will discuss this further in the last section of this chapter.

Anyway, try to keep up with all these innovations, releases, and new features. It's hard, if not undoable.

And it gets worse. It's not only the target cloud platforms, but also a lot of tools that we need to execute in order to migrate or develop applications. Just have a look at the Periodic Table of DevOps by XebiaLabs, which is continuously refreshed with new technology and tools.

In the final part of this book, we will have a deeper look at cutting-edge technology with AIOps, a rather new domain in managing cloud platforms but one that's gathering a lot of ground right now. Over the last year, a number of tools have been launched in this domain, from the well-known Splunk, which already had a settled name in monitoring, to relative newcomers on the market such as StackState (founded in 2015) and Moogsoft (founded in 2011). AIOps has been included in the Periodic Table:

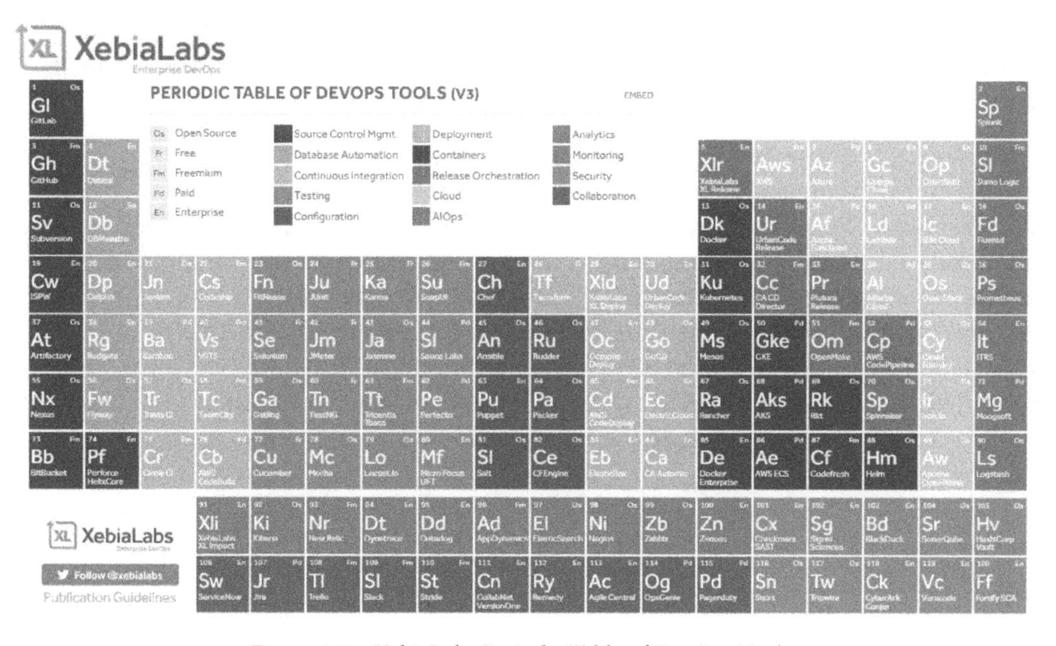


Figure 2.3 – XebiaLabs Periodic Table of DevOps Tools

> **Tip**
>
> Check out the interactive version of XebiaLab's Periodic Table of DevOps Tools at `https://xebialabs.com/periodic-table-of-devops-tools/`. For a full overview of the cloud-native landscape, refer to the following web page, which contains the *Cloud Native Trail Map of the Cloud Native Computing Foundation*: `https://landscape.cncf.io/`.

There's no way to keep up with all the developments. A business needs to have focus and that should come from the strategy that we discussed in the previous sections. In other words, don't get carried away with all the new technology that is launched.

There are three important aspects that have to be considered when managing cloud architecture: the foundation architecture, the cost of delay, and the benefit of opportunity.

## Foundation architecture

Any architecture starts with a baseline, something that we call a foundation architecture or even a reference architecture. TOGAF comprises two domains: the technical reference model and the standards information base. The technical reference model describes the generic platform services. In a multi-cloud environment, that would be the basic setup of the used platforms.

As an example, in Azure, the common practice is to have a hub and spoke-model deployed. The hub contains generic services that are applicable to all workloads in the different spokes. Think of connectivity gateways to the outside world (on-premises or the internet), bastion hosts or jump servers, management servers, and centrally managed firewalls. Although the terminology in AWS and GCP differ greatly from Azure, the base concepts are more or less the same. Within the cloud service, the client creates a virtual data center – a subscription or a **virtual private cloud** (**VPC**) – that is owned and managed by the client. In that private section of the public cloud, a transit zone is created, as well as the segments that can hold the actual workloads:

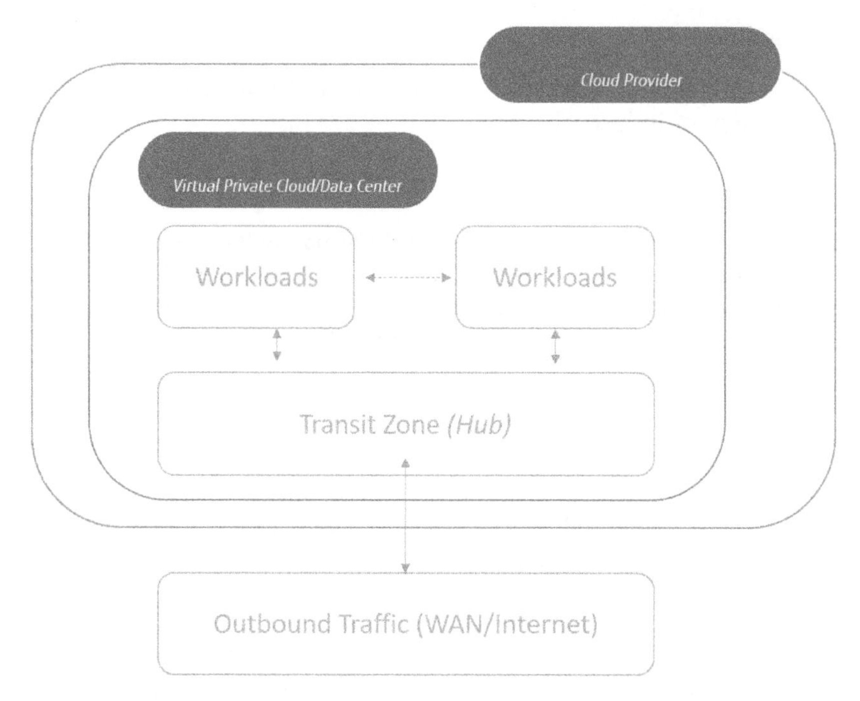


Figure 2.4 – High-level diagram of a virtual private cloud/data center

Now, how this **virtual data center** (**VDC**) or subscription is set up has to be described in the foundation architecture. That will be the baseline. Think about it: you wouldn't rebuild the physical data center every time a new application was introduced, would you? The same rule applies for a virtual data center that we're building on top of public cloud services.

The Standards Information Base is the second component that makes up our foundation architecture. We follow TOGAF: it provides a database of standards that can be used to define particular services and other components of an organization-specific architecture that is derived from the TOGAF Foundation Architecture. In short, it's a library that contains the standards. For multi-cloud, this can be quite an extensive list. Think about the following:

- Network protocol standards for communication and network security, including level of segmentation and network management.
- Standards for virtual machines; for example, type and versions of used operating systems.
- Standards for storage and storage protocols. Think of types of storage and use cases, as offered by cloud providers.

- Security baselines.
- Compliancy baselines; for example, frameworks that are applicable to certain business domains or industry branches.

> **Tip**
>
> As a starting point, you can use the **Standards Information Base (SIB)** provided by The Open Group. It contains a list of standards that might be considered when drafting the architecture for multi-cloud. The SIB is published on `https://www6.opengroup.org/sib.html`.

## Cost of delay

We have our foundation or reference architecture set out, but now, our business gets confronted with new technologies that have been evaluated: what will they bring to the business? As we mentioned previously, there's no point in adopting every single new piece of tech that is released. The magic word here is *business case.*

A business case determines whether the consumption of resources supports a specific business need. A simple example is as follows: a business consumes a certain bandwidth on the internet. It can upgrade the bandwidth, but that will take an investment. That is out-of-pocket cost, meaning that the company will have to pay for that extra bandwidth. However, it may help workers to get their job done much faster. If workers can pick up more tasks just by the mere fact that the company invests in a faster internet connection, the business case will, at the end, be positive, despite the investment.

If market demands occur and businesses do not adopt to this fast enough, a company might lose part of the market and with that lose revenue. Adopting new technology or speeding up the development of applications to cater for changing demands will lead to costs. These costs correspond with missing specific timing and getting services or products to the market in time. This is what we call cost of delay.

Cost of delay, as a piece of terminology, was introduced by Donald Reinertsen in his book *The Principles of Product Development Flow*, published by *Celeritas Publishing, 2009*:

> *"We need Cost of Delay to evaluate the cost of queues, the value of excess capacity, the benefit of smaller batch sizes, and the value of variability reduction. Cost of Delay is the golden key that unlocks many doors. It has an astonishing power to totally transform the mindset of a development organization."*

Although it's mainly used as a financial parameter, it's clear that the cost of delay can be a good driver for evaluating the business case in adopting cloud technology. Using and adopting consumption from cloud resources that are more or less agile by default can mitigate the financial risk of cost of delay.

## Benefit of opportunity

If there's something that we could call a cost of delay, there should also be something that we could call a benefit of opportunity. Where cost of delay is a risk in missing momentum because changes have not been adopted timely enough, a benefit of opportunity is really about accelerating the business by exploring future developments and related technology. It can be very broad. As an example, let's say a retailer is moving into banking by offering banking services using the same app that customers use to order goods. Alternatively, think of a car manufacturer, such as Tesla, moving into the assurance business.

The accessibility and even ease of use of cloud services enable these shifts. In marketing terms, this is often referred to as blurring. In the traditional world, that same retailer would really have much more trouble offering banking services to its customers, but with the launch of SaaS in financials apps, from a technological point of view, it's not that hard to integrate this into other apps. Of course, this is not considering things such as the requirement of a banking license from a central financial governing institution and having to adhere to different financial compliancy frameworks. The mere message is that with cloud technologies, it has become easier for businesses to explore other domains and enable a fast entrance into these domains, from a pure technological perspective.

The best example? AWS. Don't forget that Amazon was originally an online bookstore. Because of the robustness of their ordering and delivery platform, Amazon figured out that they also could offer storage systems "for rent" to other parties. After all, they had the infrastructure, so why not fully capitalize on that? Hence, S3 storage was launched as the first AWS cloud service and by all means, it got AWS to become a leading cloud provider, next to the core business of retailing. That was truly a benefit of opportunity.

With that, we have discussed how to define a strategy. We know where we're coming from and we know where we're heading to. Now, let's bring everything together and make it more tangible by creating the business roadmap and finally mapping that roadmap to our cloud strategy, thereby evaluating the different deployment models and cloud development stages.

# Creating a comprehensive business roadmap

There are stores filled with books on how to create business strategies and roadmaps. This book absolutely doesn't have any pretention to wrap this all into just one paragraph. However, for an enterprise architect, it is important to understand how the business roadmap is evaluated:

1. The mission and vision of the business, including the strategic planning of how the business will target the market and deliver its goods or services.
2. Objectives, goals, and direction. Again, this includes planning in which the business sets out when and how specific goals are met and what it will take to meet the objectives in terms of resources.
3. **Strengths, weaknesses, opportunities, and threats** (**SWOT**). The SWOT analysis shows whether the business is doing the right things at the right time or that a change in terms of the strategy is required.
4. Operational excellence. Every business has to review how it is performing on a regular basis. This is done through KPI measurements: is the delivery on time? Are the customers happy (**customer satisfaction—CSAT**)?

Drivers for a business roadmap can be very diverse, but the most common ones are as follows:

- Revenue
- Gross margin
- Sales volume
- Number of leads
- Time to market
- Customer satisfaction
- Brand recognition
- Return on investment

These are shared goals, meaning that every division or department should adhere to these goals and have their planning aligned with the business objectives. These goals end up in the business roadmap. These can be complex in the case of big enterprises, but also rather straightforward, as shown in the following screenshot:

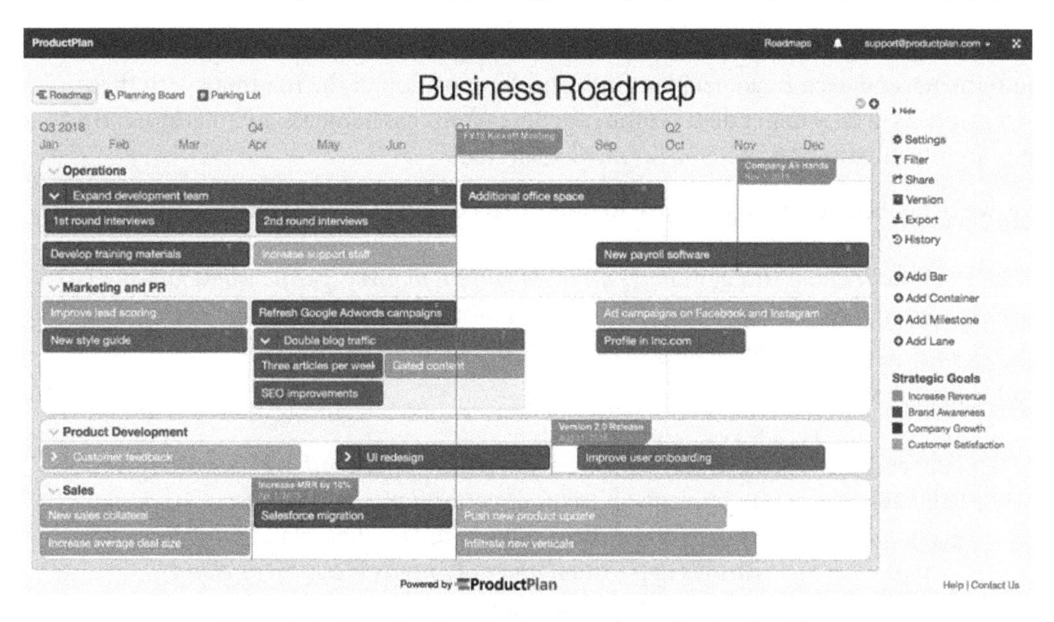


Figure 2.5 – Template for a business roadmap (by ProductPlan)

IT is the engine that drives everything: development, resource planning, CRM systems, websites for marketing, and customer apps. And these days, the demands get more challenging; the life cycle is getting shorter and the speed is getting faster. Where IT was the bottleneck for ages, it now has all the technology available to facilitate the business in every aspect. IT is no longer considered a cost center, but a business enabler.

# Mapping the business roadmap to the cloud-fit strategy

Most businesses start their cloud migrations from traditional IT environments, although a growing number of enterprises are already quite far into cloud-native development too. We don't have to exclude the other: we can plan to migrate our traditional IT to the cloud, while already developing cloud-native applications in the cloud itself. Businesses can have separate cloud tracks, running at different speeds. It makes sense to execute the development of new applications in cloud environments using cloud-native tools. Next, the company can also plan to migrate their traditional systems to a cloud platform. There are a number of ways to do that. We will be exploring these, but also look at drivers that start these migrations. The key message is that it's likely that we will not be working with one roadmap. Well, it might be one roadmap, but one that is comprised of several tracks with different levels of complexity and different approaches, at different speeds.

There was a good reason that we have been discussing the enterprise strategy, business requirements, and even financial planning. The composition of the roadmap with these different tracks is fully dependent on the outcome of our assessments and planning. And that is architecture too, let there be no mistake on that.

Here, we're quoting technology leader Radhesh Balakrishnan of RedHat:

> *"A multi-cloud strategy allows an organization to meet specific workload or application requirements – both technically and commercially – by consuming cloud services from several cloud providers."*

He adds the following:

> *"Not every department, team, business function, or application or workload will have similar requirements in terms of performance, privacy, security, or geographic reach for their cloud. Being able to use multiple cloud providers that meet their various application and data needs is critical as cloud computing has become more mature and mainstream."*

These business requirements will drive the cloud migration approach. We recognize the following technological strategies:

- **Rehost**: The application, data, and server are migrated as-is to the target cloud platform. This is also referred to as **lift and shift**. The benefits are often quite low. This way, we're not taking any advantage of cloud-native services.
- **Replatform**: The application and data are migrated to a different target technology platform, but the application architecture remains as-is. For example, let's say an application with a SQL database is moved to PaaS in Azure with Azure SQL Server. The architecture of the application itself is not changed.
- **Repurchase**: In this scenario, an existing application is replaced by SaaS functionality. Note that we are not really repurchasing the same application. We are replacing it with a different type of solution.
- **Refactor**: Internal redesign and optimization of the existing application. This can also be a partial refactoring where only parts of an application are modified to operate in an optimized way in the cloud. In the case of full refactoring, the whole application is modified for optimization in terms of performance and at lower costs. Refactoring is, however, a complicated process. Refactoring usually targets PaaS and SaaS.
- **Rearchitect**: This is one step further than refactoring and is where the architecture of an application, as such, is not modified. This strategy does comprise an architectural redesign to leverage multi-cloud target environments.

- **Rebuild**: In this strategy, developers build a new cloud-native application from scratch, leveraging the latest tools and frameworks.
- **Retire**: This strategy is valid if an application is not strategically required for the business going forward. When an application is retired, data needs to be cleaned up and often archived, before the application and underlying infrastructure is decommissioned. Of course, an application can be retired as a follow-up strategy when the functionality in an application is refactored, rearchitected, rebuilt, or repurchased.
- **Retain**: Nothing changes. The existing applications remain on their current platform and are managed as-is.

It's not easy to predict the outcomes of the business case as many parameters can play a significant role. Benchmarks conducted by institutes such as Gartner point out that total costs savings will vary between 20 and 40 percent in the case of rehost, replatform, and repurchase. Savings may be higher when an application is completely rearchitected and rebuilt. Retiring an application will lead to the highest savings, but then again, assuming that the functionality provided by that application is still important for a business, it will need to fulfill that functionality in another way – generating costs for purchase, implementation, adoption, and/or development. This all has to be taken into account when drafting the business case and choosing the right strategy.

At a high level, we can plot these strategies into three stages:

- **Traditional**: Although organizations will allow developers to work with cloud-native tools directly on cloud platforms, most of them will still have traditional IT. When migrating to the cloud, they can opt for two scenarios:

  - Lift and shift systems "as-is" to the cloud and start the application's modernization in the cloud.

  - Modernize the applications before migrating them to the target cloud platform.

  A third scenario would be a mix between the first two.
- **Rationalized**: This stage is all about modernizing the applications and optimizing them for usage in the target cloud platform. This is the stage where PaaS and SaaS are included to benefit from cloud-native technology.
- **Dynamic**: This is the final stage where applications are fully cloud-native and therefore completely *dynamic*: they're managed through agile workstreams using **continuous improvement** and **development** (**CI/CD**), fully scalable using containers and serverless solutions, and fully automated using the principle of everything as code, making IT as agile as the business requires.

It all comes together in the following model. This model suggests that the three stages are sequential, but as we have already explained, this doesn't have to be the case:

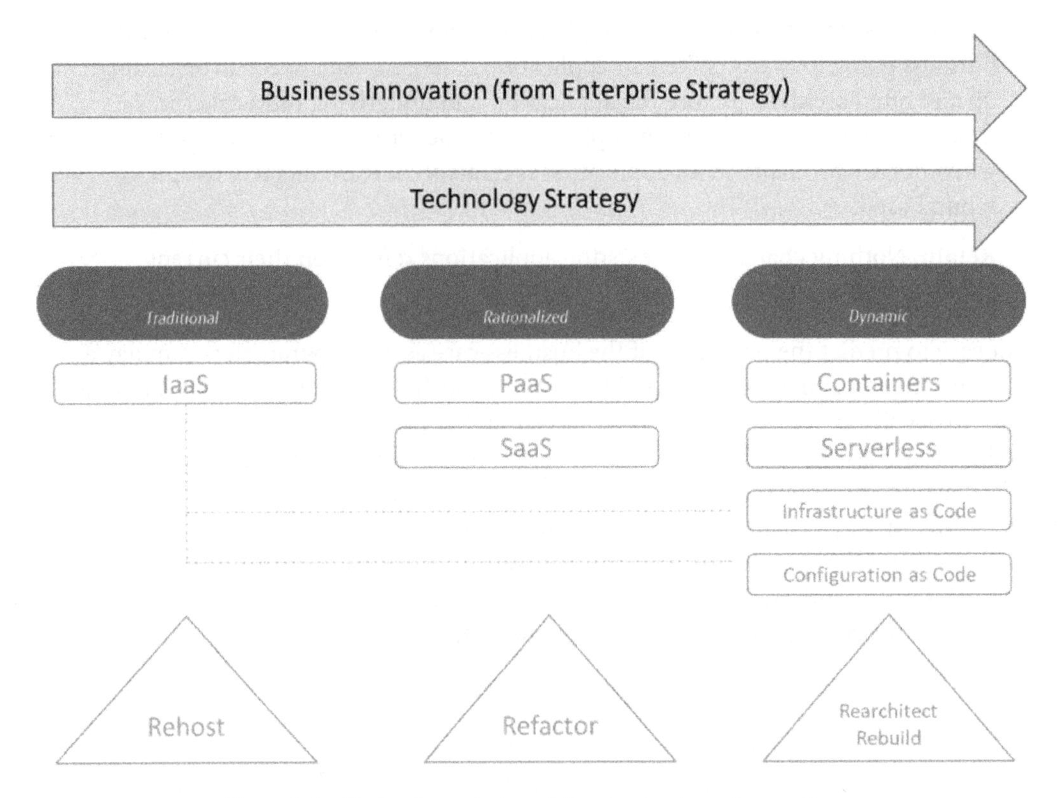


Figure 2.6 – Technology strategy following business innovation

This model shows three trends that will dominate the cloud strategy in the forthcoming years:

- **Software to service**: Businesses do not have to invest in software anymore, nor in infrastructure to host that software. Instead, they use software that is fully managed by external providers. The idea is that businesses can now focus on fulfilling business requirements using this software, instead of having to worry about the implementation details and hosting and managing the software itself. It's based on the economic theory of endogenous growth, which states that economic growth can be achieved through developing new technologies and improvements in production efficiency. Using PaaS and SaaS, this efficiency can be sped up significantly.

- **VM to container**: Virtualization brought a lot of efficiency to data centers. Yet, containers are even more efficient in utilizing compute power and storage. Virtual machines still use a lot of system resources with a guest operating system, where containers utilize the host operating system and only some supporting libraries on top of that. Containers tend to be more flexible and due to that have become increasingly popular in distributing software in a very efficient way. Even large software providers such as SAP already distribute and deploy components using containers. SAP Commerce is supported using Docker containers, running instances of Docker images. These images are built from special file structures mirroring the structures of the components of the SAP Commerce setup.
- **Serverless computing**: Serverless is about writing and deploying code without worrying about the underlying infrastructure. Developers only pay for what they use, such as processing power or storage. It usually works with triggers and events: an application registers an event (a request) and triggers an action in the backend of that application; for instance, retrieving a certain file. Public cloud platforms offer different serverless solutions: Azure Functions, AWS Lambda, and Google Knative. It offers a maximum amount of scalability against maximum cost control. One remark has to be made at this point: although serverless concepts will become more and more important, it will not be technically possible to fit everything into serverless propositions.

## The Twelve-Factor App

One final topic that we need to discuss in this chapter is the Twelve-Factor App. It's where everything comes together.

The Twelve-Factor App is a methodology for building modern apps, ready for deployment on cloud platforms, abstracted from server infrastructure. In other words, the Twelve-Factor App adopts the serverless concept. Because of the high abstraction layers, the app can scale without changing the architecture or development methodology. The format of the Twelve-Factor App is based on the book *Patterns of Enterprise Application Architecture and Refactoring*, by *Martin Fowler*, published by *Addison-Wesley Professional*, 2005. Although it was written in 2005 – lightyears ago in terms of cloud technology – it is still very relevant in terms of its architecture.

The 12 factors are as follows:

1. **Code base**: One code base is tracked in revision control, with many deployments (including Infrastructure as Code).
2. **Dependencies**: Explicitly declare and isolate dependencies.
3. **Config**: Store config in the environment (Configuration as Code).

4. **Backing services**: Treat backing services as attached resources.
5. **Build, release, run**: Strictly separate build and run stages (pipeline management, release trains).
6. **Processes**: Execute the app as one or more stateless processes.
7. **Port binding**: Export services via port binding.
8. **Concurrency**: Scale out via the process model.
9. **Disposability**: Maximize robustness with fast startup and graceful shutdown.
10. **Dev/prod parity**: Keep development, staging, and production as similar as possible.
11. **Logs**: Treat logs as event streams.
12. **Admin processes**: Run admin/management tasks as one-off processes.

More on these principles can be found at `https://12factor.net`. We will find out that a number of these 12 principles are also captured in different frameworks and embedded in the governance of multi-cloud environments, such as DevOps and Site Reliability Engineering.

# Summary

In this chapter, we explored methodologies that are used to analyze enterprise or business strategies and mapped these to a cloud technology roadmap. We also learned that it is close to impossible to keep track of all the new releases and features that are launched by cloud and technology providers. We need to determine what our business goals and objectives are and define a clear architecture that is as future-proof as possible, yet agile enough to adopt new features if the business demands this.

Enterprise architectures using frameworks such as TOGAF and IT4IT help us in designing and managing a multi-cloud architecture that is robust but also scalable in every aspect. We have also seen how IT will shift along with the business demands coming from traditional to rationalized and dynamic environments using software as a service, containers, and serverless concepts, eventually maybe adopting the Twelve-Factor methodology.

In the next chapter, we will be getting a bit more technical and will look at cloud connectivity and networking.

# Questions

1. In this chapter, we discussed the metrics surrounding availability, durability, levels of backup (including RTO/RPO specifications), and the requirements for **business continuity** (**BC**) and **disaster recovery** (**DR**). What do we call these metrics or measurements?
2. What would be the first thing to define if we created a business roadmap?
3. In this chapter, we discussed cloud transformation strategies. Rehost and replatform are two of them. Name two more.
4. In this chapter, we identified two major developments in the cloud market. The growth of serverless concepts is one of them. What is the other major development?

# Further reading

- The Twelve-Factor App (`https://12factor.net`)
- *How Competitive Forces Shape Strategy*, by Michael E. Porter, Harvard Business Review

# 3
# Getting Connected – Designing Connectivity

The first – and likely the main – challenge in multi-cloud is getting connectivity right. All major public cloud platforms have their own connectivity technology, such as Azure ExpressRoute, AWS Direct Connect, Google Dedicated Interconnect, VMware NSX, and more. They also all have their own connectivity requirements and specifics. No wonder one of the major reasons for failure is connectivity issues. Enterprises really must have a detailed network plan before they start building multi-cloud environments. In this chapter, we're going to cover the following main topics:

- Exploring the different connectivity concepts, such as VPN and direct connections to the major clouds of Microsoft Azure, AWS, and Google Cloud Platform
- Designing a network topology addressing cost, security, internet access, and service levels
- Understanding different network protocols in the cloud

# Connectivity is king – connectivity concepts in multi-cloud

Let's get back to our smartphone for a minute. Remember? You take it out of the box, and you want to start working with it. The first thing to do is to connect the phone to the outside world. It's the same with connecting to the cloud. You can make a subscription in any cloud provider and start working in it, but a company would want to have an enrollment to which its workers can securely connect from the company's domain to a specific cloud service. Basically, there are three options to enable that connection: a **virtual private network** (**VPN**), direct connections, and using a fully managed broker service from a telecom company or connectivity partner. In the next sections, we are going to have an in-depth look at each of these options.

## VPN

One of the most used technologies is the VPN. In essence, a VPN is a tunnel using the internet as a carrier. It connects from a certain IP address or IP range to the IP address of a gateway server in the public cloud.

Before we get into this, you have to be aware of what a public cloud is. If you as a business deploy services in Azure, AWS, **Google Cloud Platform** (**GCP**), or any other public cloud (remember: there are more public clouds, such as OpenStack, IBM Cloud, and Alibaba, and the basic concepts are all more or less the same), you are extending your data center to that cloud. It therefore needs a connection between your data center and that extension in the public cloud. The easiest and probably also the most cost-efficient way to get that connection fast is through a VPN. The internet is already there, and all you would have to do in theory is assign IP addresses or the IP range that is allowed to communicate to that extension, creating a tunnel. That tunnel can be between an office location (site) or from just one user connecting to the cloud. The latter is something we refer to as a point-to-site VPN.

In the public cloud itself, that connection needs to terminate somewhere, unless you want all resources to be opened up for connectivity from the outside. That is rarely the case and it's certainly not advised. Typically, a business would want to protect workloads from direct and uncontrolled outside connections. When we're setting up VPNs, we need to configure a zone in the public cloud with a gateway where the VPN terminates. From the gateway, the traffic can be routed to other resources in the cloud, using routing rules and tables in the cloud. It works the same way as in a traditional data center where we would have a specific connectivity zone or even a **demilitarized zone** (**DMZ**) before users actually get to the systems. The following architecture shows the basic principle of a VPN connection to a public cloud:

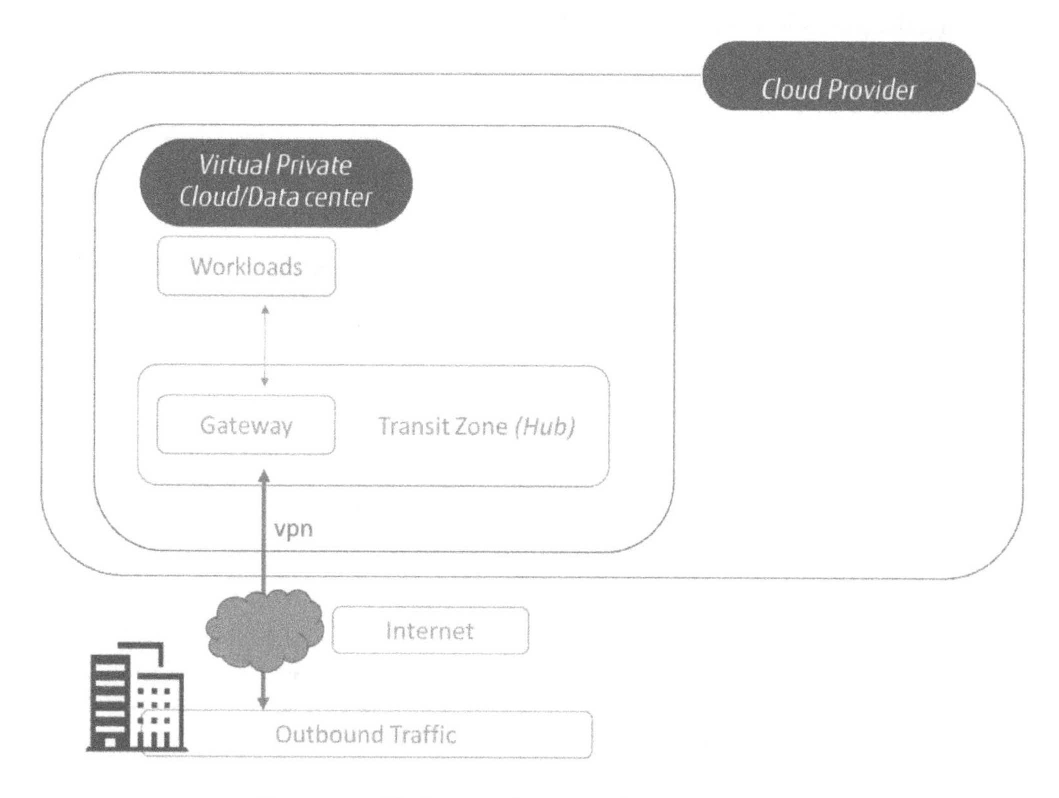


Figure 3.1 – The basic architecture of VPN connectivity

In the next section, we will look at the connectivity concepts and architectures for the three major platforms: Azure, AWS, and Google Cloud.

## Designing connectivity in Azure

Microsoft offers Azure VPN Gateway to connect an on-premises data center site-to-site to Azure. This solution uses IPsec and **Internet Key Exchange** (**IKE**) as protocols.

To connect resources from anywhere to your environment in Azure, a point-to-site solution is provided. Azure supports the following protocols on point-to-site VPN connections:

- OpenVPN, based on **Secure Socket Layer** (**SSL**) and **Transport Layer Security** (**TLS**) protocols.
- **Secure Socket Tunneling Protocol** (**SSTP**): This is Microsoft proprietary and is only supported on Microsoft Windows devices.
- IKEv2, based on IPsec. This can also be used by Apple Mac devices.

The following diagram shows the different VPN connections that Azure offers:

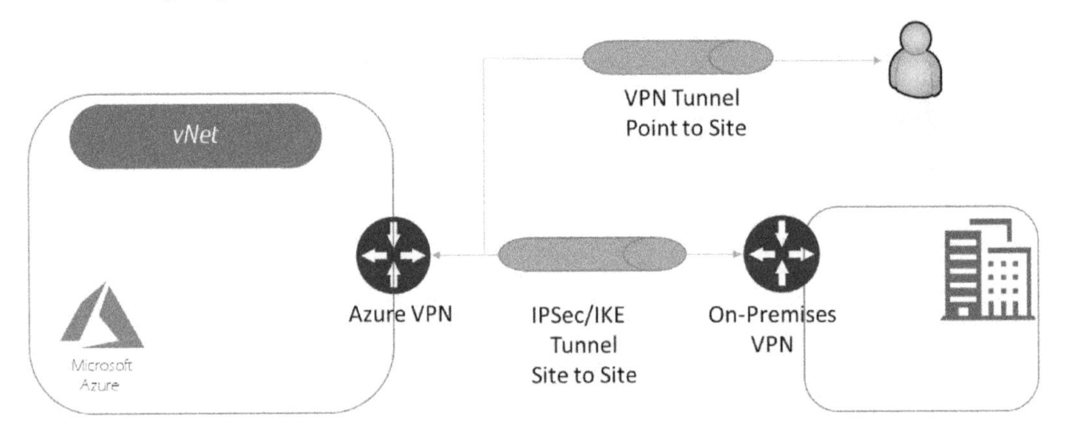


Figure 3.2 – Point-to-site and site-to-site VPN setup in Azure

As said, setting up a VPN is fast and relatively easy.

The first thing to do is set up the **virtual network (vNet)**gateway in Azure. This can be done through the Azure portal (`https://portal.azure.com`), given that you already have a subscription—without an Azure subscription, the page will generate an error. The gateway should be in its own vNet, so you need to specify that vNet. Since the gateway will serve as the endpoint of the VPN in Azure, it will need an IP address: that can be an existing IP address that your business already has for resources in Azure or a public IP address.

The next thing to do is to connect the gateway to your on-premises environment. You will need a device to do that: a VPN appliance, a network device that provides a number of features, such as routing, firewall, authentication, authorization, and strong encryption. Think of Citrix NetScaler, F5 BIG-IP, Brocade ServerIron, Juniper DX, or Cisco ACE—just to name a few popular solutions on the enterprise market. Most major hardware vendors do have virtual appliances as well, for environments with less intensive throughputs on networks. We should also mention pure software-defined networking, such as NSX by VMware.

You will need to specify the newly set up Azure gateway connection and tell the VPN appliance that traffic pointing to the gateway over the specified address range is allowed to be routed to Azure. All other traffic should be denied. With this, we have a tunnel created, sending data from a particular address (range) to a designated address that is specified and terminating on an endpoint in Azure, the vNet gateway. From the gateway, the traffic will be internally routed through the Azure subscription of your business.

The following diagram shows the position of the Azure VPN gateway:

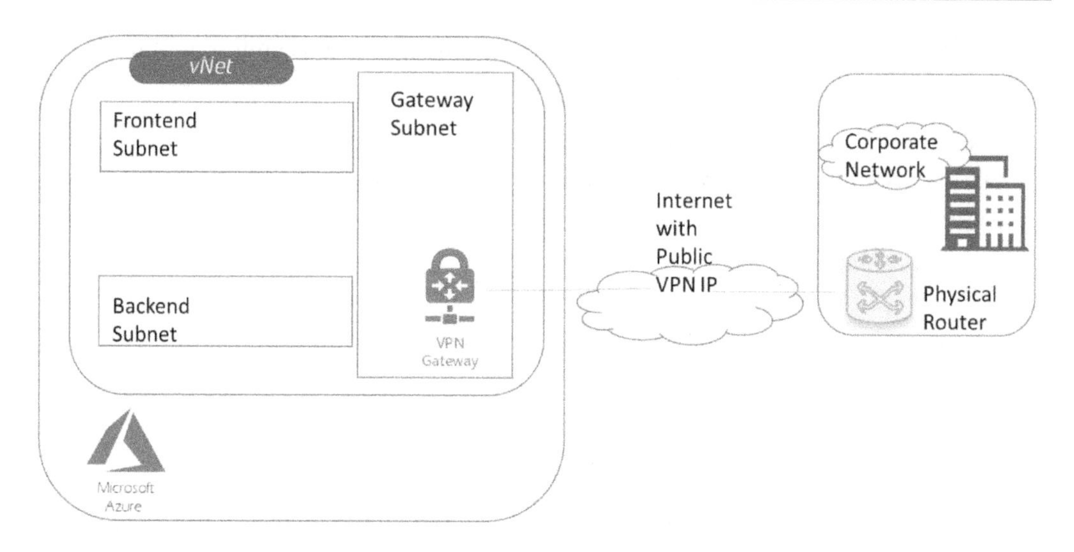


Figure 3.3 – Simplified design of the VPN gateway in Azure

> **Note**
> Find more information on designing VPN connections and the vNet gateways in Azure on `https://docs.microsoft.com/en-us/azure/vpn-gateway/vpn-gateway-howto-site-to-site-resource-manager-portal` for a site-to-site VPN and `https://docs.microsoft.com/en-us/azure/vpn-gateway/vpn-gateway-howto-point-to-site-resource-manager-portal` for a point-to-site connection.

## Designing connectivity in AWS

AWS also has two VPN types: site-to-site and Client VPN, the point-to-site solution that AWS offers. The site-to-site VPN offers an encrypted tunnel to the AWS global network. The solution comprises the use of multiple availability zones with two tunnels: one for primary traffic and a second one for redundancy. This is the default setup.

Next, in AWS, you need to deploy a customer gateway and the tunnel endpoint in AWS where the VPN is terminated. In AWS, there are two options:

- **A single site-to-site using the virtual private gateway (VPG)**: The VPG connects a **virtual private cloud (VPC)** to an external non-VPC environment. It uses IPsec as its protocol:

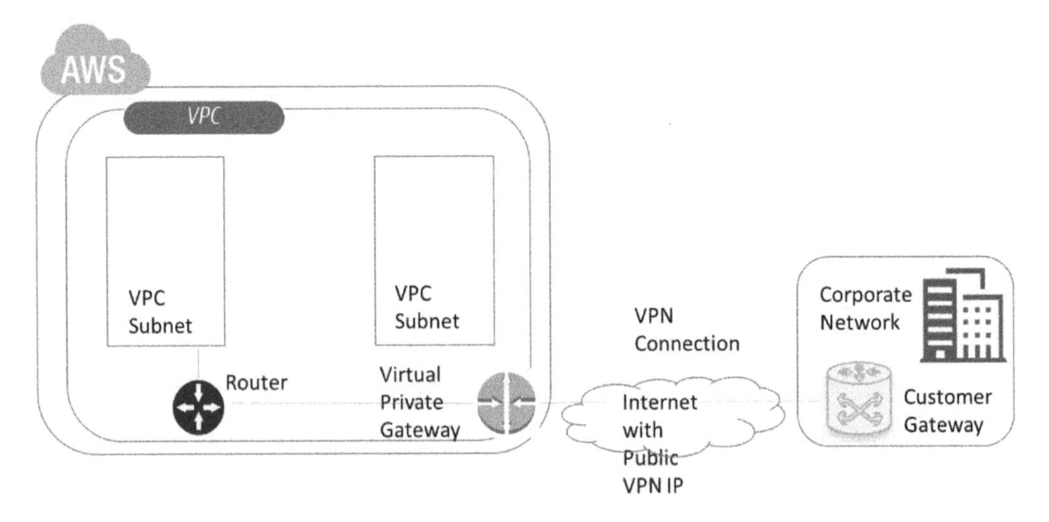


Figure 3.4 – Simplified design of a single site-to-site in AWS

- **A single site-to-site with a transit gateway**: A transit gateway enables you to scale out networks across multiple accounts and VPCs in AWS:

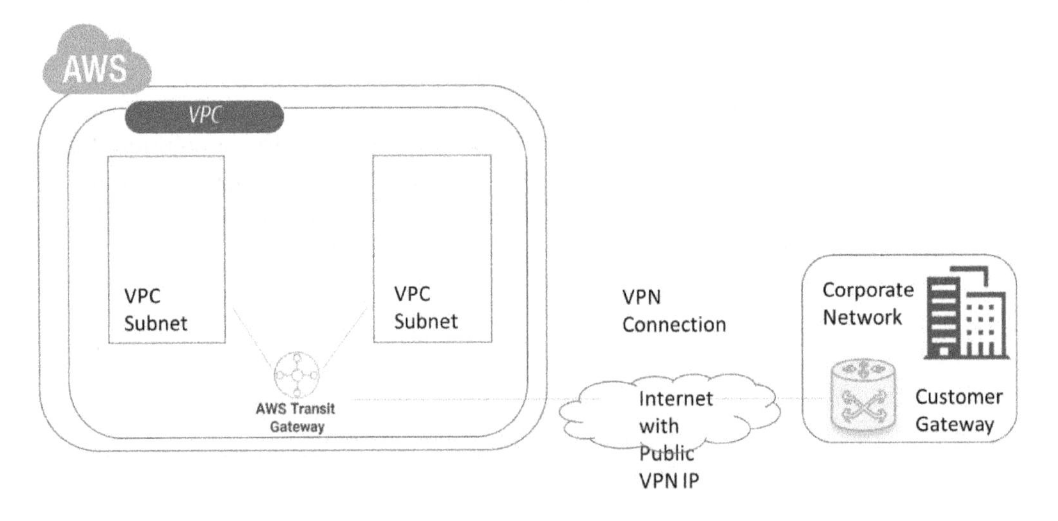


Figure 3.5 – Simplified design of a single site-to-site with AWS Transit Gateway

> **Note**
> Setting up the customer gateway, the VPG, and the actual VPN connection is documented at `https://docs.aws.amazon.com/vpn/latest/s2svpn/SetUpVPNConnections.html`.

To connect multiple sites using site-to-site VPNs, AWS offers CloudHub, which is based on the classic hub-and-spoke model. In this topology, we will have a VPG that connects to multiple customer gateways – for instance, to multiple branch offices of a business. It requires quite some network knowledge about the implementation of **Border Gateway Protocol** (**BGP**) and an **autonomous system number** (**ASN**) for each customer gateway. Next, we will have to consider routing advertising over various connections. This also requires an IP plan, since none of the connected sites can have overlapping IP ranges:

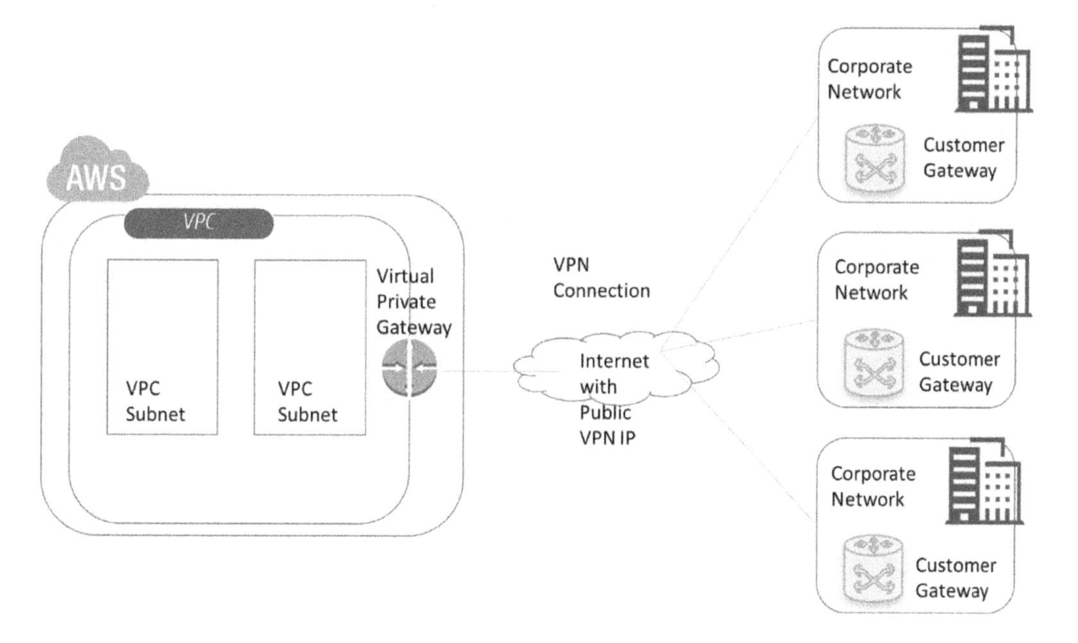


Figure 3.6 – Simplified design of AWS CloudHub

The accelerated site-to-site VPN connection is a feature that is worth mentioning here. It uses AWS Global Accelerator to route traffic from the on-premises network – typically the WAN – to the AWS location that is closest to the customer gateway device. This solution requires the use of the transit gateway. As explained, AWS deploys two tunnels: a primary and a secondary. Both tunnels get an accelerator and next, send the traffic over the AWS global network, looking for the optimized route to ensure the best possible performance of applications.

> **Note**
> More information on using AWS Global Accelerator is provided at `https://docs.aws.amazon.com/vpn/latest/s2svpn/accelerated-vpn.html`.

Client VPN is the point-to-site VPN of AWS and provides an encrypted TLS connection from any location to AWS using OpenVPN. You will need to assign a subnet within the VPC where Client VPN will be terminated, the so-called target network. Associating a subnet with a Client VPN endpoint enables you to establish the VPN sessions.

The following diagram shows the setup of the client VPN in AWS, using OpenVPN. With VPC peering, the client can *connect* to other VPCs in AWS:

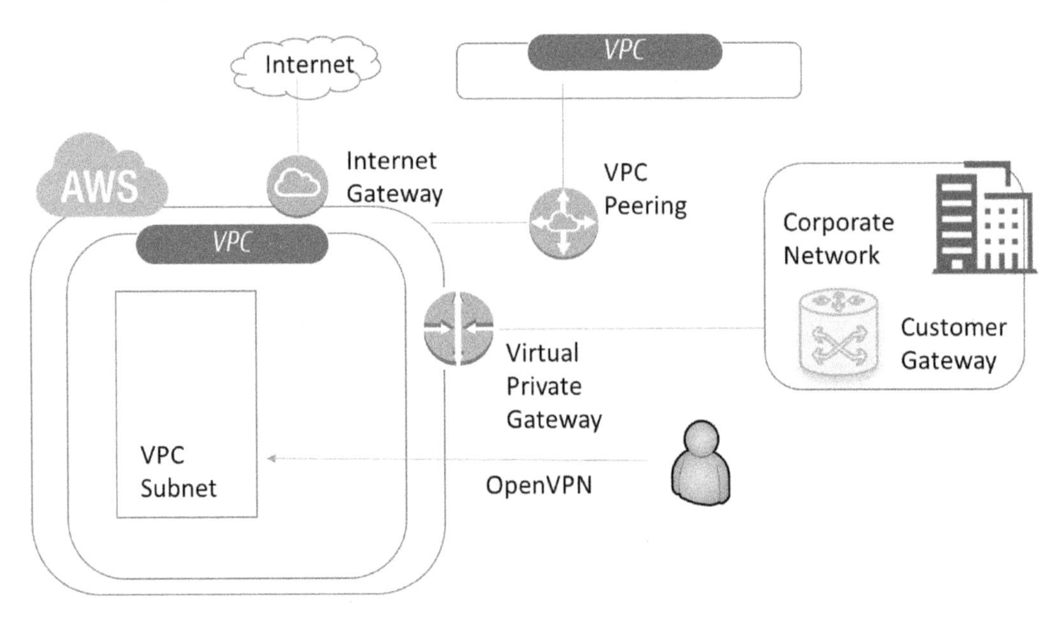


Figure 3.7 – Simplified design of AWS Client VPN

> **Note**
> Documentation on the setup and use of Client VPN is provided at `https://docs.aws.amazon.com/vpn/latest/clientvpn-admin/what-is.html`.

## Designing connectivity in GCP

Lastly, we will discuss the Google cloud VPN. Like AWS and Azure, GCP lets you connect your external environment through IPsec to GCP. For this connection, two gateways are deployed: one to encrypt the traffic and the other to decrypt the traffic.

Google offers two types of cloud VPN: **High Availability** (**HA**) and Classic VPN. Using HA VPN, you connect the on-premises network to a VPC in GCP in a single region. The setup is a bit different than with AWS and Azure. GCP automatically picks two public IP addresses for the HA VPN gateway. That gateway has two interfaces, and for each interface, you get one fixed IP address that comes from an address pool that is only used to support HA. You can connect multiple tunnels to the HA VPN gateway.

Of course, you also need VPN gateways—network devices—on-premises that point toward the HA VPN gateway. The following diagram shows how VPNs connect the corporate network to a project in GCP, using the HA Cloud VPN gateway:

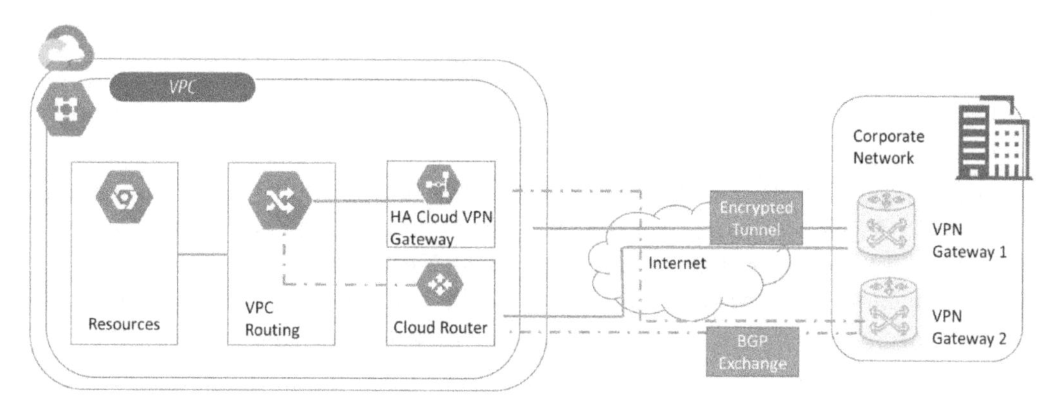


Figure 3.8 – Simplified design of HA VPN in Google Cloud

Where HA VPN utilizes two interfaces, the Classic VPN gateway—the target VPN gateway, as is referred to by Google—has only one with a single external IP address. One major difference between the two setups is that with Classic VPN, you need to specify forwarding rules in your GCP environment, whereas HA VPN takes care of that by default. The following diagram shows the Classic VPN setup, including the routing table that is needed to direct traffic within the GCP environment:

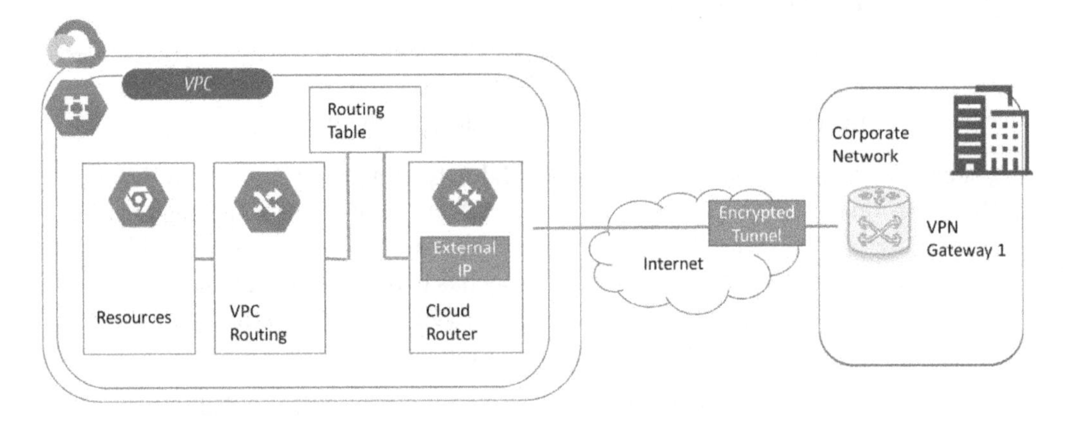


Figure 3.9 – Simplified design of the Classic VPN gateway in Google Cloud

> **Note**
>
> Documentation on the Google Cloud VPN solutions is provided at `https://cloud.google.com/vpn/docs/concepts/overview`.

We have discussed the different VPN options in the three major cloud platforms: Azure, AWS, and GCP. VPNs use the internet as a carrier and often, companies want a more reliable, direct connection to their platforms. Although VPNs certainly have cost benefits, they have limitations in terms of speed and throughput. Direct connections might be a better alternative. In the next section, we will explore these direct connections to different platforms.

## Understanding concepts of direct connectivity

VPN tunnels use the internet as a carrier. For a number of reasons, companies are often not very keen to have their traffic sent over the internet, not even when it's through secured, encrypted tunnels. A more stable, predictable, and even more secure solution is a direct connection between the router or firewall in your on-premises environment and the cloud platform that you as a business use. Down to the core, this solution is about a cable from an on-premises network device straight into a gateway device that routes directly to services that your business purchases from the cloud. The leading cloud providers all offer direct connectivity solutions. Partner interconnects to the different clouds are also available through colocations such as Equinix and Interxion. In the next sections, we will discuss the direct connectivity solutions.

### Implementing Azure ExpressRoute

Azure offers ExpressRoute as a direct connection from your network to your environments in Azure. The offering comprises three different deployment types: cloud exchange co-location, point-to-point Ethernet, and any-to-any IPVPN. The latter might be confusing since ExpressRoute does not use the public internet as a traffic carrier.

#### Point-to-point Ethernet

A point-to-point Ethernet connection provides connectivity on layer 2 or managed on layer 3. In the OSI model, layer 2 is the data link layer and layer 3 is the network layer. The main difference is that layer 3 provides routing and also takes care of IP routing, both static and dynamic, whereas layer 2 only does switching. Layer 3 is usually implemented when intra-VLAN is involved. Simply explained, layer 3 understands IP and can route traffic on an IP base, whereas layer 2 does not understand IP addresses. Having said that, a point-to-point Ethernet ExpressRoute connection will typically—or is at least recommended to—be on layer 3.

#### Any-to-any IPVPN

With this deployment, ExpressRoute integrates the **wide area network** (**WAN**) of the company with Azure, extending the on-premises environment with a virtual data center in Azure—making it literally one environment with the virtual data center as a *branch office*. Most companies will have network connectivity over MPLS, provided by a telecom provider. ExpressRoute connects this network over layer 3 to Azure.

## Azure cloud exchange co-location

This will be the preferred solution for enterprises that host their systems in a co-location. If that co-location has a cloud exchange, you can use the connections from this exchange. Typically, these will be managed layer 3 connections. The hosted environment is connected to the exchange—often in so-called meet-me rooms or racks—and from the exchange, the connection is set up to Azure.

ExpressRoute lets customers connect directly to Microsoft's network through a pair of 10 or 100 Gbps ports. Bandwidths are offered from 50 Mbps up to 10 Gbps.

The last thing you need to understand is the way ExpressRoute is set up with circuits and peering. A circuit is a logical connection between your on-premises environment and cloud services from Microsoft, such as Azure or Office 365. The connection is enabled through a connectivity provider, through a partner edge zone. Next, there are two types of peering: Microsoft peering and private peering. Microsoft peering is required when you utilize Microsoft cloud services such as Office 365 or Dynamics 365. Private peering is required to connect to the Azure cloud platform.

The following diagram shows the difference between Microsoft peering and Azure private peering:

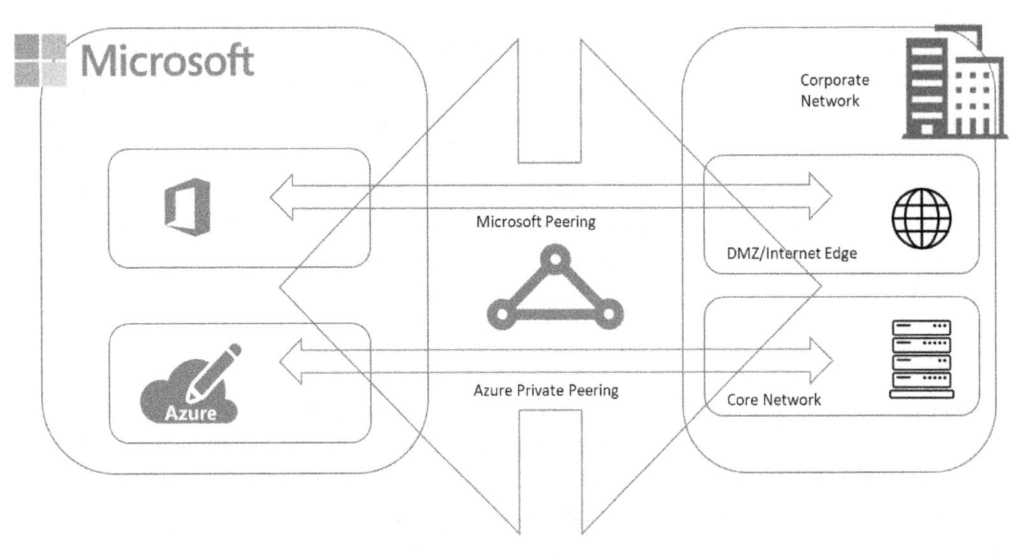


Figure 3.10 – Microsoft's ExpressRoute concept

So, what would a business need? That really depends on the planned usage. Azure is also the base platform for SaaS offerings such as Office 365. If a company with a substantial number of employees also uses Office 365, then this should be considered as well when sizing ExpressRoute.

> **Note**
> Documentation on ExpressRoute is provided at `https://docs.microsoft.com/en-us/azure/expressroute/`.

## Implementing AWS Direct Connect

The direct connection from your on-premises network to AWS is very appropriately called AWS Direct Connect. It connects your router or firewall to the Direct Connect service in your AWS region. The connection goes from your own router to a router of your connectivity partner and from there, it gets directly linked in the Direct Connect endpoint. That endpoint connects to a VPG in your AWS VPC or to the AWS services.

The link to the VPG could be compared to private peering in Azure, the link to AWS services with Microsoft peering—although the technology under the hood does differ. In AWS terminology, these peerings are called virtual interfaces. In summary, Direct Connect includes two components:

- The connection itself, from on-premises to the Direct Connect service.
- The virtual interfaces to get access to AWS services, a private virtual interface to your VPC in AWS, and a public virtual interface to gain access to AWS services, such as storage in S3 or Glacier.

The following diagram shows the basic architecture of AWS Direct Connect:

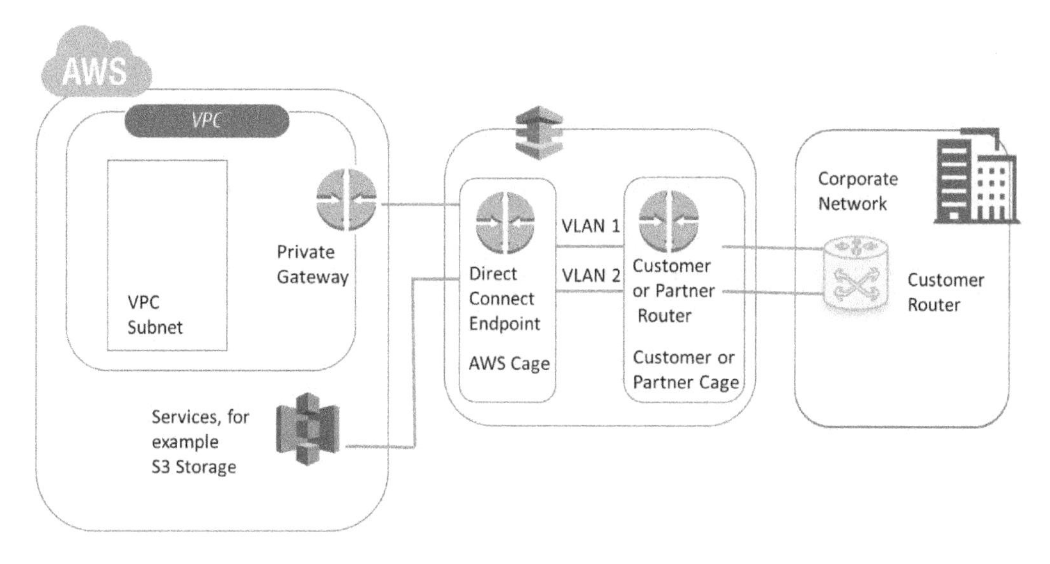


Figure 3.11 – AWS' Direct Connect concept

Direct Connect lets customers connect through 1 or 10 Gbps ports, at speeds of 50 Mbps, 100 Mbps, 200 Mbps, 300 Mbps, 400 Mbps, and 500 Mbps, through AWS Direct Connect partners. A list of these partners is provided at `https://aws.amazon.com/directconnect/partners/`.

> **Note**
> Documentation on AWS Direct Connect is provided at `https://docs.aws.amazon.com/directconnect/latest/UserGuide/Welcome.html#overview-components`.

## Implementing Google Dedicated Interconnect

Google offers Dedicated Interconnect. The principle is the same as with Direct Connect from AWS: from the router in the on-premises network, a direct link is established to the Google peering edge; this is done in a co-location facility where Google offers these peering zones. From there, the connection is forwarded to a cloud router in the GCP environment.

Dedicated Interconnect is offered as a single 10 G or 100 G link, or a link bundle that connects to the cloud router. Multiple connections from different locations or different devices to Google require separate interconnects.

The concept very much resembles the setup of AWS Direct Connect, as the following diagram shows:

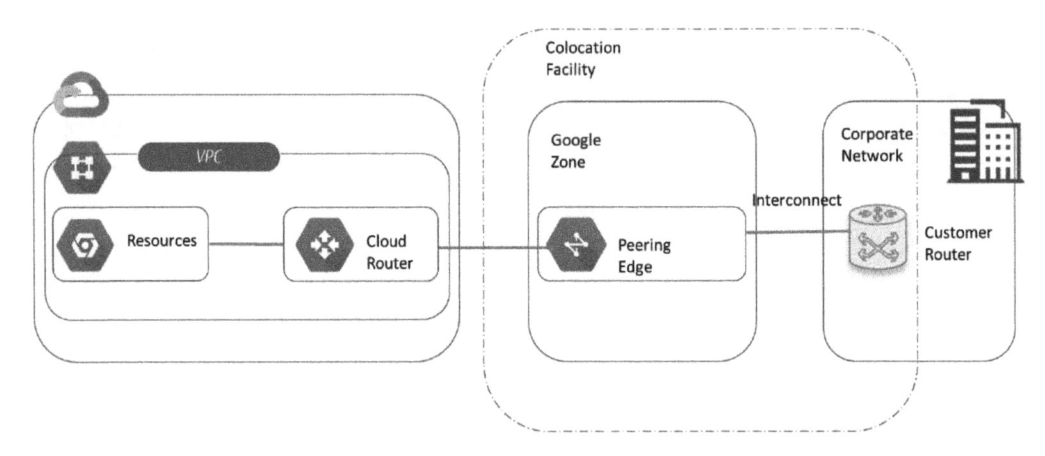


Figure 3.12 – Google's concept for Dedicated Interconnect

> **Note**
>
> Documentation on Google Dedicated Interconnect is provided at `https://cloud.google.com/interconnect/docs/concepts/dedicated-overview` and `https://cloud.google.com/network-connectivity/docs/interconnect/concepts/overview`.

## Managed dedicated connectivity through telecom companies or brokers

A lot of telecom providers offer dedicated connectivity to AWS, Azure, and GCP. For most (bigger) companies, this will likely be a preferred solution, since they typically already get their WAN connectivity through MPLS or Ethernet. Telecom companies and network providers have meet-me rooms or zones where they can connect customers to the peering zone of the preferred cloud provider. In the literature, this is also referred to as a *cloud hotel*, but basically, it's a zone within the data center where MPLS/Ethernet connections from telco-customers can be connected to either ExpressRoute, Direct Connect, or Dedicated Interconnect.

This solution offers a number of advantages for companies. First of all, these connections are fully managed by the telco, so they take away the worry for implementing and managing the connectivity yourself. Next, since telcos bundle connectivity, they typically have more options in offering more granular solutions in terms of desired bandwidths. Lastly, enterprises that are truly multi-cloud have the option to get multiple connections to different cloud platforms delivered through one connectivity provider.

To avoid misunderstanding, companies will almost always have to use a telco to get dedicated connections since their data centers have the facilities for the peering or (partner) edge zones of the cloud providers.

Major hosting facilities, data center providers, and co-locators offer cloud exchanges. Some good examples are Equinix, Digital Realty, and NTT. All these companies have global coverage in terms of data centers and connectivity exchanges, including backbone connectivity over the internet. They also offer direct connectivity as a service to the major cloud providers.

## Software-defined networking

Imagine that you're driving a car. To get you smoothly from A to B, we have invented roads. Although the layout of roads might differ from country to country, the foundation architecture of a road is usually the same all over the world. The soil is flattened and next, a layer of a hard substance is added on top. That can be cobblestones, concrete plates, or tarmac. It works better if connected roads are more or less made of the same materials: your drive will then be smoother than when roads constantly change in terms of topping material.

It's the same with networks. Networks are the roads where we travel on with workloads. Data and workloads travel easier when these networks have the same topology (and if there are not too many roadblocks, but that's more security-related). That's architecture, really.

To stay with the analogy of the road, we could define software-defined networking as a sort of magic tarmac. It creates a homogenous network on top of the physical network devices, connecting different environments, even on different platforms, with each other without having to change the physical network topology. The truth is that it sounds a bit easier than it is in real life. There are quite a number of prerequisites that need to be fulfilled.

The big idea is, of course, that if you can virtualize the use of servers and the use of storage devices, then you should be able to do exactly the same with networks. In other words: tell your network that it's in fact not only one physical network, but it can represent multiple networks connecting different environments.

There are many **software-defined networking** (**SDN**) solutions, such as Cisco ACI, HPE Aruba, and Big Switch, but one worthwhile to discuss in a bit more detail at this point is VMware's NSX as a leading proposition in SDN and the **Software Defined Data Center** (**SDDC**).

VMware's NSX comprises virtual networking and security. It's a network hypervisor, so it abstracts the network logic from the actual network and security devices, such as firewalls. By doing this, NSX enables micro-segmentation, but it also leverages the network layer in such a way that it can be extended to other platforms. NSX is part of the foundation underneath VMware on AWS: a business can create a VPC in AWS and connect it seamlessly with their on-premises VMware environment using NSX to *extend* the on-premises network and security parameters to the public cloud.

> **Note**
> At the time of writing, GCP and Azure have also joined the VMC propositions. More information can be found at `https://cloud.google.com/vmware` and `https://azure.microsoft.com/en-us/services/azure-vmware/`.

On-premises and AWS become one data center. As VMware states itself, VMware NSX Cloud enables a common and consistent way to secure and manage cloud-native workloads across the public cloud, as well as on-premises workloads from a single pane of glass, meaning that with NSX, enterprises always have one single view on both their on-premises environment and their systems in AWS.

Under the hood, it uses a built-in encrypted IPsec VPN tunnel between the on-premises systems and the VPCs in AWS, on top of the AWS global infrastructure. The following diagram shows the high-level architecture of VMware on AWS, extending the on-premises data center to AWS using VMware technology:

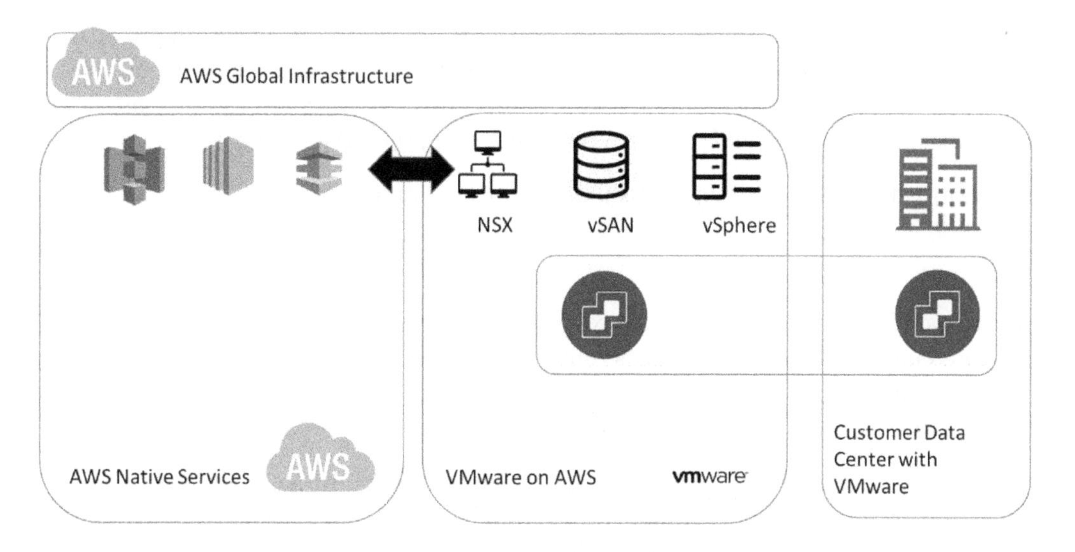


Figure 3.13 – Concept for VMware on AWS

In this section, we looked at the different options that the major platforms offer to enable direct connectivity to their platforms. These dedicated connections offer a more reliable, stable solution than VPN tunneling. In the next sections, we will study the various parameters that we need to consider when designing our connectivity solution.

# Designing a network topology for multi-cloud – thinking ahead

Before designing the network topology, we need to answer one question: what does the business require in terms of connectivity? But there are a few more things to carefully consider before you start designing and implementing VPNs or ordering direct connectivity.

The first step is assessment. A company will already have a network. You will need to assess how that network is configured. How do users connect to systems? How do they access the internet? How is traffic routed through systems? How are these systems protected from a network perspective? Where are firewalls, the proxy, and the reverse proxy situated? Yes, this is all important before we start designing a connection to a public cloud.

## Prerequisites for creating a network design

As already explained, most companies will use network services from a telecom provider. Part of the assessment, therefore, is to explore the offerings the telco has in terms of delivery and the management of public cloud connections. For instance, can they provide direct connections from a *cloud hotel* or a peering zone in their data center?

When creating the network design, we should address a number of areas.

### Cost

As we discussed in the previous chapter, costs include more than just the cash spent on equipment. Obviously, a company needs routers and firewalls on-premises to establish a connection – unless they are 100% cloud-based. These are CAPEX costs: investments that are typically depreciated over a fixed period or during their lifetime.

Other costs are the costs for the virtual equipment in the cloud: the gateway router and firewall. As with anything in the cloud, you can purchase these on a pay-as-you-go basis, where the business pays a monthly fee for the services they use. This is OPEX. Next, there is the cost of the used bandwidth. Lastly, we will need an engineer that implements the solution and perhaps manages it, if we're not opting for a fully managed service.

Calculating costs can become complicated. Something that is often forgotten is that public cloud providers also calculate costs for the traffic itself: incoming and outgoing to the cloud platform. These are really small amounts per Gb, but you have to realize that the volume of traffic can raise pretty fast and that inbound/outbound data traffic costs can become quite high. In ExpressRoute, Direct Connect, and Dedicated Interconnect, inbound (ingress) traffic is included, while outbound (egress) traffic is charged.

Just as an example, we ordered a connection using Azure VPN Gateway, as shown in the following screenshot:

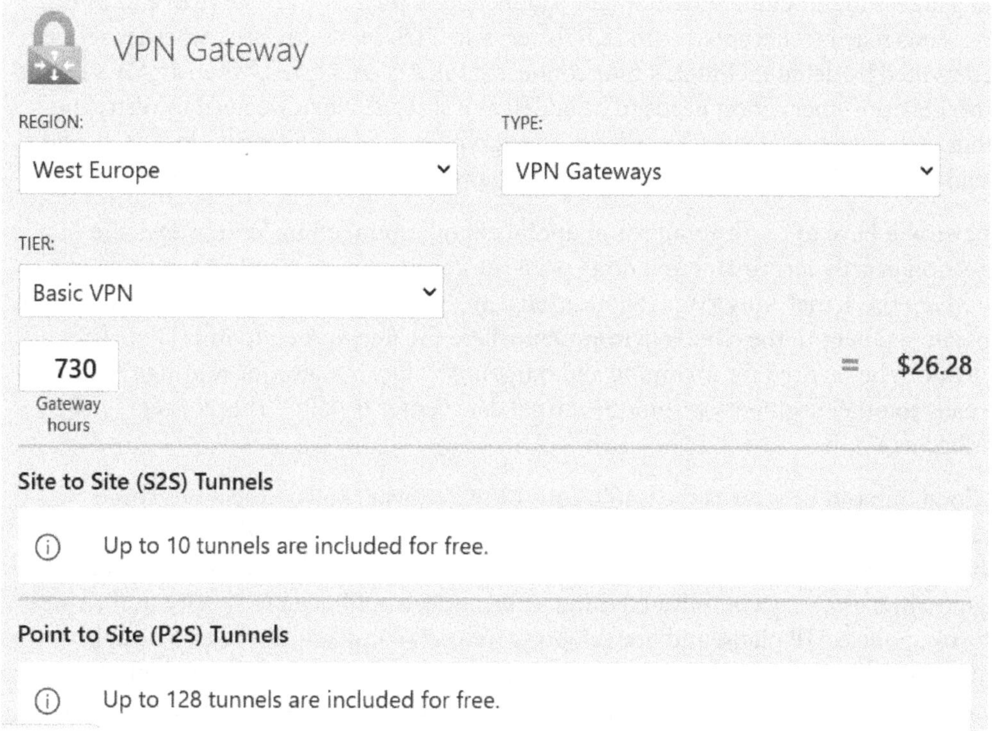

Figure 3.14 – Ordering the VPN Gateway functionality in the Azure cost model

In this calculation, we have only ordered a basic VPN for 730 hours, assuming that we need the connection the whole month through. There are no additional costs as long we don't implement more than 10 site-to-site tunnels or more than 128 point-to-site tunnels. Just for the gateway, Azure will charge us 26.28 USD per month.

But that's not all. You will also need to calculate the bandwidth. Up to 5 Gb is provided for free, but from there you will be charged 0.09 cents per Gb.

This is just a very simple example, but hopefully it makes clear that we need to think a couple of things through when it comes to costs. In this example, we only have a VPN gateway and bandwidth, nothing else. But let's assume that you would like to monitor and protect your connection, which takes us to the next point.

## Security

Obviously, we need to secure our connection to prevent non-authorized people from gaining access to our cloud environment. Connections such as VPN services and direct connections may be encrypted with IKE, IPsec, and TLS. First, do check whether services are encrypted by default. Google's Interconnect service is encrypted, whereas AWS Direct Connect is not—encryption needs to be added as a service. Next, we need to verify the settings. Be aware that it takes knowledge of encryption and protocols to do so. Oh, and remember—encryption is not only for data in transit but also for data at rest.

Then, we will have to think about the endpoints of our connection. Where does the connection exactly terminate? You don't want the connection to terminate in the same zone where the actual workloads (applications) are, so it is strongly recommended to have a separate segment in the cloud environment where the network endpoints land. This segment can be secured for incoming and outgoing traffic, but also for routing the traffic internally to other segments within the virtual data center or VPC. This concept is often described as a hub.

The cloud hub can be seen as the traffic control center, where all connections come together and traffic is routed in the right direction. What is the right direction then? This is where the specified address traffic should go and where it is allowed to go to. You can imagine a hub as a very complicated thing. A business would need to specify traffic rules, protocols, policies, IP plans, and firewall ports for each connection, and also be able to monitor them. As long as a business stays within their own tenant within one platform, they're OK. But the fact is that a lot of PaaS and SaaS services are connected from outside the tenant, and therefore it needs to be connected in the proper way.

A major problem that businesses face is security with the public services that they use in the cloud. PaaS and SaaS often require the use of public IPs, and that's exactly what businesses typically do not allow in their private tenant. A solution to this is **network address translation** (**NAT**), but this does bring new challenges to the table. Obviously, cloud providers have thought this through and have come up with more sophisticated solutions.

AWS has already offered PrivateLink for a while. AWS PrivateLink provides private connectivity between VPCs, AWS services, and on-premises applications, securely on the Amazon network. Microsoft introduced Private Link for Azure in late 2019. Private Link provides a private connection between your virtual environment in Azure to a PaaS service, either from Microsoft or a Microsoft partner. The PaaS service isn't exposing data to the public internet using a private link. Private Link uses a private endpoint so that gateways with NAT—translating from public to private addresses—are no longer required:

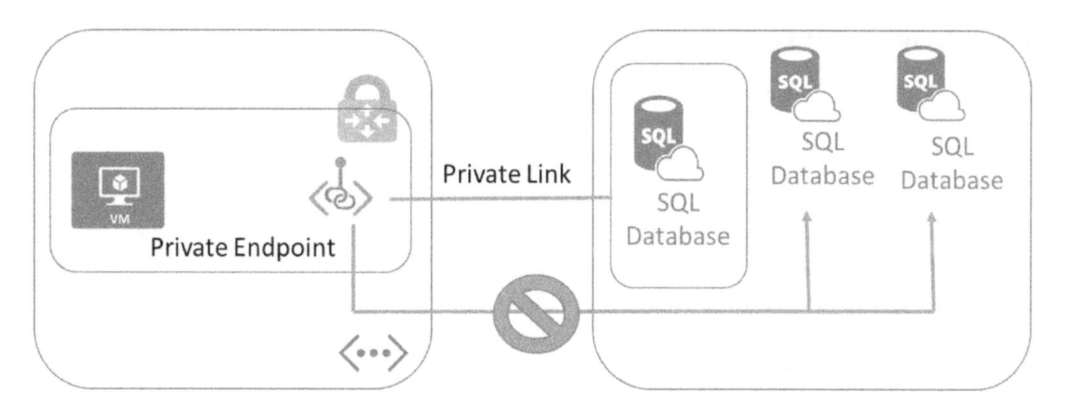


Figure 3.15 – Concept for Private Link (Azure)

## Internet access

When it comes to internet access, we have two options:

- **Internet breakout from the public cloud**: In this case, you access the internet through the public cloud. Your environment in the public cloud is internet-facing. That certainly requires strong security administration.
- **Internet breakout from an on-premises network or through a connectivity provider**: This is the setup where users access the internet from the company's network and not through the cloud. Traffic to the cloud environment is only allowed through a secured VPN or direct connections.

Large enterprises with multiple locations can have local internet breakouts, with internet access close to the users at every location. Local breakouts are meant to drive down the amount of traffic going over the WAN. With the enormous growth in the usage of SaaS and other cloud services, the amounts of traffic traveling over WAN and next via the internet to these cloud services will increase drastically. Therefore, local internet breakouts to spread the traffic are a good solution for larger companies. Traffic that has to travel within the cloud needs to be routed and load balanced as well.

Cloud providers have their respective backbones and technology to control and load balance the traffic, making sure that it's reaching its targeted destination, based on DNS. In Azure, that's Traffic Manager, while in AWS, the service is called Route 53, and GCP offers Cloud DNS.

### Service levels and support

Public clouds such as AWS, Azure, and Google offer very high service levels on their services within their platforms. However, often, these service levels are only guaranteed if you have a dedicated connection to your environment. A VPN using the internet as a carrier is less stable than a dedicated connection to the platform, but as we have seen, these connections can be complicated to set up and manage, especially when you take the security of the connection in scope as well. It takes people—network engineers—with the right skills to do this. A business needs to consider the level of required technical support. In a lot of cases, it's absolutely worthwhile to consider a fully managed service from a network provider or telco.

# Understanding network protocols in multi-cloud

We came across a lot of acronyms and terms in this chapter. If you're not a network engineer, some of these acronyms might not directly ring a bell. Yet, things such as BGP, ASN, and TLS are crucial in understanding how connections work. The good news is, any public cloud is internet-based. Without the internet, we wouldn't have the cloud in the first place. So, protocols such as IP, HTTP, and HTTPS are really crucial. But what about the rest? In terms of cloud connectivity, there is quite some more that needs to be taken into consideration. After all, we do want our connections to be secure and only going in the direction we want them to go. On top of that, we have to enable connections to set up communication between targeted resources. That requires these resources to speak the same language.

Cloud computing is hosted over the internet through a network connection. The required and crucial protocols are as follows:

- **IP**: Basic internet protocol.
- **HTTP/HTTPS**: **HyperText Transfer Protocol** (**HTTP**) communicates over ports `80` and `8080`. **HTTPS** (**Hyper Text Transfer Protocol Secure**) using encryption over TLS and SSL communicates through port `443`. Most **application programming interfaces** (**APIs**) communicate over HTTPS. These are the most commonly used ports in the public cloud.
- **TCP/UDP**: **Transmission Control Protocol** (**TCP**) and **User Datagram Protocol** (**UDP**).

- **SMTP**: **Simple Mail Transfer Protocol** (**SMTP**) is required for mail communication between servers and communicates over port `25`.
- **BGP**: BGP is used by all major cloud providers. It's used to exchange routing and reachability information among **autonomous systems** (**ASes**) on the internet, such as cloud platforms and services. BGP communicates through port `179`.

One thing we have to note here is IP, the basic internet protocol. We have two versions of IP: that is, IPv4 and IPv6. The latter was deemed required since the number of IP addresses on IPv4 was limited and running out, but with the adoption of NAT and major enterprises giving back huge unused ranges, it's not really an issue at this time. However, for current and future use of trillions of **Internet of Things** (**IoT**) devices, the use of IPv6 is becoming more useful again. Implementing IPv6 is rather complex since it has a completely different syntax.

IPv4 addresses have a 32-bit layout, whereas IPv6 has 128-bit addresses. An IPv4 address will look something like `196.128.x.x`. Converted to IPv6, that would be `0:0:0:0:0:ffff:c480:101`. It's not hard to imagine that mapping IPv4 to IPv6 is extremely complicated. Hence, all cloud platforms support IPv6, but not for all services. For instance, in AWS, you would need to create a non-default VPC and put a request in for an IPv6 **classless inter-domain routing** (**CIDR**) block, an IP addressing scheme that replaces the older system based on classes that we use in IPv4. If you want to use IPv6 in the public cloud, be sure to check the availability of this protocol in different services.

After this section, you should have a basic understanding of the most important network and communication protocols that are used in cloud technology.

# Summary

In this chapter, we explored the different concepts of connectivity to public clouds. Without connectivity, nothing will work – or at least nothing will be reachable. We have learned the major differences between the VPN concepts and the direct connectivity propositions of Azure, AWS, and GCP. An important lesson is that VPN connections are fine at lower bandwidths, but enterprises typically need more than that, and they should consider moving to direct connection solutions. To design a connectivity strategy for our business, we need to take some key parameters into account—the cost, internet access, security, and service levels.

From a technology perspective, we have studied concepts such as SDN and have also learned that you can extend an on-premises network to a public cloud with concepts such as VMware's NSX. Connectivity is king and therefore you also need to have a basic understanding of the various protocols that networks use to establish a connection and enable traffic, making sure that cloud components actually understand each other. A short explanation of the difference between IPv4 and IPv6 and the level of support when it comes to the latter concluded this chapter.

Now that we have connectivity, we can start looking at what kinds of services we want to deploy in our multi-cloud. But before we get to the actual deployment, we have to create designs, starting with the service catalog that we want to provide to our business. That's the topic of the next chapter.

# Questions

1. We've explored different VPN solutions. What sort of technological solution do we typically use to terminate the VPN in the designated public cloud?
2. What's the name of the direct connect solution in Azure?
3. SDN is considered to be a solution that a growing number of companies will adopt in the future. What's the leading proposition in the SDN space?
4. A major challenge in public clouds is the use of public services with public IP addresses. Companies want to have the option to use these services, yet make them private. Name the technology to enable this.

# 4
# Service Designs for Multi-Cloud

All cloud providers offer a cloud adoption framework that helps businesses to implement governance and deploy services, while controlling service levels and **key performance indicators** (**KPIs**) in the cloud. In multi-cloud environments, businesses would have to think about how to implement governance over different cloud components, coming from different providers, but still be able to manage it as a single environment.

This chapter will introduce the base pillars for a unified service design and governance model, starting with identities. Everything in the cloud is an identity. It requires a different way of thinking – users, a VM, a piece of code even. We will look at different pillars in multi-cloud governance and study the various stages in cloud adoption, using the cloud adoption frameworks of cloud providers. We will also learn how important identities in the cloud are and how we can create a service and governance design for multi-cloud environments.

In this chapter, we will cover the following topics:

- Introducing the scaffold for multi-cloud environments
- Cloud adoption stages
- Translating business KPIs into cloud SLAs
- Using cloud adoption frameworks to align between cloud providers
- Understanding identities and roles in the cloud
- Creating the service design and governance model

# Introducing the scaffold for multi-cloud environments

How does a business start in the cloud? You would be surprised, but a lot of companies still just start without having a plan. How difficult can it get, after all? You get a subscription and begin deploying resources. That probably works fine with really small environments, but you will soon discover that it literally grows over your head. Think of it—would you start building a data center just by acquiring a building and obtaining an Ethernet cable and a rack of servers? Of course not. So why would you just start building without a plan in the public cloud? You would be heading for disaster – and that's no joke. As we already saw in *Chapter 1, Introduction to Multi-Cloud*, a business will need a clear overview of costs, a demarcation on who does what, when, and why in the cloud, and, most important, it all needs to be secure by protecting data and assets, just as a business would do in a traditional data center.

If there's one take-away from this book, it's this: you are building a data center. You are building it using public clouds, but it's a data center. Treat it as a data center.

Luckily, all major cloud providers feel exactly the same way and have issued cloud adoption frameworks. Succinctly put, these frameworks help a business in creating the plan and, first and foremost, help to stay in control of cloud deployments. These frameworks do differ on certain points, but they also share a lot of common ground.

Now, the subtitle of this paragraph contains the word *scaffold*. The exact meaning of **scaffold** is a structure to support the construction and maintenance of buildings, the term was adopted by Microsoft to support build and manage environments that are deployed in Azure. It's quite an appropriate term, although in the cloud, it would not be a temporary structure. It's the structure that is used as the foundation to build and manage the environments in a cloud landing zone.

Scaffolding comprises a set of pillars, which will be covered in the following sections.

## Identity and access management (IAM)

Who may do what, when, and why? This is key in the public cloud, so we will devote more words to identity and access later on in this chapter, under the heading *Understanding identities and roles in the cloud*. The most important thing to bear in mind is that virtually everything in the cloud is an identity. We are not only talking about persons here, but also about resources, functions, APIs, machines, workloads, and databases that are allowed to perform certain actions. All these resources need to be uniquely identified in order to authenticate them in your environment.

Next, specific access rules need to be set for these identities: they need to be authorized to execute tasks. Obviously, identity directory systems such as Active Directory or OpenLDAP are important as identity providers or identity stores. The question is whether you want this store in your public cloud environment or whether you want an authentication and authorization mechanism in your environment, communicating with the identity store. As stated previously, under the heading *Understanding identities and roles in the cloud*, we will look into this in more detail later on in this chapter.

## Security

Here's a bold statement: platforms such as Azure, AWS, and GCP are likely the most secure platforms in the world. They have to be, since thousands of companies host their systems on these platforms. Yet, security remains the responsibility of the business itself. Cloud platforms will provide you with the tools to secure your environment. Whether you want to use these tools and to what extent is entirely down to the business. Security starts with policies. Typically, businesses will have to adhere to certain frameworks that come with recommendations or even obligations to secure systems. Next to these industry standards, there are horizontal security baselines, such as the **Center for Internet Security** (**CIS**). The CIS baseline is extensive and covers a lot of ground in terms of hardening resources in the cloud. The baseline has scored and non-scored items, where the scored items are obviously the most important. Auditors will flag on these items when the baseline is not met.

One framework deserves a bit more attention: MITRE ATT&CK. Having a baseline implemented is fine, but how do you retain control over security without being aware of actual attack methods and exploited vulnerabilities? MITRE ATT&CK is a knowledge base that is constantly evaluated with real-world observations in terms of security attacks and known breaches. The key words here are real-world. They keep track of real attacks, and mitigation of these attacks, for the major public clouds – Azure, AWS, and GCP – but also for platforms that are enrolled on top of these platforms, such as Kubernetes for container orchestration.

> **Tip**
> The MITRE ATT&CK matrices can be found at `https://attack.mitre.org/`.

There's a lot to say about securing your cloud platform. *Chapter 16, Defining Security Policies for Data*, provides best practices in relation to cloud security.

## Cost management

You've heard this one before: the public cloud is not as cheap as the traditional stack that I run in my own data center. That could be true. If a business decides to perform a lift and shift from traditional workloads to the public cloud, without changing any parameters, you will realize that hosting that workload 24/7/365 in the public cloud is probably more expensive than having it on the on-premises system. There are two explanations for that:

- Businesses have a tendency not to fully calculate all related costs to workloads that are hosted on on-premises systems. Very often, things such as power, cooling, but also labor (especially involved in changes) are not taken into consideration.
- Businesses use the public cloud like they use the on-premises systems, but without the functionality that clouds offer in terms of flexibility. Not all workloads need to be operational 24/7/365. Cloud systems offer a true pay-as-you-go model, where businesses only pay for the actual resources they consume—even all the way down to the level of CPUs, memory, storage, and network bandwidth.

Cost management is of the utmost importance. You want to be in full control of whatever your business is consuming in the cloud. But that goes hand in hand with IAM. If a worker has full access to platforms and, for instance, enrolls a heavy storage environment for huge data platforms such as data lakes, the business will definitely get a bill for that. Two things might go wrong here:

- First of all, was that worker authorized to perform that action?
- Second, has the business allocated a budget for that environment?

Let's assume that the worker was authorized, and that budget is available. Then we need to be able to track and trace the actual consumption and, if required, be able to put a charge back in place to a certain division that uses the environment. Hence, we need to be able to identify the resources. That's where naming and tagging in resources comes into play. We have to make sure that all resources can uniquely be identified by name. Tags are used to provide information about a specific resource; for example, who owns the resource, and hence will have to pay to use that resource.

*Chapter 12, Defining Naming Convention and Asset Tagging Standards*, provides best practices on how to define naming and tagging standards. *Chapter 13, Validating and Managing Bills*, will explore billing and cost management further.

## Monitoring

We need visibility on and in our platform. What happens and for what reason? Is our environment still healthy in terms of performance and security? Cloud providers offer native monitoring platforms: Azure Monitor, AWS CloudWatch, Google Cloud Monitoring (previously known as Stackdriver), and vRealize for VMware. The basic functionality is comparable all in all: monitoring agents collect data (logs) and metrics, and then store these in a log analytics space where they can be explored using alert policies and visualization with dashboards. All these monitoring suites can operate within the cloud itself, but also have APIs to major **IT Service Management** (**ITSM**) systems such as ServiceNow, where the latter will then provide a single pane of glass over different platforms in the IT environment.

There are quite a number of alternatives to the native toolsets and suites. Good examples of such tools are Splunk and Datadog. Some of these suites operate in the domain of AIOps, a rather new phenomenon. AIOps does a lot more than just execute monitoring: it implies intelligent analyses conducted on metrics and logs. In *Chapter 19, Optimizing Multi-Cloud Environments with AIOps*, we will cover AIOps, since it is expected that this will become increasingly popular in multi-cloud environments.

## Automation

We have already talked about costs. By far the most expensive factor in IT is costs related to labor. For a lot of companies, this was the driver to start off-shoring labor when they outsourced their IT. But we already noticed that IT has become a core business again for these companies. For example, a bank is an IT company these days. Where they almost completely outsourced their IT in the late nineties and at the beginning of the new millennium, we now see that their IT functions are back in house. However, there is still the driver to keep costs down as far as possible. With concepts such as Infrastructure as Code, Configuration as Code, repositories to store that code, and have deployment of code fully automated using DevOps pipelines, these companies try to automate to the max. By doing this, the amount of labor is kept to a minimum.

Costs are, however, not the only reason to automate, although it must be said that this is a bit of an ambiguous argument. Automation tends to be less fault tolerant than human labor (*robots do it better*). Automation only works when it's tested thoroughly. And you still need good developers to write the initial code and the automation scripts. True, the cloud does offer a lot of good automation tools to make the life of businesses easier, but we will come to realize that automation is not only about the tools and technology. It's also about processes; methodologies such as **Site Reliability Engineering** (**SRE**) – invented by Google – are gaining a lot of ground. We will cover this in *Chapter 20, Introducing Site Reliability Engineering in Multi-Cloud*, of this book.

> **Tip**
> The respective cloud adoption frameworks can be found as follows: The Azure Cloud Adoption Framework – `https://azure.microsoft.com/en-us/cloud-adoption-framework/#cloud-adoption-journey`; AWS – `https://aws.amazon.com/professional-services/CAF/`; GCP – `https://cloud.google.com/adoption-framework/`.

These pillars are described in almost all cloud adoption frameworks. In the following sections, we will study these pillars as we go along the various stages involved in cloud adoption.

# Cloud adoption stages

You may have come across one other term: the **cloud landing zone**. The landing zone is the foundation environment where workloads eventually will be hosted. Picture it all like a house. We have a foundation with a number of pillars. On top of that we have the house with a front door (be aware that this house should not have a back door), a hallway, and a number of rooms. These rooms will be empty: no decoration, no furniture. That all has yet to be designed and implemented, where we have some huge shops (portals) from where we can choose all sorts of solutions to get our rooms exactly how we want them. The last thing to do is to actually move the residents into the house. And indeed, these residents will likely move from room to room. Remember: without scaffolding, it's hard to build a house in the first place.

This is what cloud adoption frameworks are all about: it's about how to adopt cloud technology. Often, this is referred to as a journey. Adoption is defined by a number of stages, regardless of the target cloud platform. The following diagram shows the subsequent stages in cloud adoption:

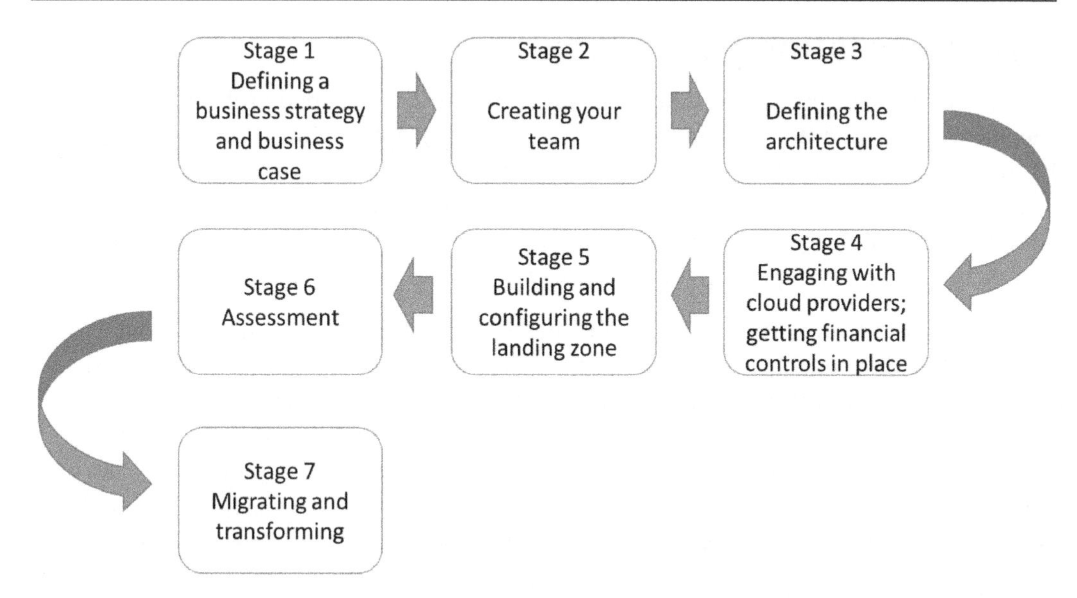


Figure 4.1 – The 7 steps in cloud adoption

Let's discuss each stage in detail in the following sections.

# Stage 1 – defining a business strategy and business case

In *Chapter 2, Business Acceleration Using a Multi-Cloud Strategy*, we looked extensively at the business strategy and how to create a business case. A business needs to have clear goals and know where cloud offerings could add value. We have also looked at technical strategies such as rehost, replatform, and rebuild. Rebuild might not always be the cheapest solution when it comes to **total cost of ownership** (**TCO**). That's because businesses tend to forget that it takes quite some effort in rearchitecting and rebuilding applications to cloud-native environments. These architecture and build costs should be taken into consideration. However, the native environment will undoubtedly bring business benefits in terms of flexibility and agility. In short, this first stage is crucial in the entire adoption cycle.

## Stage 2 – creating your team

Let's break this one immediately: there's no such thing as the T-shaped professional, someone who can do everything in the cloud: from coding applications to configuring infrastructure. The wider the T, the less deep the stroke under the T gets. In other words, if you have professionals who are generic and basically have a knowledge of all cloud platforms, they will likely not have a deep understanding of one specific cloud technology. But also, a software developer is not a network engineer, or vice versa.

Of course, someone who's trained in architecting and building cloud environments in Azure or AWS will probably know how to deploy workloads, a database, and have a basic understanding of connectivity. But what about firewall rules? Or specific routing? Put another way: a firewall specialist might not be very skilled in coding in Python. If you have these type of people in your team, congrats. Pay them well, so they won't leave. But you will probably have a team with these skills mixed. You will need developers and staff that are proficiently trained in designing and configuring infrastructure, even in the cloud.

Some adoption frameworks do mention this as the cloud center of excellence or – as AWS calls it – the Cloud Adoption Office, the team where this team with all the required skills are brought together. Forming this center of excellence is an important step in adopting cloud technology.

## Stage 3 – defining the architecture

This is the stage where you will define the landing zone—the foundation platform where the workloads will be hosted. In the previous chapter, we looked at connectivity, since it all starts with getting the cloud platforms connected. Typically, these connections will terminate in a transit zone or hub, the central place where inbound and outbound traffic is regulated and filtered by means of firewalls, proxies, and gateways. This will be the place where administrators of the cloud platform will enter the environment. Most administrators will access systems through APIs or the consoles, but in some cases, it might be recommended to use a jump server, a stepping stone, or a Bastion server, the server that forms the entrance to the environment before they can access any other servers. Typically, third parties such as system integrators use this type of server. In short, this transit zone or hub is crucial in the architecture.

The next thing is to define the architecture according to your business strategy. That defines how your cloud environment is set up. Does your business have divisions or product lines? It might be worthwhile to have the cloud environment corresponding to the business layout, for instance, by using different subscriptions or the **Virtual Private Cloud** (**VPC**) per division or product line.

There will be applications that are more generically used throughout the entire business. Office applications are usually a good example. Will these applications be hosted in one separate subscription? And what about access for administrators? Does each of the divisions have their own admins controlling the workloads? Has the business adopted an agile way of working, or is there one centralized IT department that handles all of the infrastructure? Who's in charge of the security policies? These policies might differ by division or even workload groups. These security policies might also not be cloud friendly or applicable in a cloud-native world. They might need to be updated based on feedback from your cloud SMEs.

One major distinction that we can already make is the difference between systems of record and systems of engagement, both terms first used by Microsoft. Systems of record are typically backend systems, holding the data. Systems of engagement are the frontend systems, used to access data, work with the data, and communicate said data. We often find this setup reflected in the tiering of environments, where tier 1 is the access layer, tier 2 the worker (middleware), and tier 3 the database layer. A common rule in architecture is that the database should be close to the application accessing the database. In the cloud, this might work out differently, since we will probably work with **Platform as a Service (PaaS)** as a database engine.

These are the types of questions that are addressed in the cloud adoption frameworks. These are all very relevant questions that require answers before we start. And it's all architecture. It's about mapping the business to a comprehensive cloud blueprint. *Chapter 5, Successfully Managing the Enterprise Cloud Architecture*, of this book is all about architecture.

## Stage 4 - engaging with cloud providers; getting financial controls in place

In this stage, we will decide on which cloud platform we will build the environment and what type of solutions we will be using: **Infrastructure as a Service (IaaS)**, PaaS, **Software as a Service (SaaS)**, containers, or serverless. These solution should derive from the architecture that we have defined in stage 3. We will have to make some make-or-buy decisions: can we use native solutions, off the shelf, or do we need to develop something customized to the business requirements?

During this stage, we will also have to define business cases that automatically come with make-or-buy analyses. For instance, if we plan to deploy **virtual machines (VMs)** on IaaS, we will have to think of the life cycle of that VM. In the case of a VM that is foreseen to live longer than, let's say for the sake of argument, 1 year, it will be far more cost efficient to host it on reserved instances as opposed to using the pay-as-you-go deployment model. Cloud providers offer quite some discounts on reserved instances, for a good reason: reserved instances mean a long-term commitment and, hence, a guaranteed income. But be aware: it's a long-term commitment. Breaking that commitment comes at a cost. Do involve your financial controller to have it worked out properly.

Development environments will generally only exist for a shorter time. Still, cloud providers do want business to develop as much as possible on their cloud platforms and offer special licenses for developers that can be really interesting. At the end of the day, cloud providers are only interested in one thing: consumption of their platforms. There are a lot programs that offer all sorts of guidance, tools, and migration methods to get workloads to these platforms.

## Stage 5 – building and configuring the landing zone

There are a number of options to actually start building the landing zone. Just to have the right understanding: the landing zone is the foundation platform, typically the transit zone or hub and the basic configuration of VNets, VPCs, or projects. We aim to have it automated as much as we can, right from the start. Hence, we will work according to the Infrastructure as Code and Configuration as Code, since we can only automate when components are code-based. *Chapter 8, Defining and Using Infrastructure Automation Tools and Processes*, is about automation.

However, there are, of course, other ways to start your build, for instance, using the portals of the respective cloud providers. If you are building a small, rather simple environment with just a few workloads, then the portal is a perfect way to go. But assuming that we are working with an enterprise, the portal is not a good idea to build your cloud environment. It's absolutely fine to start exploring the cloud platform, but as the enterprise moves along and the environments grow, we need a more flexible way of managing and automating workloads. As has already been said, we want to automate as much as we can. How do we do that? By coding our foundation infrastructure and defining that as our master code. That master code is stored in a repository. Now, from that repository we can fork the code if we need to deploy infrastructure components. It is very likely that every now and then, we have to change the code due to certain business requirements. That's fine, as long we as merge the changed, approved code back into the master repository. By working in this way, we have deployed an infrastructure pipeline, shown as follows:

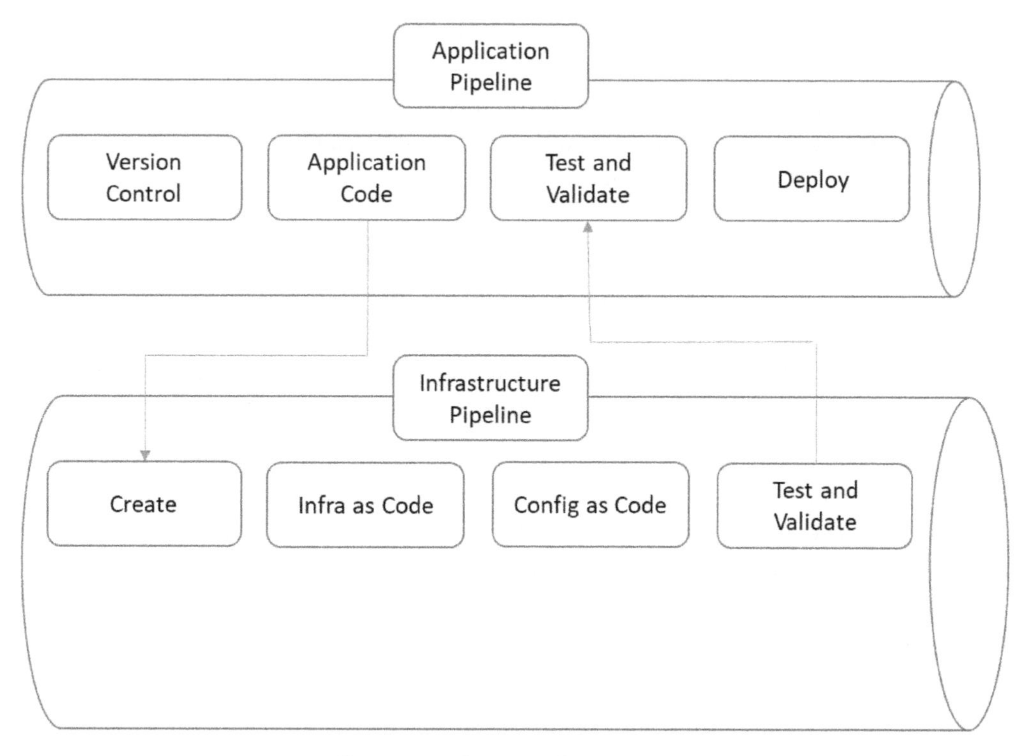


Figure 4.2 – Basic pipeline structure

In a multi-cloud environment, the biggest challenge would be to have a consistent repository and pipeline that could expand over multiple cloud platforms. After all, although the base concepts of AWS, Azure, and GCP are more or less the same, they do differ in terms of applied technology.

> **Note**
>
> In this section, we are mainly talking about IaaS components. A popular tool in this area is Terraform, an open source software by HashiCorp that is specifically designed to deploy data center infrastructure. Terraform supports the three major clouds that we are focusing on in this book, but also – among others – VMware, IBM Cloud, Open Telekom Cloud by T-Systems, Oracle Cloud, and OVHcloud. Terraform abstracts the code of these clouds into cloud-agnostic code, based on HCL or JSON. **HashiCorp Configuration Language** (**HCL**) is the native language of Terraform, while **JavaScript Object Notation** (**JSON**) is more commonly known as a programming language.

If you search for alternatives, you may find tools such as Ansible, Chef, Puppet, or SaltStack. However, these are configuration tools and work quite different from a provisioning tool such as Terraform. Of course, there are alternatives, such as CloudFormation, but at the time of writing, this is more limited than Terraform when it comes to supporting all cloud platforms.

When we're talking true agnostic, we should definitively talk about containers and Kubernetes. Remember one of the two major shifts? One of them was VMs to containers and that is certainly true for infrastructure components. The big difference between VMs and containers is the way they handle operating systems. Whereas a VM needs to have its own operating system, containers use the operating system of the host. That makes a container not just much lighter than a VM, but also much more flexible and truly agnostic.

You can use the container on any platform. However, you will need an orchestrating platform to land the containers on. This is what Kubernetes provides. You can enroll Kubernetes on every platform using **Azure Kubernetes Services** (**AKS**), **Elastic Kubernetes Services** (**EKS**) on AWS, or **Google Kubernetes Engine** (**GKE**) or **Pivotal Kubernetes Services** (**PKS**) on VMware platforms. The following diagram shows the difference in concepts between VMs and containers:

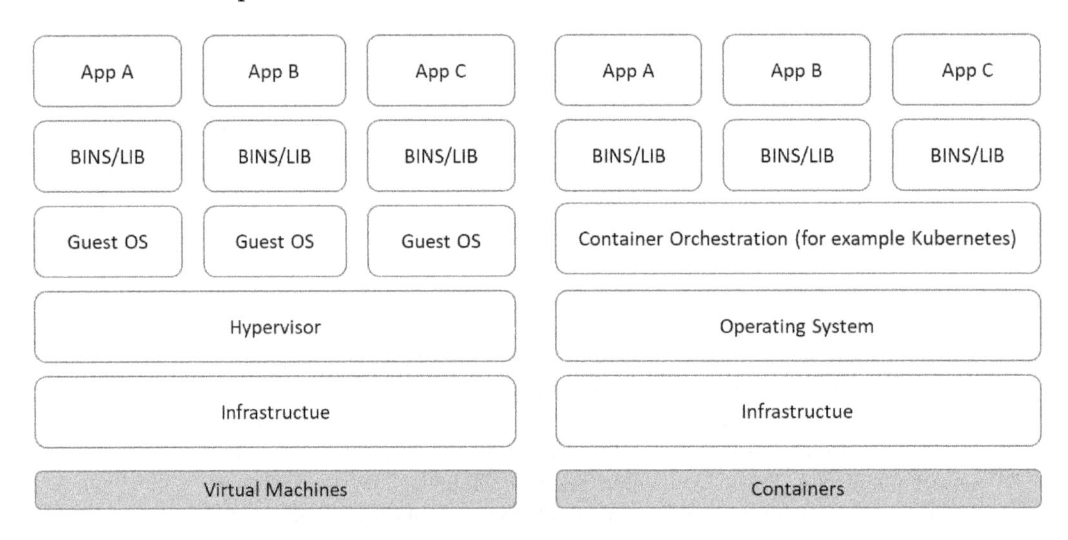


Figure 4.3 – VMs versus containers

In the next chapter, we will explore the build and configuration of the landing zone in much more detail.

## Stage 6 - assessment

The assessment phase is a vital step to ensuring proper migration to a target cloud environment. Before we start migrating or rebuilding applications in our landing zone, we need to know what we have. First and foremost, we need to assess our business strategy. Where do we want to go with our business and what does it take to get there? The next question would be: is our current IT estate ready to deliver that strategy? Which applications do we have and what business function do they serve? Are applications and the underlying infrastructure up to date or are they (near) end of service, even end of life? What support contracts do we have, and do we need to extend these during our transformation to the cloud or can we retire these contracts?

You get the point: a proper assessment takes some time, but don't skip it. Our end goal should be clear; at the end of the day, all businesses want to become a digital company that takes data-driven decisions. We need an environment in which we can disclose data in a secure way and make the environment as flexible and scalable as possible, so it can breathe at business speed. The problem is our traditional IT environment, which has been built out over many years. If we're lucky, everything will be well documented, but the hard reality is that documentation is rarely up to date. If we start our transformation without a proper assessment, we are bound to start pulling bricks out of an old wall without knowing how stable that wall really is. Again, here too, we require scaffolds.

## Stage 7 - migrating and transforming

Now we have our landing zone and we're ready to start deploying services and workloads into our cloud environments. This is what we call cloud transformation. This is the stage where we will implement our technical strategies that we discussed in *Chapter 2, Business Acceleration Using a Multi-Cloud Strategy*, such as rehost, replatform, rebuild, retain, and retire. Following the assessment, we have defined for each application or application group what the business focus is and what the technical strategy is. In this final stage, we will shift our applications to the new platform, apply new cloud services, or rebuild applications native to the cloud. Obviously, we will do that in a DevOps way of working, where we do all the building and configuration from code as we discussed in stage 5.

DevOps comprises epics and features. Don't overcomplicate things. The epic could be *implementing new cloud architecture*, where transformation of an application or application group can be the feature. With the knowledge that we acquired from the assessment phase, combined with the technical strategy, the DevOps team should be able to do a good refinement, breaking down the feature into tasks that can be executed and completed in a limited number of sprints. We will explore this further in *Chapter 18, Defining and Designing Processes for Test, Integration, Deployment, and Release Using CI/CD*, where we will also discuss the **continuous improvement/continuous delivery** (**CI/CD**) pipeline.

There are two really important items in a transformation stage: going live and the exit strategy. Before going live, testing is required. The need for good testing is really underestimated. It is very strongly advised to run the full test cycle: unit, integration, end user test. From a process point of view, no company should allow anything to go live before all test findings have proven to be addressed. The same applies to the exit strategy: no company should allow anything to go live without a clearly defined exit strategy; how to roll back or move environments out of the cloud again, back to the original state. It's one more reason to consider a – parallel – rebuild of environments, so that there's always the old environment as a fallback when things turn out not to be working as designed. Of course, testing should prevent things from going wrong, but we have to be realistic too: something will break.

# Translating business KPIs into cloud SLAs

Frankly, infrastructure in the cloud should be a black box to a business. Infrastructure is like turning on the water tap. Some IT companies refer to operating cloud infrastructure as liquid or fluid IT for that reason: it was simply there, all the time. As a consequence, the focus on SLAs shifted to the business itself. Also, that is part of the cloud adoption. As enterprises are moving ahead in the adoption process, a lot of businesses are also adopting a different way of working. If we can have flexible, agile infrastructure in the cloud, we can also speed up the development of environments and applications. Still, also in the cloud, we have to carefully consider service-level objectives and KPIs.

Let's have a look at the cloud SLA. What would be topics that have to be covered in a SLA? The **A** stands for **agreement** and, from a legal perspective, it would be a contract. Therefore, an SLA typically has the format and the contents that belong to a contract. There will be definitions for contract duration, start date, legal entities of the parties entering into the agreement, and service hours. More important are the agreements on the KPIs. What are we expecting from the cloud services that we use and we are paying for? And who do we contact if something's not right or we need support for a certain service? Lastly, what is the exact scope of the service?

These are all quite normal topics in any IT service contract. However, it doesn't work the same way when we're using public cloud services. The problem with the SLA is that it's usually rightsized per business. The business contracts IT services, where the provider tailors the services to the needs of that business. Of course, a lot of IT providers standardize and automate as much as they can to obtain maximum efficiency in their services, but nonetheless, there's room for tweaking and tuning. In the public cloud, that room is absolutely limited. A company will have a lot of services to choose from to tailor to its requirements, but the individual services are as they are. Typically, cloud providers offer an SLA per service. Negotiating the SLA per service in a multi-cloud environment is virtually impossible.

It's all part of the service design: the business will have to decide what components they need to cater for their needs and assess whether these components are fit for purpose. The components – the services themselves – can't be changed. In IaaS, there will be some freedom, but when we're purchasing PaaS and SaaS solutions, the services will come out of the box. The business will need to make sure that an SaaS solution really has the required functionality and delivers at the required service levels.

Common KPIs in IT are availability, durability, **Recovery Time Objective** (**RTO**) and **Recovery Point Objective** (**RPO**) – just to name a few important ones. How do these KPIs work out in the major public clouds?

Availability is defined as the time when a certain system can actually be used.

Availability should be measured end to end. What do we mean with this? Well, a VM with an operating system can be up and functioning alright, but if there's a failure in one software component running on top of that VM and the operating system, the application will be unusable, and hence unavailable to the user. The VM and operating system are up (and available), but the application is down. This means that the whole system is unavailable and this has some serious consequences. It also means that if we want to obtain an overall availability of 99.9 percent of our application, this means that the platform can't have an availability below that 99.9 percent. And then nothing should go wrong.

In traditional data centers, we needed to implement specific solutions to guarantee availability. We would have to make sure that the network, compute layers, and storage systems can provide for the required availability. Azure, AWS, and GCP largely take care of that. It's not that you get an overall availability guarantee on these platforms, but these hyperscalers - Azure, AWS, and Google Cloud - do offer service levels on each component in their offerings. By way of an example, a single-instance VM in Azure has a guaranteed connectivity of 99.9 percent. Mind the wording here: the connectivity to the VM is guaranteed. Besides, you will have to use premium storage for all disks attached to the VM. You can increase the availability of systems by adding availability, zones, and regions in Azure. Zones are separate data centers in an Azure region. At the time of writing, Azure has 58 regions worldwide. In summary, you can make sure that a system is always online somewhere around the globe in Azure, but it takes some effort to implement such a solution using load balancing and traffic manager over the Azure backbone. That's all a matter of the following:

- Business requirements (is a system critical and does it have to have high availability?)
- The derived technical design
- The business case, since the high-availability solution will cost more money than a single-ended VM

It's not an easy task to compare the service levels between providers. As with a lot of services, the basic concepts are all more or less the same, but there are differences. Just look at the way Azure and AWS detail their service levels on compute. In Azure, these are VMs. In AWS, the service is called **EC2 - Elastic Compute Cloud** in full. Both providers work with service credits if the monthly guaranteed uptime of instances is not met and, just to be clear, system infrastructure (the machine itself!) is not available. If uptime drops below 99.99 percent over a month, then the customer receives a service credit of 10 percent over the monthly billing cycle. Google calculates credits if the availability drops below 99.5 percent.

> **Note**
>
> In GCP, all service levels are defined as **service level objectives** (**SLOs**). That's because Google has fully adopted SRE on their platform. In the SLA for GCP, you will encounter some different terms such as **service level indicators** (**SLIs**) and error budgets. We will discuss this in a bit more detail in *Chapter 20, Introducing SRE in Multi-Cloud Environments.*

Again, requirements for service levels should come from the business. For each business function and corresponding system, the requirements should be crystal clear. That ultimately drives the architecture and system designs. The cloud platforms offer a wide variety of services to compose that design, making sure that requirements are met. To put it in slightly stronger terms, the hyperscalers offer the possibility to have systems that are ultimately resilient. Where, in traditional data centers, **disaster recovery (DR)** and business continuity meant that a company had to have a second data center as a minimum, cloud platforms offer this as a service. Azure, AWS, and GCP are globally available platforms, meaning that you can actually have systems available across the globe without having to do enormous investments. The data centers are there, ready to use. Cloud providers have native solutions to execute backups and store these in vaults in different regions, or they offer third-party solutions from their portals so that you can still use your preferred product.

However, it should be stressed once again that the business should define what their critical services and systems are, defining the terms for recovery time and recovery points. The business should define the DR metrics and, even more important, the processes when a DR plan needs to be executed. Next, it's up to IT to fulfill these requirements with technical solutions. Will we be using a warm standby system, fully mirrored from the production systems in a primary region? Are we using a secondary region and what region should that be then? Here, compliancy and public regulations such as the **General Data Protection Regulation (GDPR)** or data protection frameworks in other parts of the world also play an important role. Or will we have a selection of systems in a second region?

One option might be to deploy acceptance systems in another region and leverage these to production in case of a failover in DR. That implies that acceptance systems are really production-like. How often do we have to back up the systems? A full backup once a week? Will we be using incremental backups and, if so, how often? What should be the retention time of backup data? What about archiving? It's all relatively easy to deploy in cloud platforms, but there's one reason to be extremely careful in implementing every available solution. It's not about the upfront investment, as with traditional data centers (the real cash out for investment in capital expenditure, or CAPEX), but you will be charged for these services (the operational expenditure, or OPEX) every month.

In short, the cloud needs a plan. That's what we will explore in the next sections, eventually in creating a service design.

# Using cloud adoption frameworks to align between cloud providers

The magic word in multi-cloud is a single pane of glass. What do we mean by that? Imagine that you have a multi-cloud environment that comprises a private cloud running VMware, a public cloud platform in AWS, and you're also using SaaS solutions from other providers. How would you keep track of everything that happens in all these components? Cloud providers might take care of a lot of things, so you need not worry about, for example, patches and upgrades. In SaaS solutions, the provider really takes care of the full stack, from the physical host all the way up to the operating systems and the software itself. However, there will always be things that you, as a company, will remain responsible for. Think of matters such as IAM and security policies. Who has access to what and when?

This is the new reality of complexity: multi-cloud environments consisting of various solutions and platforms. How can we manage that? Administrators would have to log in to all these different environments. Likely, they will have different monitoring solutions and tools to manage the components. That takes a lot of effort and, first and foremost, a lot of different skills. It surely isn't very efficient. We want to have a single pane of glass: one ring to rule them all.

Let's look at the definition of a single pane of glass first. According to TechTarget (`https://searchconvergedinfrastructure.techtarget.com/definition/single-pane-of-glass`), it's *"a management console that presents data from multiple sources in a unified display. The glass, in this case, is a computer monitor or mobile device screen."* The problem with that definition is that it's purely a definition from a technological perspective: just one system that has a view of all the different technology components in our IT landscape. However, a single pane of glass goes way beyond the single monitoring system. It's also about unified processes and even unified automation. Why is the latter so important? If we don't have a unified way of automation, we'll still be faced with a lot of work in automating the deployment and management of resources over different components in that IT landscape. So, a single pane of glass is more an approach that can be visualized in a triangle:

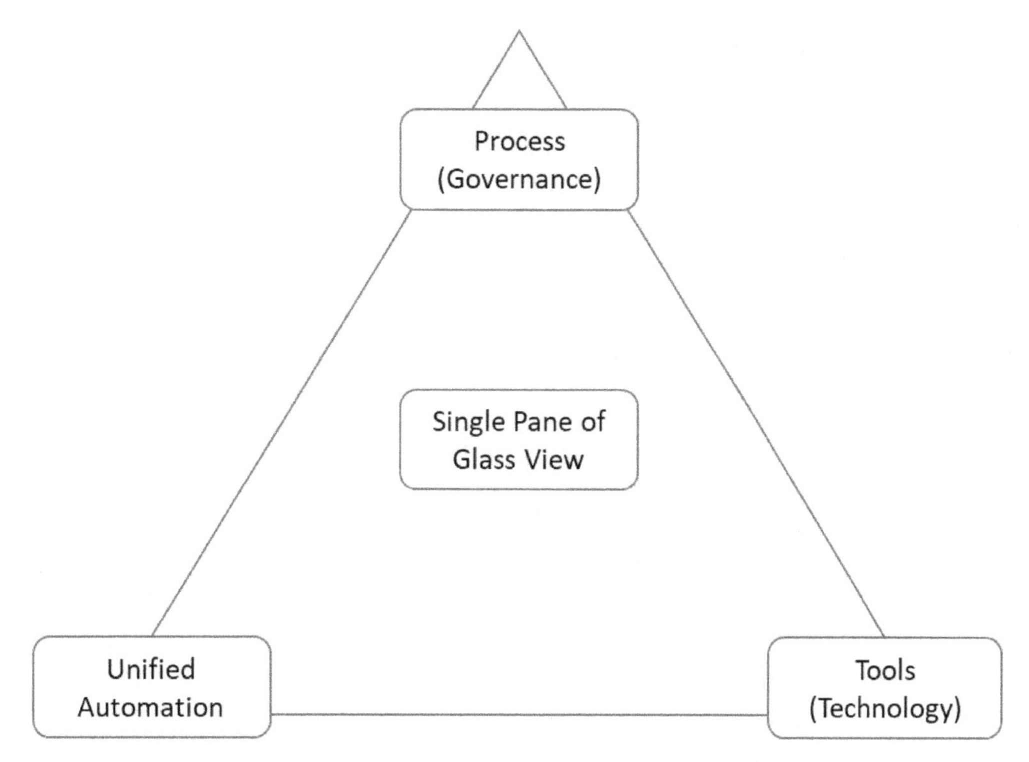


Figure 4.4 – Graphic representation of a single pane of glass

Do such systems exist that embrace that approach? Yes, there are full IT service management systems such as BMC Helix Multi-Cloud Management and ServiceNow with the Now platform. There are certainly more alternatives, but these are considered to be the market leaders, according to Gartner's Magical Quadrant for ITSM systems.

ITSM, that's what where talking about. The tool – the technology – is one thing, but the processes are just as important. IT service management processes include, as a minimum, the following processes:

- **Incident management**: Tracking and resolving incidents in the platform itself or resources hosted on the platform
- **Problem management**: Tracking and resolving recurring incidents
- **Change management**: Tracking and controlled implementation of changes to the platform or resources hosted on the platform
- **Configuration management**: Tracking the state of the platform and the resources hosted on the platform

The cornerstone in ITSM is knowledge: you have to have an indisputable insight into what your platform looks like, how it is configured, what type of assets live on your platform, and which assets and resources are deployed on the platform. Assets and resources are often referred to as configuration items and they are all collected and tracked in a **Configuration Management Database** (**CMDB**) or master repository (**Master Data Records**, **MDRs**). Here, the challenge in the cloud really starts. With scalable, flexible resources and even resources that might only live for a very brief period of time in our estate, such as containers or serverless functions, we are faced with the risk that our CMDB or asset repository will never be as accurate as we would like it to be, although the leading ITSM systems have native APIs to the monitoring tools in the different clouds that are truly responsive and collect asset data in (near) real time.

The agility of the cloud makes change management probably the most important process in multi-cloud environments. Pipelines with infrastructure and config as code help. If we have a clear process in how the code is forked, tested, validated, and merged back in the master branch, then changes are fully retrievable. If a developer skips one step in the process, we are heading for failure and worse – without knowing what went wrong.

All cloud adoption frameworks stress the importance of governance and processes on top of the technology that clouds provide. All frameworks approach governance from the business risk profiles. That makes sense: if we're not in agreement in how we do things in IT, at the end of the day, the business is at risk. Basically, the ultimate goal of service management is to reduce business risks that emanate from a lack of IT governance. IT governance and ITSM is a common language between technology providers, for a very good reason.

Back to our *one ring to rule them all*. We have unified processes, defined in ITSM. There are different frameworks for ITSM (ITIL or Cobit, for example), but they all share the same principles. Now, can we have one single dashboard to leverage ITSM, controlling the life cycle of all our assets and resources? We already mentioned BMC Helix and ServiceNow as technology tools. But can we also have our automation through these platforms? Put another way, can we have automation that is fully cross-platform? This is something that Gartner calls **hyperautomation**.

Today, automation is often executed per component or, in the best cases, per platform. By doing that, we're not reaching the final goal of automation, which is to reduce manual tasks that have be executed over and over again. We're not reducing the human labor and, for that matter, we're not reducing the risk of human error. On the contrary, we are introducing more work and the risk of failure by having automation divided into different toolsets on top of different platforms, all with separate workflows, schedules, and scripts. Hyperautomation deals with that. It automates all business processes and integrates these in a single automated life cycle, managed from one automation platform.

Gartner calls this platform **Hybrid Digital Infrastructure Management** (**HDIM**). Machine learning, **Robotic Process Automation** (**RPA**), and subsequent AIOps are key technologies in HDIM. One remark has to be made: the time of writing is April 2020 and Gartner anticipates that AI-enabled automation and HDIM will be advanced enough for broad, large-scale adoption in 2023.

In summary, cloud adoption frameworks from Azure, AWS, and GCP all support the same principles. That's because they share the common IT service management language. That helps us to align processes across platforms. The one challenge that we have is the single dashboard to control the various platforms and have one source of automation across the cloud platforms – hyperautomation. With the speed of innovation in the cloud, that is becoming increasingly complex, but we will see more tools and automation engines coming to market over the next years, including the rise and adoption of AIOps.

# Understanding identities and roles in the cloud

Everything in the cloud has an identity. There are two things that we need to do with identities: authenticate and authorize. For authentication, we need an identity store. Most enterprises will use **Active Directory** (**AD**) for that, where AD becomes the central place to store identities of persons and computers. We won't be drilling down into the technology, but there are a few things you should understand when working with AD. First of all, an AD works with domains. You can deploy resources – VMs or other virtual devices – in a cloud platform, but if that cloud platform is not part of your business domain, it won't be very useful. So, one of the key things is to get resources in your cloud platform domain-joined. For that, you will have to deploy domain services with domain controllers in your cloud platform or allow cloud resources access to the existing domain services. By doing that, we are extending the business to the cloud platform.

That sounds easier than it is in practice. Azure, AWS, and GCP are public clouds. Microsoft, Amazon, and Google are basically offering big chunks of their platforms to third parties: businesses that host workloads on a specific chunk. But they will still be on a platform that is owned and controlled by the respective cloud providers. The primary domain of the platform will be `onmicrosoft.com` or `aws.amazon.com`: this makes sense if you think of all the (public) services they offer on their platforms.

If we want our own domain on these platforms, we will need to ring-fence a specific chunk by attaching a registered domain name to the platform. Let's, for example, have a company with the name `myfavdogbiscuit.com`. On Azure, we can specify a domain with `myfavdogbiscuit.onmicrosoft.com`. Now we have our own domain on the Azure platform. The same applies obviously for AWS and GCP. Resources deployed in the cloud domains can now be domain-joined, if the domain on the cloud platform is connected to the business domain. That connection is provided by domain controllers. The following diagram shows the high-level concept for AD Federation:

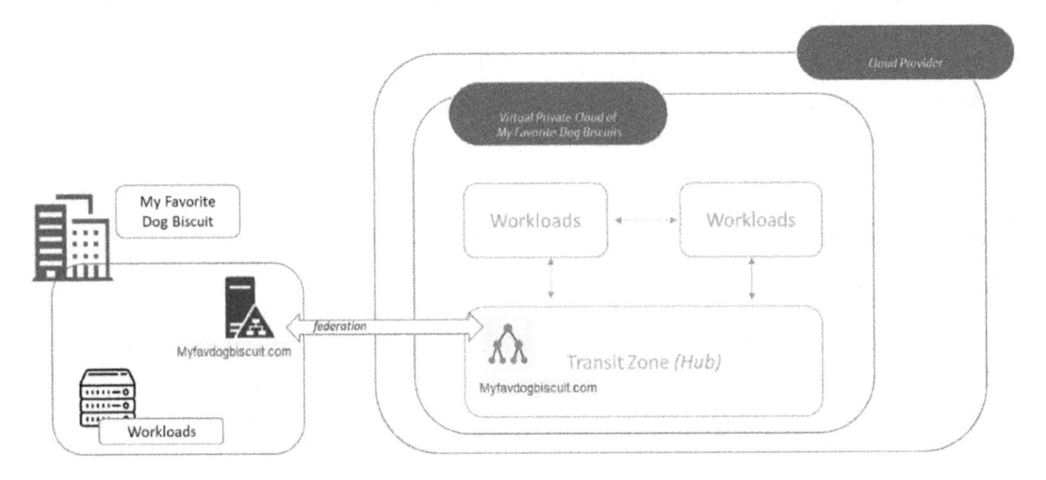


Figure 4.5 – Active Directory Federation

In AD, we have all our resources and persons that are allowed inside our domain. Authentication is done through acknowledgement: an identity is recognized in the domain or rejected. This AD uses Kerberos to verify an identity. It's important to know that all cloud providers support AD, the underlying **Lightweight Directory Access Protocol** (**LDAP**) standard, and Kerberos.

If a resource or person can't be identified in the directory, it simply won't get access to that domain, unless we explicitly grant them access. That can be the case when a person doesn't have an account in our domain, but needs to have access to resources that are on our platform. We can grant this person access using a business-to-consumer connection. In Azure, that is conveniently called B2C, in AWS it's called Cognito, and in GCP, Cloud Identity.

We have identified a person or a resource using the directory, but now we have to make sure that this resource can only do what we want or allow it to do – and nothing more. This is what we call authorization: we specify what a resource is allowed to do, when certain criteria are met. First, we really want to make sure that the resource is whoever it claims it is. For people logging in, it is advised to use multi-factor authentication. For compute resources, we will have to work with another mechanism and typically that will be based on keys: a complex, unique hash that identifies the resource.

One more time: we have defined identities in our environment, either human personnel or system identities. How can we define what an identity is allowed in our environment? For that we need **Role-Based Access Control** (**RBAC**). RBAC in Azure, IAM in AWS, and Cloud Identity in GCP let you manage access to (parts of) the environment and what identities can do in that environment. We can also group identities for which a specific RBAC policy applies.

We have already concluded that all cloud platforms support AD and the underlying protocols. So, we can federate our AD with domains in these different clouds. Within Azure, the obvious route to do so would be through connecting AD to Azure AD. Although this might seem like these are similar solutions, they are totally different things. AD is a real directory, whereas Azure AD is merely a tool to verify identities within Azure. It does not have the authentication mechanisms that AD has, such as Kerberos. Azure AD will authenticate using AD. And with that it's quite similar to the way the other platforms federate with AD. In both AWS and GCP, you will need identities that can be federated against AD. In other words, your AD will always remain the single source of truth for identity management, the one and only identity store.

*Chapter 15, Identity and Access Management and Account Federation*, is all about access management and account federation. In that chapter, we will further explore RBAC, but also things such as privileged access and eligible accounts.

# Creating the service design and governance model

The final thing to do is to combine all the previous sections into a service design and governance model for multi-cloud environments. So, what should the contents be of a service design? Just look at everything we have discussed so far. We need a design that covers all the topics: requirements, identities and access management, governance, costs, and security. Let's discuss these in detail.

## Requirements

This includes the service target that will comprise a number of components. Assuming that we are deploying environments in the public cloud, we should include the public cloud platform as such as a service target. The SLA for Microsoft Online Services describes the SLAs and KPIs committed to by Microsoft for the services delivered on Azure. These are published on `https://azure.microsoft.com/en-us/support/legal/sla/`. For AWS, the SLA documentation can be found at `https://aws.amazon.com/legal/service-level-agreements/`. Google published the SLAs for all cloud services on GCP at `https://cloud.google.com/terms/sla/`. These SLAs will cover the services that are provided by the respective cloud platforms; they do not cater for services that a business builds on top of these cloud-native services. By way of an example, if a business builds a tiered application with frontends, worker roles, and databases, and defines that as a service to a group of end users, this service needs to be documented separately as a service target.

Next, we will list the relevant requirements that have to be addressed by the service target:

- **Continuity requirements**: This will certainly be relevant for business-critical services. Typically, these are addressed in a separate section that describes RTO/RPO, backup strategies, the business continuity plans, and DR measures.
- **Compliance requirements**: You will need to list the compliance frameworks that the company is constrained by. These can be frameworks related to privacy, such as the EU GDPR, but also security standards such as ISO 27001. Keep in mind that Microsoft, AWS, and Google are US-based companies. In some industry sectors outside the US (this applies typically to EU countries), working with US-based providers is allowed only under strict controls. The same applies to agreements with Chinese providers such as Alibaba, one of the upcoming public clouds. Always consult a legal advisor before your company starts deploying services in public clouds or purchasing cloud services.
- **Architectural and interface requirements**: Enterprises will likely have an enterprise architecture, describing how the company produces goods or delivers services. The business architecture is, of course, very important input for cloud deployment. It will also contain a listing of various interfaces that the business has, for example, with suppliers of components or third-party services. This will include interfaces within the entire production or delivery chain of a company – suppliers, HR, logistics, and financial reporting.

- **Operational requirements**: This section has to cover life cycle policies and maintenance windows. An important requirement that is set by the business is so-called blackout periods, wherein all changes to IT environments are halted. That may be the case, for example, at year-end closing or in the case of expected peaks in production cycles. The life cycle includes all policies related to upgrades, updates, patches, and fixes to components in the IT environment.
- **As with the continuity requirements, this is all strongly dependent on the underlying cloud platform**: Cloud providers offer a variety of tools, settings, and policies that can be applied to the infrastructure to prevent downtime of components. Load balancing, backbone services, and planning components over different stacks, zones (data centers), and even regions are all possible countermeasures to prevent environments from going offline for any reason, be it planned or unplanned. Of course, all these services do cost money, so a business has to define which environments are business-critical so as to set the right level of component protection and related operational requirements.
- **Security and access requirements**: As stated previously, cloud platforms all offer highly sophisticated security tools to protect resources that are deployed on their platforms, yet security policies and related requirements should really be defined by the business using the cloud environments. That all starts with who may access what, when, and why. A suitable RBAC model must be implemented for admin accounts.

Next, we will look at the **Risks, Assumptions, Issues, and Dependencies (RAID)** and the service decomposition.

## RAID

A service design and governance model should contain a RAID log. This RAID log should be maintained so that it always represents the accurate status, providing input to adjust and adapt principles, policies, and the applied business and technical architecture.

## Service decomposition

The next part is service decomposition, in other words, the product breakdown of the services. What will we be using in our cloud environment?

- **Data components**: What data is stored, where, and in what format, using which cloud technology? Think of SQL and NoSQL databases, data lakes, files, queues, but also in terms of the respective cloud storage solutions, such as Blob in Azure, S3, Glacier, or Google Cloud Storage.
- **Application components**: Which applications will be supported in the environment, and how are these built and configured? This defines which services we need to onboard and makes sure there's a clear definition between at least business-critical systems and systems that are not critical. A good method is to have systems categorized, for example, into gold, silver, and bronze, with gold denoting business-critical systems, silver denoting other important production and test systems, and bronze development systems.

  However, be careful in categorizing systems. A development system can be critical in terms of finances. Just imagine having a hundred engineers working on a specific system under time pressure to deliver and the development systems become unavailable. This will surely lead to delays, a hundred engineers sitting idle, and thereby costing a lot of money. We cannot stress enough how important business cases are.
- **Infrastructure components**: VMs, load balancers, network appliances, firewalls, databases, storage, and so on. Remember that these will all configure items in a CMDB or MDR.

- **Cloud-native components**: Think of PaaS services, containers, and serverless functions. Also, list how cloud components are managed: through portals, CLIs or code interfaces such as PowerShell or Terraform.
- **Security components**: Security should be intrinsic on all layers. Data needs to be protected, both in transit and at rest, applications need to be protected from unauthorized access, infrastructure should be hardened, and monitoring and alerting should be enabled on all resources.

  Typically, backup and restoration are also part of the security components. Backup and restore are elements related to protecting the IT estate, but ultimately protecting the business by preventing the loss of data and systems. Subsequently, for business-critical functions, applications, and systems, a **business continuity and disaster recovery** (**BCDR**) plan should be identified. From the BCDR plan, requirements in terms of RPO/RTO and retention times for backups are derived as input for the architecture and design for these critical systems.

As you can tell, we follow the **The Open Group Architecture Framework** (**TOGAF**) **Architecture Development Method** (**ADM**) cycle all the way: business requirements, data, applications, and the most recent technology. Security is part of all layers. Security policies are described in a separate section.

## Roles and responsibilities

This section in the service design defines who's doing what in the different service components, defining roles and what tasks identities can perform when they have specific roles. Two models are detailed in the following sections.

## Governance model

This is the model that defines the entities that are involved in defining the requirements for the service, designing the service, delivering the service, and controlling the service. It also includes lines of report and escalation. Typically, the first line in the model is the business setting the requirements, the next line is the layer comprising the enterprise architecture, responsible for bridging business and IT, and the third line is the IT delivery organization. All these lines are controlled by means of an audit as input for risk and change control:

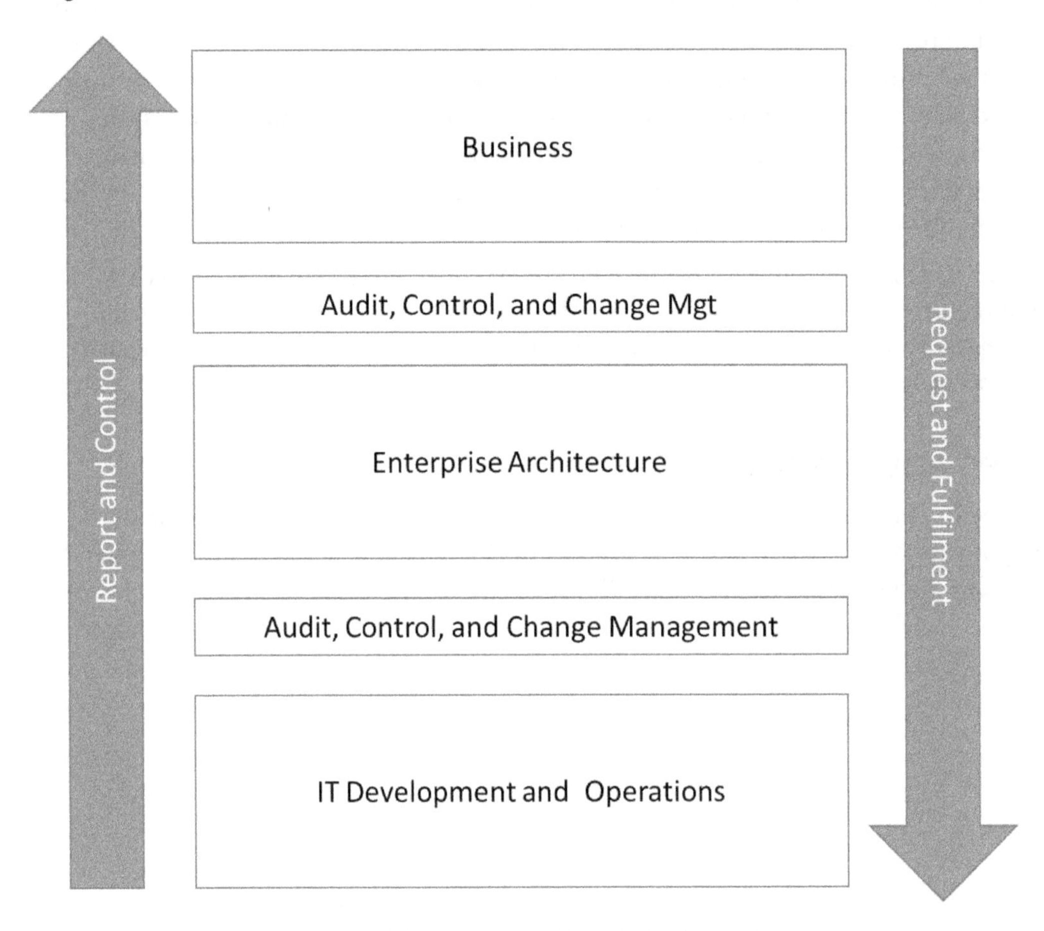


Figure 4.6 – Governance model (high-level example)

Now, this is a very simple, straightforward presentation of a governance model. It can have many variations. For one, IT delivery is often done in Agile teams, working according to DevOps principles. The main principle stays intact, even with Agile teams. Even Agile teams need to be controlled and work under definitions of change management. Just one tip: don't overcomplicate models, keep it as simple as possible.

## Support model

The support model describes who's delivering the support on the various components. Is that solely an internal IT operations division, or do we need to have support contracts from third parties? For that matter, an enterprise will very likely require support from the cloud provider. The support model also defines to what degree that support needs to be provided. In some cases, having the option to have an occasional talk with a subject matter expert from a provider might be sufficient, but when a company has outsourced its cloud operations, full support can be a must.

An important topic that needs to be covered in the support model is the level of expertise that a company requires in order to run its business in cloud platforms. As we already noticed in *Chapter 2, Business Acceleration Using a Multi-Cloud Strategy*, there's a strong tendency to insource IT operations again, since the way IT is perceived has dramatically changed. For almost every company, IT has become a core activity and not just a facilitator. Since more and more companies are deploying services in the cloud, they are also building their own cloud centers of excellence, but with the subject matter expertise and support of cloud providers.

If we follow all the stages so far as a full cycle, then we will end up with a service catalogue, describing exactly what services are in scope, how they are delivered, and who's supporting these services.

# Processes

This section defines what processes are in place and how these are managed. All processes involved should be listed and described:

- Incident management
- Problem management
- Change management
- Asset management and CMDB (or MDR)
- Configuration management
- Reporting
- Knowledge base

These are the standard processes as used in ITSM. For cloud environments, it's strongly advised to include the automation process as a separate topic. In the DevOps world that we live in, we should store all code and scripts in a central repository. The knowledge base can be stored in Wikipages in that repository. The DevOps pipeline with the controlled code base and knowledge wikis must be integrated in the ITSM process and the ITSM tooling. Remember: we want to have a single-pane glass view of our entire environment.

There's one important process that we haven't touched yet and that's the request and request fulfilment. The request starts with the business demand. The next step in the process is to analyze the demand and perform a business risk assessment, where the criticality of the business function is determined and mapped to the required data. Next, the request is mapped to the business policies and the security baseline. This sets the parameters on how IT components should be developed and deployed, taking into account the fact that RBAC is implemented and resources are deployed according to the services as described in the service decomposition. That process can be defined as request fulfilment.

If different services are needed for specific resources, than that's a change to the service catalogue.

# Costs

This section covers the type of costs, and how these are monitored and evaluated. It contains the model that clearly describes how costs are allocated within the business, the so-called charge back. The charge back is usually based on the subscription model in the public cloud, the RBAC design, and the naming and tagging standards that have been deployed to resources. Costs should be evaluated at regular intervals and subsequently businesses should have a clear delegation of control when it comes to costs. Budgets need to be set and cost alerts implemented to manage and, if so required, set IT spend limits. We will talk about Amex Armageddon, where the company credit card is simply pulled out and, at the end of the day, no one knows who's spending what in the cloud – or for what reason. You wouldn't be the first company to run a Hadoop cluster without even knowing it.

Be aware that costs in the public cloud are not just the costs per deployed resource, in terms of a fee for a VM or a connection. Data ingress and outgress are charged, too, on various levels: in network connectivity, firewall throughput, and databases. In fact, a lot of items are chargeable. It all depends on the type of solution that you deploy and, as the saying goes, many roads lead to Rome.

One thing that really must be included are licenses. Obviously, a lot of software is licensed. But the public cloud brings an extra dimension to licensing: scalability. Be sure that software that's licensed for your company can actually scale up, down, and out within the terms of that license. The public cloud offers various licensing models, such as enterprise agreements, premium agreements, or agreements through resellers, but all of these come with different conditions.

*Chapter 13, Validating and Managing Billing*, is all about FinOps, financial operations, and covers cost management, licensing, billing, and financial controlling. Business financial control must be involved and the rules of FinOps in multi-cloud environments should be understood.

## Security

We said it a few times: security is intrinsic. What do we mean by that? Security is part of every single layer in the multi-cloud environment, from the business, via enterprise architecture, to the actual deployment and management of platforms, and is embedded in every single service and service component.

This section contains a business risk assessment in using different cloud solutions and how these risks have been mitigated. This is done through a gap analysis between the business security frameworks the company must adhere to and the security frameworks that cloud providers actively support and have integrated in their standards. The good news is that the major platforms support most of the industry-leading frameworks, yet it's the responsibility of the company to prove that when it's audited. Hence, this section also describes how the environment is audited (internal/external), at what frequency, and what the process is for mitigating audit findings. These mitigation actions must follow the change process in order to document the change itself, the adapted solution, and possibly the change to the service catalogue.

It's probably needless to say, but still we'll stress that CISO and internal auditing should be involved at all times. *Chapter 17, Defining, Designing, and Using Security Monitoring and Management Tools*, is all about security operations – SecOps.

Wait a minute… where's our architecture? You're right: we need an architecture. That's what we will be digging into in the next chapter.

# Summary

In this chapter, we've explored the main pillars in cloud adoption frameworks, and we learned that the different frameworks have quite some overlap. We've identified the seven stages of cloud adoption up until the point where we can really start migrating and transforming applications to our cloud platforms. In multi-cloud environments, control and management is challenging. It calls for a single pane of glass approach, but, as we have also learned, there are just a few tools – the one ring to rule them all – that would cater for this single pane of glass.

One of the most important things to understand is that you first have to look at identities in your environment: who, or what, if we talk about other resources on our platform, is allowed to do what, when, and why? That is key in setting out the governance model. The governance model is the foundation of the service design.

In the last paragraph of this chapter, we've looked at the different sections in such a service design. Of course, it all starts with the architecture and that's what we'll be studying in the next chapter: creating and managing our architecture.

# Questions

1. You are planning a migration of a business environment to the public cloud. Would an assessment be a crucial step in designing the target environment in that public cloud?
2. You are planning a cloud adoption program for your business. Would you consider cost management as part of the cloud adoption framework?
3. IAM plays an important role in moving to a cloud platform. What is the most commonly used environment as an identity directory in enterprise environments?

# Further reading

Alongside the links that we mentioned in this chapter, check out the following books for more information on the topics that we have covered:

- *Mastering Identity and Access Management with Microsoft Azure*, by Jochen Nickel, published by Packt Publishing
- *Enterprise Cloud Security and Governance*, by Zeal Vora, published by Packt Publishing

# 5
# Managing the Enterprise Cloud Architecture

In the previous chapters, we've learned about different cloud technology strategies, looked at a model for identity and access management, and started drafting a multi-cloud network topology and a service model, including governance principles. Where do we go from here? From this point onward, you will be – as a business – managing your IT environments in multi-cloud. Successfully managing this new estate means that you will have to be very strict in maintaining the enterprise architecture. Hence, this chapter is all about maintaining and securing the multi-cloud architecture.

This chapter will introduce the methodology to create an enterprise architecture for multi-cloud using **The Open Group Architecture Framework** (**TOGAF**). We will study how to define architecture principles for various domains such as security, data, and applications. We will also learn how we can plan and create the architecture in different stages. Lastly, we will discuss the need to validate the architecture and how we can arrange it.

In this chapter, we will cover the following topics:

- Defining architecture principles for multi-cloud
- Creating the architecture artifacts
- Working under the architecture for multi-cloud and avoiding pitfalls
- Change management and validation as the cornerstone
- Validating the architecture

Let's get started!

# Defining architecture principles for multi-cloud

We'll start this chapter again from the perspective of the enterprise architecture. As we have seen, the **Architecture Development Method** (**ADM**) cycle in TOGAF is a guiding and broadly accepted framework used to start any enterprise architecture. In *Chapter 2, Business Acceleration Using a Multi-Cloud Strategy*, we learned that the production cycle for architecture starts with the business, yet there are two steps before we actually get to defining the business architecture: we have a preliminary phase where we set out the framework, and the, there's the architecture principles. These feed into the very first step in the actual cycle, known as architecture vision, as shown in the following diagram:

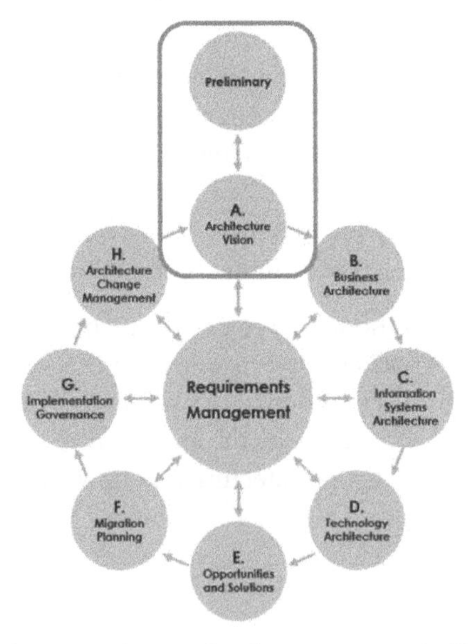


Figure 5.1 – The preliminary phase and architecture vision in TOGAF's ADM cycle

The key to any preliminary phase is the architecture principles; that is, your guidelines for fulfilling the architecture. There can be many principles, so the first thing that we have to do is create principle groups that align with our business. The most important thing to remember is that principles should enable your business to achieve its goals. Just to be very clear on this aspect: going to the cloud is not a business goal, just like cloud first is not a business strategy. These are technology statements at best, nothing more. But principles should do more: they have to support the architectural decisions being made and for that reason, they need to be durable and consistent.

When businesses decide that the cloud might be a good platform to host business functions and applications, the most used principles are flexibility, agility, and being cost-efficient. The latter is already highly ambiguous: what does cost-efficient mean? Typically, it means that the business expects that moving workloads to cloud platforms is cheaper than keeping them on-premises. This could be the case, but the opposite can also be true if incorrect decisions in the cloud have been made by following bad architectural decisions based on ambiguous principles. In short, every principle should be challenged:

- Does the principle support the business goals?
- Is the principle clear so that it can't be subject to multiple interpretations?
- Is the principle leading toward a clearly defined solution?

Some suggested groups for defining principles are as follows:

- Business
- Security and compliance
- Data principles
- Application principles
- Infrastructure and technology principles
- Usability
- Processes

Let's talk about each category in detail.

## Business principles

Business principles start with business units setting out their goals and strategy. These adhere to the business mission statement and, from there, describe what they want to achieve in the short and long term. This can involve a wide variety of topics:

- Faster response to customers
- Faster deployment of new products (time to market)
- Improve the quality of services or products
- Engage more with employees
- Real digital goals such as releasing a new website or web shop

As with nearly everything, these goals should be **SMART**, which is short for **specific, measurable, attainable, relevant, and timely**. For example, a SMART formulated goal could be *"the release of the web shop for product X in the North America region on June 1."* It's scoped to a specific product in a defined region and targeted at a fixed date. This is measurable as a SMART goal.

Coming back to TOGAF, this is an activity that is performed in phase B of the ADM cycle; that is, the phase in the architecture development method where we complete the business architecture. Again, this book is not about TOGAF, but we do recommend having one language to execute the enterprise architecture in. TOGAF is generally seen as the standard in this case. The business principles drive the business goals and strategic decisions that a business makes. For that reason, these principles are a prerequisite for any subsequent architectural stage.

## Security and compliance

Though security and compliance are major topics in any architecture, the principles in this domain can be fairly simple. Since these principles are of extreme importance in literally every single aspect of the architecture, it's listed as the second most important group of principles, right after the business principles.

Nowadays, we talk a lot about zero trust and security by design. These can be principles, but what do they mean? Zero trust speaks for itself: organizations that comply with zero trust do not trust anything within their networks and platforms. Every device, application, or user is monitored. Platforms are micro-segmented to avoid devices, applications, and users from being anywhere on the platform or inside the networks: they are strictly contained. The pitfall here is to think that zero trust is about technological measures only. It's not. Zero trust is foremost a business principle and looks at security from a different angle: zero trust assumes that an organization has been attacked, with the only question left being what the exact damage was. This is also the angle that frameworks such as MITRE ATT&CK take.

Security by design means that every component in the environment is designed to be secure from the architecture of that component: built-in security. This means that platform and systems, including network devices, are hardened and that programming code is protected against breaches via encryption or hashing. This also means that the architecture itself is already micro-segmented and that security frameworks have been applied. An example of a commonly used framework is the **Center for Internet Security** (**CIS**). CIS contains 20 critical security controls that cover various sorts of attacks on different layers in the IT stack. As CIS themselves rightfully state, it's not a one size fits all. An organization needs to analyze what controls should be implemented and to what extent.

We'll pick just one as an example: data protection, which is control 13. The control advises that data in transit and data at rest is encrypted. Note that CIS doesn't say what type of **Hardware Security Modules** (**HSMs**) an organization should use or even what level of encryption. It says that an organization should use encryption and secure this with safely kept encryption keys. It's up to the architect to decide on what level and what type of encryption should be used.

In terms of compliance principles, it must be clear to what international, national, or even regional laws and industry regulations the business has to adhere to. This includes laws and regulations in terms of privacy, which is directly related to the storage and usage of (personal) data.

An example of a principle is that the architecture must comply with the **General Data Protection Regulation** (**GDPR**). This principle only contains six words, but it means a lot of work when it comes to securing and protecting environments where data is stored (the systems of record) and how this data is accessed (systems of engagement). Technical measures that will result from this principle will vary from securing databases, encrypting data, and controlling access to that data with authentication and authorization. In multi-cloud, this can be even more challenging than it already was in the traditional data center. Using different clouds and PaaS and SaaS solutions, your data can be placed anywhere in terms of storage and data usage.

## Data principles

As we mentioned previously, here's where it really gets exciting and challenging at the same time in multi-cloud environments. The most often used data principles are related to data confidentiality and, from that, protecting data. We briefly touched on two important technology terms that have become quite common in cloud environments earlier in this chapter:

- **Systems of record**: Systems of record are data management or information storage systems; that is, systems that hold data. In the cloud, we have the commonly known database, but due to the scalability of cloud platforms, we can now deploy huge data stores comprising multiple databases that connect thousands of data sources. Public clouds are very suitable to host so-called data lakes.
- **Systems of engagement**: Systems of engagement are systems that are used to collect or access data. This can include a variety of systems: think of email, collaboration platforms, and content management systems, but also mobile apps or even IoT devices that collect data, send it to a central data platform, and retrieve data from that platform.

A high-level overview of the topology for holding systems of record and systems of engagement is shown in the following diagram, with **Enterprise Resource Planning (ERP)**, **Content Management** (**CMS**), and **Customer Relationship Management** (**CRM**) systems being used as examples of systems of record:

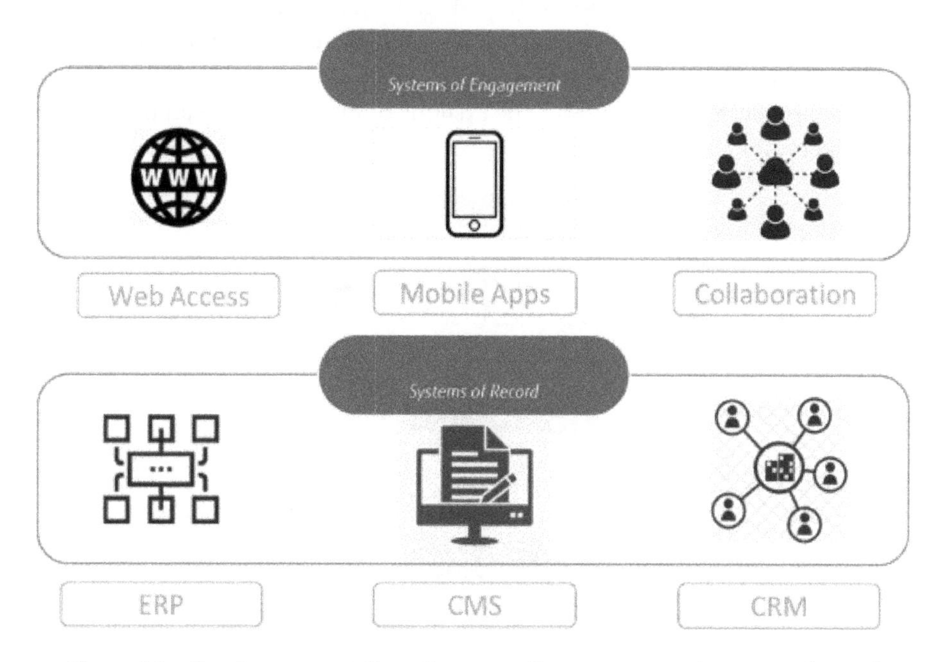


Figure 5.2 – Simple representation of systems of engagement and systems of record

The ecosystem of record and engagement is enormous and growing. We've already mentioned data lakes, which are large data stores that mostly hold raw data. In order to work with that data, a data scientist would need to define precise datasets to perform analytics. Azure, AWS, and Google all have offerings to enable this, such as Data Factory and Databricks in Azure, EMR and Athena in AWS, and BigQuery from Google.

Big data and data analytics have become increasingly important for businesses in their journey to become data-driven: any activity or business decision, for that matter, is driven by actual data. Since clouds can hold petabytes of data and systems need to be able to analyze this data fast to trigger these actions, a growing number of architects believe that there will be a new layer in the model. That layer will hold "systems of intelligence" using machine learning and **artificial intelligence (AI)**. Azure, AWS, and Google all offer AI-driven solutions, such as Azure ML in Azure, SageMaker in AWS, and Cloud AI in Google. The extra layer – the systems of intelligence – can be seen in the following diagram:

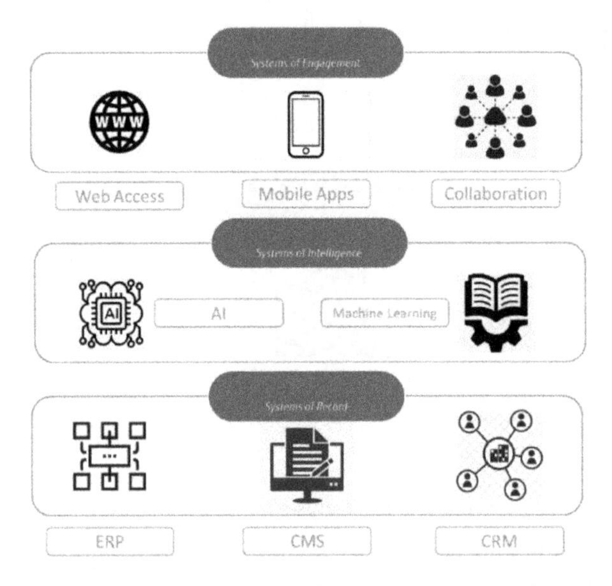


Figure 5.3 – Simple representation of the systems of intelligence layer

To be clear: systems of record or engagement don't say anything about the type of underlying resource. It can be anything from a physical server, to a **virtual machine (VM)**, a container, or even a function. Systems of record or engagement only say something about the functionality of a specific resource.

## Application principles

Data doesn't stand on its own. If we look at TOGAF once more, we'll see that data and applications are grouped into one architectural phase, known as phase C, which is the information systems architecture. In modern applications, one of the main principles for applications is that these have a data-driven approach, following the recommendation of Steven Spewak's enterprise architecture planning. Spewak published his book in 1992, but his approach is still very relevant, even – and perhaps even more – in multi-cloud environments.

Also mentioned in Spewak's work, the business mission is the most important driver in any architecture. That mission is data-driven: enterprises make decisions based on data, and for that reason, data needs to be relevant, but also accessed and usable. These latter principles are related to the applications disclosing the data to the business. In other words, applications need to safeguard the quality of the data, make data accessible, and ensure that data can be used. Of course, there can be – and there is – a lot of debate regarding, for instance, the accessibility of data. The sole relevant principle for an application architecture is that it makes data accessible. To whom and on what conditions are security principles.

In multi-cloud, the storage data changes, but also the format of applications. Spewak wrote his methodology at the beginning of the nineties, even before the internet really became big and ages before we saw something that we call the cloud today. Modern applications are usually not monolithic or client-server-based these days, although enterprises can still have a large base of applications with legacy architectures. Cloud-native apps are defined with roles and functions and build on the principles of code-based modularity and the use of microservices. These apps communicate with other apps using APIs or even triggers that call specific functions in other apps. These apps don't even have to run on the same platform; they can be hosted anywhere. Some architects tend to think that monolithic applications on mainframes are complex, so use that as a guideline to figure out how complex apps in multi-cloud can get.

However, a lot of architectural principles for applications are as valid as ever. The technology might change, but the functionality of an application is still to support businesses when it comes to rendering data, making it accessible, and ensuring that the data is usable.

Today, popular principles for applications are taking the specific characteristics of cloud-native technology into consideration. Modern apps should be enabled for mobility, be platform-independent using open standards, support interoperability, and be scalable. Apps should enable users to work with them any time, any place, anywhere.

One crucial topic is the fact that the requirements for applications change at almost the speed of light: users demand more and more from apps, so they have to be designed in an extremely agile way so that they can adopt changes incredibly fast in development pipelines. Cloud technology does support this: code can easily be adapted. But this does require that the applications are well-designed and documented, including in runbooks.

## Infrastructure and technology principles

Finally, we get to the real technology: machines, wires, nuts, and bolts. Here, we're talking about virtual nuts and bolts. Since data is stored in many places in our multi-cloud environment and applications are built to be cloud-native, the underlying infrastructure needs to support this. This is phase D in TOGAF, the phase in architecture development where we create the target technology architecture, which comprises the platform's location, the network topology, the infrastructure components that we will be using for specific applications and data stores, and the system interdependencies. In multi-cloud, this starts with drafting the landing zone: the platform where our applications and data will land. As we saw in *Chapter 3, Getting Connected – Designing Connectivity*, this begins with connectivity. Hence, the network architecture is the first component that needs to be detailed in the infrastructure and technology architecture.

One of the pitfalls of this is that architects create long, extensive lists with principles that infrastructure and technology should adhere to, all the way up to defining the products that will be used as a technology standard. However, a catalogue with products is part of a portfolio. Principles should be generic and guiding, not constraining. In other words, a list of technology standards and products is not a principle. A general principle could be about bleeding edge technology: a new, non-proven, experimental technology that imposes a risk when deployed in an environment because it's still unstable and unreliable.

Other important principles for infrastructure can be that it should be scalable (scale out, up, and down) and that it must allow micro-segmentation. We've already talked about the Twelve-Factor App, which sets out specific requirements to the infrastructure. These can be used as principles. The principles for the Twelve-Factor App were already set out in 2005, but as we already concluded in *Chapter 2, Business Acceleration Using a Multi-Cloud Strategy*, they are still very accurate and relevant.

The Twelve-Factor App sets the following three major requirements for infrastructure:

- The app is portable between different platforms, meaning that the app is platform-agnostic and does not rely on a specific server of systems settings.
- There's little to no difference between the development stage and the production stage of the app so that continuous development and deployment is enabled. The platform that the app is deployed on should support this (meaning that everything is basically code-based).
- The app supports scaling up without significant changes needing to be made to the architecture of the app.

In the next section, we will discuss the principles for usability and processes. We will also touch upon transition and transformation to cloud environments.

## Principles for usability

This principle group might look at bit odd in a multi-cloud architecture. Often, usability is related to the ease of use of apps, with clear interfaces and transparent app navigation from a user's perspective. However, these topics do imply certain constraints on our architecture. First of all, usability requires that the applications that are hosted in our multi-cloud environment are accessible to users. Consequently, we will have to think of how applications can or must be accessed. This is directly related to connectivity and routing: do users need access over the internet or are certain apps only accessible from the office network? Do we then need to design a **Demilitarized Zone** (**DMZ**) in our cloud network? And where are jump boxes positioned in the multi-cloud?

Keep in mind that multi-cloud application components can originate from different platforms. Users should not be bothered by that: the underlying technical setup should be completely transparent for users. This also implies architectural decisions: something we call technology transparency. In essence, as architects, we constantly have to work from the business requirements down to the safe use of data and the secured accessibility of applications to the end users. This drives the architecture all the way through.

## Principles for processes

The last group of principles are concerned about processes. This is not about the **IT System Management** (**ITSM**) processes, but about the processes of deployment and automation in multi-cloud. One of the principles in multi-cloud is that we will automate as much as we can. This means that we will have to define all the tasks that we would typically do manually into an automated workflow. If we have a code-only principle defined, then we can subsequently set a principle that states that we must work from the code base or master branch. If we fork the code and we do have to make changes to it, then a principle is that altered code can only be committed back to the master code if it's tested in an environment that is completely separated from acceptance and production. This is related to the life cycle process of our environment.

So, processes here do focus more on our way of working. Today, a lot of companies are devoted to agile and DevOps. If that's the defined way of working, then it should be listed as a principle; for example, development is done through the **Scaled Agile Framework** (**SAFe**) or the Spotify model. Following that principle, a company should also define the teams, their work packages, and how epics, features, product backlogs, and so on are planned. However, that's not part of the principle anymore. That's a consequence of the principle.

As with all principles, the biggest pitfall is making principles too complex. Especially with processes, it's important to really stick to describing the principle and not the actual process.

# Transition and transformation

We have done a lot of work already. Eventually, this should all add up to an architecture vision: a high-level view of the end state of our architecture and the objective of that architecture. However, an architecture is more than just a description or a blueprint of that end state. An architecture should also provide a roadmap; that is, a guide on how we will reach that end state. To be honest, there's nothing new under the sun here. On the contrary, this is how IT programs are typically run: it's all about transition and transformation. We will get to this in a bit.

Let's assume that our end state is a full cloud adoption. This means that the business has all of their IT systems, data, and applications in a cloud. Everything is code-based and automated, deployed, and managed from CI/CD pipelines. We've adopted native cloud technology such as containers and serverless functions. In *Chapter 2, Business Acceleration Using a Multi-Cloud Strategy*, we defined this as the dynamic phase, but that's a technical phase. The dynamic phase can be part of the end state of our architecture. However, we need to be absolutely sure that this dynamic technology does fit the business needs and that we are ready to operate this environment in the end state. We will refer to this end state as the **Future Mode of Operation** (**FMO**).

How do we get to this FMO? By starting at the beginning – the current situation, the **Current Mode of Operation** (**CMO**), or **Present Mode of Operation** (**PMO**). A proper assessment of the existing landscape is crucial to get a clear, indisputable insight into the infrastructure, connections, data, and applications that a business has in their IT environment. From there, we can start designing the transition and transformation to the FMO.

If we combine the methodology of Spewak, which we discussed at the beginning of this section, with CMO-FMO planning, the model will look as follows:

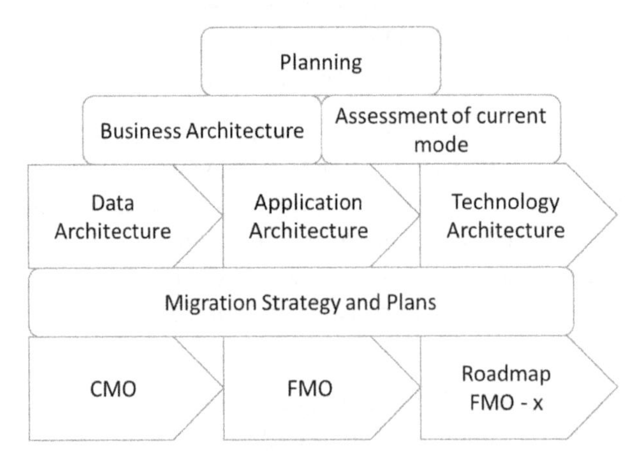


Figure 5.4 – Spewak's Enterprise Architecture model plotted with transition planning

If we don't change anything in our application and we simply move it to a public cloud using IaaS or bare-metal propositions, then we can talk about transition. The technology phase would be the standard phase. Transition just means that we move the workloads, but we don't change anything at all in terms of the technology or services. However, we are also not using the cloud technologies to make our environment more agile, flexible, or cost-efficient. If we want to achieve that, we will need to make a transformation: we need to change the technology under the data and applications. This is a job that needs to be taken care of through architecture. Why are we changing? What are we changing? How are we changing applications? And also, how do we revert changes if things don't work as planned; that is, what is our fallback solution?

There's one debate that needs discussing in terms of transition and transformation. As explained already, transition means that we are not changing the underlying technology and services. We just move an environment from A to B – as it is. But is that true when we are shifting environments to a public cloud? Moving an application to Azure, AWS, or GCP does always imply that we are changing something: either the underlying platform or the services.

By moving an application to a major public cloud, the services will almost definitively change. We are introducing a third party to our landscape: a public cloud provider. Hence, we are introducing an agreement to our landscape. That agreement comprises terms and conditions on how our applications will be hosted in that public cloud. This is something the architecture should deal with in a clear change management process.

# Creating the architecture artifacts

Basically, the hierarchy in documents that cover the architecture starts with the enterprise architecture. It's the first so-called architecture artifact. The enterprise architecture is followed by the high-level design and the low-level design, which covers the various components in the IT landscape. We will explore this in more detail in the following sections. Keep in mind that these sections are merely an introduction to the creation of these artifacts. You will find samples of these artifacts ay `https://publications.opengroup.org/i093`, where you can download a ZIP file containing relevant templates.

## Creating a business vision

Creating a business vision can take years, but it's still a crucial artifact in the architecture. It sets out what the business wants to achieve. This should be a long-term outlook since it will drive architectural decisions. Though cloud environments enable the agile deployment of services, it should never become ad hoc.

A business vision focuses on the long-term goals in terms of finance, quality of services/products, sustainability of the business, and, above all, the potential growth of the business and market domains that it's targeting. The business vision is the input for the enterprise architecture. It's the only document that will not be produced by architects, although the enterprise architect might be an important stakeholder that gives their view on the vision. After all, the vision must be realistic and obtainable. In other words, the architecture must be able to support the vision and help achieve its goals.

## Enterprise architecture

The enterprise architecture is the first document that will be written by architects. Typically, this is the deliverable that is created by a team of architects, led by the enterprise or business architect. He or she will work together with domain architects. The latter can also be a cloud architect, or an architect specialized in cloud-native development. The enterprise architecture describes the business structures and processes and maps these to the need and use of information. In essence, the enterprise architecture bridges between the business and IT.

## Principles catalog

This document lists all the architecture principles that have to be applied to any architecture that will be developed. We discussed this in detail in the first section of this chapter. Principles are assembled per architecture domain.

## Requirements catalog

This document lists all the requirements that a business has issued in order to achieve its goals, since these are set out in the business vision. Coming from a business vision to a requirements catalog is a long haul, so there are intermediate steps in creating the enterprise architecture and the principles catalog. From there, business functionality must be translated into requirements regarding the use of data and application functionality. Since not everything is known in detail at this stage, the catalog also contains assumptions and constraints. At the end, the catalog holds a list of building blocks that represent solutions to the business requirements.

## High-level design

This is not an official TOGAF document. TOGAF talks about a solution concepts diagram. In practice, a lot of people find it hard to read just a diagram and grasp the meaning of it. High-level design provides the solution concepts and includes the rationales of why specific concepts have been chosen to fulfill the requirements. Typically, a high-level design is created per architecture domain: data, application, and technology. Cloud concepts are part of each of these domains. Networking, computing, and storage are concepts that fit into the technology design. Data logics and data streams are part of the data design. Application functions must be described in the design for applications.

## Low-level design

The documents that contain the nitty-gritty details per building block. Low-level designs for data comprise data security and data transfer. Application designs contain the necessary software engineering diagrams and distribution patterns. Technology designs hold details on core and boundary (networks and security), including lists of used ports; IP plan and communication protocols; platform patterns and segmentation' processing units (VMs, containers, and so on); storage division; interfaces; and so on.

One note that has to be made here is that in *Chapter 4, Service Design for Multi-Cloud*, we agreed that we would work with everything as code. So, does it make sense to have everything written out in documents that are stored in some cabinet or drawer, never to be looked at again? Still, documenting your architecture is extremely important, but we can also have our documentation in wikis that can easy be searched through and directly linked to the related code that are ready to be worked with or even deployed. In today's world of multi-cloud, DevOps, and CI/CD pipelines, this will be the preferred way of working.

Working in DevOps pipelines and having documentation in wikis enforces the fact that the cycle of creating and maintaining these artifacts never stops. Code and wikis can easily be maintained and are more agile than chunky documents. Keep in mind that artifacts will constantly be updated. This is the ground principle of continuous architecture (Reference: *Continuous Architecture*, by Murat Erder and Pierre Pureur, 2016). Continuous architecture doesn't focus on solutions, for a good reason.

In multi-cloud, there are a zillion solutions and solution components (think of PaaS) already available and a zillion more on their way. Continuous architecture focuses on the quality of the architecture itself and describes how to design, build, test, and deploy solutions, as in DevOps pipelines. Other than this, it has a strong focus on continuous validation of the architecture, which is something we will explore in the last section of this chapter; that is, *Validating the architecture.*

# Working under architecture for multi-cloud and avoiding pitfalls

So far, we've looked at the different components of an architecture and what it should achieve. We've been discussing the conditions and prerequisites for the architecture and the service design, all of which have sprouted from business needs. Next, we explored the basic principles of an architecture for cloud environments. Now, the next phase is to really start putting the architecture together. The big question is, where do we start? The geeky answer might be, open Visio and load the stencils for either cloud platform you will be working in. But that's not how you create a good architecture – that really takes some thorough thinking.

Assuming that we have a clear understanding of the requirements and that we have agreed upon the principles, we will execute five stages to create our multi-cloud architecture.

## Stage 1 – security architecture

As we mentioned previously, there is a lot of debate about security by design and privacy by design. At the time of writing, we are in the midst of the global Coronavirus pandemic (April 2020) and a lot of countries are turning their hope to apps that alert people if they have been in contact with a COVID-19 patient. In some countries, it's leading to fierce debates about privacy safeguards for these apps. Such apps should be designed while following the principles of security by design and privacy by design. The big questions are, as always, what should we protect and to what extent? Or, maybe more accurate formulated, how far must – or should – we go? Regarding the coronavirus pandemic, these were more moral questions, but in architecture design, they should always be addressed at the lowest level. This starts with a clear view of what (data) we have to protect and how we protect it.

In the security architecture, we are focusing on data protection. After all, data is the most important asset in your multi-cloud environment. The architecture should have one goal: safeguarding the integrity of data. The best way to start thinking of a security architecture is to think from the angle of possible threats. How do you protect the data, how do you prevent the application from being breached, and what are the processes in terms of security policies, monitoring, and following up alerts? The latter is a subject for **Security Operations** (**SecOps**).

Designing an architecture for security is not an easy task. We will have to explore a lot of different layers and decide what the protective measures should be for each layer, as well as how these must be implemented. These layers are as follows:

- **Perimeter**: The outside boundary of your environment, this is the first access layer. Typically, this the first layer of defense. **Distributed Denial of Service** (**DDoS**) attacks where environments are flooded with requests so that they eventually collapse are often targeted on this layer.
- **Network**: Switches, routers, routing tables, peerings (what is allowed to communicate directly to what in the environment), micro-segmentation in VLANs, vNets, projects, and so on. Typically, these are delivered as managed services in cloud platforms, but even then, we need to think about hardening. This means that no ports or routes are left open without a monitored and clearly defined usage. This is typically the case for routing tables, peering, security groups, and other service gateways that allow traffic in/out of the cloud network. If ports or routes are unintentionally left open without surveillance, it allows attacks to come in through these vulnerabilities. Typically, these are so-called brute-force attacks: attackers simply start battering on your doors – routers, switches, firewalls – scanning all the ports on the devices until they find an open door.
- **Compute**: The virtual machines and the hardening of these machines. Virtual machines must be protected from viruses and other malware. Systems must be hardened.
- **Application**: Protection of the application and the different components within the application. Think of, for example, a web part and a worker role. These components form one application, but when we're using microsegmentation and microservices, a security principle could be to have protective measures on each component.
- **Data**: The storage of data, access, encryption, and encryption keys. This is your biggest asset. It's the deepest layer in your architecture, but it is always the treasure that attackers will be targeting. If hackers succeed in finding vulnerabilities in the other layers of defense, they will eventually get to the data – the one thing that they're after. No matter how well you have set up your layers of defense, you will need to take protective measures to safeguard the integrity of the data.

This is not about tools, such as Azure Security Center or any other toolset that you can use to set up layers of defense in the cloud. Tools allow teams to satisfy requirements. The tools that are used to satisfy the security requirements might differ between clouds, but as long as the requirements are met, they should be sufficient. The architecture at this stage can lead to a set of requirements that a certain tool should adhere to, but it starts with thinking of protecting the layers in the first place and the possible attacks that can be executed at these different layers.

## Stage 2 - architecture for scalability

The killer feature in public cloud is scalability. Where developers had to wait for hardware being ready in the data center before they could actually start their work, we now have capacity right at our fingertips. But scalability goes beyond that: it's about the full agility and flexibility in the public cloud and being able to scale out, scale up, and scale down whenever business requirements call for that. Let's explore what these terms mean.

Scale out is also referred to as horizontal scaling. When we scale out an environment, we usually add systems such as virtual machines to that environment. In scale up – or vertical scaling – we add resources to a system, typically CPUs, memory, or disks in a storage system. Obviously, when we can scale out and up, we can also go the opposite direction and scale systems down. Since we are paying for what we really use in the public cloud, the costs will down immediately, which is not the case if we have invested in physical machines sitting in a traditional, on-premises environment. You will be able to lower the usage of these physical machines, but this will not lower the cost of that machine since it's fully **CAPEX** – **capital expenditures or investments**.

> **Important Note**
>
> Public clouds offer various deployment models. Pay as you go is one such deployment models. Azure, AWS, and GCP also offer reserved instances, which are interesting if businesses use these instances for a longer period of time, such as 3 or 5 years. Cloud providers offer discounts on reserved instances, but the "downside" is that the business has to commit to the usage of these reserved instances for that period of time. Scaling down these systems is then typically not allowed, unless businesses pay termination fees.

Typical domains for the scalability architecture are virtual machines, databases, and storage, but network and security appliances should also be considered. For example, if business demands for scaling their environment up or out increases, typically, the throughput also increases. This has an impact on network appliances such as switches and firewalls: they should scale too. However, you should use the native services from the cloud platforms to avoid scaling issues in the first place.

Some things you should include in the architecture for scalability are as follows:

- **Definition of scale units**: This concerns scalability patterns. One thing you have to realize is that scaling has an impact. Scaling out on virtual machines has an impact on scaling the discs that these machines use and thus the usage of storage.

  But there's one more important aspect that an architect must take into account: can an application handle scaling? Or do we have to rearchitect the application so that the underlying resources can scale out, up, or down without impacting the functionality and – especially – the performance of the application? Is your backup solution aware of scaling?

  Defining scale units is important. Scale units can be virtual machines, including memory and discs, database instances, storage accounts, and storage units such as blobs or buckets. We must architect how these units scale and what the trigger is to start the scaling activity.

- **Allowing for autoscaling**: One of the ground principles in the cloud is that we automate as much as we can. If we have done a proper job on defining our scale units, then the next step is to decide whether we allow autoscaling on these units, or allow an automated process for dynamically adding or revoking resources to your environment. First of all, the application architecture must be able to support scaling in the first place. Autoscaling adds an extra dimension. The following aspects are important when it comes to autoscaling:

  - The trigger that executes the autoscaling process.

  - The thresholds of autoscaling, meaning to what level resources may be scaled up/out or down. Also, keep in mind that a business must have a very good insight into the related costs.

  One specific challenge of scaling is monitoring. All assets are stored in the CMBD or master data records. Unless there's a native API that feeds into the CMDB in near real time, administrators will not immediately see that autoscaling has called for extra resources.

- **Partitioning**: Part of architecting for scalability is partitioning, especially in larger environments. By separating applications and data into partitions, controlling scaling and managing the scale sets becomes easier and prevents large environments from suffering from contention. Contention is an effect that can occur if application components use the same scaling technology, but resources are limited due to set thresholds, which is often done to control costs.

In the next stage, we will design the architecture to make sure that our systems are not just scalable but also have high availability.

## Stage 3 – architecture for availability

Platforms such as Azure, AWS, and GCP are just there, ready to use. And since these platforms have global coverage, we can rest assured that the platforms will always be available. Well, these platforms absolutely have a high availability score, but they do suffer from outages. This is rare, but it does happen. The one question that a business must ask itself is whether they can live with that risk, or what the costs of mitigating that risk is and whether the business is willing to invest in that mitigation. That's really a business decision at the highest level. It's all about business continuity.

Let's assume that the availability of the cloud platform is taken as a given. Here, we still have to think about the availability of our systems that are deployed on that platform. Requirements for availability also sprout from business requirements. From experience, this will take time to debate. If you ask a CFO what the most critical systems are in the business, chances are that they will point toward the financial systems. But if he or she is the CFO of a company that manufactures cars, then the most critical systems are probably production systems that need to put the cars together. If these systems stop, the business stops. If the financial system stops, the CFO may not get financial reports, but this doesn't halt the production process instantly. Still, the CFO is a major stakeholder in deciding what critical systems require specific architecture for availability.

Availability is about accessibility, retention, and recovery. When we architect for availability, we have to do so at different layers. The most common are the compute, application, and data layers. But it doesn't make sense to design availability for only one of these layers. If the virtual machines fail, the application and the database won't be accessible, meaning that they won't be available.

In other words, you need to design availability from the top of stack, from the application down to the infrastructure. If an application needs to have an availability of 99.9 percent, this means that the underlying infrastructure needs to be at a higher availability rate. The underlying infrastructure comprises the whole technology stack: compute, storage, and network.

A good availability design counters for failures in each of these components, but also ensuring the application – the top of stack – can operate at the availability that has been agreed upon with the business and its end users.

However, failures do occur, so we need to be able to recover systems. Recovery has two parameters:

- **Recovery Point Objective (RPO)**: RPO is the maximum allowed time that data can be lost for. An RPO could be, for instance, 1 hour of data loss. This means that the data that was processed in 1 hour since the start of the failure can't be restored. However, it's considered to be acceptable.
- **Recovery Time Objective (RTO)**: RTO is the maximum duration of downtime that is accepted by the business.

RPO and RTO are important when designing the backup, data retention, and recovery solution. If a business requires an RPO for a maximum of 1 hour, this means that we must take backups every hour. A technology that can be used for this is snapshotting or incremental backups. Taking full backups every hour would create too much load on the system and, above that, implies that a business would need a lot of available backup storage.

It is crucial that the business determines which environments are critical and need a heavy regime backup solution. Typically, data in such environments also needs to be stored for a longer period of time. Standard offerings in public clouds often have 2 weeks as a standard retention period for storing backup data. This can be extended, but it needs to be configured and you need to be aware that it will raise costs significantly.

One more point that needs attention is that backing up data only makes sense if you are sure that you can restore it. So, make sure that your backup and restore procedures are tested frequently – even in the public cloud.

## Stage 4 – architecture for operability

This part of the architecture covers automation in the first place, but also monitoring and logging. A key decision in monitoring is not what monitoring tool we will use, but what we have to monitor and to what extent.

In multi-cloud, monitoring has to be cross-platform since we will have to see what's going on in the full chain of components that we have deployed in our multi-cloud environment. This is often referred to as end-to-end monitoring: looking at systems from an end user perspective. This is not only related to the health status of systems, but whether the systems do what they should do and are free from bugs, crashes, or hangs. It's also maybe even more related to the performance of these systems. From an end user perspective, there's nothing more frustrating that systems that respond slowly. And here's where the big debate starts: define slow.

Where an architect can decide that a system that responds within 1 second is fast, the end user might have a completely different idea of this. Even if they agree that the performance and responsiveness of system is slow, the next question is how to determine what the cause of degrading performance is. Monitoring the environment from the end user's perspective, all the way down to the infrastructure, is often referred to as end-to-end. There are monitoring environments that really do end-to-end, typically by sending transactions through the whole chain and measuring health (heartbeat) and performance by determining how fast transactions are processed. Keep in mind that this type of monitoring usually deploys agents on various components in your environment. In that case, we will have to take into consideration how much overhead these agents create on systems, thus taking up extra resources such as CPU and memory. The footprint of agents should be as small as possible, also given the fact that there will undoubtedly more agents or packages running on our systems. Just think of endpoint protection, such as virus scanning, as an example.

Monitoring systems collect logs. We will also need to design where these logs will have to go to and how long these will have to be stored. The latter is important if systems are under an audit regime. Auditors can request logs.

The last topic we need to cover in terms of operability is automation. If we are going to talk about automation, then we should also discuss the architectural setup for the CI/CD pipeline, something that we explored briefly in in the previous chapter. Automation is basically about creating maximum efficiency in the environment. Not just in the deployment of resources, but also in operating these resources.

An example of this is automatically switching off VMs if they are not used; for example, VMs that are only used in the day and can be suspended at night. However, as an architect, we have to be sure that the applications and databases that are running on these systems can support this. Not all applications and certainly not databases can simply be put into suspension mode. Complex databases take time to build and synchronize their tables.

# Stage 5 – architecture for integration

The biggest challenge in multi-cloud environments is integration. Systems on different platforms will still need to be able to communicate with each other. For that, we need an integration architecture. In application architecture, a common technology used to set up integration is **Application Programming Interfaces** (**APIs**). Obviously, the underlying infrastructure will need to support these APIs, often to allow certain communication protocols and enable routes, such as to allow communication to go through a firewall.

The integration architecture also requires thinking about the APIs themselves. On what layer do they communicate and what type of API is it – private, a specific partner API, or public? Be aware of the fact that most cloud providers use RESTful APIs, where access to these APIs is only granted through API tokens or certificates. The majority of these APIs use XML or JSON as their format.

The first step in the integration architecture is to define what needs to be able to communicate with what and what type of communication it comprises: one-way, bi-directional, or multi-directional using specific rules and triggers. In multi-cloud, the event-driven architecture is increasingly gaining ground: connections are only executed when certain requirements have been met, triggering an event to initiate communication. This is becoming popular since it prevents open connections all the time. Connections and communication are only executed when an event calls for it.

Apache Kafka is a leading product in this space. In essence, Kafka handles real-time data streams. It can import and export data feeds that are connecting from and to different systems. It receives, stores, and sends data feeds that have been triggered by events. In public, clouds Kafka is often used as a message broker and for data streaming. Azure itself offers Event Hub and Logic Apps for data streaming and application integration, respectively, while AWS has Kinesis and GCP Google Pub/Sub.

> **Tip**
>
> It's beyond the scope of this section to really start deep diving into integration architectures and the named concepts. We would like to point you to a blog by Andrew Carr on Scott Logic, comparing Kafka with Event Hubs, Kinesis, and Google Pub/Sub. This blog can be found at `https://blog.scottlogic.com/2018/04/17/comparing-big-data-messaging.html`.

Architecting scalability, availability, and operability are topics that we will cover in depth as part of BaseOps, the main subject of part 2 of this book.

## Pitfalls in architecture

It's easy and tempting to skip steps in the architecture. It's one of the biggest pitfalls in working under an architecture.

Let's say we have a problem, but we already know what the fix is. Under the flag of fix first, talk later, or use a temporary solution, a lot of architectural changes are implemented. Keep this in mind: there's nothing more permanent than a temporary solution, especially when it's not documented. If an urgent fix is really the only way to keep the business running, then go ahead. But do document it and when it leads to a change in the architecture, evaluate and decide whether this is something that you want in your landscape – if it fits the architecture - or whether you have to design a permanent solution that adheres to the architecture and the architectural principles.

One other pitfall is falling for the newest technology. In the literature, this is called bleeding or cutting edge: technology that might be a great opportunity but is still so new that it may also cause issues in terms of reliability and stability. All the major cloud platforms have a life cycle where they announce new technology and make it available through private and public reviews before they issue it to the general public. This allows organizations that use these platforms to test the new technology and provide Azure, AWS, and GCP with feedback regarding debugging and improvements. This is obviously not the type of technology you want in your production environment from day 1, yet organizations do want to find out whether it would bring advantages and business benefits. It's advised that you create sandboxes in your environment that are meant for testing beta versions and features that are in preview. They should not already be a part of the architecture.

Finally, the last pitfall is making it all too complicated. Always take a step back and have this one principle as the main guideline at all times: keep it as simple as possible, yet be accurate and complete.

# Change management and validation as the cornerstone

We are working under architecture from this point onward. This implies that the changes that are made to the systems in our environment are controlled from the architecture. Sometimes, these changes have an impact on the architecture itself, where we will need to change the architecture. In multi-cloud environments, that will actually happen a lot.

Cloud platforms are flexible in terms of use and thus our architecture can't be set in stone: it needs to allow improvements to be made to the environments that we have designed, thereby enabling that these improvements are documented and embedded in the architecture. Improvements can be a result of fixing a problem or mitigating an issue to enhancements. Either way, we have to make sure that changes that are the result of these improvements can be validated, tracked, and traced. Change management is therefore crucial in maintaining the architecture.

Since we have already learned quite a bit from TOGAF, we will also explore change management from this angle: phase H. Phase H is all about change management: keeping track of changes and controlling the impact of changes on the architecture. But before we dive into the stages of proper change management, we have to identify what type of changes we have in IT. Luckily, that's relatively easy to explain since IT organizations typically recognize two types: standard and non-standard changes. Again, catalogs are of great importance here.

Standard changes can be derived from a catalog. This catalog should list changes that have been foreseen from the architecture as part of standard operations, release, or life cycle management. A standard change can be to add a VM. Typically, these are quite simple tasks that have either been fully automated from a repository and the code pipeline or have been scripted. Non-standard changes are often much more complex. They have not been defined in a catalog or repository, or they consist of multiple subsequent actions that require these actions to be planned.

In all cases, both with standard and non-standard changes, a request for change is the trigger for executing change management. Such a request has a trigger: a drive for change. In change management for architecture, the driver for change always has a business context: what problem do we have to solve in the business? The time to market for releasing new business services is too slow, for instance. This business problem can relate to not being able in deploying systems fast enough, so we would need to increase deployment speed. The solution could lie in automation – or designing less complex systems.

That is the next step: defining our architecture objectives. This starts with the business objective (getting services faster to the market) and defining the business requirements (we need faster deployment of systems), which leads to a solution concept (automatic deployment). Before we go to the drawing board, there are two more things that we must explore.

Here, we need to determine what the exact impact of the change will be and who will be impacted: we need to assess who the stakeholders are, everyone who needs to be involved in the change, and the interests of these people. Each stakeholder can raise concerns about the envisioned change. These concerns have to be added to the constraints of the change. Constraints can be budgetary limits but also timing limits: think of certain periods where a business can't absorb changes.

In summary, change management to architecture comprises the following:

1. Request for change
2. The request is analyzed through change drivers within the business context
3. Definition of business objectives to be achieved by the change
4. Definition of architecture objectives
5. Identifying stakeholders and gathering their concerns
6. Assessment of concerns and constraints to the change

These steps have to be documented well so that every change to the architecture can be validated and audited. Changes should be retrievable at all times. Individual changes in the environment are usually tracked via a service, if configured. However, a change can comprise multiple changes within the cloud platform. We will need more sophisticated monitoring to do a full audit trail on these changes, to determine who did what. But having said that, it remains of great importance to document changes with as much detail as possible.

# Validating the architecture

You might recognize this from the process where we validate the architecture of software. It is very common to have an architecture validation in software development, but any architecture should be validated. But what do we mean by that and what would be the objective? The first and most important objective is quality control. The second objective is that improvements that need to be made to the architecture need to be considered. This is done to guarantee that we have an architecture that meets our business goals, addresses all the principles and requirements, and that it can be received for continuous improvement.

Validating the architecture is not an audit. Therefore, it is perfectly fine to have the first validation procedure be done through a peer review: architects and engineers that haven't been involved in creating the architecture. It is also recommended to have an external review of your cloud architecture. This can be done by cloud solutions architects from the different providers, such as Microsoft, AWS, and Google. They will validate your architecture against the reference architectures and best practices of their platforms, such as the **Azure Reference Architecture** (**AZRA**) or the AWS Well-Architected Framework. These companies have professional and consultancy services that can help you assess whether best practices have been applied or help you find smarter solutions to your architecture. Of course, an enterprise would need a support agreement with the respective cloud provider, but this isn't a bad idea.

The following is what should be validated at a minimum:

- **Security**: Involve security experts and the security officer to perform the validation process.
- **Interoperability**: After security, interoperability is probably the most important thing to validate when we architect a multi-cloud environment. We don't want standalone platforms or systems that can't communicate with each other: they must be able to communicate through well-programmed interfaces.
- **Scalability**: At the end of the day, this is what multi-cloud is all about. Cloud environments provide organizations with great possibilities in terms of scaling. But as we have seen in this chapter, we have to define scale sets, determine whether applications are allowing for scaling, and define triggers and thresholds, preferably all automated through auto-scaling.
- **Availability**: Finally, we have to validate whether the availability of systems is guaranteed, whether the backup processes and schemes are meeting the requirements, and whether systems can be restored within the given parameters of RTO and RPO.

In summary, validating our architecture is an important step to make sure that we have completed the right steps and that we have followed the best practices.

# Summary

In the cloud, it's very easy to get started straight away, but that's not a sustainable way of working for enterprises. In this chapter, we've learned that, in multi-cloud, we have to work according to a well-thought and designed architecture. This starts with creating an architecture vision and setting principles for the different domains such as data, applications, and the underlying infrastructure.

We have also explored topics that make architecture for cloud environments very specific in terms of availability, scalability, and interoperability. If we have designed the architecture, we have to manage it. If we work under the architecture, we need to be strict in terms of change management. Finally, it's good practice to have our architectural work validated by peers and experts from different providers.

With this, we have learned how to define an enterprise architecture in different cloud platforms by looking at the different stages in creating the architecture. We have also learned that we should define principles in various domains that determine what our architecture should look like. Now, we should have a good understanding that everything in our architecture is driven by the business and that it's wise to have our architecture validated.

Now, we are ready for the next phase. In the next chapter, we will design the landing zones.

# Questions

1. In cloud architectures, we often work with layers. There are two main layers: systems of engagement and systems of record. However, we can also add a third layer. Please name that layer.
2. What would be the first artifact in creating the architecture?
3. True or false: There are two types of changes – standard and non-standard changes.

# Further reading


- The official page of The Open Group Architecture Framework: `https://www.opengroup.org/togaf`.
- *Enterprise Architecture Planning*, by Steven Spewak, John Wiley & Sons Inc.

# Section 2 – Getting the Basics Right with BaseOps

**Basic operations** (**BaseOps**) is about getting and keeping the basics right, from the start to the management of the landing zone – the foundation.

The following chapters will be covered in this section:

- *Chapter 6, Designing, Implementing, and Managing the Landing Zone*
- *Chapter 7, Designing Resilience and Performance*
- *Chapter 8, Defining Automation Tools and Processes*
- *Chapter 9, Defining and Using Monitoring and Management Tools*

# 6
# Designing, Implementing, and Managing the Landing Zone

This section of the book is all about the basic operations in multi-cloud, or BaseOps. We'll be learning about the basics, starting with managing the landing zone – the foundation of any cloud environment. Before a business can start migrating workloads or develop applications in cloud environments, they will need to define that foundation. Best practices for landing zones include the hub and spoke-model in Azure, AWS Landing Zone, and the definition of projects in Google Cloud. In multi-cloud, this landing zone expands over multi-cloud concepts and technologies.

This chapter describes how to design the landing zones for the major cloud platforms and explores the BaseOps principles for managing them. We will learn how to design the landing zones in Azure, AWS, and GCP, how to define policies to manage the landing zone, and get a deeper understanding of handling accounts in these landing zones. We will also learn that there are platforms where we can manage different clouds from just one console via orchestration. In this chapter, we're going to explore the foundational concepts of the major cloud providers; that is, Azure, AWS, and GCP. We'll also design the basic landing zones in the major clouds, manage the foundation environments in multi-cloud, learn how to abstract policies from resources on the different cloud platforms by exploring Infrastructure as Code and Configuration as Code, and understand the need for demarcation in the cloud.

In this chapter, we will cover the following topics:

- Understanding BaseOps and the foundational concepts
- Creating a multi-cloud landing zone and blueprint
- Managing the landing zone using policies
- Orchestrating policies for multi-cloud
- Global admin galore – the need for demarcation
- Let's get started!

# Understanding BaseOps and the foundational concepts

**BaseOps** might not be a familiar term to all, although you could guess what it means: **basic operations**. In cloud environments, this is more often referred to as cloud operations. BaseOps is mainly about operating the cloud environment in the most efficient way possible by making optimal use of the cloud services that major providers offer on the different layers: network, compute, storage, but also PaaS and SaaS.

The main objective of BaseOps is to ensure that cloud systems are available to the organization and that these can safely be used to do the following:

- Monitor network capacity and appropriately route traffic.
- Monitor the capacity of compute resources and adjust this to the business requirements.
- Monitor the capacity of storage resources and adjust this to the business requirements.

- Monitor the availability of resources, including health checks for backups and ensuring that systems can be recovered when required.
- Monitor the perimeter and internal security of systems, ensuring data integrity.
- Overall, manage systems at the service levels and use **Key Performance Indicators (KPIs)**, as agreed upon by the business.
- Assuming that the systems are automated as much as possible, part of BaseOps is also being able to monitor and manage the pipeline.

At the end of the day, this is all about the quality of service. That quality is defined by service levels and KPIs that have been derived from the business goals. BaseOps must be enabled to deliver that quality via clear procedures, skilled people, and the proper tools.

We have already explored the business reasons regarding why we should deploy systems in cloud environments: the ultimate goal is to have flexibility, agility, but also cost efficiency. This can only be achieved if we standardize and automate. All repetitive tasks should be automated. Identifying these tasks and monitoring whether these automated tasks are executed in the right way, is part of BaseOps. The automation process itself is development, but the one reason we should have DevOps in the first place is so that we can execute whatever the developer invents. Both teams have the same goal, for that matter: protect and manage the cloud systems according to best practices.

We can achieve these goals by executing the activities mentioned in the following sections.

## Defining and implementing the base infrastructure – the landing zone

This is by far the most important activity in the BaseOps domain. It's really the foundation of everything else. The landing zone is the environment on the designated cloud platform where we will host the workloads, the applications, and the data resources. The starting principle of creating a landing zone is that it's fully provisioned through code. In other words, the landing zone contains the building blocks that form a consistent environment where we can start deploying application and data functionality, as we discussed in *Chapter 4, Service Design for Multi-cloud*, where we talked about scaffolding. In the *Creating a multi-cloud landing zone and blueprint* section of this chapter, we will deep dive into creating landing zones on the different major platforms; that is, Azure, AWS, and GCP.

# Defining standards and policies for the base infrastructure

The base infrastructure typically consists of networking and environments that can host, compute, and storage resources. You could compare this with the **Hyperconverged Infrastructure** (**HCI**), which refers to a physical box that holds compute nodes, a storage device, and a switch to make sure that compute nodes and storage can actually communicate. The only addition that we would need is a router that allows the box to communicate with the outside world. The cloud is no different: the base infrastructure consists of compute, storage nodes, and switches to enable traffic. The major difference with the physical box is that, in the cloud, all these components are code.

But as we have already learned, this wouldn't be enough to get started. We also need an area that allows us to communicate from our cloud to the outside and to access our cloud. Next, we will need to control who accesses our cloud environment. So, a base infrastructure will need accounts and a way to provision these accounts in a secure manner. You've guessed it: even when it comes to defining the standard and policies for setting up a base infrastructure, there are a million choices to make. Landing zone concepts make it a lot easier to get started fast.

As a rule of thumb, the base infrastructure consists of five elements:

- Network
- Compute nodes
- Storage nodes
- Accounts
- Defense (security)

The good news is that all cloud providers agree that these are the base elements of an infrastructure. Even better, they all provide code-based components to create the base infrastructure. From this point onward, we will call these components building blocks. The issue is that they offer lots of choices in terms of the different types of building blocks and how to deploy them, such as through blueprints, templates, code editors, command-line programming, or through their respective portals. As we mentioned previously, we will explore the landing zone solutions in this chapter.

Defining standard architecture principles (architecture patterns and reference architecture)

A way to define a reference architecture for your business is to think outside-in. Think of an architecture in terms of circles. The outer circle is the business zone, where all the business requirements and principles are gathered. These drive the next inner circle: the solutions zone. This is the zone where we define our solutions portfolio. For example, if the business has a demand for analyzing large sets of data (business requirement), then a data lake could be a good solution.

The solution zone is embedded between the business zone at the outer side and the platform zone at the inner side. If we have, for instance, Azure as our defined platform, then we could have Azure Data Factory as a solution for the specific data lake requirement. The principle is that from these platforms, which can also be third-party PaaS and SaaS platforms, the solutions are mapped to the business requirements. By doing so, we create the solutions portfolio, which contains specific building blocks that make up the solution.

The heart of this model – the utmost inner circle – is the integration zone, from where we manage the entire ecosystem in the other, outer circles.

Security should be included in every single layer or circle. Due to this, the boundary of the whole model is set by the intrinsic security zone:

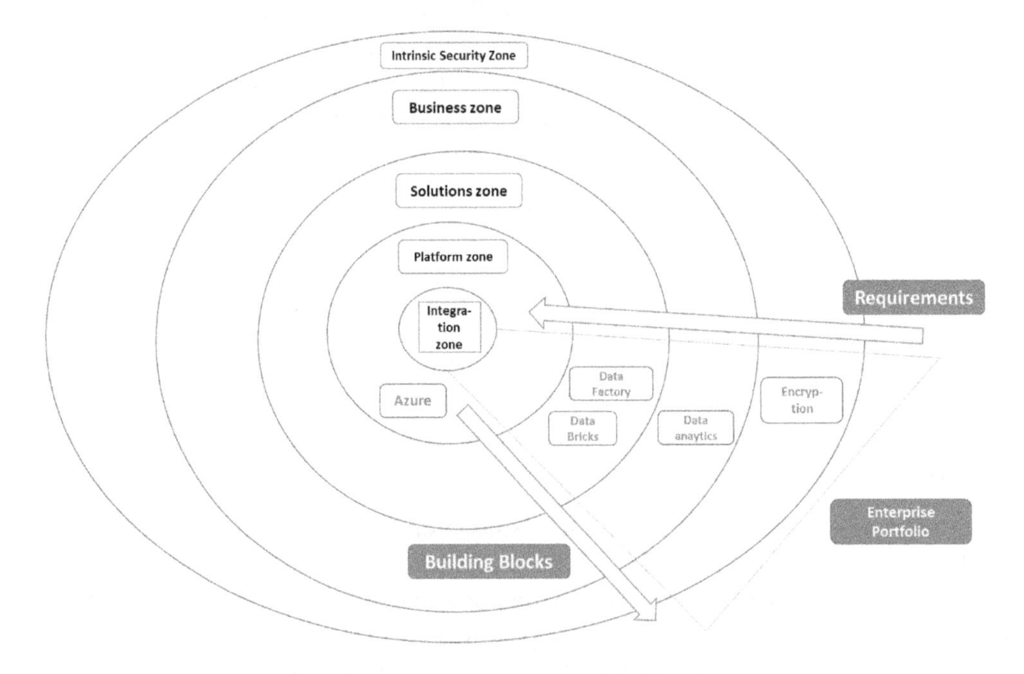


Figure 6.1 – Circular model showing the layers of the enterprise portfolio

The preceding diagram shows this model with an example of the business requiring data analytics, with Data Factory and Data Bricks as solutions coming from Azure as the envisioned platform. The full scope forms the enterprise portfolio.

# Managing the base infrastructure

Even if we have only deployed a landing zone, there are still quite a number of building blocks that we will have to manage from that point onward.

For a network, we will have to manage, at a minimum, the following:

- Provisioning, configuring, and managing virtual networks (vNets, VPCs, subnets, internet facing public zones, and private zones)
- Provisioning and managing routing, **Network Address Translation** (NAT), **Network Access Control** (NAC), **Access Control Lists** (ACL), and traffic management
- Provisioning and managing load balancing, network peering, and network gateways for VPNs or dedicated connections

- Provisioning and managing DNS
- Network monitoring
- Detect, investigate, and resolve incidents related to network functions

For compute, we will have to manage, at a minimum, the following:

- Provisioning, configuring, and the operations of virtual machines. This often includes managing the operating system (Windows, various Linux distributions, and so on).
- Detect, investigate, and resolve incidents related to the functions of virtual machines.
- Patch management.
- Operations of backups (full, iterative, and snapshots).
- Monitoring, logging, health checks, and proactive checks/maintenance.

Do note that compute in the cloud involves more than virtual machines. It also includes things such as containers, container orchestration, functions, and serverless computing. However, in the landing zone, these native services are often not immediately deployed. You might consider having the container platform deployed as part of the base infrastructure. Remember that, in the cloud, we do see a strong shift from VM to container, so we should prepare for that while setting up our landing zone.

In most cases, this will include setting up the Kubernetes cluster. In Azure, this is done through **Azure Kubernetes Services** (**AKS**), where we create a resource group that will host the AKS cluster. AWS offers its own cluster service through **Elastic Kubernetes Service** (**EKS**). In GCP, this is the **Google Kubernetes Engine** (**GKE**). The good news is that a lot of essential building blocks, such as Kubernetes DNS, are already deployed as part of setting up the cluster. Once we have the cluster running, we can start deploying cluster nodes, pods (a collection of application containers), and containers. In terms of consistently managing Kubernetes platforms across multi-cloud platforms, there are multiple agnostic solutions that you can look at, such as Rancher or VMWare's Tanzu Mission Control.

For storage, we will have to manage, at a minimum, the following:

- Provisioning, configuring, and the operations of storage, including disks for managed virtual machines
- Detect, investigate, and resolve incidents related to the functions of storage resources
- Monitoring, logging, health checks on local and different redundant types of storage solutions (zone, regional, globally redundant), and proactive checks/maintenance, including capacity checks and adjustments (capacity allocation)

Next, we will have to manage the accounts and make sure that our landing zone – the cloud environment and all its building blocks – is secure. Account management involves creating accounts or account groups that need access to the cloud environment. These are typically created in Active Directory.

In the *Global admin galore – the need for demarcation* section of this chapter, we will take a deeper look at admin accounts and the use of global admin accounts. Security is tightly connected to account, identity, and access management, but also to things such as hardening (protecting systems from outside threats), endpoint protection, and vulnerability management. From day 1, we must have security in place on all the layers in order to prevent, detect, assess, and mitigate any breach. This is part of SecOps. *Section 4* of this book is all about securing our cloud environments.

# Defining and managing infrastructure automation tools and processes (Infrastructure as Code and Configuration as Code)

In the cloud, we work with code. There's no need to buy physical hardware anymore; we simply define our hardware in code. This doesn't mean we don't have to manage it. To do this in the most efficient way, we need a master code repository. This repository will hold the code that defines the infrastructure components, as well as how these components have to be configured to meet our principles in terms of security and compliancy. This is what we typically refer to as the desired state.

Azure, AWS, and Google offer native tools to facilitate infrastructure and configuration as code, as well as tools to automate the deployment of the desired state. In Azure, we can work with Azure DevOps and Azure Automation, both of which work with **Azure Resource Manager** (**ARM**). AWS offers CloudFormation, while Google has Cloud Resource Manager and Cloud Deployment Manager. These are all tied into the respective platforms, but the market also offers third-party tooling that tends to be agnostic to these platforms. We will explore some of the leading tools later in this chapter, in the *Orchestrating policies for multi-cloud* section.

For source code management, we can use tools such as GitHub, Azure DevOps, AWS CodeCommit, and GCP Cloud Repositories.

# Defining and implementing monitoring and management tools

We've already discussed the need for monitoring. The next step is to define what tooling we can use to perform these tasks. Again, the cloud platforms offer native tooling: Azure Monitoring, Application Insights, and Log Analytics; AWS CloudTrail and CloudWatch; and Google Stackdriver monitoring. And, of course, there's a massive set of third-party tools available, such as Splunk and Nagios. These latter tools have a great advantage since they can operate independent of the underlying platform. This book won't try to convince you that tool A is preferred over tool B; as an architect, you will have to decide what tool fits the requirements - and the budget, for that matter.

Security is a special topic. The cloud platforms have spent quite some effort in creating extensive security monitoring for their platforms. Monitoring is not only about detecting; it's also about triggering mitigating actions. This is especially true when it comes to security where detecting a breach is certainly not enough. Actually, the time between detecting a vulnerability or a breach and the exploit can be a matter of seconds, which makes it necessary to enable fast action. This is where **SIEM** comes into play: **Security Incident and Event Management**. SIEM systems evolve rapidly and, at the time of writing, intelligent solutions are often part of the system.

An example of this is Azure Sentinel, an Azure-native SIEM solution: it works together with Azure Security Center, where policies are stored and managed, but it also performs an analysis of the behavior it sees within the environments that an enterprise hosts on the Azure platform. Lastly, it can automatically trigger actions. For instance, it can block an account that logs in from the UK one minute and from Singapore the next - something that wouldn't be possible without warp-driven time travelling.

In other words, monitoring systems do become more sophisticated and developments become as fast as lighting.

## Supporting operations

Finally, once we have thought about all of this, we need to figure out who will be executing all these tasks. We will need people with the right skills to manage our multi-cloud environments. As we have said already, the truly T-shaped engineer or admin doesn't exist. That would be the five-legged sheep. Most enterprises end up with a group of developers and operators that all have generic and more specific skills. Some providers refer to this as the **Cloud Center of Excellence** (**CCoE**), and they mark it as an important step in the cloud journey or cloud adoption process of that enterprise. Part of this stage would be to identify the roles this CCoE should have and get the members of the CCoE on board with this. The team needs to be able to build and manage the environments, but they will also have a strong role to fulfil to evangelize new cloud-native solutions.

> **Tip**
>
> Just as a reading tip, please have a look at an excellent blog post on forming a CCoE by Amazon's Enterprise Strategist Mark Schwartz: `https://aws.amazon.com/blogs/enterprise-strategy/using-a-cloud-center-of-excellence-ccoe-to-transform-the-entire-enterprise/`.

In this section, we have learned what we need to cover to set up our operations in multi-cloud. The next step is building our landing zones on the cloud platforms.

# Creating a multi-cloud landing zone and blueprint

All the major cloud providers offer a methodology that can be used to create a landing zone on their respective platforms. In this section, we will explore the landing zone concepts for Azure, AWS, and GCP.

## Configuring the landing zone on Azure

The landing zone in Azure is part of the **Cloud Adoption Framework** (**CAF**) and implements a set of cloud services to get us started with building or migrating workloads to the Azure platform. The landing zone creates all the necessary building blocks to enable a business to start using the cloud platform.

We talked about the analogy of constructing a house previously, when we discussed scaffolding. Consider the landing zone to be the empty house. A house has a foundation; that is, a front door that provides access to the house and rooms where we can place furniture. These rooms have already been designed to cater for specific needs. The kitchen has connections for cooking equipment and a tap for running water. So does the bathroom: it has taps, a shower, a bath, but also a floor that doesn't get damaged when it gets wet. We can compare this to the landing zone: it already has rooms that have been set up for specific usage, such as to cater for outside connectivity.

Preparing these rooms for usage is something Microsoft calls **refactoring**. CAF guides the business in setting up security, identity, and access management, naming conventions, cost management, and so on. All these topics are deployed as part of the landing zone. Once we've finished building the landing zone, we will have a base platform that is secure and defined a naming and tagging convention for, where **Role-Based Access Control** (**RBAC**) is in place and where we have a clear insight into the costs that we are generating in the platform.

Now, what do we need for that?

First of all, we need a subscription to Azure. Next, we need to deploy rooms, the different segments in our environment where we will host our systems. In Azure, we typically deploy the hub and spoke model. This derives from the fact that Azure offers shared services, which are used across the different rooms, such as monitoring and backup services. These shared services land in the hub. The spokes connect to the hub so that they can consume the shared services from there, instead of having to deploy all these services separately into the different spokes.

The landing zone consists of code: it's Infrastructure as Code, so it drives the Azure architecture completely from code, from the very start. To do this, it uses ARM templates in JSON format. We can actually blueprint the code so that we can easily launch new spokes in a very consistent way. The blueprint would, for instance, contain code that shows how the spokes connect to the hub and how shared services are consumed. Azure offers various sample landing zone blueprints to get us started really fast. However, do check if the blueprint meets the compliancy and security requirements of your specific business.

The landing zone blueprint will provide the following:

- Virtual networks with subnets for gateways, Azure Firewall, and an Azure Bastion server (a jumpbox, which is the management server that administrators use to enter the environments in the cloud)
- Storage account for logging and monitoring
- An Azure Migrate project

Be aware that this landing zone is not fit to host sensitive data or mission-critical applications yet. The blueprint is deployed under the assumption that the subscription is already associated with an Azure Active Directory instance. Also, the landing zone blueprint makes the assumption that no Azure policies have to be applied. In other words, you will have an empty house with a few empty rooms that you will still need to decorate yourself, meaning that you will have to implement baselines and policies.

This gets you started. By refactoring the landing zone and adding services to improve performance, reliability, cost efficiency, and security, you will get it ready to actually host workloads:

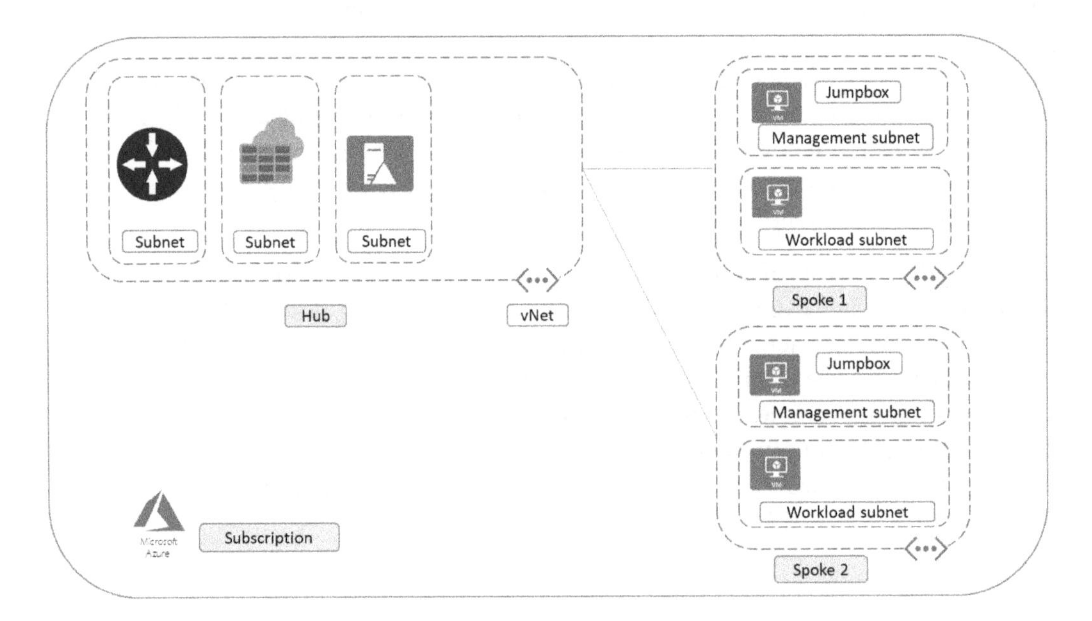


Figure 6.2 – Basic setup of Azure landing zone B

The preceding diagram shows a basic setup for a landing zone in Azure containing a hub to host the generic services and two spokes to host the workloads. These spokes have two subnets: one for management and one for the actual workloads, such as applications.

> **Tip**
> More information about Azure Landing Zone can be found at `https://docs.microsoft.com/en-us/azure/cloud-adoption-framework/ready/landing-zone/`.

## Creating a landing zone in AWS

AWS offers AWS Landing Zone as a complete solution, based on the Node.js runtime. Like Azure, AWS offers numerous solutions so that you can set up an environment. All these solutions require design decisions. To save time in getting started, AWS Landing Zone sets up a basic configuration that's ready to go. To enable this, AWS Landing Zone deploys the so-called AWS **Account Vending Machine** (**AVM**), which provisions and configures new accounts with the use of single sign-on.

To grasp this, we must understand the way AWS environments are configured. It is somewhat comparable to the hub and spoke model of Azure, but instead of hub and spokes, AWS uses accounts. AWS Landing Zone comprises four accounts that follow the **Cloud Adoption Framework** (**CAF**) of AWS:

- **Organization account**: This is the account that's used to control the member accounts and configurations of the landing zone. It also includes the so-called manifest file in the S3 storage bucket. The manifest file sets parameters for region and organizational policies. The file refers to AWS CloudFormation, a service that we could compare to ARM in Azure. CloudFormation helps with creating, deploying, and managing resources in AWS, such as EC2 computing instances and Amazon databases. It supports Infrastructure as Code.
- **Shared services account**: By default, Landing Zone manages the associated accounts through **SSO**, short for **single sign-on**. The SSO integration and the AWS managed AD is hosted in the shared services account. It automatically peers new accounts in the VPC where the landing zone is created. AVM plays a big role in this.
- **Log archive account**: AWS Landing Zone uses CloudTrail and Config Logs. CloudTrail monitors and logs account activity in the AWS environment that we create. It essentially keeps a history of all actions that take place in the infrastructure that is deployed in a VPC. It differs from CloudWatch in that it's complementary to CloudTrail. CloudWatch monitors all resources and applications in AWS environments, whereas CloudTrail tracks activity in accounts and logs these activities in an S3 storage bucket.

- **Security account**: This account holds the key vault–the directory where we store our accounts–for cross-account roles in the Landing Zone and two security services that AWS provides: GuardDuty and Amazon SNS. GuardDuty is the AWS service for threat detection, the **Simple Notification Service** (**SNS**) that enables sending of security notifications. The Landing Zone implements an initial security baseline that comprises (among other things) central storage of config files, configuration of IAM password policies, threat detection, and Landing Zone notifications. For the latter, CloudWatch is used to send out alerts in case of, for example, root account login and failed console sign-in.

The following diagram shows the setup of the landing zone in AWS:

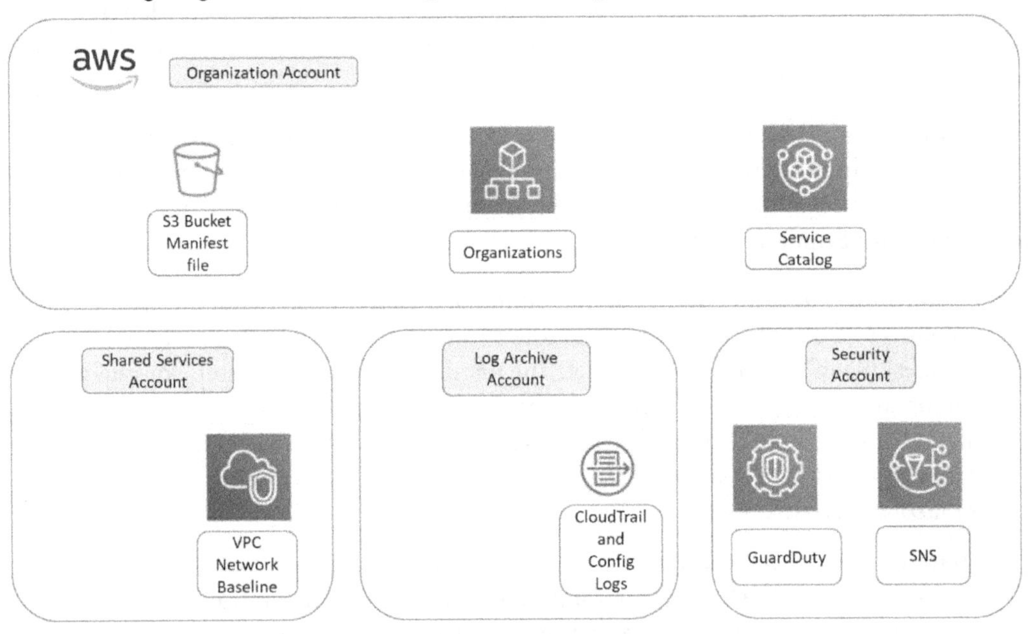


Figure 6.3 – The AWS Landing Zone solution

The one thing that we haven't discussed yet is the **Account Vending Machine** (**AVM**), which plays a crucial role in setting up the Landing Zone. The AVM launches the basic accounts in the Landing Zone with a predefined network and the security baseline. Under the hood, AVM uses Node.js templates that set up organization units wherein the previously described accounts are deployed with default, preconfigured settings. One of the components that is launched is the AWS SSO directory allows federated access to AWS accounts.

> **Tip**
>
> More information about AWS Landing Zone can be found at `https://aws.amazon.com/solutions/aws-landing-zone/`.

## Creating the landing zone in GCP

GCP differs a lot from Azure and AWS, although the hub and spoke model can also be applied in GCP. Still, you can actually tell that this platform has a different vision of the cloud. GCP focuses more on containers than on IaaS by using more traditional resources. Google talks about a landing zone as somewhere you are planning to deploy a Kubernetes cluster in a GCP project using GKE, although deploying VMs is, of course, possible on the platform.

In the landing zone, you create **Virtual Private Cloud** (**VPC**) network and set Kubernetes network policies. These policies define how we will be using isolated and non-isolated pods in our Kubernetes environment. Basically, by adding network policies, we create isolated pods, meaning that these pods – which hold a number of containers – only allow defined traffic, where non-isolated pods accept all traffic from any source. The policy lets you assign IP blocks and deny/allow rules to the pods. The next step is to define service definitions to the Kubernetes environment in the landing zone so that pods can actually start running applications or databases. The last step to create the landing zone is to configure DNS for GKE.

As we mentioned previously, Google very much advocates the use of Kubernetes and containers, which is why GCP is really optimized for running this kind of infrastructure. If we don't want to use container technology, then we will have to create a project in GCP ourselves. The preferred way to do this is through Deployment Manager and the gcloud command line. You could compare Deployment Manager to ARM in Azure: it uses the APIs of other GCP services to create and manage resources on the platform. One way to access this is through the Cloud Shell within the Google Cloud portal, but GCP also offers some nice tools to get the work done. People who are still familiar with Unix command-line programming will find this really recognizable and easy to work with.

The first step is enabling these APIs; that is, the Compute Engine API and the Deployment Manager API. By installing the Cloud SDK, we get a command-line tool called gcloud that interfaces with the Deployment Manager. Now that we have gcloud running, we can simply start a project with the `gcloud config set project` command, followed by the name or ID of the project itself; for example, `gcloud config set project [Project ID]`. Next, we must set the region where we will be deploying our resources. It uses the very same command; that is, `gcloud config set compute/region`, followed by the region ID; that is, `gcloud config set compute/region [region]`.

With that, we're done! Well, almost. You can also clone samples from the Deployment Manager GitHub repository. This repository also contains good documentation on how to use these samples.

> **Tip**
> To clone the GitHub repository for Deployment Manager into your own project, use the `git clone https://github.com/GoogleCloudPlatform/deploymentmanager-samples` command or go to `https://github.com/terraform-google-modules/terraform-google-migrate`. There are more options, but these are the commonly used ways to do this.

The following diagram shows a basic setup for a GCP project:

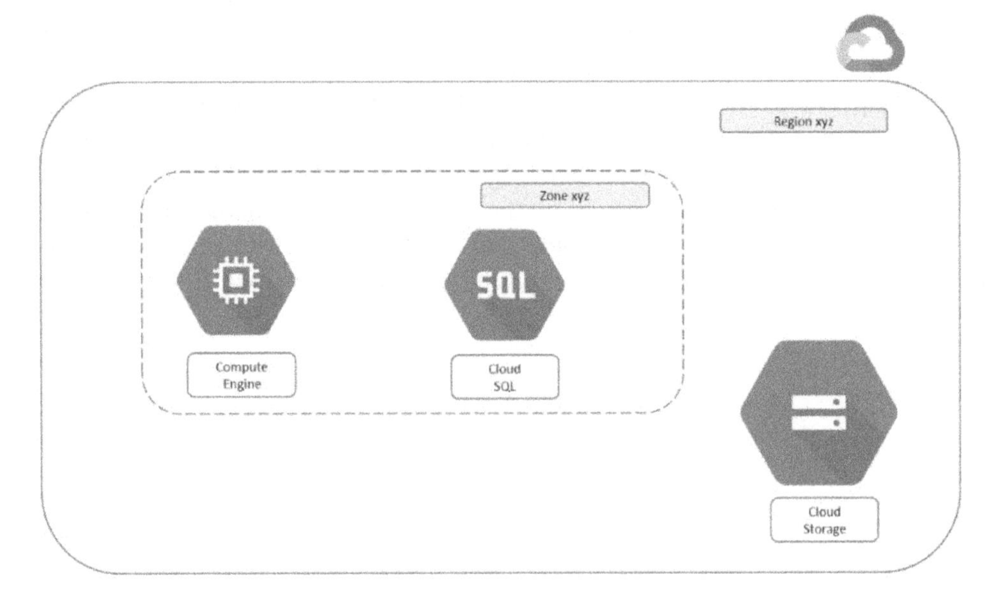


Figure 6.4 – Basic setup of a project in GCP, using Compute Engine and Cloud SQL

With that, we have created landing zones in all three major cloud platforms and by doing so, we have discovered that, in some ways, the cloud concepts are similar, but that there are also some major differences in the underlying technology. Now, let's explore how we can manage these landing zones using policies, as well as how to orchestrate these policies over the different platforms.

# Managing the landing zone using policies

When we work in cloud platforms, we work with code. Everything we do in the cloud is software- and code-defined. This makes the cloud infrastructure absolutely very agile, but it also means that we need some strict guidance in terms of how we manage the code, starting with the code that defines our landing zone or foundation environment. As with everything in IT, it needs maintenance. In traditional data centers and systems, we have maintenance windows where we can update and upgrade systems. In the cloud, things work a little differently.

First of all, the cloud providers apply maintenance whenever it's needed. There's no way that they can agree upon maintenance windows with thousands of customers spread across the globe. They simply do whatever needs to be done to keep the platform healthy, ready for improvements and the release of new features. Enterprises don't want to be impacted by these maintenance activities, so they will have to make sure that their code is safe at all times.

The next thing we need to take into account is the systems that the enterprise has deployed on the platform, within their own virtual cloud or project. These resources also need maintenance. If we're running VMs, we will need to patch them every now and then. In this case, we are patching code. We want to make sure that, with these activities, administrators do not accidently override certain security settings or worse, delete discs or any critical code that is required for a specific function that a resource fulfills. This is something that we must care about from the very start, when setting up the landing zones. From that point onward, we must start managing. For that, we use can policies and management tooling.

In this section, we have set up the landing zones. In the next section, we'll learn how to manage them.

## Managing basic operations in AWS

This time, we'll start with AWS first. AWS offers CloudFormation Guardrails. This is a very appropriate name since it really keeps your environment on the rails. Guardrails come with four principal features for which it sets policies in JSON format. To create policies, AWS offers Policy Generator. In Policy Generator, you define the type of policy first and then define the conditions, meaning when the policy should be applied:

- **Termination protection**: Here, AWS talks about stacks and even nested stacks. Don't get confused – a stack is simply a collection of AWS resources that can be managed as one unit from the AWS Management Console. An example of a stack can be an application that comprises a frontend server, a database instance using a S3 bucket, and network rules. Enabling termination protection prevents that stack from being deleted unintendedly. Termination protection is disabled by default, so you need to enable it, either from the management console or by using command-line programming.
- **Deletion policies**: Where termination protection has entire stacks as scope, deletion policies target specific resources. To enable this, you must set `DeletionPolicy` attributes within the CloudFormation templates. Now, this policy comes with a lot of features. For instance, the policy has a retain option so that whenever a resource is deleted, it's still kept as an attribute in your AWS account. You can also have CloudFormation take a snapshot of the resource before it gets deleted. It's absolutely worthwhile to have a very good understanding of deletion policies in terms of compliancy and audit obligations. Keep in mind that deletion policies are set per resource.
- **Stack policies**: These policies are set to define actions for a whole stack or group of resources. An action could be to update all database instances.
- **IAM policies**: These policies define the access controls; that is, who is allowed to do what and when? Access controls can be set with fine granularity for whole stacks, specific resource groups, or even single resources and only allow specific tasks to define the roles that users can have. In other words, this is the place where we manage RBAC. The last section of this chapter, *Global admin galore – the need for demarcation*, is all about IAM and the separation of duties.

> Tip
>
> More information on Guardrails policies in AWS can be found ay `https://aws.amazon.com/blogs/mt/aws-cloudformation-guardrails-protecting-your-stacks-and-ensuring-safer-updates/`.

## Managing basic operations in Azure

When we look at Azure, we must look at a service called **test-driven development** (**TDD**) for landing zones in Azure. TDD is particularly known in software development as it aims to improve the quality of software code. As we have already discussed, the landing zone in Azure is expanded through the process of refactoring, an iterative way to build out the landing zone. Azure provides a number of tools that support TDD and help in the process of refactoring the landing zone:

- **Azure policy**: This validates the resources that will be deployed in Azure against the business rules. Business rules can be defined as cost parameters or thresholds, as well as security parameters such as checking for hardening of resources or consistency with other resources. For instance, they can check if a certain ARM template has been used for deployment. Policies can also be grouped together to form an initiative that can be assigned to a specific scope, such as the landing zone. A policy can contain actions, such as denying changes to resources or deploy after validation. Azure policy offers built-in initiatives that can be specifically used to execute TTD: it will validate the planned resources in the landing zone against business rules. A successful validation will result in a so-called definition of done and, with that, accept that resources may be deployed.
- **Azure blueprints**: With blueprints, you can assemble policies, initiatives, and deployment configurations in one package so that they can be reused over and over again in case an enterprise wants to deploy multiple landing zones in different subscriptions. Microsoft Azure offers various blueprint samples, including policies for testing and deployment templates. The good thing is that these can easily be imported through Azure DevOps so that you have a CI/CD pipeline with a consistent code repository right from the start.
- **Azure Graph**: Azure Landing Zone is deployed based on the principle of refactoring. So, in various iterations, we will be expanding our landing zone. Since we are working according to the principles of TTD, this means that we must test whether the iterations are successfully implemented, that resources have been deployed in the right manner, and that the environments have interoperability. For these tasks, Azure offers Graph. It creates test sets to validate the configuration of the landing zone. Azure Graph comes with query samples, since it might become cumbersome to get started with the settings and coding that Graph uses.
- **Azure quickstart templates**: If we really want to get going fast, we can use the quickstart templates, which provide default settings for the deployment of the landing zone itself and its associated resources.

> **Tip**
>
> More information on test-driven development in Azure Landing Zone can be found at `https://docs.microsoft.com/en-us/azure/cloud-adoption-framework/ready/considerations/azure-test-driven-development`.

In all cases, Azure uses ARM templates, based on JSON.

## Managing basic operations in GCP

As we have seen, GCP can be a bit different in terms of public cloud and landing zones. This originates from the conceptual view that Google has, which is more focused on container technology using Kubernetes. Still, GCP offers extensive possibilities in terms of setting policies for environments that are deployed on GCP. In most cases, these policies are comprised of organizations and resources that use IAM policies:

- **Organizations**: In GCP, we set policies using constraints. A constraint is an attribute that is added to the service definition. Just as an example, we'll take the service Compute Engine that deploys VMs to our GCP project. In Compute Engine projects, logging in for operating systems by default is disabled. We can enable this and set a so-called Boolean constraint, named after George Boole, who invented this type of logic as an algebraic system in the nineteenth century: a statement or logical expression is either true or false. In this case, we set Compute Engine to true. Next, we must set a policy that prevents that login from being disabled: `constraints/compute.requireOsLogin`. A lot of policies and constraints in GCP work according to this principle.

> **Tip**
>
> More on organization policy constraints in GCP can be found at `https://cloud.google.com/resource-manager/docs/organization-policy/org-policy-constraints`.

- **Resource policies**: Cloud IAM policies set access controls for all GCP resources in JSON or YAML format. Every policy is defined by bindings, an audit configuration, and metadata. This may sound complex, but once you understand this concept, it does make sense. First, let's look at bindings. Each binding consists of a member, a role, and a condition. The member can be any identity. Remember what we set previously: in the cloud, basically everything is an identity. This can be users, but also resources in our cloud environment that have specific tasks so that they can access other resources and have permission to execute these tasks. Thus, a member is an identity: a user, a service account, a resource, or group of resources. The member is bound to a role that defines the permission that a member has. Finally, we must determine under what condition a member may execute its role and what constraints are valid. Together, this makes a binding.

  However, the binding is only one part of the policy. We also have an AuditConfig to log the policy and the metadata. The most important field in the metadata is `etag`. The `etag` field is used to guarantee that policies are used in a consistent way across the various resources in the project. If a policy is altered on one system, the `etag` field makes sure that the policies stay consistent. Inconsistent policies will lead to resource deployments to fail.

  Policies can have multiple bindings and can be set on different levels within GCP. However, be aware that there are limitations. As an example, GCP allows a maximum of 1,500 members per policy. So, do check the documentation thoroughly, including the best practices for using policies.

> TIP
>
> Extensive documentation on Cloud IAM Policies in GCP can be found at `https://cloud.google.com/iam/docs/policies`.

In this section, we have learned how to create policies by enabling the basic operations (BaseOps) of our landing zones in the different clouds. The next section talks about orchestrating policies in a true multi-cloud setup, using a single repository.

# Orchestrating policies for multi-cloud

So far, we've looked at the different ways we can set policies in the major cloud platforms. Now, what we really want in multi-cloud is a single repository where we can store and manage all our policies. Can we do this? From a technological perspective, we probably can: all cloud providers support JSON as a programming format. The problem is that these platforms have different concepts of deploying policies. What's the solution to this problem?

To think of a solution, we must start thinking in terms of layers and abstract logic from the code itself. What do we mean by this? A policy has a certain logic. As an example, from a security perspective, we can define that all the VMs in our environment must be hardened by following the guidelines of **CIS**, the baseline of the **Center for Internet Security**. What type of VM we're talking about is irrelevant, as is the type of operating system it runs or on what platform the VM is hosted on. The logic only says that the VM needs to be hardened by following the recommendations of the CIS framework. It's completely abstracted from the code that deploys the VM. If we do this, we can store the policies themselves in a single repository. The only thing we need to do then is add the specific code that is required to deploy the VM to our target cloud platform.

This is basically what HashiCorp's Terraform application does. Terraform abstracts policies from code so that it can deploy Infrastructure as Code on various cloud platforms from a single source of truth. For this, it uses the definition of the desired state: the code that launches the infrastructure resources is completely abstracted from the actual configuration of that resource. It's important to note that Terraform is idempotent and convergent, meaning that only the required changes are applied to return the environment to the desired state.

This point will help you gain a better understanding of **desire state configuration** (**DSC**). First of all, DSC is often associated with Microsoft PowerShell. This makes sense since DSC was indeed introduced with Windows Server 2012 R2. However, nowadays, the term desired state is more broadly used to abstract Infrastructure as Code from the actual configuration of that infrastructure. It is commonly used in CI/CD pipelines. Here, development teams can build the necessary systems and when these are pushed to production, the desired state gets deployed. An example is installing a backup agent or bringing resources under monitoring. The following diagram shows the simplified model of desired state:

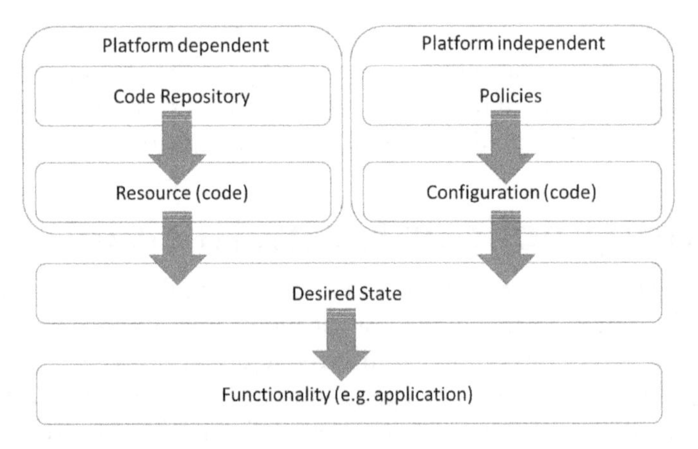


Figure 6.5 – High-level model of desired state using Infrastructure as Code and Configuration as Code

Let's get back to Terraform. The syntax that Terraform uses allows us to fully abstract resources and providers. It defines blocks that can hold any type of resource, from a VM to a container, but also certain services, such as DNS. This is defined in the **HashiCorp Configuration Language** (**HCL**). The next step is to deploy these blocks to our target cloud. This is done by initializing a project in that cloud. For this, the Terraform `init` command is used. `init` will read the Terraform configuration files and import the providers needed to connect to various clouds and services.

The next step is to use the Terraform `plan` command, which is used to create the execution plan. This determines what actions are necessary to achieve the desired state specified in the configuration files. The last step is to use the Terraform `apply` command, which deploys the actions to reach the desired state.

Terraform will now apply the blocks to the cloud and, at the same time, create a so-called state file. This state file is used to apply future changes to the infrastructure: before changes are applied in an execution plan that is automatically created by the Terraform software, it runs a refresh of the actual environment to update the state file. This way, Terraform always holds the latest version of the actual deployed code and keeps environments in sync at all times.

> **Tip**
>
> You can use Terraform to deploy landing zones in Azure, AWS, and GCP. In Azure, this will create a basic setup that enables activity logs and a subscription for Azure Security Center. For AWS, the Terraform HCL scripts call the AWS Landing Zone solution that we described in this chapter. You can find the Terraform code for Azure at `https://docs.microsoft.com/en-us/azure/cloud-adoption-framework/ready/landing-zone/terraform-landing-zone`. The code for AWS has been made publicly available by the Mitoc Group on GitHub: `https://github.com/MitocGroup/terraform-aws-landing-zone`.

If you are already familiar with configuration tools such as Chef or Puppet, you will find that there's some overlap in the functionality of Terraform and some other tools. The big difference is that Terraform actually provisions new infrastructure resources, where most other tools are more focused on adding configuration settings to resources that have been previously deployed. This does not mean that configuration tools are useless; on the contrary. These tools have other use cases; there's no good or bad.

The key to multi-cloud is the single pane of glass view. We will discuss this frequently in this book. However, this is a complicated area. Companies such as ServiceNow target their development at creating platforms from which enterprises can do multi-cloud orchestration from just one console. At the time of writing, the latest release of ServiceNow is Orlando. It contains a product for Policy and Compliance Management that provides a centralized process for creating and managing policies, cross-cloud.

In summary, yes, you can deploy code and policies that are agnostic to different cloud platforms. However, it does require tooling. Throughout this section, we've explored some of the leading tools on the market, at time of writing. All of this requires a thorough understanding of abstracting the infrastructure resources from functionality and policies, resulting in the desired state of the resources.

# Global admin galore – the need for demarcation

Typically, when we talk about demarcation in cloud models, we refer to the matrix or delineation of responsibility: who's responsible for what in IaaS, PaaS, and SaaS computing? The following diagram shows the very basics of this matrix:

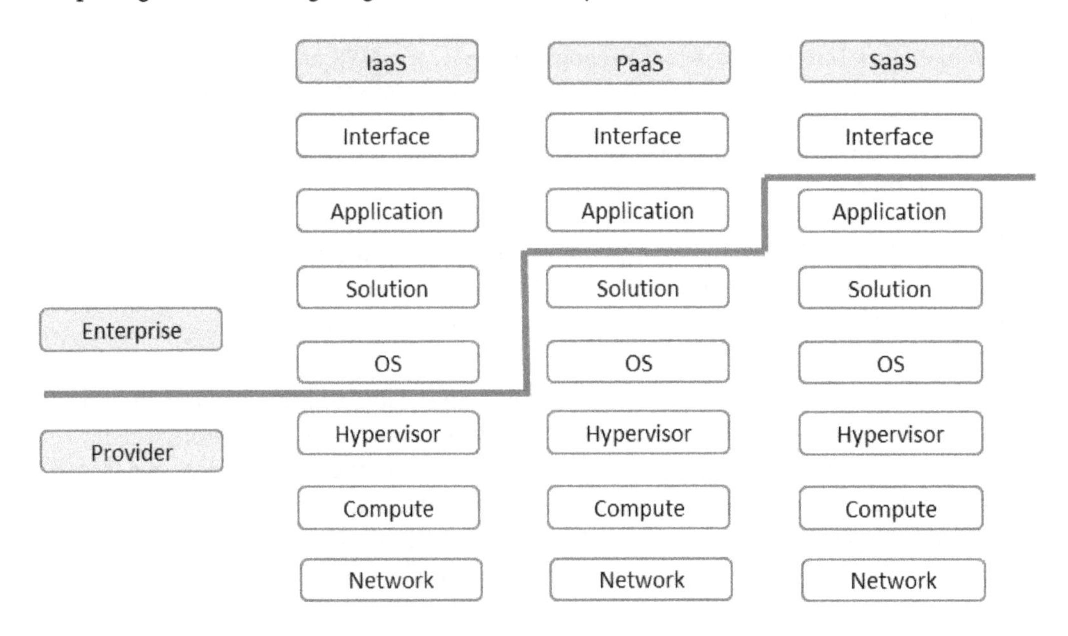


Figure 6.6 – Demarcation model in cloud deployment

However, we need a much more granular model in multi-cloud. We have been discussing policies throughout this chapter and by now, we should have come to the conclusion that it's not very easy to draw some very sharp lines when it comes to responsibilities in our multi-cloud environment. Just look at the solution stack – even in SaaS solutions, there might be certain security and/or compliancy policies that the solution needs to adhere to. Even something such as an operating system might already be causing issues in terms of hardening: are monitoring agents from a PaaS provider allowed or not? Can we run them alongside our preferred monitoring solution? Or will that cause too much overhead on our systems? In short, the world of multi-cloud is not black and white. On the contrary, multi-cloud has an extensive color scheme to work with.

So, how do we get to a demarcation model that will work for our enterprise? Well, that's architecture. First, we don't need global admins all over our estate. This is a major pitfall in multi-cloud. We all know the cases: the database administrator that needs global admin rights to be able to execute certain actions or worse, solutions that require service accounts with such roles. It's global admin galore. Do challenge these requests and do challenge software providers – or developers, for that matter – when it comes to why systems would need the highest possible access rights in the environment.

That's where it starts: policies. In this case, a good practice is the **Policy of Least Privilege** (**PoLP**). This states that every identity is granted the minimum amount of access that is necessary to perform the tasks that have been assigned to that identity. Keep in mind that an identity, in this case, doesn't have to be a user: it can be any resource in the environment. When we are talking about users, we're addressing this as **Least-Privileged User Account or Access** (**LPUA**). PoLP helps in protecting data as data will only be accessible when a user or identity is explicitly granted access to that data. But there are more reasons to adhere to this policy. It also helps in keeping systems healthy as it minimizes risks or faults in systems. These faults can be unintended or the result of malicious conduct. We should follow the rule of least privilege at all times. We will discuss this in more detail in *Chapter 15*, *Implementing Identity and Access Management*, which is all about identity and access management.

Regarding this very first principle, there are a few more considerations that need to be made at this stage. These considerations translate into controls and with that, into deliverables that are part of BaseOps, since they are absolutely part of the foundational principles in multi-cloud. The following table shows these controls and deliverables:

| Control | Deliverable |
| --- | --- |
| A policy document is available and active that describes how user/admin accounts are generated, maintained, and disposed throughout their life cycle. | Policy and approvals |
| An RBAC authorization matrix is available that describes the access delegation from data or system owners. | Authorization matrix |
| User accounts are created by following established approval procedures that adhere to LPUA. | List of user accounts |
| Periodic checks are performed to ensure the continuous validity of accounts; for example, the account is needed and in active use, the correct role has been applied, and so on. | Checklist |
| Unauthorized access (attempts) to system resources are logged in an audit trail and periodically reported to and reviewed by the CISO/Security Manager. | Report of unauthorized access attempts |

Demarcation and separation of duties is very strongly related to identity and access management. That will be discussed in full in *Chapter 15, Designing Identity and Access Management.*

# Summary

In this chapter, we have designed and set up our landing zones in the different major cloud platforms. We have learned that the foundational principles might be comparable, but the actual underlying implementation of the landing zone concepts do differ.

Next, we explored the principles of Infrastructure as Code and Configuration as Code. With tools such as Terraform, we can manage multi-cloud from one code base using configuration policies that have been abstracted from the resource code. We then learned how to define policies and how to apply these to manage our landing zones. Finally, we learned that there's a need for a redundant demarcation model in multi-cloud. This all adds up to the concept of BaseOps: getting the basics right.

Part of keeping the basics right is making sure that our environments are resilient and performing well. That's what we will be discussing in the next chapter, which is all about creating availability and scalability in the cloud.

# Questions

1. A basic infrastructure in the cloud consists of five major domains, three of which are network, compute, and storage. What are two other domains?
2. What is the best practice deployment model for the landing zone in Azure?
3. AWS offers a service called Landing Zone. In enrolls four accounts. In which account is single sign-on managed?
4. A good practice in managing identity and access management is PoLP. What does PoLP stans for?

# Further reading

- *VMware Cross-Cloud Architecture,* by Ajit Pratap Kundan, Packt Publishing
- *Azure for Architects,* by Ritesh Modi, Packt Publishing
- *Architecting Cloud Computing Solutions,* by Kevin L. Jackson, Packt Publishing

# 7
# Designing Resilience and Performance

An important topic in any multi-cloud architecture is the resilience and performance of our environments. The cloud providers offer a variety of solutions. We will have to decide on the type of solution that fits the business requirements and mitigates the risks of environments not being available, not usable, or not secured. Some questions we might ask include, how do we increase availability, how do we ensure that data is not lost when an outage occurs, and how do we arrange disaster recovery? These are questions that arise from having a good understanding of the business risks that are related to transforming cloud environments.

In this chapter, we're going to gather and validate business requirements for resilience and performance. We will then get a deeper understanding of backup and disaster recovery solutions in Azure, AWS, and GCP. We will also learn how to optimize our environments using advisory tools and support plans. In the last section of this chapter, we will learn how to define **Key Performance Indicators** (**KPIs**) to measure performance in our cloud environments.

We will cover the following topics in this chapter:

- Starting with business requirements
- Exploring solutions for resiliency in different cloud propositions

- Optimizing your multi-cloud environment
- Performance KPIs in a public cloud – what's in it for you?

Let's get started!

# Starting with business requirements

In *Chapter 6, Designing, Implementing, and Managing the Landing Zone*, we talked a little bit about things such as availability, backup, and disaster recovery. In this chapter, we will take a closer look at the requirements and various solutions that cloud platforms offer to make sure that your environment is available, accessible, and, most of all, safe to use. Before we dive into these solutions and the various technologies, we will have to understand what the potential risks are for our business if we don't have our requirements clearly defined.

In multi-cloud, we recognize risks at various levels, again aligning with the principles of enterprise architecture.

## Understanding data risks

The biggest risk concerning data is ambiguity about the ownership of the data. This ownership needs to be regulated and documented in contracts, as well as with the cloud providers. International and national laws and frameworks such as **General Data Protection Regulation** (**GDPR**) already define regulations in terms of data ownership, but nonetheless, be sure that it's captured in the service agreements as well. First of all, involve your legal department or counselor in this process.

We should also make a distinction between types of data. Is it business data, metadata, or data that is concerning the operations of our cloud environments? In the latter category, you can think of the monitoring logs of the VMs that we host in our cloud. For all these kinds of data, there might be separate rules that we need to adhere to in order to be compliant with laws and regulations.

We need to know and document where exactly our data is. Azure, AWS, and GCP have global coverage and will optimize their capacity as much as they can by providing resources and storage from the data centers where they have that capacity. This can be a risk. For example, a lot of European countries specify that specific data cannot leave the boundaries of the **European Union** (**EU**). In that case, we will need to ensure that we store data in cloud data centers that are in the EU. So, we need to specify the locations that we use in the public cloud: the region and the actual country where the data centers reside.

We also need to ensure that when data needs to be recovered, it's recovered in the desired format and in a readable state. Damaged or incomplete data is the risk here. We should execute recovery tests on a regular basis and have the recovery plans and the actual test results audited. This is to ensure that the data integrity is guarded at all times. This is particularly important with transaction data. If we recover transactions, we need to ensure that all the transactions are recovered, but also that the transactions are not doubled during the recovery procedure. For this, we also need to define who's responsible for the quality of the data, especially in the case of SaaS.

To help with structuring all these requirements, a good starting point would be to create a model for data classification. Classification helps you decide what type of solution needs to be deployed to guarantee the confidentiality, integrity, and availability of specific datasets. Some of the most commonly used data categories are public data, company confidential data, and personal data.

## Understanding application risks

The use of SaaS is becoming increasingly popular. Many companies have a strategy that prefers SaaS over PaaS over IaaS. In terms of operability, this might be the preferred route to go, but SaaS does come with a risk. In SaaS, the whole solution stack is managed by the provider, including the application itself. A lot of these solutions work with shared components, and you have to combat the risk of whether your application is accessible to others or whether your data can be accessed through these applications. A solution to mitigate this risk is to have your own application runtime in SaaS.

One more risk that is associated with the fact that the whole stack – up until the application itself – is managed by the provider is that the provider can be forced out of business. At the time of writing, the world is facing the coronavirus pandemic and a lot of small businesses are really struggling to survive. We are seeing businesses going down and even in IT, it's not always guaranteed that a company will keep its head above water when a severe crisis hits the world. Be prepared to have your data safeguarded whenever an SaaS provider's propositions might be forced to stop the development of the solution or worse, to close down business.

Also, there's the risk that the applications fail and have to be restored. We have to make sure that the application code can be retrieved and that applications can be restored to a healthy state.

## Understanding technological risks

We are configuring our environments in cloud platforms that share a lot of components, such as data centers, the storage layer, the compute layer, and the network layer. By configuring our environment, we merely **silo**. This means that we are creating a separated environment – a certain area on these shared services. This area will be our virtual data center. However, we are still using the base infrastructure of Azure, AWS, GCP, or any other cloud.

It's like a huge garden where we claim a little piece of ground, put a fence around it, and state from that point onward that that piece of ground is now our property, while the garden as a whole still belongs to some landlord. How do we make sure that no one enters that piece of ground without our consent? In the cloud, we have technological solutions for this, such as account management, IAM, firewalls, and network segmentation.

Even the major cloud providers can be hit by outages. It's up to the enterprise to guarantee that their environments will stay available, for instance, by implementing redundancy solutions when using multiple data centers, zones, or even different global regions.

Monitoring is a must, but it doesn't have any added value if we're looking at only one thing in our stack or at the wrong things. Bad monitoring configuration is a risk. As with security, the platforms provide their customers with tools, but the configuration is up to the company that hosts its environment on that platform.

Speaking of security, one of the biggest risks is probably weak security. Public clouds are well-protected as platforms, but the protection of your environment always remains your responsibility. Remember that clouds are a wonderful target for hackers, since they're a platform hosting millions of systems. That's exactly the reason why Microsoft, Amazon, and Google spend a fortune securing their platforms. Make sure that your environments on these platforms are also properly secured and implement endpoint protection, hardening of systems, network segmentation, firewalls, and vulnerability scanning, as well as alerting, intrusion detection, and prevention. You also need to ensure you have a view of whatever is happening on the systems.

However, do not overcomplicate things. Protect what needs to be protected but keep it manageable and comprehensible. The big question is, what do we need to protect, to what extent, and against which costs? This is where gathering business requirements begins.

Although we're talking about technological, application, and data risks, at the end of the day, it's about business requirements. These business requirements drive data, the applications, and the technology, including the risks. So far, we haven't answered the question of how to gather these business requirements.

First of all, the main goal of this process is to collect all the relevant information that will help us create the architecture, design our environments, implement the right policies, and configure our multi-cloud estate as the final product. Now, this is not a one-time exercise. Requirements will change over time and especially in the cloud era, the demands and therefore the requirements are changing constantly at an ever-increasing speed. So, gathering requirements is an ongoing and repetitive process.

How do we collect the information we need? There are a few key techniques that we can use for this:

- **Assessment**: A good way to do this is to assess whether we're assessing resilience and performance from the application layer. What does an application use as resources and against which parameters? How are backups scheduled and operated? What are the restore procedures? Is the environment audited regularly, what were the audit findings, and have these been recorded, scored, and solved? We should also include the end user experience regarding the performance of the application and under what conditions, such as office rush hour, when the business day starts, and normal hours.
- **Stakeholder interviews**: These interviews are a good way to understand what the business need is about. We should be cautious, though. Stakeholders can have different views on aspects such as what the business-critical systems are.
- **Workshops**: These can be very effective to drill down a bit deeper into the existing architectures, the design of systems, the rationales behind demands, and the requirements, while also giving us the opportunity to enforce decisions, since all stakeholders will ideally be in one room. A risk of this is that discussions in workshops might become too detailed. A facilitator can help steer this process and get the desired result.

Once we have our requirements, then we can map to the functional parameters of our solution. A business-critical environment can have the requirements that it needs to be available 24/7, 365 days a year. The system may hold transactions, where every transaction is worth a certain amount of money. Every transaction that's lost means that the company is losing money. The systems handle a lot of transactions every minute, so every minute of data loss equals an amount of real financial damage. This could define the **recovery point objective** (**RPO**) – the maximum amount of data loss the company finds acceptable – which should be close to 0. This means that we have to design a solution that is highly available, redundant, and guarded by a disaster recovery solution with a restore solution that guarantees an RPO of near 0 – possibly a solution that covers **data loss prevention** (**DLP**).

Is it always about critical systems, then? Not necessarily. If we have development systems wherein a lot of developers are coding, the failure of these systems could actually trigger a financial catastrophe for a company. The project gets delayed, endangering the time to market of new services or products, and the developers will sit idle, but the company will still have to pay them. It's always about the business case, the risks a company is willing to accept, and the cost that the company is willing to pay to mitigate these risks.

# Exploring solutions for resiliency in different cloud propositions

This chapter is about resilience and performance. Now that we have gathered the business requirements and identified the risks, we can start thinking about solutions and align these with the requirements. The best way to do this is to create a matrix with the systems, the requirements for resilience, and the chosen technology to get the required resilience. The following table shows a very simple example of this, with purely fictional numbers:

| System or system group/ category | Business level | RTO | RPO | Solution |
|---|---|---|---|---|
| | | | | |
| Application X | Critical | <2 hours | <2 hours | Standby (failover) systems, DR |
| Application Y | Important | >2 hours <8 hours | >2 hours <8 hours | Full daily backup, increments with snapshots |
| Application Z | Non-critical | <48 hours | <48 hours | Weekly backup, daily incrementals |

Resilient systems are designed in such a way that they can withstand disruptions. Regardless of how well the systems might be designed and configured, sooner or later, they will be confronted with failures and, possibly, disruptions. Resilience is therefore often associated with quality attributes such as redundancy and availability.

## Creating backups in the Azure cloud with Azure Backup and Site Recovery

Azure Backup works with the principle of snapshots. First, we must define the schedule for running backups. Based on that schedule, Azure will start the backup job. During the initial execution of the job, the backup VM snapshot extension is provisioned on the systems in our environment.

Azure has extensions for both Windows and Linux VMs. These extensions work differently from each other: the Windows snapshot extension works with Windows **Volume Shadow Copy Services (VSS)**. The extension actually takes a full copy of the VSS volume. On Linux machines, the backup takes a snapshot of the underlying system files.

Next, we can take backups of the disks attached to the VM. The snapshots are transferred to the backup vault. By default, backups of operating systems and disks are encrypted with Azure Disk Encryption. The following diagram shows the basic setup for the Azure Backup service:

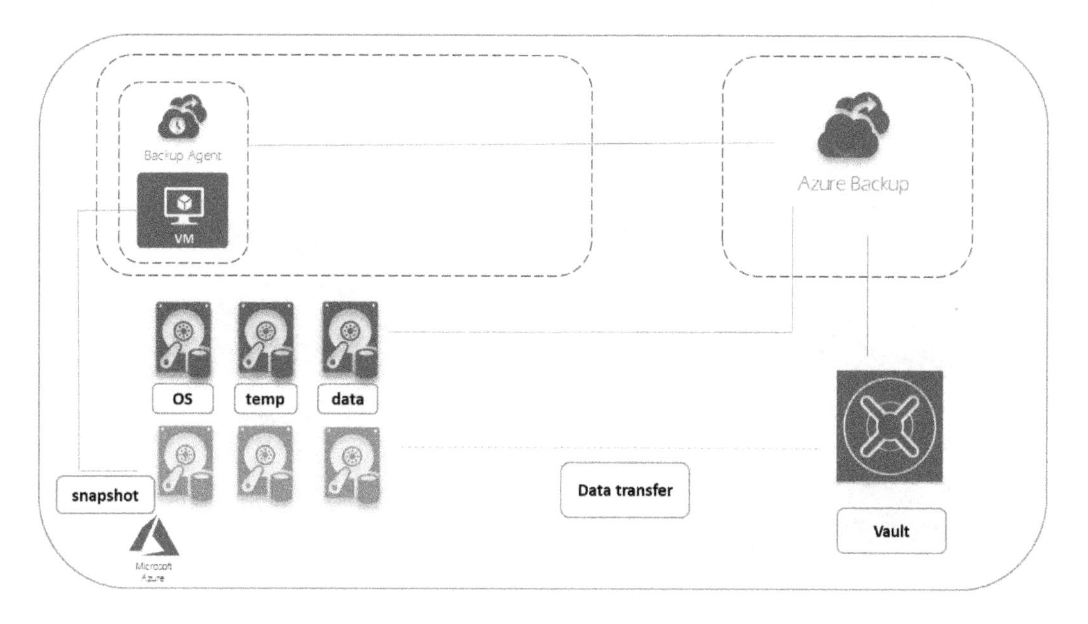


Figure 7.1 – High-level overview of the standard backup components in Azure

We can create backups of systems that are in Azure, but we can also use Azure Backup for systems that are outside the Azure cloud.

## Backing up non-Azure systems

Azure Backup can be used to create backups of systems that are not hosted in Azure itself. For that, it uses different solutions. **Microsoft Azure Recovery Services** (**MARS**) is a simple solution to do this. In the Azure portal, we have to create a Recovery Services vault and define the backup goals.

Next, we need to download the vault credentials and the agent installer that must be installed on the on-premises machine or machines that are outside Azure. With the vault credentials, we register the machine and start the backup schemes. A more extensive solution is **Microsoft Azure Backup Server** (**MABS**). MABS is a real VM – running Windows Server 2016 or 2019 – that controls the backups within an environment, in and outside Azure. It can execute backups on a lot different systems, including SQL Server, SharePoint, and Exchange, but also VMware VMs – all from a single console.

MABS, like MARS, uses the recovery vault, but in this case, backups are stored in a geo-redundant setup by default. The following diagram shows the setup of MABS:

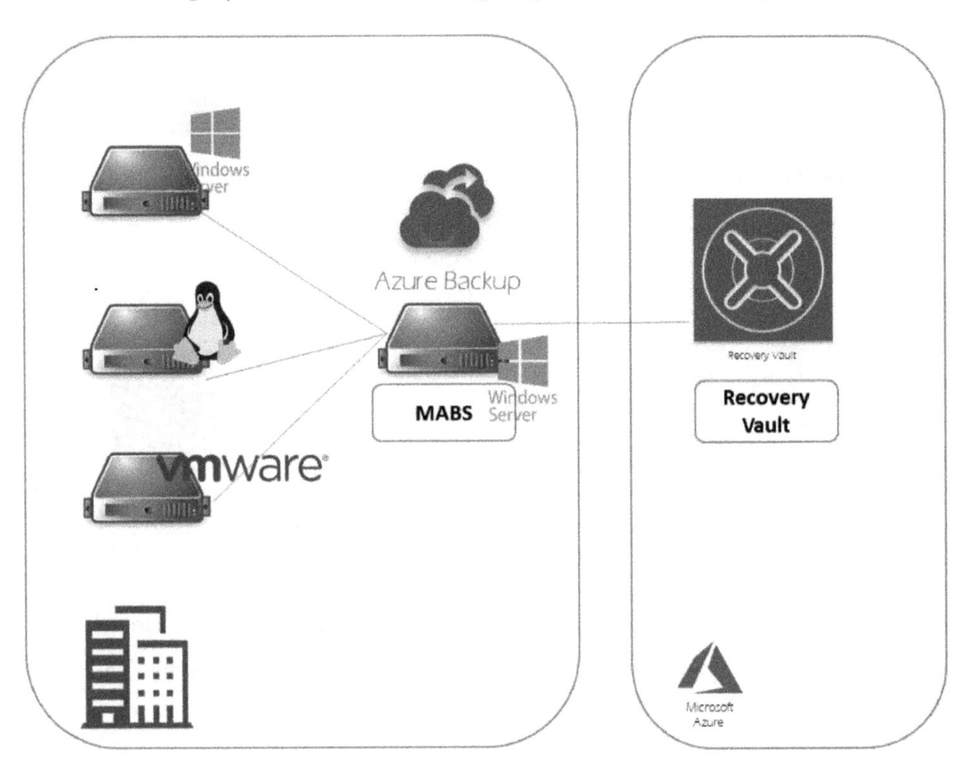


Figure 7.2 – High-level overview of the setup for Microsoft Azure Backup Server

> **Tip**
>
> Documentation on the different backup services that Azure provides can be found at `https://docs.microsoft.com/en-us/azure/backup/`.

Before we dive into the recovery solutions for Azure and the other cloud providers, we will discuss the generic process of disaster recovery. Disaster recovery has three stages: detect, response, and restore. First of all, we need to have monitoring in place that is able to detect whether critical systems are failing and that they are not available anymore. It then needs to trigger actions to execute mitigating actions, such as failover to standby systems that can take over the desired functionality, and ensure that business continuity is safeguarded. The last step is to restore the systems back to the state that they were in before the failure occurred. In this last step, we also need to make sure that the systems are not damaged in such a way that they can't be restored.

Recovery is a crucial element in this process. However, recovery can mean that systems are completely restored back to their original state where they still were fully operational, but we can also have a partial recovery where only the critical services are restored and, for example, the redundancy of these systems must be fixed at a later stage. Two more options are cold standby and warm standby. With cold standby, we will have systems that are reserved that we can spin up when we need them. Until that moment, these systems are in shut down modus. In warm standby, the systems are running, but not yet operational in production modus. Warm standby servers are much faster to get operational than cold standby servers, which merely have reserved capacity available.

> **Tip**
>
> Donald Firesmith wrote an excellent blog post about resilience for the Software Engineering Institute of Carnegie Mellon University. You can find it at `https://insights.sei.cmu.edu/sei_blog/2019/11/system-resilience-what-exactly-is-it.html`.

## Understanding Azure Site Recovery

**Azure Site Recovery** (**ASR**) offers a solution that helps set up disaster recovery in Azure. In essence, it takes copies of workloads in your environment and deploys these to another location within Azure. If the primary location where you host the environments becomes unavailable because of an outage, ASR will execute a failover to the secondary location, where the copies of your systems are. As soon as the primary location is back online again, ASR will execute the failback to that location again.

Under the hood, ASR uses Azure Backup and the snapshot technology for this solution. The good news is that it works with workloads in Azure, but you can also use ASR for non-Azure workloads, such as on-premises systems and even systems that are in AWS, for instance. You can replicate workloads from one Azure region to another, VMware and Hyper-V VMs that are on-premises, Windows instances that are hosted in AWS, and also physical systems.

A bit of bad news is that this is not as simple as it sounds. You will need to design a recovery plan and assess whether workloads can actually failover from the application and data layer. Then, probably the trickiest part is getting the network and boundary security parameters right: think of switching routes, reserved IP addressing, DNS, and replicating firewall rules.

Azure has solutions for this as well, such as DNS routing with traffic manager, which helps with DNS switching in case of a failover, but still, this takes some engineering and testing to get this in place. The last thing that really needs serious consideration is what region you will have the secondary location in. A lot of Azure regions do have dual zones (data centers), but there are some regions that only have one zone, and you will need to choose another region for failover. Be sure that you are still compliant in that case.

The following diagram shows the basic concept of ASR. It's important to remember that we need to set up a cache storage account in the source environment. During replication, changes that are made to the VM are stored in the cache before being sent to storage in the replication environment:

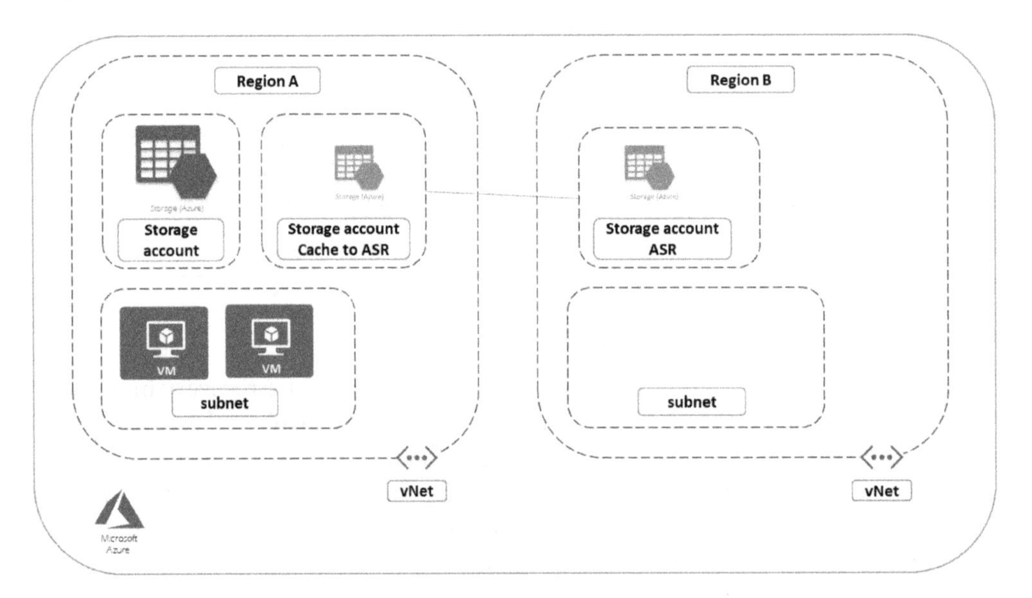


Figure 7.3 – High-level overview of ASR

> **Tip**
> More information on ASR can be found at `https://docs.microsoft.com/en-us/azure/site-recovery/`.

With that, we have covered Azure. In the next section, we will look at backup and disaster recovery in AWS and GCP.

# Working with AWS backup and disaster recovery

In this section, we will explore the backup and disaster recovery solutions in AWS. We will learn how to create backups based on policies and on tags. We will also look at the hybrid solution for AWS.

## Creating policy-based backup plans

As in Azure, this starts with creating a backup plan that's comprised of backup rules, frequency, windows, and defining and creating the backup vault and the destination where the backups should be sent. The backup vault is crucial in the whole setup: it's the place where the backups are organized and where the backup rules are stored. You can also define the encryption key in the vault that will be used to encrypt the backups. The keys themselves are created with AWS **Key Management Service** (**KMS**). AWS provides a vault by default, but enterprises can set up their own vaults.

With this, we have defined a backup plan, known as backup policies in AWS. These policies can now be applied to resources in AWS. For each group of resources, you can define a backup policy in order to meet the specific business requirements for those resources. Once we have defined a backup plan or policy and we have created a vault, we can start assigning resources to the corresponding plan. Resources can be from any AWS service, such as EC2 compute, DynamoDB tables, **Elastic Block Store** (**EBS**) storage volumes, **Elastic File System** (**EFS**) folders, **Relational Database Services** (**RDS**) instances, and storage gateway volumes.

## Creating tag-based backup plans

Applying backup plans or policies to resources in AWS can be done by simply tagging the plans and the resources. This integration with tags makes it possible to organize the resources and have the appropriate backup plan applied to these resources. Any resource with a specific tag will then be assigned to the corresponding backup plan. An example, if we have set out policies for business-critical resources, we can define a tags an that says `BusinessCritical` as a parameter for classifying these resources. If we have defined a backup plan for `BusinessCritical`, every resource with that tag will be assigned to that backup plan.

The following diagram shows the basic concept of AWS Backup:

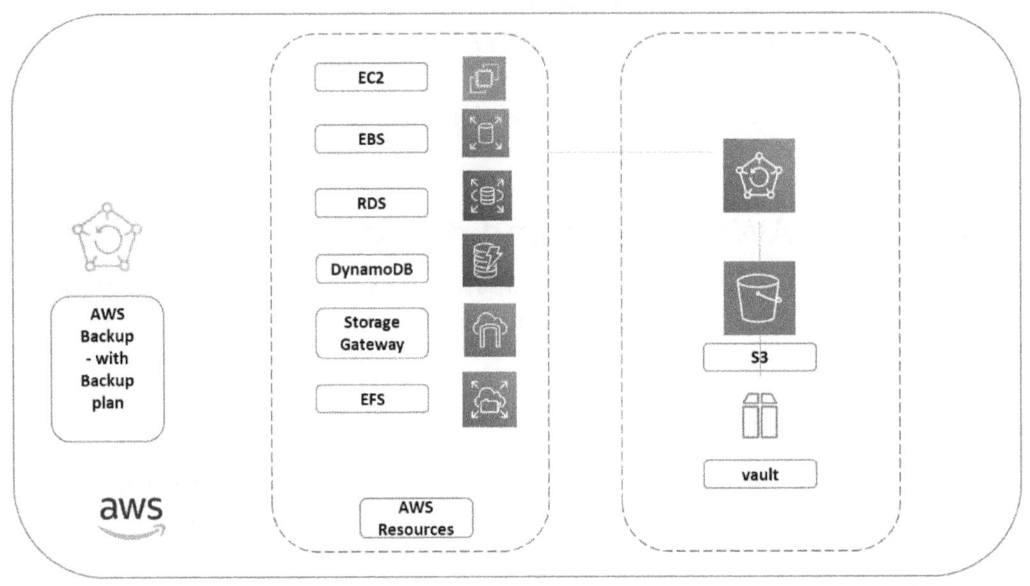


Figure 7.4 – High-level overview of AWS Backup

Similar to Azure, we can also create backups of systems that are outside of AWS using the hybrid backup solution of AWS. We'll describe this in the next section.

## Hybrid backup in AWS

AWS calls backing up resources in AWS a native backup, but the solution can be used for on-premises workloads too. This is what AWS calls hybrid backup. For this, we'll have to work with the AWS Storage Gateway. We can compare this to MABS, which Microsoft offers. In essence, the on-premises systems are connected to a physical or virtual appliance over industry-standard storage protocols such as **Network File System** (**NFS**), **Server Message Block** (**SMB**), and **internet Small Computer System Interface** (**iSCSI**). The appliance – the storage gateway – connects to the AWS S3 cloud storage, where backups can be stored. You can use the same backup plans for hybrid backup that you do for the native backup. The following diagram shows the principle of hybrid backup:

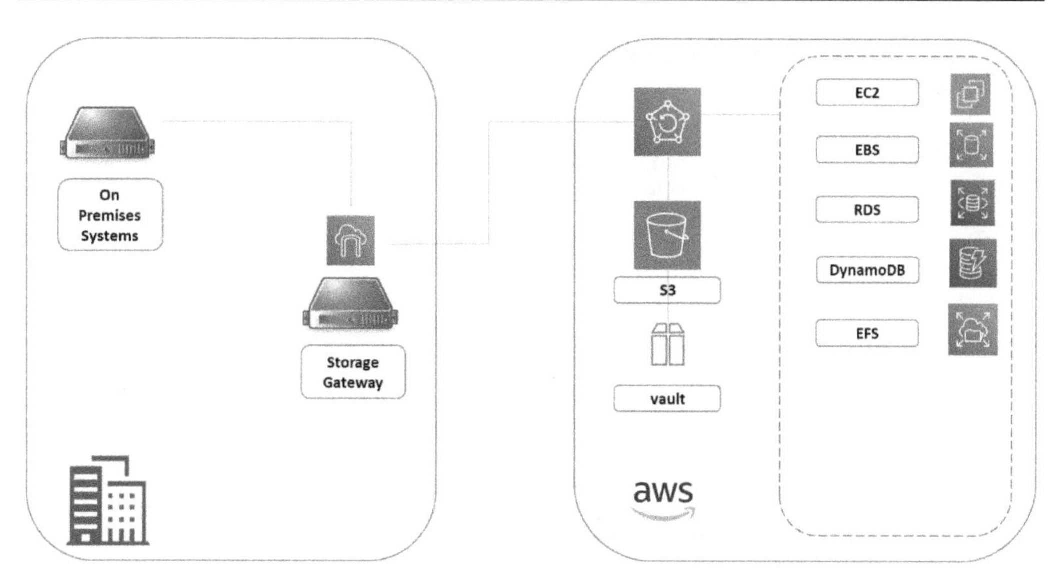


Figure 7.5 – High-level overview of hybrid backup in AWS

Now, let's learn about the disaster recovery options available in AWS.

## AWS disaster recovery and cross-region backup

AWS allows us to perform cross-region backups, meaning that we can make backups according to our backup plans and replicate these to multiple AWS regions. However, this occurs on the data layer. We can do this for any data service in AWS: RDS, EFS, EBS, and Storage Gateway volumes. So, with Storage Gateway included, it also works for data that is backed up on-premises. Next to this, AWS also has another proposition that's a **Business Continuity and Disaster Recovery** (**BCDR**) solution: CloudEndure **disaster recovery** (**DR**). This solution doesn't work with snapshots, but keeps target systems for DR continuously in sync with the source systems with continuous data protection. By doing this, they can even achieve sub-second recovery points and barely lose any data. CloudEndure supports a lot of different systems, including physical and virtualized machines, regardless of the hypervisor. It also supports enterprise applications such as Oracle and SAP.

This principle is shown in the following diagram:

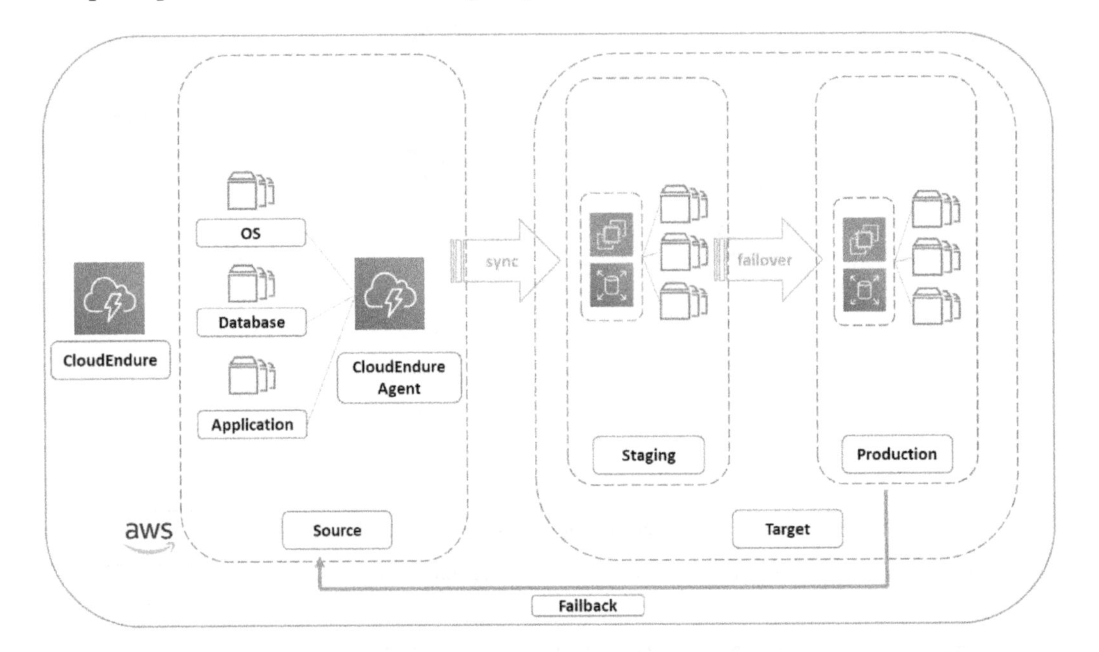


Figure 7.6 – High-level overview of the CloudEndure concept in AWS

CloudEndure uses agents on the source systems and a staging area in AWS where the system duplicates are stored on low-cost instances. In case of a failover, the target DR systems are booted and synced from this staging area. The failback is done from the DR systems in AWS.

> **Tip**
>
> More information on AWS Backup can be found at `https://docs.aws.amazon.com/aws-backup/latest/devguide/whatisbackup.html`. Documentation on CloudEndure can be found at `https://aws.amazon.com/cloudendure-disaster-recovery/`.

## Creating backup plans in GCP

GCP also uses the snapshot technology to execute backups. The first snapshot is a full backup, while the ones that follow are iterative and only back up the changes that have been made since the last snapshot. If we want to make a backup of our data in GCP Compute Engine, we have to create a persistent disk snapshot. It's possible to replicate data to a persistent disk in another zone or region, thus creating geo-redundancy and a more robust solution.

As with AWS and Azure, you will first have to design a backup plan, or in GCP, a snapshot schedule so that backups are taken at a base frequency. Next, we have to set the storage location. By default, GCP chooses the region that is closest to the source data. If we want to define a solution with a higher availability, we will need to choose another region ourselves where we wish to store the persistent disks.

Be aware that, in GCP, we work with constraints. If we have defined a policy with a constraint that data can't be stored outside a certain region and we do pick a region outside of that boundary, the policy will prevent the backup from running.

GCP proposes to flush the disk buffers prior to the backup as a best practice. You don't need to stop the applications before snapshots are taken, but GCP does recommend this so that the application stops writing data to disk. If we stop the application, we can flush the disk buffer and sync the files before the snapshot is created. For Unix programmers, this will be very familiar, since GCP lets you connect with SSH to the disk and `sudo sync` to execute the synchronization process. All of this is done through the command-line interface.

But what about Windows? We can run Windows-based systems in GCP and we can take backups of these systems. GCP uses VSS for this, which is the Volume Shadow Copy Services of Windows. Before we do that, GCP recommends unmounting the filesystem and then taking the snapshots. We can use PowerShell for this.

> **Tip**
>
> More information on backups in Compute Engine from GCP can be found at `https://cloud.google.com/compute/docs/disks/create-snapshots`. Specific documentation and how-to information about creating snapshots of Windows systems can be found at `https://cloud.google.com/compute/docs/instances/windows/creating-windows-persistent-disk-snapshot`.

## Disaster recovery planning

GCP lets us define the **Recovery Time Objective** (**RTO**) and **Recovery Point Objective** (**RPO**) first when planning a DR strategy. Based on the requirements, we define the building blocks within GCP to fulfill the strategy. These building blocks comprise Compute Engine and Cloud Storage. In Compute Engine, we can define how we want our VMs to be deployed and protected from failures. The key components here are persistent disks, live migration, and virtual disk import. We discussed the creation of persistent disks as part of backing up in GCP. Live migration keeps VMs up by migrating them into a running state to another host. Virtual Disk Import lets you import disks from any type of VM to create new VMs in Compute Engine. These newly created machines will then have the same configuration as the original machines. The supported formats are **Virtual Machine Disk** (**VMDK**), which is issued by VMware, and **Virtual Hard Drive** (**VHD**), which is used by Microsoft and RAW.

As you can tell, GCP does not offer a predefined solution for DR. And again, there's much more focus on containers with GKE. GKE has some built-in features that you can use to create highly available clusters for containers. Node auto repair checks the health status of cluster nodes: if nodes don't respond within 10 minutes, they get automatically remediated. If we're running nodes in a multi-region setup, GKE offers multi-cluster ingress for Anthos as a load balancing solution between the clusters. This solution was previously offered as **Kubernetes Multicuster Ingress** (**Kubemi**). For all of this, we do need a solution to route the traffic across the GCP regions and to make sure that DNS is pointing to the right environments. This is done through Cloud DNS using Anycast, the Google global network, and Traffic Director.

Lastly, Google does suggest looking at third-party tools when we have to set up a more complex DR infrastructure solution. Some of the tools that are mentioned in the documentation include Ansible with Spinnaker and Zero-to-Deploy with Chef on Google Cloud.

> **Tip**
>
> More information on disaster recovery planning in GCP can be found at `https://cloud.google.com/solutions/dr-scenarios-planning-guide`.

So far, we have discussed backup solutions from the cloud provider themselves. There's a risk of doing this: we are making our businesses completely dependent on the tools of these providers. From an integration perspective, this may be fine, but a lot of companies prefer to have their backups and DR technology delivered through third-party tooling. Reasons to do this can sprout from compliancy obligations, but also from a technological perspective. Some of these third-party tools are really specialized in these types of enterprise cloud backup solutions, can handle many more different types of systems, and data and be truly cloud agnostic. Examples of such third-party tools include Cohesity, Rubrik, Commvault, and Veeam.

# Optimizing your multi-cloud environment

Systems need to be available, but if their performance is bad, they're still of no use at all. The next step is to optimize our cloud environments in terms of performance. Now, performance is probably one of the trickiest terms in IT. What is good performance? Or acceptable performance? The obvious answer is that it depends on the type of systems and the SLA that the business has set. Nonetheless, with all the modern technology surrounding us every day, we expect every system to respond fast whenever it's called. Again, it's all about the business case. What does a business perceive as acceptable, what are the costs of improving performance, and is the business willing to invest in these performance enhancements?

Cloud providers offer tools we can use to optimize environments that are hosted on their platforms. In this section, we will briefly look at these different tools and how we can use them.

## Using Trusted Advisor for optimization in AWS

It all honesty, getting the best out of AWS – or any other cloud platform – is really not that easy. There's a good reason why these providers have an extensive training and certification program. The possibilities are almost endless, and the portfolios for these cloud providers grow bigger every day. We could use some guidance while configuring our environments. AWS provides that guidance with Trusted Advisor. This tool scans your deployments, references them against best practices within AWS, and returns recommendations. It does this for cost optimization, security, performance, fault tolerance, and service limits.

Before we go into a bit more detail, there's one requirement we must fulfill in order to start using Trusted Advisor: we have to choose a support plan, although a couple of checks are for free, such as a check on **Multi-Factor Authentication** (**MFA**) for root accounts and IAM use. Also, checks for permissions on S3 (storage) buckets are free. Note that basic support is included at all times, including AWS Trusted Advisor on seven core checks, mainly focusing on security. Also, the use of the Personal Health Dashboard is included in basic support.

Support plans come in three levels: developer, business, and enterprise. The latter is the most extensive one and offers full 24/7 support on all checks, reviews, and advice on the so-called well-architected framework, as well as access to AWS support teams. The full service does come at a cost, however. An enterprise that spends 1 million dollars in AWS every month would be charged around 70 USD per month on this full support plan. This is because AWS typically charges the service against the volumes that a customer has deployed on the platform. The developer and business plans are way lower than that. The developer plan can be a matter of as little as 30 dollars per month, just to give you an idea.

However, this full support does include advice on almost anything that we can deploy in AWS. The most interesting parts, though, are the service limits and performance. The service limits perform checks on volumes and the capacity of a lot of different services. It raises alerts when 80 percent of a limit for that service has been reached and it then gives advice on ways to remediate this, such as providing larger instances of VMs, increasing bandwidth, or deploying new database clusters. It strongly relates to the performance of the environment: Trusted Advisor checks the high utilization of resources and the impact of this utilization on the performance of those resources.

> **Tip**
>
> The full checklist for Trusted Advisor can be found at `https://aws.amazon.com/premiumsupport/technology/trusted-advisor/best-practice-checklist/`.

One more service that we should mention in this section is the free Personal Health Dashboard, which provides us with very valuable information on the status of our resources in AWS. The good news is that not only does it provide alerts when issues occur and impact your resources, but it also guides us through remediation. What's even better is that the dashboard can give you proactive notifications when planned changes might affect the availability of resources. The dashboard integrates with AWS CloudWatch, but also with third-party tooling such as Splunk and Datadog.

## Optimizing environments using Azure Advisor

Like AWS, Azure offers support plans and a tool to help optimize environments, called Azure Advisor. But no, you can't really compare the support plans and the tools with one another. The scopes of these services are completely different. Having said that, Azure Advisor does come at no extra cost in all support plans.

Let's start with the support plans. Azure offers four types of plans: basic, developer, standard, and professional direct. The basic plan is free, while the most extensive one is professional direct, which can be purchased at 1,000 USD per month. But again, you can't compare this to the enterprise plan of AWS. Put another way, every provider offers free and paid services – the difference per provider is which services are free or must be paid for.

Indeed, Azure Advisor comes at no extra cost. It provides recommendations on costs, high availability, performance, and security. The dashboard can be launched from the Azure portal and it will immediately generate an overview of the status of the resources that we have deployed in Azure, as well as recommendations for improvements. For high availability, Azure Advisor checks whether VMs are in deployed in an availability set, thereby remediating fault tolerance for VMs. Be aware of the fact that Azure Advisor only advises that the actual remediation needs to be done by the administrator. We could also automate this with Azure Policy and Azure Automation, but there's a good reason why Azure Advisor doesn't already do this. Remediation actions might incur extra costs and we want to stay in control of our costs. If we automate through Policy and Automation, that's a business decision and architectural solution that will be included in cost estimations and budgets.

On the other hand, Azure Advisor does provide us with some best practices. In terms of performance, we might be advised to start using managed disks for our app, do a storage redesign, or increase the sizes of our VNets. It's always up to us to follow up, either through manual tasks or automation.

The different cloud providers offer a great deal of tools so that we can keep a close eye on the platforms themselves and the environments that we deploy on these platforms. Next to Advisor, we will use Azure Monitor to guard our resources and Azure Service Health to monitor the status of Azure services. Specific for security monitoring, Azure offers Azure Security Center and the Azure-native **Security Information and Event Manager** (**SIEM**) tool known as Sentinel. Most of these services are offered on a pay-as-you-go basis: an amount per monitored item. In *Chapter 9, Defining and Using Monitoring and Management Tools*, we will explore the different monitoring options for the major clouds that we've discussed in this book.

> **Tip**
> More information on Azure Advisor can be found at `https://docs.microsoft.com/en-us/azure/advisor/advisor-get-started`.

## Optimizing GCP with Cloud Trace and Cloud Debugger

GCP offers two interesting features in terms of optimizing environments: Cloud Trace and Cloud Debugger. Both can be accessed from the portal. From this, you can tell that GCP is coming from the cloud-native and native apps world.

Cloud Trace is really an optimization tool: it collects data on latency from the applications that you host on instances in GCP, whether these are VMs, containers, or deployments in App Engine or the native app environment in GCP. Cloud Trace measures the amount of time that elapses between incoming requests from users or other services and the time the request is processed. It also keeps logs and provides analytics so that you can see how performance evolves over a longer period of time. Cloud Trace uses a transaction client that collects data from App Engine, load balancers, and APIs. It gives us good insight into the performance of apps, dependencies between apps, and ways to improve performance.

Cloud Trace doesn't only work with GCP assets, but with non-Google assets too. In other words, we can use Cloud Trace in AWS and Azure as a REST API using JSON.

Cloud Debugger is another tool and it's used to debug code in apps that you run in GCP. Debugger will analyze the code while the application is running. It does this by taking a snapshot of the code, although you can use it on the source code as well. It integrates with versioning tools such as GitHub. Debugger supports the most commonly used programming languages to code apps, at least when it runs in containers on GKE. In this case, Java, Python, Go, Node.js, Ruby, PHP, and .Net Core are supported. In Compute Engine, .NET Core is not supported at the time of writing.

Cloud Trace and Cloud Debugger are part of the operations suite – previously known as Stackdriver – of GCP and is a charged service.

> **Tip**
> More information on Cloud Trace can be found at `https://cloud.google.com/trace/docs/overview/`. Documentation on Cloud Debugger can be found on `https://cloud.google.com/debugger/docs`.

# Performance KPIs in a public cloud – what's in it for you?

As we mentioned in the previous section, performance is a tricky subject and, to put it a bit more strongly, if there's one item that will cause debates in service-level agreements, it's going to be performance. In terms of KPIs, we need to be absolutely clear about what performance is, in terms of measurable objectives.

What defines performance? It's the user experience. What about how fast an application responds and processes a request? Note that *fast* is not a measurable unit. A lot of us can probably relate to this: a middle-aged person may think that an app on their phone responding within 10 seconds is fast, while someone younger may be impatiently tapping their phone a second after they've clicked on something. They have a relative perception of *fast*. Thus, we need to define and agree on what is measurably fast. One thing to keep in mind is that without availability, there's nothing to measure, so resilience is still a priority.

What should we measure? There are a few key metrics that we must consider:

- **CPU and memory**: All cloud providers offer a wide variety of instance sizes. We should look carefully at what instance is advised for specific workloads. For instance, applications that run massive workflow processes in-memory require a lot of memory in the first place. For example, SAP S4/HANA instances can require up to 32 GB of RAM or more. For these workloads, Azure, AWS, and GCP offer large, memory-optimized instances that are next to complete SAP solutions. If we have applications that run heavy imaging or rendering processes, we might want to look at specific instances for graphical workloads that use GPUs. So, it comes down to the right type of instance and infrastructure, as well as the sizing. You can't blame the provider for slow performance if we choose a low-CPU, low-memory machine underneath a heavy-duty application. Use the Advisor tools to fulfill the best practices. We will come back to this in *Chapter 11, Defining Principles and Guidelines for Resource Provisioning and Consumption*.
- **Responsiveness:** How much time does it take for a server to get a response to a request? There are a lot of factors that determine this. To start with, it's about the right network configuration, the routing, and the dependencies in the entire application stack. It does matter whether we connect through a low bandwidth VPN or a high-speed dedicated connection. And it's also about load balancing. If, during peak times, the load increases, we should be able to deal with that. In the cloud, we can scale out and up, even in a fully automated way. In that case, we need proper configuration for the load balancing solution.

- **IO througput**: This is about throughput rates on a server or in an environment. Throughput is a measure of **Requests Per Second** (**RPS**), the number of concurrent users, and the utilization of the resources, such as servers, connections, firewalls, and load balancers. One of the key elements in architecture is sizing. From a technological perspective, the solution can be well-designed, but if the sizing isn't done correctly, then the applications may not perform well or be available at all. The Advisor tools that we have discussed in this chapter provide good guidance in terms of setting up an environment, preparing the sizes of the resources, and optimizing the application (code) as such.

The most important thing about defining KPIs for performance is that all stakeholders – business, developers, and administrators – have a mutual understanding of what performance should look like and how it should be measured.

# Summary

In this chapter, we discussed the definitions of resilience and performance. We explored the various backup and disaster recovery solutions that hyperscalers offer. We also learned how to optimize our environments using different advisory tools that cloud providers offer. We then learned how to identify risks in the various layers: business, data, applications, and technology. We studied the various methods we can use to mitigate these risks. One of the biggest risks is that we "lose" systems without the ability to retrieve data from backups or without the possibility to failover to other systems.

To prevent systems from going down, which brings with it the risk of data loss and with that, losing business, we need to design resiliency in our environments. For real business-critical systems, we might want to have disaster recovery, but at a minimum, we need to have proper backup solutions in place. Due to this, we learned about the backup and disaster recovery solutions available in the major cloud platforms.

We also learned how to optimize our environments in the cloud by using some cloud-native, handy advisory tools. Lastly, we studied KPIs and how to use them to measure the performance of our systems in the cloud.

In the next chapter, we will study the use of automation and automation tools in the cloud. We'll be looking at concepts such as Infrastructure as Code and Configuration as Code from automated pipelines.

# Questions

1. What do the terms RPO and RTO stand for?
2. What tool would you use to capture failures in application code that's running in Google Cloud?
3. True or false: We can use the backup solutions in Azure and AWS for systems that are hosted on-premises too.

# Further reading

- *Reliability and Resilience on AWS*, by Alan Rodrigues, Packt Publishing
- *Architecting for High Availability on Azure*, by Rajkumar Balakrishan, Packt Publishing

# 8
# Defining Automation Tools and Processes

One of the major advantages of cloud environments is the fact that we can automate almost anything. We don't want too many manual tasks in our cloud environment. We also want to automate as much as we can in the management of the infrastructure. How do we automate cross-cloud, what processes do we need to have in place, and who's going to be responsible for managing the automation templates?

This chapter will introduce the core principle of automation in abstracting environments in layers. We will look at the automation tools that are integrated with the platforms of the major providers: Azure, AWS, and Google Cloud. Next, we will study how we can design an automation process, starting with storing our source code in a single repository, and then we will apply version control to that code. We will also briefly discuss the main pitfalls when defining automation.

In this chapter, we're going to cover the following main topics:

- Understanding cross-cloud infrastructure automation
- Creating automation processes using a code repository and workflows
- Using automation tools
- Designing automation for multi-cloud

# Cross-cloud infrastructure automation

Before we can start thinking about automation itself, we need to virtualize all of our components in IT. Automation simply doesn't work if we have to drag physical devices into a data center – unless we have robots or drones to do that. So, it starts with virtualization, and this is exactly why companies such as VMware still play such an important role in the cloud arena. Their **software-defined data center** (**SDDC**) concept is basically the blueprint for building clouds. We have to virtualize the full stack: compute, storage, and networks.

Only virtualized entities can be stored in a repository, and from there programmatically provisioned on-demand. However, we want this to be truly multi-cloud, hence the interoperability of these virtualized components is key in automation.

Virtualization is the starting point, but we want it to be truly agnostic and cross-platform. Then we'll find that a lot of systems are still very dependent on settings in the underlying physical infrastructure, even in the public clouds of the hyperscalers, the major cloud providers: Azure, AWS, and Google Cloud. Let's take virtual machines as an example: we can tell the physical host that it can share its processor (CPU) and memory among multiple virtual machines by using a hypervisor, but all of these virtual machines still will need their own guest operating system.

One way to overcome this issue is by using containers. As we saw in *Chapter 4*, *Service Design for Multi-Cloud*, containers don't have their own operating system; they use the operating system of the physical host. Yet containers do require a platform that can host and orchestrate these containers. This is where Kubernetes typically comes in. The main platforms all have Kubernetes services (AKS, EKS, PKS, and GKE), but also, for the use of containers, we need to build and configure infrastructure. The use of containers doesn't mean that we can skip infrastructure build.

In essence, it comes down to abstracting layers. We have to make sure that the application layer is not depending on the infrastructure layer: it needs to be completely unaware of the infrastructure it's hosted on. Let's first look at a logical view of these layers:

- **Access layer**: The access layer comprises the network and interfaces. We need networking to get connections from the outside into the environments that are hosted on the cloud platforms and connections within the platforms so that applications can communicate with each other or with, for example, databases. The access layer also contains the interconnects to the services layer; this can be a real portal or any command interface that we can use to order and configure services in the services layer.
- **Application layer**: This layer holds the application code and the configuration code of the application. It's completely separated from all the other layers.

- **Services layer**: This is the layer where **Infrastructure as a Service (IaaS)**, **Platform as a Service (PaaS)**, and **Software as a Service (SaaS)** are positioned. IaaS contains services for servers or storage. PaaS is for managed services, such as AWS Elastic Beanstalk or RedHat OpenShift. SaaS contains full-stack business services, such as office automation – for example, Office365.
- **Resources layer**: This is the layer where the building blocks are for the services in the services layer. In this layer, we have a physical pool of resources for the CPU, disks, **network interface cards (NICs)**, and so on. These are all the resources that are needed to build a server and make it accessible over a network connection. This layer also contains a pool of logical resources, such as operating systems and runtime scripts.

The following diagram shows the concept of abstracting the data center in order to virtualize it and providing a logical view in deploying environments on a cloud platform:

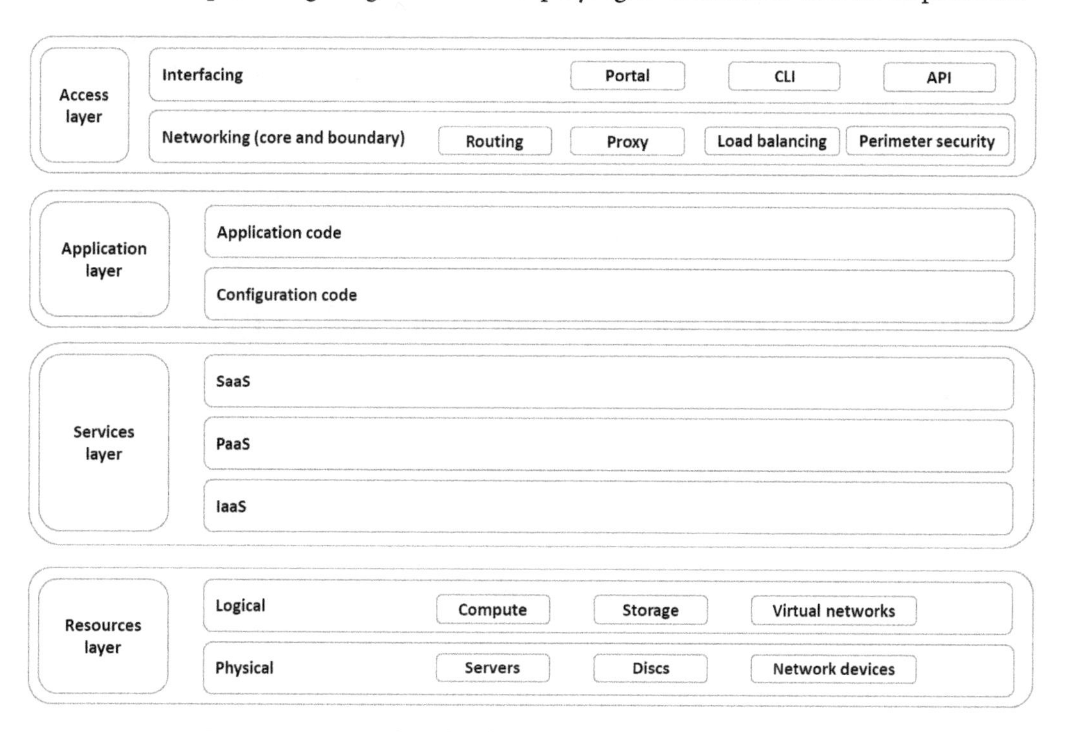


Figure 8.1 – Logical model of abstracting layers in an environment

You can imagine how deploying IT environments used to be a very intensive, costly process that took a lot of effort and time before we found a way to get our infrastructure defined as code. Besides defining the architecture, we really needed to do a proper sizing of the physical machines that we would need in our data center. A mistake in the sizing or ordering the wrong machines could lead to a situation where the capacity would either not be enough or be too much. After ordering the machines, we would need to install them in the data center, and only then could we actually start deploying our workloads – a process that could easily take up two months of the total throughput time.

Now, we have the technology to virtualize the entire data center, and even better: we use existing data centers that Azure, AWS, and Google Cloud provide. They have already figured out a lot of the building blocks that we can use from the resource, services, and access layer to compose our environments. These building blocks are code. Putting the building blocks together is the only thing left to do. Cloud automation is exactly about the steps of putting it all together. If we have found a way to put building blocks from the different layers together and we know that we want to repeat this process frequently, then it makes sense to automate the steps that form this process. It will save us time and thus costs; but also, with automation, the risk of errors will be lower than with manual intervention.

In the next section, we will dive into the process of automation and how we can use catalogs and libraries for the automation process.

# Automation processes using a code repository and workflows

In *Chapter 4, Service Design for Multi-Cloud*, we briefly discussed the **continuous integration** (**CI**)/**continuous delivery** (**CD**) pipeline. In this section, we will explore this further since the CI/CD pipeline is a crucial part of our automation. A high-level diagram of the pipeline is shown here:

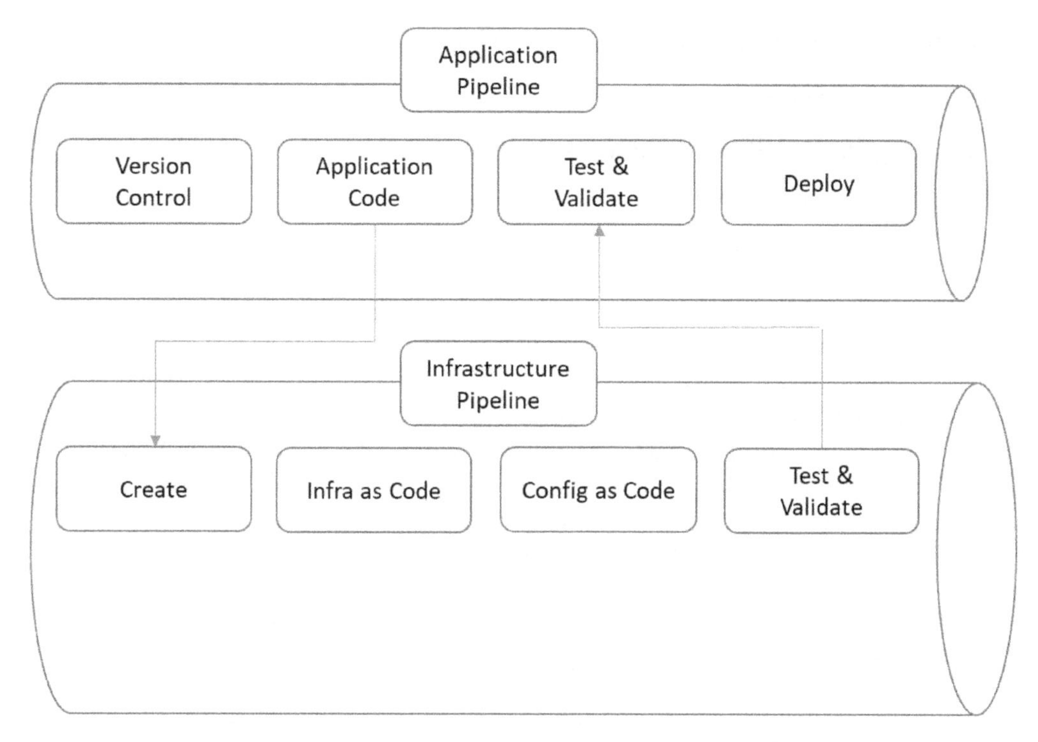


Figure 8.2 – High-level overview of the CI/CD concept

The pipeline begins with version control and the actual application code. To start version control, we will need source code. This source code is typically stored in a source code repository. An example of an independent repository is Git, such as GitHub, BitBucket, or GitLab. However, each cloud has its own, and an enterprise can even host their own repository on-premises. The automation pipeline configuration starts with a request to change the code – or to fork the code. By forking, we are creating a new branch where we can develop the code further. This forked code can then be submitted back to the master branch when it's validated and tested.

In any case, the request will trigger a process in the CI pipe that will prepare the code for the next stage. This is the build phase, where the code is packaged into components that can be deployed into our environment. This package will contain not only the application code but also the packages for the required resources where the code is to be deployed. Resources can be a virtual machine, a storage block, or a container. Finally, before we get to deployment, all of these packages need to be tested and validated against the desired state and policies, after which the whole deployment process finishes.

Common processes to automate infrastructure in cloud environments are as follows:

- Auto-provisioning of virtual machines
- Deploying **Desired State Configuration** (**DSC**) to infrastructure components
- Deploying backup schedules
- Automation of workflows for scaling and failover scenarios (for example, disaster recovery)

The most important automation task is to create **infrastructure as code** (**IaC**) and store that in the repository. With automation tools, we can fork items from the repository. This is the reason why abstraction in layers is crucial. Every item or component is defined in code: virtual machines, storage blocks, network parameters, and containers. Depending on the application code and the packages that have been defined to run this application code, the automation tool will know how it should assemble components and next deploy them into our environment. If an application requires, for instance, a number of containers, the tool can create these containers and also configure them to land on a Kubernetes node, connect storage, configure load balancing, and apply the network policies. This entire workflow can be set as a process within the automation.

But there's more that automation tooling can do and can bring benefits besides the automated deployment of environments. Automation can also be used to manage environments. We can use automation to perform tasks such as scaling or trigger remediation actions when the performance of an application is degrading. This is why automation tooling needs to be integrated with monitoring. If this monitoring detects that an environment is experiencing peak load or the performance decreases, it can trigger the automation to execute predefined actions: for example, add extra virtual machines, increase storage capacity, and add load balancing. On the other hand, if environments or components are detected to be idle, automation can be triggered to remove these components if they are not needed anymore, and with that, save costs.

Be aware that provisioning, managing, and removing components is tied into a process – a workflow that needs to be defined carefully. Just removing a virtual machine, for instance, can cause failures if that machine has connections to other components in the environment. Automation needs to be aware of these connections and other interactions.

The very same applies if we auto-deploy new workloads to our environment: with what other components should these workloads interface? Automation is not something that you just turn on and then wait for the magic to happen. We will need to define and design the workflows in the automation tool. The following diagram shows an example of a workflow to automate the deployment of a virtual machine:

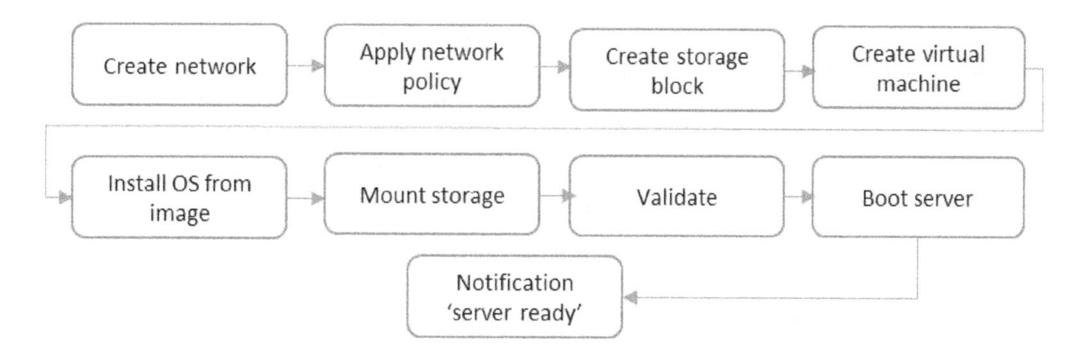


Figure 8.3 – Conceptual workflow for the deployment of a virtual machine

In the next section, we will explore various automation tools and how we should get started with automation.

# Exploring automation tools

There's a whole world to discover when it comes to cloud automation; there are a lot of tools available on the market. The cloud platforms themselves offer native tooling. We'll look at these first.

## Azure Automation

Azure Automation offers a variety of solutions to automate repetitive tasks in infrastructure that is deployed in Azure. Using DSC can help in keeping the infrastructure up to standard, consistent, and compliant. It may be good to recap DSC first since it's an important aspect of cloud automation.

We're automating for two main reasons: to drive operational costs down and to prevent human error by having administrators doing too many manual and repetitive tasks. DSC is one way to start with automation. If we run a server farm, we might get to a point where we discover that over time, the settings on these servers have changed and actually differ from each other. If there's a good reason to allow these differences, then this is not necessarily an issue and should be documented with an updated DSC.

In larger server farms, it can be a cumbersome, time-consuming task checking and manually updating servers. We want that process to be automated with a tool that monitors whether servers still have the right settings and policies applied, and if that's not the case, automatically remediate these settings and policies. Servers that are newly deployed will also automatically get these settings and policies. This is the benefit of standardization that a DSC provides.

Azure Automation is the tool to manage DSC: it handles configuration and update management. But the most interesting part of Azure Automation is the process automation. Azure uses runbook automation for this. This means that you can create runbooks graphically, in PowerShell or using Python. Runbooks let you deploy and manage workloads in Azure, but also on systems that you host on-premises or in other clouds, such as AWS. You can even integrate runbooks with webhooks into the monitoring systems. This can be ITSM platforms, such as ServiceNow. And, of course, Azure Automation integrates perfectly with Azure DevOps, where we can define complete DevOps projects, including CI/CD pipelines.

The key concept in runbooks is the worker that executes a specified job that we create. Workers can be shared among different resources in Azure, but they can only be assigned to one job at the time. From a trigger in CI/CD, or monitoring, the job gets started and a worker is assigned to that job. Next, it fulfills the actual runbook – for instance, applying a policy to a virtual machine.

Remember that everything in the cloud is basically an identity: in this case, the identity is a worker that is assigned to a job. That worker will need access to resources where it needs to execute the job. This means that we have to make sure that workers have the right permissions and are authenticated against Active Directory. Otherwise, the job will fail.

> **Tip**
> More information on Azure Automation and runbooks can be found at `https://docs.microsoft.com/en-us/azure/automation/`.

## AWS OpsWorks

As with a lot of tools within AWS, OpsWorks integrates with third-party tooling. The functionality of OpsWorks is comparable to DSC with PowerShell and Azure Automation, but OpsWorks integrates with either Chef Automate or Puppet Enterprise. There's also a native service for OpsWorks that is called OpsWorks Stacks.

Stacks works with layers. A layer can be a group of virtual machines, deployed from the **Elastic Compute Cloud (EC2)** service in AWS. That layer will deploy the web servers or the database servers. Next, Stacks can deploy the application layer on the infrastructure. Although Stacks is a native service, it does use Chef as its underlying technology. In fact, it uses Chef's recipes to automate the deployment of layers, as well as install the applications and scripts. It also applies autoscaling, if demanded, and installs monitoring on the stacks.

OpsWorks with Chef Automate goes a step further. This service requires Chef servers in your environment that hold cookbooks. It doesn't only deploy a server stack, but it also applies configuration policies, implements access controls based on **Lightweight Directory Access Protocol** (**LDAP**) or **Security Assertion Markup Language** (**SAML**), and configures the integrations. You can define workflows for full deployments – also for containerized environments, compliance, and security checks using industry-led security frameworks, such as the one by the **Center of Internet Security** (**CIS**).

Again, Chef also works with layers. The main parts of these layers are attributes and resources. Attributes contain details on the systems that we want to install: the nodes. Chef evaluates the current state of the node and the desired state. To reach the desired state, it uses resources describing the desired state in the packages, templates, and services that it retrieves from AWS. Under the hood, Chef works with JSON and Ruby, so when working with Chef, it's advisable to have an understanding of these script languages.

Chef provides the full cloud-native menu to create an application landscape using cookbooks. It does require knowledge on how to define these cookbooks. As mentioned, we will explore this in much more detail in *Chapter 18, Design Process for Test, Integration, Deployment, and Release Using CI/CD*. The best part is the fact that you can use cookbooks that have been developed and tested by a community already and that can be downloaded from GitHub.

One other toolset that we can use is OpsWorks for Puppet Enterprise. In this case, we will deploy Puppet master servers that control the infrastructure in AWS. Puppet works with modules that contain the desired state for infrastructure components in AWS. With Puppet, you can, as with Chef, deploy, configure, and manage systems, whether they are in AWS using EC2 or on-premises. It will deploy the systems, install operating systems, configure databases, and enroll desired state policies, all from workflows that you can define yourself in the development kit or use from Puppet Forge, where a large community contributes to the Puppet modules.

Puppet Enterprise will be discussed in *Chapter 18, Design Process for Test, Integration, Deployment, and Release Using CI/CD*, in more detail too.

> Tip
>
> More information on AWS OpsWorks can be found at `https://docs.aws.amazon.com/opsworks/latest/userguide/welcome.html`.

## Automation in Google Cloud Platform

By now, it should be clear that by abstracting environments into separate identifiable layers, it's possible to automate deployments and management of our environments. We can deploy complete application stacks and configure them with the policies that we have defined, ensuring that all these stacks are consistent and compliant. Management is also made a lot more efficient since we do have the stack as a whole, but, for instance, update parts of the stack without having to touch other components. Since it is all code, we only need to manage the code and not the underlying physical hardware, such as servers, switches, routers, computer racks, and cables. All those physical parts are taken care of by the cloud provider.

In **Google Cloud Platform** (**GCP**) (`https://cloud.google.com/solutions/devops/devops-tech-deployment-automation`), we have exactly the same concept as we have seen in Azure and AWS. GCP automates deployments in packages and scripts. Very simply explained, packages contain the *what*, while scripts contain the *how*. Packages hold the artifacts that have to be deployed, whereas scripts define how the packages are deployed. With scripts, the target environment in GCP is prepared by defining the project (similar to an AWS VPC or Azure vNet) where the systems will be hosted, followed by the actual deployment of the packages, and finally, test scripts are executed to make sure that the systems can be accessed and that they function as designed.

## Exploring other automation tools

We discussed the native tooling that is integrated with Azure, AWS, and GCP. We also mentioned that there many more tools available on the market. Chef, Puppet, Terraform, Spinnaker – originally created at Netflix – and Ansible are just a couple of them. Keep in mind that all of these tools have strong assets, but might not always be the right tool for the goals that you have set. The saying goes that if a hammer is the only tool you have at your disposal, then every problem looks like a nail. Better said: the tool should fit your needs. It's important to review the toolset on a frequent basis. That's a team effort: allow developers and solution builders in the cloud to evaluate toolsets and have them recommend improvements.

Just look at the periodic table of DevOps tools at `https://xebialabs.com/periodic-table-of-devops-tools/`, which is created and maintained by Xebia Labs. It changes regularly for a good reason.

# Architecting automation for multi-cloud

Automation seems like the holy grail in the cloud, but there are some major pitfalls that we should avoid. The three main reasons why automation projects in the cloud fail are as follows:

- **Making automation too complex**: As with anything in the cloud, you should have a plan before you start. We have to think about the layers: which components in which layer are we deploying and are these repetitive actions? Think of the easiest way to perform these actions so that they are really simple to repeat. For example, spinning up a virtual machine is very likely such a task. What would you do to create a virtual machine? You determine where the machine should land, create the machine, and next install the operating system. These are three basic steps that we can automate.
- **Trying to automate everything**: For instance, consider the usage of PaaS solutions. A lot of cloud-native applications use PaaS that can be triggered by just one command. The trigger to that command is something we can include in the automation script, but not the service itself. You could, perhaps, but you shouldn't: it would be too complicated. This pitfall is tightly related to the first one: making automation too complex.
- **Disregarding dependencies**: Automation doesn't make sense if the process fails with the first component that isn't available in the automation script. What do we mean with that? The automation script makes calls to components in the cloud environment. That's where orchestration comes in. With automation, we make calls to a number of specific services offered by cloud providers, but these calls have to be made in a particular order.

  For example, if we deploy a database from an automation script, we should first provision and confirm that the database server is up and running with an operating system before we deploy the database and, at last, the actual data itself. A good practice in automation is that services can be automated independently so that they don't crash if another component is not available. If an automation script that deploys a database doesn't find a virtual machine to instantiate, it should simply hold and wait for the server to come online, and not proceed to the installation of the database. This phenomenon is called lock-step.

So, how do we start? The answer to that question is with version control. We can't start automating if we don't have a repository where we have our code stored in a logical way. That starts with the source code, but all the iterations to all the different components – files – to the code need to be filed in a repository that is shared and accessible to everyone who's working with it. This not only ensures that the code can be reused and improved upon in every iteration but also that it can be traced who changed the code and how it has changed. In the case of system failure, we can trace the changes back in the versions that we have at the time of failure.

For version control, we can use Git, but there are more tools available, such as Subversion. The thing that really matters is that we have to bring all the code under version control. From the following list, you will definitively recognize the different abstracted layers:

- Application code.
- Runtime scripts.
- Deployment scripts for any building block in the environment. These can be image building scripts, as well as Chef recipes or Puppet modules.
- Buildpacks for containers.
- Scripts for the packaging and provisioning of components, such as databases, and in the case of containerization, Kubernetes nodes and pods.
- Configuration files for the desired state, such as AWS CloudFormation files, Azure DSC, and Terraform files.
- Configuration files for the core and boundary, such as firewall configuration settings and DNS parameter files.

From the source code and version control, we will design the automation process. If we have done a proper job in layering and versioning, then we can work from three categories to start designing the automation:

- Application code
- System configuration
- Application configuration

From the application, we define what resources we need in the systems layer. Then, we create the flow to configure the systems to the desired state so that they are ready to run the application code. Let's take a simple web application as an example, containing a web server, application server, and a database for which we're using a PaaS service. How would we automate the deployment of this stack? In the following diagram, a more detailed workflow for this is presented, adjacent to the workflow in *Figure 8.3*:

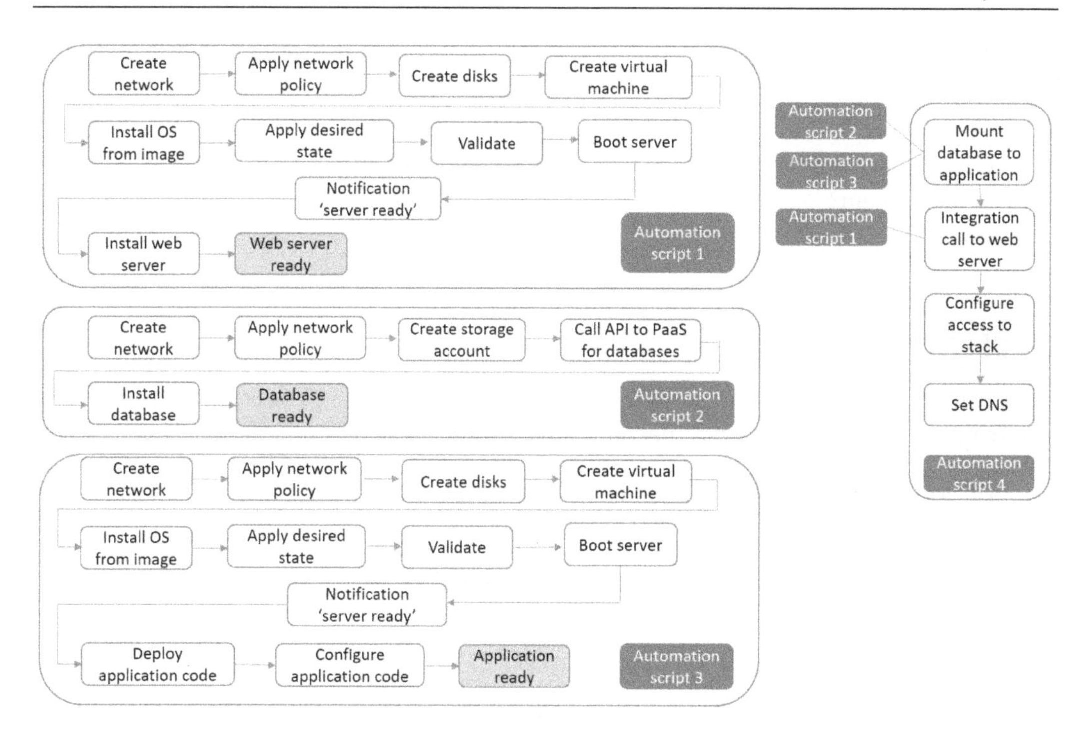


Figure 8.4 – Script design for automating an application with a database on PaaS and a web server

In *Chapter 1*, *Introduction to Multi-Cloud*, we introduced the 12-factor app. The 12-factor app is truly automated. The first of the 12 factors is the code base: the single repository where we will have all the code stored. The second factor is about making sure that components have very clear – explicit – descriptions of dependencies. The third factor is about configuration: configuration is strictly separated from the application code itself. There we have our layers once more.

# Summary

In this chapter, we have discussed the basic principles of automation. We have learned how to abstract our environment in different layers: applications, systems, and configurations. We have studied tools that enable automation in Azure, AWS, and GCP, as well as found that there are many more tools that we can use to automate deployment and management of systems in multi-cloud environments. We have learned how to start designing the automation process and that version control is crucial in automation.

Now, if we have deployed our systems, we want to keep a close eye on them. That's what the next chapter is all about: monitoring and management.

# Questions

1. In what layer would CPUs be if we abstract the data center into layers?
2. AWS OpsWorks has two options to integrate with configuration management. Can you name them?
3. True or false: version control is crucial in automation.

# Further reading

As well as the links that we have mentioned in this chapter, check out the following books for more information on the topics that we have covered:

- *VMware Cross-Cloud Architecture* by Ajit Pratap Kundan, Packt Publishing
- Blog post by Tim Warner on DSC (`https://4sysops.com/archives/powershell-desired-state-configuration-dsc-part-1-introduction/`)
- The principles of the 12-factor app: `https://12factor.net/`

# 9

# Defining and Using Monitoring and Management Tools

We're getting to the last section on basic operations, or BaseOps, in multi-cloud environments. This chapter is about monitoring your multi-cloud environment. How do we keep track of the health of our cloud resources? We will be using the native monitoring tools of different cloud providers, but we'll also explore some tools that provide a single-pane-of-glass view—one overall dashboard where we have a unified view of our entire environment.

In this chapter, we will first define the monitoring and management processes, before we take a look at the different tools of Azure, AWS, and Google Cloud Platform. We will also learn about what tools we can use to manage our environments. We will get a deeper understanding of what we should monitor in the seven layers of the **Open System Interconnections** (**OSI**) model and how we can consolidate monitoring data so that it becomes relevant to the business. Lastly, we will briefly explore two platforms that offer a single-pane-of-glass view: ServiceNow and BMC Helix.

In this chapter, we're going to cover the following topics:

- Defining monitoring and management processes
- Exploring the different native monitoring and management tools of major cloud providers
- Understanding how to consolidate and interpret monitoring data
- Understanding the concept of the single-pane-of-glass view

# Defining monitoring and management processes

This section of the book is all about BaseOps, and we will be looking at the Cloud Adoption Framework offered by the major cloud providers and hyperscalers—Azure, AWS, and Google Cloud Platform. These frameworks share a lot of basic principles. We can identify five domains in the frameworks:

- Governance
- Cost management
- Security
- Automation
- Monitoring

In the previous chapters, we covered governance, service design, policies, implementing landing zones in different clouds, resilience, and performance. Lastly, we learned how we can automate the deployment and management of our environments. We now have one final thing to discuss in terms of BaseOps, and that's monitoring.

Monitoring is crucial in the professional management of IT systems. It doesn't make sense to monitor everything in your environment, but that's what a lot of companies still do: they simply turn monitoring on and then wait until the alerts come in. But in a larger enterprise estate in a multi-cloud environment, the overwhelming amount of alerts would likely make it difficult to extract the most important warnings and critical events that need attention. As with everything that we have already discussed, we need a plan. That plan needs to come from the business requirements: they set the stage. These requirements define how we have to manage our systems in the cloud and what we should monitor.

It helps to think in layers, as we did when we discussed automation in *Chapter 8, Defining Automation Tools and Processes*. If we're talking about end-to-end monitoring, then we mean that we are monitoring from the perspective of the end user: this type of monitoring views all layers. The top layer is the business layer, where the end user sits and kicks off the business process. That can be any process, but typically it's a transaction on a frontend system, such as a web page. That transaction has to be processed by a function that is embedded in an application. This is the second layer: the application and the interfaces of the application to databases and other systems that it communicates with in order to process the transaction.

Applications, databases, and interfaces use infrastructure—virtual machines, a network, storage, or a container platform. This is the infrastructure layer, but **Platform as a Service (PaaS)** is also involved in this layer. Infrastructure consists of different components, something that we learned in the previous chapter. The final layer is the components or resources layer. The following diagram shows the conceptual model of the layers. You will find that it overlaps with *figure 8.1* in *Chapter 8, Defining Automation Tools and Processes*:

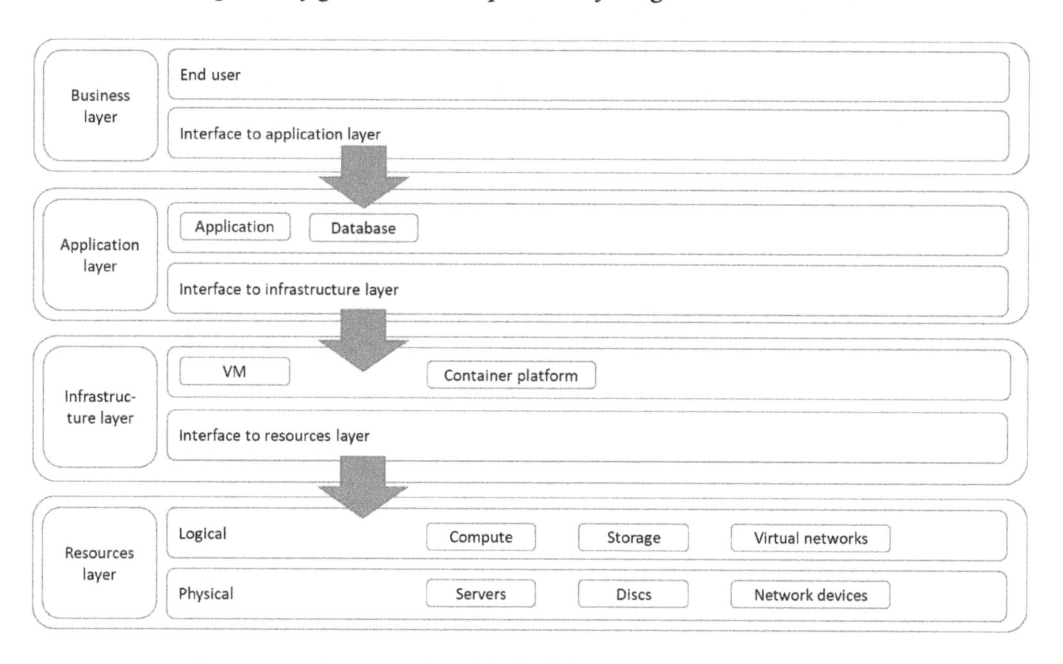


Figure 9.1 – Conceptual model of a full end-to-end monitoring stack

For each of these layers, we can have separate monitoring tools. However, we want to have the end user's view. Resources might be up and running and performing well, but if something's wrong in the application layer, the end user will be confronted with a failing system—even though the monitoring of our resources tells us that everything is fine. It's a common joke in IT: *all lights green, yet nothing works*. Hence, we want event monitoring or the aforementioned end-to-end monitoring: monitoring systems that can correlate between the different layers and provide us with a full-stack view.

The main topics that we want to monitor in the stack are explained in the following sections.

## Cloud health

Sometimes this is referred to as *heartbeat* monitoring, and basically, that's exactly what it is. We want to know whether the cloud platform on which we are hosting our environment is still there and healthy. Are systems and services still running correctly, for instance? Hyperscalers have dashboards that provide us with insights as to the status of their platforms. At `https://status.aws.amazon.com/`, we can check the status of all services in all regions of AWS, seeing whether they are running normally and whether services are suffering from incidents. Azure has a similar dashboard at `https://status.azure.com/en-us/status`. Google provides the health status of Google Cloud Platform at `https://status.cloud.google.com/`.

Now, if you check the health status of, for instance, Azure, via the dashboard, you will find that services in some regions are not reported. The explanation for this is very simple: Azure doesn't offer all services in every region. The following screenshot shows that CloudSimple and large instances for the large in-memory ERP system SAP HANA are not provided in Middle Eastern and African data centers of Azure:

Americas | Europe | Asia Pacific | Middle East and Africa

| PRODUCTS AND SERVICES | *NON-REGIONAL | SOUTH AFRICA WEST | SOUTH AFRICA NORTH | UAE CENTRAL | UAE NORTH |
|---|---|---|---|---|---|
| COMPUTE | | | | | |
| Azure VMware Solution by CloudSimple | | | | | |
| Virtual Machines | | ✓ | ✓ | ✓ | ✓ |
| SAP HANA on Azure Large Instances | | | | | |

Figure 9.2 – The Azure status dashboard, showing services in the Middle East region

AWS mentions the specific data centers where a service is running:

| Service | Status |
|---|---|
| Amazon Managed Streaming for Apache Kafka (Frankfurt) | Service is operating normally |
| Amazon Managed Streaming for Apache Kafka (Ireland) | Service is operating normally |
| Amazon Managed Streaming for Apache Kafka (London) | Service is operating normally |
| Amazon Managed Streaming for Apache Kafka (Paris) | Service is operating normally |

Figure 9.3 – The health status of an AWS service

The preceding screenshot shows an example for the **Amazon Managed Streaming for Apache Kafka** service in the Europe region of AWS, running in the data centers of Frankfurt, Ireland, London, and Paris.

## Cloud performance

Performance is related to health but is more to do with the responsiveness of systems. The responsiveness of a system determines its performance level. When is a system *slow*? To be able to answer that question, we have to define what acceptable performance is. It comes back to what the business requirements are. Say that the expectation is that if someone pays for an article on a website, the transaction must go through in seconds. Requesting a complex calculation regarding a star orbiting somewhere in outer space, though, might take some time. Accuracy of processing in both instances is important, but the actual processing *times* will differ greatly. Both indicators—the quality of the processing outcome and the processing time—are important in terms of defining cloud performance and determine how we should monitor these indicators.

## Governance

As part of implementing the guardrails of the Cloud Adoption Framework, we have designed a model for **Role-Based Access Control** (**RBAC**). RBAC defines who is authorized to perform certain actions against specific conditions: who is allowed to do what, when, and how. It's tightly related to security, but governance monitoring does a bit more than that. It also monitors the usage of APIs within cloud environments and checks what processes are triggered to get access to systems. For example, if an administrator—or a system API calling for a system account—creates a new account, monitoring will follow the authorization path before the account gets acknowledged.

## Security

Security monitoring is more or less self-explanatory This is about checking for vulnerabilities in our environments and getting alerts if a vulnerability is spotted. Security monitoring is about prevention and defense: preventing intrusion by viruses, malicious access, or traffic patterns trying to flood systems so that they eventually collapse, as in **Distributed Denial of Service** (**DDoS**) attacks. If someone or something manages to get through defensive lines, then mitigating actions should be triggered immediately to control the damage, for instance, automatically shutting down systems.

## Cloud usage (analytics)

We want to know what we use in the cloud in terms of resources, virtual machines, network, storage, and services. For example, we can monitor the utilization of the processors (CPUs) that we use in our virtual machines. If we measure the utilization over a long period of time, we can analyze this data and see whether we need to adjust the sizing of the machines. If CPUs are under-utilized, we might want to downscale and save costs. Alternatively, if we found from performance monitoring that systems responded slowly, we should analyze whether CPUs are being over-utilized. In that case, we should consider the scaling out or scaling up of our system. These analytics will also report trends of what we can expect in terms of the capacity required in the near and more distant future.

Now that we have defined what we can and maybe even must monitor in cloud environments, it's time to explore the tooling that cloud providers have to offer. The question is, how we can consolidate all this data from monitoring systems and provide us with a single-pane-of-glass view? We will see how in the next sections.

# Exploring monitoring and management tools

In this section, we will first study the native monitoring that Azure, AWS, and Google Cloud Platform have to offer. After that, we will take a brief look at some other popular end-to-end monitoring systems that are on the market and are more cross-cloud.

Before we dive into the tools, we should get a high-level understanding of how monitoring works. Typically, these tools work with agents that collect data on the health and performance of resources. This is often raw data that is compiled into a more comprehensible format so it can be analyzed. From there, it gets visualized, for instance, in graphical presentations in dashboards that can be viewed from a console.

Monitoring can also lead to triggers: a system can suffer from malfunctions or other issues. In that case, the monitoring service will send out an alert that triggers a response. That response can be either to start a scaling process if systems run out of resources such as processor power or memory capacity, or an automated process to start a failover mechanism.

The following diagram shows a high-level overview of basic monitoring functionality:

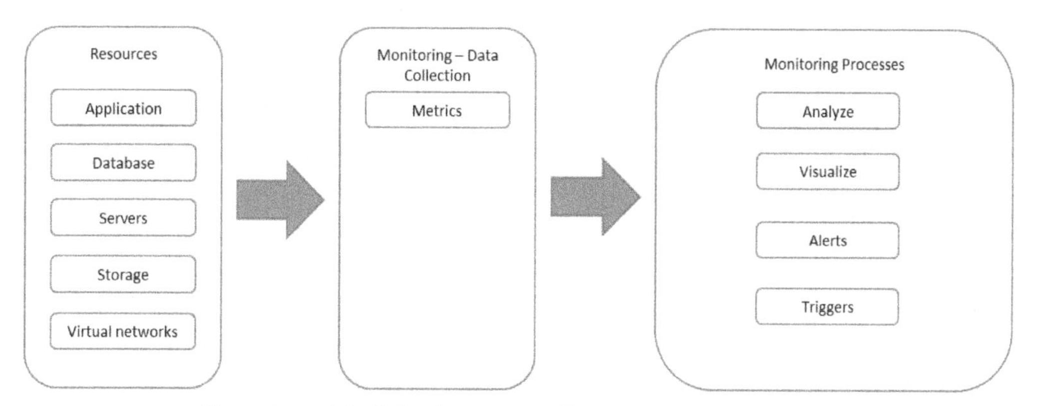


Figure 9.4 – A high-level overview of basic monitoring principles

These are the basic principles of monitoring. In the next sections, we will discuss the services for monitoring in Azure, AWS, and Google Cloud Platform.

## Azure Monitor and Lighthouse

Azure Monitor is available from the Azure portal at `https://portal.azure.com`. The key components of Azure Monitor are metrics and logs, the two types of data stores in Azure Monitor. This is the place where Azure Monitor collects all the data that it can retrieve from resources and services that are used in Azure. Metrics contain real-time data on the status of resources, and logs are collections of data that can be used to trace events. To analyze logs, you can use Log Analytics to get deeper insights into the performance of resources and services. Log Analytics is a separate module in Azure that is used to analyze monitored metrics.

Azure Monitor collects a lot of data that can be immediately viewed from the dashboard in the Azure portal. Azure Monitor can monitor resources that have been deployed on resources both within Azure and outside Azure, including other cloud platforms and on premises.

Next, there are additional services that can widen the monitoring scope of Azure Monitor. Two important services are Application Insights and Azure Monitor for containers. Application Insights is a separate service in Azure that monitors applications that are hosted in Azure, but it can be used for on-premises applications too. It keeps track of the operations of applications and reports failures in web application code and connected services.

We are moving from the more traditional environments of virtual machines to containers, and of course Azure Monitor is prepared for that. This service collects metrics on the usage of processors and memory for Kubernetes resources such as nodes, controllers, and the containers themselves. Azure Monitor for containers connects to **Azure Kubernetes Services (AKS)** for this. However, be aware that it only monitors the infrastructure that is used for containers. It does not monitor the contents of the container; for that, you will need different tooling.

In terms of the management of the environments in Azure, there's an offering that deserves to be discussed. In 2019, Microsoft launched Azure Lighthouse. The challenge that a lot of enterprises have is that they have not got just one tenant in a public cloud. Typically, an enterprise will have multiple tenants and subscriptions, just as they have multiple divisions, business groups, or delivery units. The problem they then face is monitoring and managing all these different tenants and subscriptions. For this, Lighthouse is the solution.

Lighthouse offers centralized management and monitoring across multiple tenants and subscriptions. It's basically the single pane of glass for all environments that an enterprise runs in the Azure cloud.

> **Tip**
> More information on Azure Monitor can be found at `https://docs.microsoft.com/en-us/azure/azure-monitor/overview`.

In this section, we explored the different tools that Azure provides for monitoring. In the next sections, we will discuss the monitoring propositions of AWS and Google Cloud Platform.

## AWS CloudWatch and Control Tower

AWS CloudWatch is available through the CloudWatch console at `https://console.aws.amazon.com/cloudwatch/`. The key components are comparable to Azure Monitor's. AWS CloudWatch uses metrics and statistics, although the core is the metrics repository. Data from resources is collected in metrics and translated into graphical overviews that are presented on the console. CloudWatch collects a lot of metrics, from almost every kind of resource that AWS offers. Obviously, there are metrics on compute, storage, and networks in AWS, but also on services such as data and video streams with Kinesis and IoT environments in AWS, as well as data analytics with SageMaker.

CloudWatch integrates with a number of other services in AWS, of which **Simple Notification Service** (**SNS**) and **Elastic Compute Cloud** (**EC2**) auto-scaling are the most important ones to mention. SNS is basically the pub/sub messaging mechanism in AWS. It can trigger the auto-scaling process to increase the capacity of resources.

As with Azure, AWS will start collecting metrics as soon as we deploy our first account on the platform. A lot of AWS services automatically call the CloudWatch API to start monitoring. This applies to compute in EC2, storage in **Elastic Block Store** (**EBS**), and database instances in **Relational Database Services** (**RDS**). However, we still need to configure the monitoring in terms of how we want metrics to be presented, at what frequency, and what type of alerts we find to be valuable. In AWS CloudWatch, we can create alerts for specific items.

One service needs to be highlighted, since it's the solution for end-to-end monitoring in AWS: CloudWatch Synthetics. In Synthetics, we create canaries. These are scripts that simulate processes as an end user would execute in AWS.

In terms of management, AWS offers Control Tower. It's the centralized management console for all accounts that an enterprise enrolls in AWS, making sure that all of these accounts are consistent and compliant with the frameworks that the enterprise has to adhere to. The landing zone that we discussed in *Chapter 6, Designing, Implementing, and Managing the Landing Zone*, is part of Control Tower. It holds all organization units, users, accounts, and all the resources that are subject to compliance and security regulations within the enterprise and that are enforced to environments in AWS.

To keep track of all these items in AWS, the platform offers guardrails. We can have preventative and detective guardrails. These are rules that make sure that units, accounts, users, and resources are always consistent with the policies that have been set for environments. These rules can have different labels: mandatory, strongly recommended, and elective.

Control Tower comes with a dashboard so that the team that is concerned with the overall management of the systems has a single-pane-of-glass view encompassing all environments that have been deployed to AWS.

> **Tip**
> More information on AWS CloudWatch can be found at `https://docs.aws.amazon.com/AmazonCloudWatch/latest/monitoring/WhatIsCloudWatch.html`. More information on Control Tower can be found at `https://docs.aws.amazon.com/controltower/latest/userguide/what-is-control-tower.html`.

Lastly, we will look at monitoring in Google Cloud Platform, before we discuss some other important tools in terms of monitoring and managing container platforms.

# Google Cloud Platform's Cloud Monitoring and Operations Suite

Cloud monitoring in Google Cloud Platform is really easy. You don't need to install or configure anything: as soon as you start using systems or services in Google Cloud Platform, Cloud Monitor will start collecting metrics. This is done through Cloud Run, a fully managed service by Google Cloud Platform.

Cloud Monitoring in Google Cloud Platform has one more service to offer, and that is Cloud Run on GKE. **GKE** is **Google Kubernetes Engine**. Google offers a separate service to monitor the Kubernetes clusters where you host containers. The service is actually named Cloud Monitoring for Anthos, since it targets the Anthos stack of Google.

Anthos—a suite of Google services that runs on VMware vSphere or Hyper-V instances—helps in transforming legacy applications on virtual machines to containers so that they can run on Kubernetes. Anthos is a truly hybrid, multi-cloud environment, since you can manage the containers on Anthos from other clouds as well, such as AWS. It's again an indicator that Google Cloud Platform is much more focused on cloud-native and containerization than other major providers.

Cloud Monitoring is available from the console at `https://console.cloud.google.com/getting-started`. You don't need to configure the monitoring, but you can add custom metrics. This service uses OpenCensus, an open source monitoring library. Here we can add specific metric data that we want to retrieve from monitoring our resources in Google Cloud Platform. If we want to do so for container monitoring, we have to do the same with Knative metrics. Knative is a Kubernetes-based platform used to deploy and manage modern serverless workloads.

So, Google Cloud Platform's Cloud Monitoring is a fully integrated service that we don't need to configure. However, we can get more out of it if we add metrics with uptime checks and alerts.

Cloud Monitoring for Google Cloud Platform and AWS is part of Google Cloud's operations suite, which was formerly called Stackdriver. The operations suite contains also Cloud Logging, Error Reporting, and automation services such as Cloud Debugger and Cloud Trace, which we discussed in *Chapter 8, Defining and Using Automation Tools and Processes*.

> **Tip**
> More information on Cloud Monitoring in Google Cloud Platform can be found at `https://cloud.google.com/run/docs/monitoring`.

## VMware's Tanzu

The world is moving more and more toward containers, and that's something that we haven't discussed in depth in terms of management. How can we manage cross-cloud and multi-cloud containers? One product that should be mentioned here is VMware's Tanzu, and particularly Tanzu Mission Control.

We have seen that all major cloud providers have their own implementation of container orchestration. They all use Kubernetes to launch and control cluster nodes to host containers, but they all have their own flavor: Azure has AKS, AWS has EKS, Google works with GKE, and on VMware platforms, we can use **Pivotal Kubernetes Services** (**PKS**). But the major advantage of containers is that because they don't rely on their own operating system, they can be really cloud independent. But how do we control Kubernetes environments cross-cloud then?

VMware monitors and operates the different Kubernetes environments on all these aforementioned clouds with Tanzu, and more specifically Tanzu Mission Control, which was introduced in 2019. We can attach Kubernetes environments in any cloud—Azure, AWS, or Google Cloud Platform, to name the big ones—to Tanzu, and from there we have centralized management of identity, centralized access to the clusters, centralized policy management so that all our clusters operate in the same way, and one monitoring system watching over all our clusters.

> **Tip**
> More information on Tanzu Mission Control can be found at `https://tanzu.vmware.com/mission-control`.

# Other end-to-end monitoring tools

We have already introduced the term end-to-end monitoring. What does it mean? Typically, we mean that the monitoring is looking at systems from the end user's perspective. To understand this, we have to understand the **OSI** model. That model contains seven layers. The following diagram represents the model:

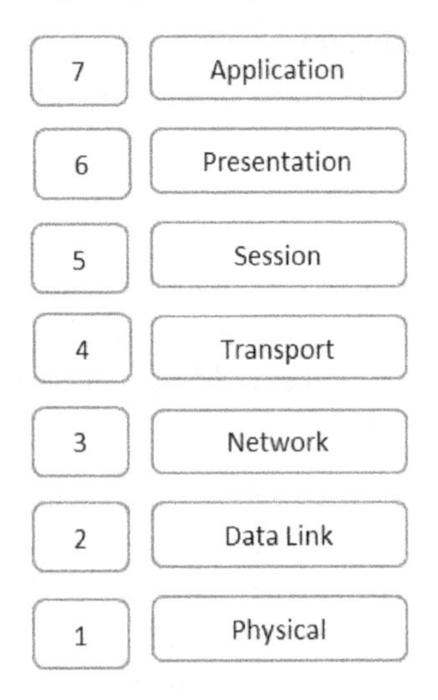


Figure 9.5 – The seven-layer OSI model

Now, let's explain what's happening in these layers in a bit more detail, to get a better understanding of what each layer represents. Just a note: these are technical layers and not the layers that we talked about in the first section of this chapter. There, we talked about three layers at a very high level: business, applications, and technical. That corresponds with the **The Open Group Architecture Framework** (**TOGAF**) that we explored in *Chapter 5, Successfully Managing an Enterprise Cloud Architecture*; the OSI model is really about the technology stack:

- **Layer 1**: This is the physical layer, or the hard-wired layer. This is the layer where all the physical devices are.
- **Layer 2**: This is the data link layer, where the data is translated in a format that can travel over a network.
- **Layer 3**: This is the network layer, where the routing of the data is defined.

- **Layer 4**: This is the transport layer. This concerns how data is actually sent or transmitted according to specified network protocols.
- **Layer 5**: This is the session layer. If we have defined how data should be routed and it's sent, then we have to make sure that the addressee components are aware of the incoming traffic and that they are able to receive it. The session layer takes care of that; it's where ports are assigned and connections are established.
- **Layer 6**: This the presentation layer. Up until this point, we have been talking about raw data. We need to be able to get it into a comprehensible format. For example, raw data for a picture may be translated into JPEG format so that we view the picture itself and not just the data. That is what happens in this layer.
- **Layer 7**: This is the application layer. This the layer where the end user interacts with the underlying systems. Layer 7 is often referred to as the human interface layer.

What does end-to-end monitoring do? It sends an agent from layer 7 all the way down to layer 1, retrieving metrics in all the layers it traverses. Typically, the monitoring mechanism will issue a transaction from layer 7 through the stack and measure the performance of this transaction. If the transaction fails, the monitoring mechanism can determine where it failed and why. If we go one step further than just the monitoring mechanism, then we can imagine that the monitoring mechanism will trigger processes to mitigate the failures: that's where automation comes in. Ultimately, we have systems that are able to predict and prevent failures because they actually learn from the information they receive from the monitoring agents. Then, we're talking about AIOps, something that we will cover in *Chapter 19, Optimizing Multi-Cloud Environments with AIOps.*

There's a wide range of products available when we're looking at end-to-end monitoring. It would take another book to name them all, but examples include Lakeside, Splunk, Datadog, and CheckMK. All these suites have products that target cloud environments, all from the end user's perspective. For instance, Lakeside offers SysTrack Cloud Edition for this; CheckMK is a popular open source monitoring environment for infrastructure and applications.

Splunk and Datadog are a bit different and are more in the league of AIOps. Splunk Cloud claims to be the monitoring environment that truly enables operational intelligence. Splunk Cloud is cross-cloud and works across business use cases. A use case could be anti-fraud, where we have to combine data from different sources to detect fraud. The monitoring tool of Splunk will collect data that might hint at fraud operations in cloud environments. The power is in the search engine that Splunk uses, the **Search Processing Language**. You can ask the monitoring system to correlate data from different systems to gain insight into a full chain of application delivery and its performance.

# Consolidating and interpreting data from monitoring systems

The only thing a business needs to be interested in here is how events in IT impact the business' operations. To be able to discern this, we need to consolidate and interpret monitoring data.

The big question is this: when is data from monitoring relevant to the business? It doesn't make sense to inform a business leader about the performance of CPUs in virtual machines, but it does make sense to inform him or her when system capacity is lacking and hindering the speed of processing transactions. In that case, the business might lose money since transactions might be processed too slowly or, worse, dropped because of timeout failures.

When is data relevant to a business? In short, data should enable business decisions. Deploying extra virtual machines or scaling out environments are not business decisions. These are technical decisions. A business decision would be to launch a new product at a given moment. In that case, we should know whether our environment is ready for that. From monitoring data, we should analyze how our systems have been performing with the existing product portfolio. Would systems have enough capacity to absorb extra traffic? Such questions and their answers drive architecture: if we find from monitoring data that systems are not ready from a technological point of view or are not expected to be able to absorb extra load, then we might have to re-architect systems.

One of the major pitfalls in monitoring is that a lot of companies treat it as reactive. Monitoring is, in that case, just a tool that starts alerting when systems fail. But by then, we are already far too late. The business might already be impacted on a large scale.

Before the end user starts to see that their requests are processed in a slower way, our monitoring system should alert about system components reaching certain capacity thresholds or interfaces that are suffering faults. We can do that by collecting a lot of data so that we know how systems respond under normal conditions, the baseline. Any deviation from those conditions will lead to an alert. These alerts can be proactive, so that we can adjust before something really breaks.

To summarize: the business is only interested in what happens at layer 7, the layer where the actual interactions between users and systems are. How quickly can end users access systems, how fast can transactions be processed, and how fast can new products be launched? To answer these questions, we have to collect a lot of data from our systems so that we know what the critical thresholds are and so that we can anticipate demand on the business.

The monitoring data must be easy to understand for business decision makers; for example, say that our current systems can hold an extra 10,000 visitors to the company's website per day. The rationale for such a statement should come from the monitoring data.

Monitoring is very important to get to the right decisions in development and operations, or DevOps. But monitoring is obviously also highly important in terms of financial reporting. That is part of **Financial Operations**, or **FinOps**, which is part of *Chapter 13, Validating and Managing Bills.*

# Discovering the single-pane-of-glass view

We have come across the term single-pane-of-glass view a couple of times during this chapter. But what do we really mean by that? Typically, we mean that we have one console from which we can monitor and manage environments from multiple platforms. Imagine that we have cloud environments in Azure, AWS, and Google Cloud Platform. We might even have on-premises systems in privately owned data centers. If we want our system administrators to manage these environments, the chances are fairly high that they would need to log in to every single platform. For Azure, they would need to log in through the Azure portal, for AWS through the AWS portal, and so on. That is not very efficient.

The solution for this is to have one console where we can view the environments independently from the platform they run and, even better, manage the environments from this single console. Imagine it like a Swiss Army knife: a tool that we can use for different purposes. Knife, screwdriver, scissors—but it's still only one tool.

Sounds fantastic, but the reality is that these tools are extremely complicated to develop and keep up to date with all the new features that are constantly being released on various cloud platforms. That one tool, providing the single pane of glass, will have to integrate with all the cloud platforms. APIs that enable this would have to be re-evaluated constantly. It's the reason why there are just a few tools on the market that can actually do this. These two suites are the only ones in the leader section of the Gartner Magic Quadrant: ServiceNow and BMC Helix. Of course, there are alternatives, such as Cherwell and Provance, but in the enterprise market, the share that ServiceNow and BMC Helix hold is dominant.

Both ServiceNow—Orlando being the most recent release at the time of writing—and BMC Helix provide a platform to perform IT services management, multi-cloud operations, multi-cloud cost management, the management of security and compliance policies in multi-cloud environments, and monitoring all in one suite. They integrate with the native tools of the major cloud platforms. For example, their APIs connect to Azure Monitor, CloudWatch, and Google's Cloud Monitoring to retrieve data from the cloud platforms and consolidate that data in the management platform integrated into ServiceNow or BMC Helix.

These suites have a large portfolio of modules that enterprises can use to run many services from one console. But there's one pitfall: these platforms will take care of all the essential services, but there will always be services that can't be viewed and managed from this one, integrated console—serverless functions, for instance. These multi-tool platforms will never capture every function for each cloud platform, which is absolutely not a shortcoming. It's simply something that we have to take into account.

# Summary

In this chapter, we have learned what it takes to set up good monitoring by defining the monitoring process on different layers and by deciding what we should monitor in our environments. We have learned that it's better to have end-to-end monitoring in place, looking at systems the way the end user would experience the behavior of these systems.

We have studied the OSI model and have gained an understanding of how monitoring can retrieve data from the various layers. We have learned that we need to consolidate and interpret monitored data to make it valuable to a business, enabling it to be used to make business decisions. We now also should have an understanding of the concept of the single-pane-of-glass view.

We are now able to decide how we will monitor systems. We are also able to tell the difference between different monitoring systems and methods of monitoring. Lastly, we have learned about the various options that cloud providers offer and how we can use them.

This concludes our section on BaseOps. The next part of this book will address FinOps in multi-cloud environments. We will begin with license management in multi-cloud environments.

# Questions

1. True or false: end-to-end monitoring typically uses agents to simulate transactions through a systems stack.
2. Both Azure and AWS have operational suites that make the management of multiple environments on their platforms possible from one console. Name the two consoles that are used for this.
3. What would you recommend in terms of monitoring: reactive or proactive monitoring?
4. What would you use VMware's Tanzu Mission Control for?

# Further reading

- *Kubernetes on vSphere* by Boskey Savla, VMware
- *ServiceNow IT Operations Management* by Ajaykumar Guggilla, Packt Publishing

# Section 3 – Cost Control in Multi-Cloud with FinOps

Building and running a data center in public clouds might be more cost efficient than the traditional way, but they do still cost money. Hence, you need ways to control costs. **Financial operations** (**FinOps**) is all about cost control.

The following chapters will be covered in this section:

# 10
# Managing Licenses

Building and running a data center in public clouds can be more cost-efficient than going the traditional way. However, running a data center in public clouds also costs money. it does still cost some money. Hence, as ever, you still need ways to control costs. **FinOps—financial operations**—is all about cost control. This chapter focuses on the starting point for managing FinOps in multi-cloud environments: licenses.

To use cloud platforms and their services, you need an agreement with these platforms; in some cases, it requires specific licenses. There are several ways to engage with a cloud provider. Examples include enterprise agreements, which cover a variety of IT services, but there is more to it all that you should know about, such as, for example, licenses for the software you use in the cloud. Do you have everything covered? Next, you'll have to create a subscription hierarchy and set up root accounts for multi-cloud components.

After completing this chapter, you will have a good understanding of different license types and how we can manage licenses and contracts. We will learn that the management of contracts is crucial to the avoidance of the risks of working with software that isn't properly licensed and overspending on licenses. We will discover that licensing in cloud environments work differently from licensing in on-premises systems.

In this chapter, we're going to cover the following topics:

- Exploring different types of license agreements
- Software licenses in cloud platforms
- Managing licenses and contracts

- Using third-party brokers for licenses
- Setting up account hierarchy for enterprises

# Types of license agreements

How do a lot of us start the journey in the public cloud? By simply pulling out a credit card? If you're just a person who wants to try some technology in the public cloud, that's OK. However, for enterprises, this isn't the way to go. Enterprises will likely have quite massive environments hosted in the cloud and therefore it's advisable to have agreements with cloud providers, ensuring the best financial offers and the safeguarding of service levels. Those are the two main reasons to obtain a license agreement:

- Financial benefits, especially for the long term
- Service level agreements, safeguarded in the license agreement

License agreements are complicated, but in essence, there are three types of agreements to start using services in the public cloud:

- **Consumption-based**: This is often referred to as the pay-as-you-go model. The enterprise only pays for the actual usage in the public cloud, without any upfront commitment. Cloud providers issue a monthly invoice with the actual consumption of resources. These resources—for example, virtual machines, database instances, and storage units—are charged against the rates that are published on the public portals of the providers.
- **Commitment-based**: For most enterprises, this is the preferred model. In this case, the enterprise commits to the usage of a specific amount of resources in the cloud for a longer period of time, typically 1, 3, or 5 years. Now, public clouds such as Azure, AWS, and Google Cloud Platform were invented to enable maximum flexibility and agility. If we allow enterprises to have committed resources for a longer period of time, then this will have an impact on the resources that a public cloud can offer to other customers. For that reason, public cloud providers want to be certain that enterprises do really commit to the consumption of these reserved resources. Typically, an enterprise will need to pay upfront for these resources, whether they use them or not. Cloud consumption has become a formal contract that entitles an enterprise to have these resources available at all times.

- **Limited agreements**: These are agreements that are limited by time to an amount of resources that a customer can use. Typically, these are the type of agreements that are used for trial periods where resources are not charged for a specific period of time. Not all services will be part of these agreements—such as really heavy instances with a lot of memory and terabytes of storage—and after 1, 2, or 3 months, the environment will be suspended by the cloud provider. A limited agreement can also hold a certain amount of credits that can be used for a given time. If the credit amount is used, the trial period ends.

In this section, we learned about the different types of contracts and license agreements in public clouds. The next section is about licensing software that we use in our cloud environments.

# Software licenses in cloud platforms

When an enterprise uses software, it needs to purchase licenses for its usage. That goes for both proprietary and open source software. The main difference between these two categories is that open source software does allow modifications and changes in the software, as long as the changes are contributed to the software's development as a whole. Proprietary software is typically closed source, that is, the source code may not be modified.

As with a lot of licenses, this can become quite complicated. If a product that a company uses is not sufficiently licensed, the company can be forced to pay fines along with the license fees it should actually have paid from the start. Using non-licensed software is illegal. That doesn't change when we're moving environments to the cloud.

How do you know when a software product is properly licensed? There are just a few types of software licenses—with a lot of variations—but stripped to their essence, they come down to these categories:

- **License on user basis**: This is often the model that is used for end user licenses and it's probably the most straightforward way of licensing. For each user, there's a license that entitles the use of the software. A good example of this is Microsoft Office 365, for which a company can order a license per user, per month. In that case, there's a one-to-one relationship between the user and the use of the specific software product.

- **Licenses based on resources**: This is a more complicated licensing model. An example are software licenses based on the usage of a specific number of CPUs or the number of database instances. This is still a popular way of licensing proprietary software: the license fee is calculated according to how many CPUs or instances are being used. The issue in cloud infrastructure is that resources are quite often shared resources, virtualized on top of the real physical machine. Which CPU is licensed then? Typically, the license in cloud environments is based on the virtual CPU, in that case. Keep in mind that support agreements on software might change as soon as the software is deployed in cloud environments. Not all software is supported when used in Azure, AWS, or Google Cloud Platform.
- **Lump sum fee**: Software is purchased and paid in full upfront. For software vendors, this is not a very attractive model, since they will only receive a one-time payment. But for companies, this is also not very attractive, since they will be confronted with high, upfront, cash-out investments.

Let's come back to the question, How do you know when a software product is properly licensed? For that, special **Software Asset Management** (**SAM**) tools can be very convenient. SAM tools do a lot more than just make an inventory of all the software that a company uses: these solutions evaluate the whole life cycle of software, from purchase to deployment and, indeed, to utilization.

A SAM tool keeps track of who or what resources use the software that's in the scope of the tool and makes sure that usage is compliant and covered by licenses. Popular tools in this space include Flexera's FlexNet Manager Suite, Snow License Manager, and also the SAM tooling inside the bigger suites of BMC Helix and ServiceNow that we have discussed in previous chapters. In BMC, this is called Remedy Asset Management; in ServiceNow, SAM is part of the **IT Operations Management** (**ITOM**) module.

# Managing licenses and contracts

In the previous section, we discussed the licenses that we need in order to use software in our cloud environments. But the usage of the cloud platforms itself is licensed too, as we have seen in the first section. So, we have a cloud platform, cloud services such as **Platform as a Service** (**PaaS**) and **Software as a Service** (**SaaS**), and we have software that we run in these environments. For all these components, we need licenses. Companies find themselves confronted with two major challenges:

- **Costs**: One of the key drivers to move systems to cloud platforms is because it's believed to be cheaper than keeping systems on premises. That's not always the case, though. A major cost factor is licenses and contracts to allow the usage of cloud services, especially when companies make the mistake of thinking that the existing licenses that they have for their on-premises environments will cover them for the cloud as well. That's rarely the case. The reason for this is that cloud deployment models work in a completely different manner.

  Here's a simple example: if we run software on an on-premises system, you can easily predict that this system will not change very often. The license will cover the usage of the software on that particular system for quite a long time. In cloud platforms, these systems can and will change because of scaling, or because they're automatically switched off when not in use. Sometimes, paying the cloud provider for the license might be advantageous for systems that are not run 24/7, as the cost savings of stopping systems might be greater than a negotiated enterprise discount with a software company. The licenses that are often tied to a product license key on the software itself need to cater to that.

  Some major providers have bundles for this that allow enterprises to buy licenses that they can use on various systems, both on premises as well as in the cloud. Microsoft, for instance, has enterprise agreements that bundle a lot of licenses in one agreement. For larger organizations and enterprises, this can be very interesting, since these enterprise agreements often come with savings at higher volumes. This is referred to as volume licensing. Be aware of the fact that sometimes the cost per unit might change between the cloud and on premises. Therefore, the same software run on premises might cost twice as much to run in the cloud on the same-sized machine.

  In AWS, it might be worthwhile to look at volume-based discounts.

- **Management**: It's a cumbersome task to manage all these licenses. Some companies decide to outsource this. For the cloud, this can be done through a partner or reseller program, or a **Cloud Solution Provider (CSP)**. Cloud providers such as the ones that we discuss in this book—Azure, AWS, Google Cloud Platform—often work with partners. These can be big system integrators, but also smaller companies that specialize in a specific cloud service. These partners can be entitled to resell services on cloud platforms.

  In that case, an enterprise doesn't purchase cloud services directly from Azure, AWS, or Google, but through a partner of these hyperscalers. These partners can acquire licenses for various cloud services on behalf of their customers. The big benefit of this model is that a company doesn't have to worry about the licenses themselves; it will be taken care of by the CSP, who manages this completely.

  To be clear, a CSP is not the same as a third-party broker or reseller for software. A CSP really engages with their customer and will work on cloud solutions jointly with the customers and the platforms. To make life easier, the CSP can take care of the licensing in the cloud too, so that a customer is sure that all used services are covered with the appropriate contracts.

> **Tip**
> Hire someone who really understands software licensing and knows how to negotiate tariffs, especially when your enterprise hits big figures for consumption. Account managers from Microsoft, AWS, Google, VMware, or any other provider will gladly work with you to find the best solution.

We've discussed different deployment types, such as PaaS and SaaS, and how we can work through a CSP. For software licenses, we can work with a third-party broker, something that we will talk about in the next section. We will also explore the benefits of **Application Life Cycle Management** (**ALM**).

# Using third-party brokers for licenses

You can use third-party management, or brokers, to take care of licenses. Although large enterprises often have contract, license, or purchasing managers to deal with contractual relationships with IT services companies and software vendors, a lot of companies tend to work through a third party that is specialized in this area. These third-party managers take care of all the external relationships that a company has with service or software providers.

In most cases, we talk about upstream third-party management. Upstream means that the third party handles vendors and suppliers, rather than being downstream, where a company is a reseller or distributor of IT services or software themselves. In fact, we're adding an extra layer between the company that uses the software and the services and the supplier of these services and software.

This third-party layer will make sure that licenses are kept up to date using software life cycle management. This is often tied into the process of ALM. ALM ensures that all steps in application development are followed through, from design to testing and eventually production. Part of ALM is that in all stages, the appropriate software licenses are in place. But life cycle management also means that software is kept up to date when particular software runs out of support. For example, in January 2020, Windows Server 2008 lost support, meaning that Microsoft doesn't update the operating system anymore from that point onward. Companies using that software now have to upgrade to a newer version or—in this example—move their systems to Azure, where Server 2008 is still supported.

Third-party brokers come with some special points of attention. For one, relying on third-party management doesn't take away the responsibility of a company to ensure that all required licenses are in place and contractual obligations are met. Following the verdicts of American courts, for instance, companies are legally responsible to manage risks with third-party brokers (reference: `https://www.occ.gov/news-issuances/bulletins/2013/bulletin-2013-29.html`).

We've listed a couple of good reads on this subject under *Further reading*.

# Setting up an account hierarchy

It's important to understand from what level enterprise management wants to see costs. Enterprises usually want a full overview of the total spend, so we need to make sure that they can view that total spend: from the top level all the way down to subscriptions that are owned by specific business divisions or DevOps teams. These divisions or teams might have a full mandate to run their own subscriptions, but at the top level, the enterprise will definitely want to see the costs that these units are accruing at the end of the day.

This starts with the setup of the tenants, the subscriptions, and the accounts in public cloud platforms. This has to be set up following a specific hierarchy. The good news for financial controllers is that these structures in the public cloud closely follow the rules of the **Chart of Accounts** (**COA**) hierarchy that is used for financial reporting. This hierarchy has one top level. There can be many accounts underneath, but at the end of the day, they are all accountable to that top level. There's no difference when setting up an account hierarchy in the public cloud.

In Azure, we work with enterprise enrollment, the top level where we can manage our enterprise administrators and view all usage across all accounts in our Azure environment. The next level is the departments. Beneath the departments, we can create accounts. Both the top level—enterprise enrollment—and the departments are created through the Enterprise Agreement portal at `https://ea.azure.com`.

> **Important note**
>
> Be aware that you need an enterprise account in Azure before you can enter the portal.

Now we can create accounts. These will be the account owners, who can view all of their subscriptions. The account owners will have the rights to create subscriptions and appoint service administrators that can manage the subscriptions. The following diagram shows the account hierarchy in Azure:

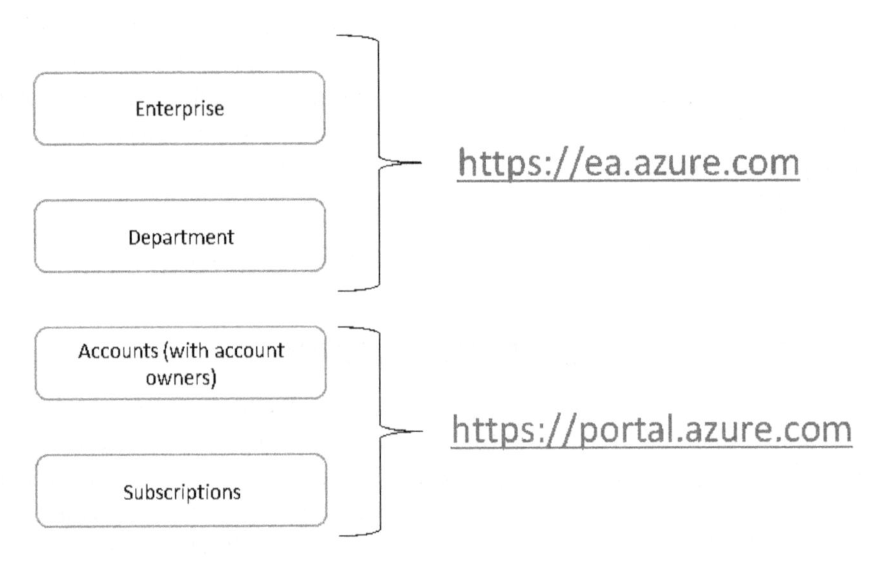


Figure 10.1 – A high-level overview of enterprise enrollment in Azure

We can also enroll multiple accounts in AWS and centrally manage them. For this, AWS offers a service called AWS Organizations, where we can provision accounts using AWS CloudFormation and group them into organizational units that we can manage from AWS Organizations. Organizations also allows us to have a centralized cost management platform in AWS.

To start enterprise enrollment, AWS advises contacting a sales representative directly. This is indeed strongly advised, since AWS has some interesting enterprise volume-driven discount programs such as **EDP**—the **Enterprise Discount Program**—that would be part of an Enterprise Agreement with AWS.

The setup in **Google Cloud Platform** (**GCP**) is very similar to Azure. In GCP, we also have a top level, the organization resource. This resource requires an organization node. We create the organization node through Cloud Identity. The node can match the corporate internet domain. Beneath the organization node, we can view and manage every resource and account that is deployed under the organization.

The second level in Azure was departments; in GCP, these are called **folders**. The final layer in the hierarchy is the projects in GCP. Projects are functionally similar to subscriptions in Azure. Everything in GCP is created and managed through the Google Cloud console or the `gcloud` tool. In the console, we create an organization ID. Whoever creates this ID is automatically assigned as the super-administrator.

This concludes the section about understanding the hierarchy of enterprise organizations in the major public clouds. The main conclusion is that the models resemble one another very much, for a very good reason: at the top level, it is best for an enterprise administrator to have one single view of everything that is deployed in a cloud environment.

# Summary

This chapter was about the licensing of cloud platforms themselves and the software used within them. We have learned that there are different types of agreements for the usage of cloud services: purely consumption-based, commitment-based, and limited agreements, which are mainly used for trial periods.

We have seen that license agreements for software might change if we deploy software on cloud resources and that it might be worthwhile to implement SAM. Since licenses and contracts can become very complex, some companies decide to outsource the task of managing licenses to third-party brokers.

In the last section, we learned how we should set up enterprise enrollment in Azure, looked at organizations and accounts in AWS, and explored organizations, folders, and projects for the potential segmentation of billing in GCP. These enrollments come with a specific hierarchy that we need to deploy, but we have also seen that these hierarchical models in the main public clouds are comparable.

Once we have set up our enterprise model in the cloud, we can finally start provisioning resources in a cloud environment. But how do we do that while keeping control of costs? That's what the next chapter is about.

# Questions

1. If we want to run a trial period in a public cloud, what type of agreement would fit our needs?
2. What sort of tool would you use to keep track of software licenses in your environment?
3. Which two actions do we need to perform in the enterprise portal of Azure?

# Further reading

- Effective Database Management (`https://effectivedatabase.com/the-difference-between-enterprise-software-and-software-as-a-service/`): Explains the differences between enterprise licensed software and SaaS
- *The Risk IT Framework*: ISACA, the risk assessment methodology of Isaca; information is available at `isaca.org`
- Documentation on cost management and billing in Azure: `https://docs.microsoft.com/en-us/azure/cost-management-billing/manage/ea-portal-get-started`
- Documentation on setting up a hierarchy in AWS using organizations, and documentation on setting up a billing hierarchy in AWS: `https://aws.amazon.com/organizations/`
- Documentation on setting up a hierarchy in GCP using projects, and documentation on setting up a billing hierarchy in GCP: `https://cloud.google.com/docs/enterprise/best-practices-for-enterprise-organizations`

# 11
# Defining Principles for Resource Provisioning and Consumption

Cost control starts with guidelines and principles on when and what type of resources may be deployed and by whom. The way resources are deployed in different cloud platforms is different and needs alignment when an enterprise has adopted a multi-cloud strategy. In this chapter, we will discover that resource planning should be a part of our architecture. We need to define what type of resources we are planning to provision and how we can deploy them using the different methods that Azure, AWS, and **Google Cloud Platform** (**GCP**) provide.

We will also learn how we can set budgets in our environment and how cost alerts can be set when budget thresholds are met. We will have a look at the tools that the public clouds provide in terms of cost control and management.

In this chapter, we're going to cover the following main topics:

- Avoiding Amex Armageddon with unlimited budgets
- The provisioning and consumption of resources in public cloud platforms
- The provisioning and consumption of resources in on-premises systems
- Setting guidelines and principles for provisioning and consumption
- Controlling resource consumption using cost alerts

# Avoiding Amex Armageddon with unlimited budgets

The term *Amex Armageddon* will not be familiar to you. It's a term I use when I see companies starting off in the public cloud. Very often, companies, even big ones, begin deploying resources in the public cloud without a plan. Someone simply opens an account, gets a subscription, fills in some credit card details, and starts. Often, the resources go unmonitored and don't adhere to the organization mandates, more commonly known as shadow IT. That's alright if you're a developer who wants to try out things on a Saturday afternoon, but it's certainly not OK if you're working for a company. It's the reason why Azure, AWS, and GCP have developed **Cloud Adoption Frameworks** (**CAFs**).

If you're moving a company to a public cloud, you're basically building a data center in Azure, AWS, GCP, or any other cloud. The only difference is that this data center is completely software-defined. But as with a physical data center, the virtual data center in a public cloud costs money. If you're working without a plan, it will cost you more money than necessary and probably also more than keeping applications in the physical data center. That's what I call **Amex Armageddon**.

We can avoid this by having a plan—in most cases, by following CAFs that provide guidelines to set up a business in the public cloud, which is covered in *Chapter 1, Introduction to Multi-Cloud*, *Chapter 2, Business Acceleration Using a Multi-Cloud Strategy*, and *Chapter 3, Getting Connected – Designing Connectivity*. Part of the plan is also to select the type of resources that you will have to provision in the cloud environment. Will you only use **Virtual Machines** (**VMs**) or are you planning to use other services as well? If you're only deploying VMs, what type of applications are you planning to host?

If you're only hosting a website, then there's no need to have an option to deploy big machines with lots of memory. But if you're planning to host an in-memory **Enterprise Resource Planning** (**ERP**) system, such as SAP HANA, then you will very likely need big machines with as much as 32 GB or more of memory. The point is that it makes sense to have a plan, worked out in an architecture.

In this chapter, we will first look at the different types of resources in the public cloud and how we can provision them while keeping track of costs. One method to do that is by setting budgets and defining, per the architecture, what resources we will be deploying in our cloud environment.

# The provisioning and consumption of resources in public cloud platforms

Before we dive into cost control in the provisioning of resources, we need to understand how resource provisioning works in the public cloud. There are lots of different ways to do this, but for this chapter, we will stick with the *native* provisioning tools that Azure, AWS, and GCP provide.

There are basically two types of provisioning:

- Self-provisioning
- Dynamic

Typically, we start with self-provisioning through the portal or web interface of a cloud provider. The customer chooses the resources that are needed in the portal. After confirmation that these resources may be deployed in the cloud environment, the resources are spun up and made available for usage by the provider.

The resources are billed by hour or minute unless there is a contract for **reserved instances**. Reserved instances are contracted for a longer period—1, 3, or 5 years. The customer is guaranteed availability, capacity, and usage of the pre-purchased reserved instances. The benefit of reserved instances can be that cloud providers offer discounts on these resources. Over a longer period, this may be very cost-efficient. It's a good way to set budget control: a company will know exactly what the costs will be for that period. However, it's less flexible than a pay-as-you-go model and, even more important, it requires up-front payments or investments.

Dynamic provisioning is more of an automated process. An example is a web server that experiences a spike in load. When we allow automatic scale-out or scale-up of this web server, the cloud provider will automatically deploy more resources to that web server or pool. These extra resources will also be billed on a pay-as-you-go rate.

Now, let's take a look at how these resources are deployed.

# Deploying resources in Azure using ARM

Azure works with **Azure Resource Manager** (**ARM**). This is a service that handles requests from users and makes sure that the requests are fulfilled. That request is sent to ARM. Next, ARM executes all the actions to actually deploy the VM. What it does is assign memory, the processor, and disks to a VM and makes it available to the user. ARM can do this with all types of resources in Azure: VMs, storage accounts, web apps, databases, virtual network resource groups, subscriptions, management groups, and tags.

ARM can be directly accessed from the portal. However, most developers will be working with PowerShell or the **Command-Line Interface** (**CLI**). In that case, the request goes to a **SDK**, a **software development kit**. SDKs are libraries with scripts and code templates that can be called through a command in PowerShell or the CLI. From the SDK, the resources are deployed in ARM. The following diagram shows the high-level conceptualization for ARM:

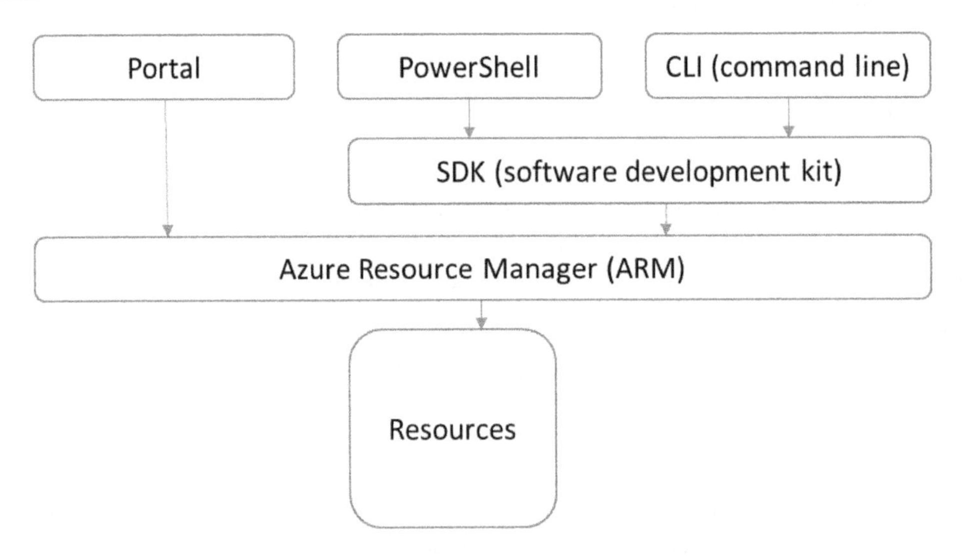


Figure 11.1 – High-level concept for ARM

In the next section, we will learn how we can deploy resources in AWS.

# Deploying resources in AWS using OpsWorks

AWS has AWS OpsWorks Stacks for the deployment of resources. It works with a cookbook repository—a term that AWS borrowed from Chef. That makes sense since under the hood, Stacks works with Chef. We've had a deeper look at Stacks in *Chapter 8*, *Defining Automation Tools and Processes*.

The stack itself is the core component for any deployment in AWS; it's the construct that holds the different resources, such as EC2, VMs, and Amazon **RDS** (short for **Relational Database Services**) database instances. OpsWorks makes sure that these resources are grouped together in a logical way and deployed as that logical group—we call this the cookbook or recipe.

It's important to remember that Stacks work in layers. The first layer is the **Elastic Load Balancing** (**ELB**) layer, which holds the load balancer. The next layer hosts the VMs, the actual servers that are deployed from EC2. The third layer is the database layer. If the stack is deployed, you can add the application from a different repository. OpsWorks can do this automatically as soon as the servers and databases are deployed, or it can be done manually.

The following diagram shows the conceptualization of an OpsWorks stack:

Figure 11.2 – High-level overview of an OpsWorks stack in AWS

The last cloud that we will discuss is GCP. In the next section, we will look at Google's Deployment Manager.

# Deploying resources in GCP using Deployment Manager

In GCP, the native programmatic deployment mechanism is Deployment Manager. We can create resources and group them logically together in a deployment. For instance, we can create VMs and a database and have them as one code file in a deployment. However, it does take some programming skills to work with Deployment Manager. To start, you will need to have the `gcloud` command-line tool installed. Next, create or select a GCP project. Lastly, resources are defined in a deployment coded in YAML. When the deployment is ready, we can actually deploy it to our project in GCP using `gcloud deployment -manager`.

As said, it does take some programming skills. Deployment Manager works with YAML files in which we specify the resource:

- **Machine type**: A set of predefined VM resources from the GCP gallery
- **Image family**: The operating system
- **Zone**: The zone in GCP where the resource will be deployed
- **Root persistent disk**: Specifies the boot sequence of the resource
- **IP address**

This information is stored in a `vm.yaml` file that is deployed by Deployment Manager.

# Benefits of cloud provisioning

The major benefit of cloud provisioning is that an organization doesn't need to make large investments in on-premises infrastructure. In the public cloud, it can deploy and scale resources whenever needed and pay for these resources as long the organization uses it. If it doesn't use the resources, it will not receive an invoice—unless a company has contracted reserved instances.

Another advantage of cloud provisioning is the agility and speed of deployment. Developers can easily deploy resources, within a few minutes. But that's a budget risk at the same time. With on-premises investments, a company knows exactly what the costs will be over a certain period: the investment itself and depreciation are a given. The cloud works differently, but an organization needs to be able to forecast the costs and control them.

A way to do this is by tagging resources. Tags allow a company to organize the resources in its cloud environment in a logical way, so they can easily be identified. By grouping resources using tags, it's also easy to see what costs are related to these resources and to which department or company division these costs should be transferred to. Defining and using tags will be explained in the next chapter, *Chapter 12, Defining Naming Convention and Asset Tagging Standards*.

We have discussed the various methods to deploy resources in the major clouds: Azure, AWS, and GCP. But in multi-cloud, we might also have on-premises environments. In the next section, we will elaborate on these on-premises resources.

# The provisioning and consumption of resources in on-premises propositions

We are talking about multi-cloud in this book. In *Chapter 1, Introduction to Multi-Cloud*, we defined that the cloud could involve public clouds such as Azure, AWS, and GCP, but also private clouds. In most cases, private clouds are still on-premises environments that take a significant investment. Companies use private clouds for different reasons, the most important one being compliancy—data and systems that aren't allowed to be moved to a public cloud.

The challenge with private clouds is that companies have to make major up-front investments to get hardware that enables the setup of a private cloud. They don't want to overspend by way of too much hardware, but they also don't want to be confronted with capacity limits on their hardware. Forecasting and capacity management are really crucial in terms of cost control on private clouds, even more so than in public clouds.

One of the advantages of deploying resources to public clouds is that a lot of stuff is taken care of by the cloud provider. If we deploy a VM in Azure or AWS through portals or other interfaces, the platforms guide you through the complete setup, and most of the activities are automated from the start. In private environments, this works differently; we have to account for networking and connecting storage.

How do we get the most out of our private clouds and how do we control costs when we provision workloads to these environments? If the whole private cloud is paid by one single entity and costs are not allocated to divisions or groups within the company, then there's no driver to keep track of costs, perhaps. However, most companies do allocate costs to different divisions.

Virtualization of the whole environment does help. That's where VMware comes in as the most important enterprise player in the field. They realized that in order to control a fully private environment, including networks and storage, you would need to virtualize it so that it would be easy to define who consumes what in the private cloud, making cost allocation possible. So, VMware doesn't just virtualize compute resources with vSphere, but also storage with vSAN and networks with NSX.

So, VMware introduced Cloud Foundation for the configuration of compute, storage, networks, security, and management. It's a deployment and management console for full deployments of private clouds running VMware, as well as for public clouds. To enable this, it uses **Hyperconverged Infrastructure** (**HCI**). HCI is hardware that comprises compute, storage, and networking devices in one single stack or machine.

There are more on-premises propositions that we might want to consider; Azure Stack, AWS Outposts, and Google Anthos are examples. These on-premises systems are managed through the consoles of the related public platforms. Take notice of the fact that Google Anthos is really a container-hosting platform, using Google Kubernetes Engine. Azure Stack and AWS Outposts are really extensions of the respective public cloud platforms and offer hybrid, on-premises infrastructure with the services that you can get from the Azure and AWS public clouds.

# Setting guidelines and principles for provisioning and consumption

This chapter is about keeping control of costs while provisioning resources to cloud environments. Let's start with saying that the sky is the limit in these clouds, but unfortunately, most companies do have limits to their budgets. So, we will need to set principles and guidelines and what divisions or developers are allowed to consume in the cloud environments, to avoid budgets being overrun.

To be able to set these guidelines and principles, we need to understand what these public clouds have to offer. Let's have a look at Azure first.

## Using the Azure pricing calculator

It's easy to get an overview of what a VM would cost us in Azure: the pricing overview on `https://azure.microsoft.com/en-us/pricing/calculator/` is a very handy tool for this.

If we open the page, we can look at the **Virtual Machines** tab, as shown in the following screenshot:

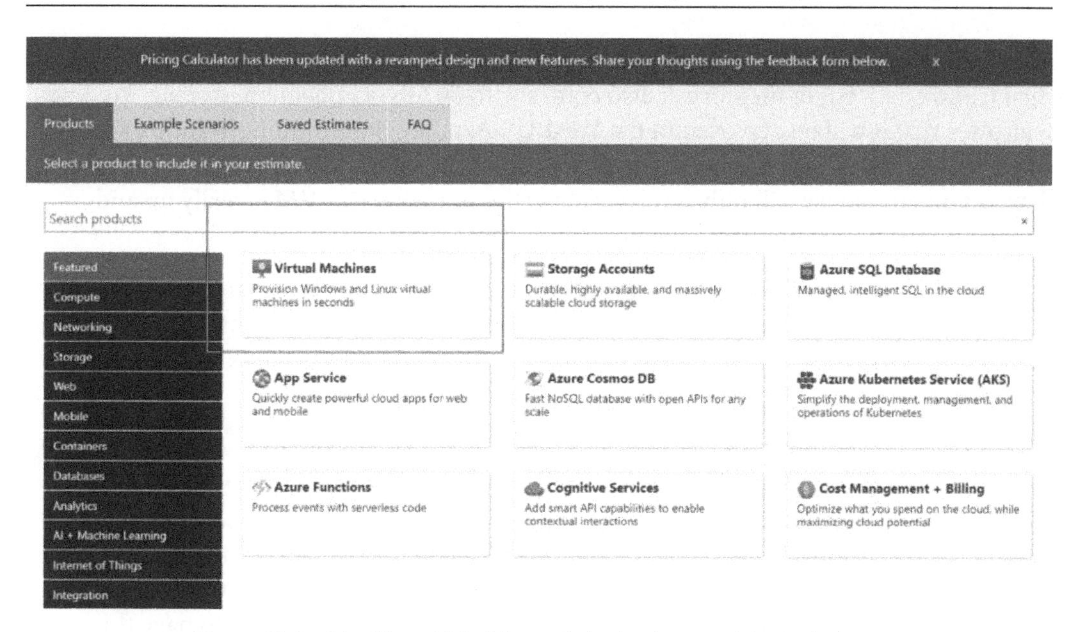


Figure 11.3 – The Virtual Machines tab in the Azure pricing calculator

The portal will display all the possible choices that are offered in terms of VMs, as shown in the following screenshot:

Virtual Machines 1 D2 v3 (2 vCPU(s), 8 GB RAM) x 730 Hours; Windows – ...

Virtual Machines

REGION: West US
OPERATING SYSTEM: Windows
TYPE: (OS Only)
TIER: Standard
INSTANCE: D2 v3: 2 vCPU(s), 8 GB RAM, 50 GB Temporary storage, $0.209/hour
VIRTUAL MACHINES: 1 × 730 Hours

Savings Options

Save up to 72% on pay-as-you-go prices with 1-year or 3-year Reserved Virtual Machine Instances. Reserved Instances are great for applications with steady-state usage and applications that require reserved capacity. Learn more about Reserved VM Instances pricing.

Compute (D2 v3)
Pay as you go
1 year reserved (~62% discount)
3 year reserved (~76% discount)
$85.41
Average per month
($0.00 charged upfront)

OS (Windows)
License included
Azure Hybrid Benefit
$67.16
Average per month
($0.00 charged upfront)

= $152.57
Average per month
($0.00 charged upfront)

Managed Disks $0.00
Storage transactions $0.05

Upfront cost $0.00
Monthly cost $152.62

Figure 11.4 – Tab details for VMs in the Azure pricing calculator

In the screenshot, the **D2 v3** VM has been selected. This is a standard VM with two virtual CPUs and 8 GB of memory. It also comes with 50 GB of ephemeral storage. We can also see that it will be deployed in the **West US** Azure region, running **Windows** as the operating system. We purchase it for 1 month, or **730** hours, but under the condition of **Pay as you go**—so we will only be charged for the time that this VM is really up and running. For the full month, this VM will cost us US$152.62.

We could also buy the machine as a reserved instance, for 1 or 3 years. In that case, the VM cost would be reduced by 62% for 1 year and 76% with a 3-year commitment. The reason Azure does this is that reserved instances mean guaranteed revenue for a longer period of time.

The D2 v3 is a general-purpose machine, but the drop-down list contains well over 130 different types of VMs, grouped in various series. The D-series are for common use. The drop-down list starts with the A-series, which are basic VMs mainly meant for development and testing. To run a heavy workload such as an SAP HANA in-memory database, an E-series VM would be more appropriate. The E64s v4 has 64 vCPUs and 500 GB of memory, which would cost around US$5,000/month. It makes sense to have this type of VM as a reserved instance.

## Using the AWS calculator

The same exercise can be done in AWS, using the calculator on `https://calculator.aws/#/`. By clicking **Create an estimate**, the following page is shown. Next, select **Amazon EC2** as the service for creating VMs:

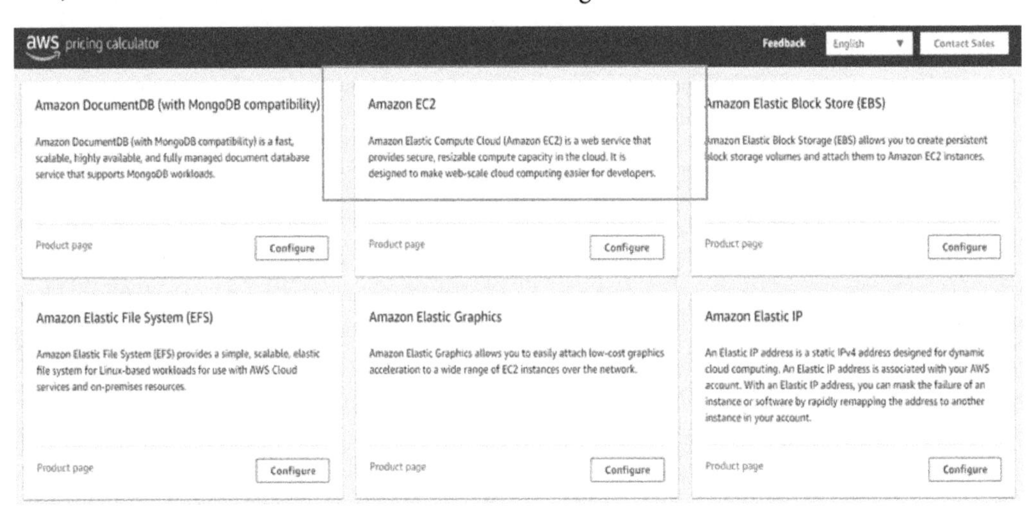


Figure 11.5 – Tab for EC2 VMs in the AWS pricing calculator

By clicking on that tab, a similar screen is displayed as in Azure. There is, however, one major difference. In Azure, the VM machine type is also taken into account

It can be done in AWS, too; the requirements of the machine can be specified by indicating how many vCPUs and how much memory a machine should have. AWS will next decide what type of VM fits the requirements. The following example shows the requirements for a machine with two vCPUs and 8 GB of memory. AWS has defined `t3a.large`—`t3a` being a specific instance size—as a suitable machine:

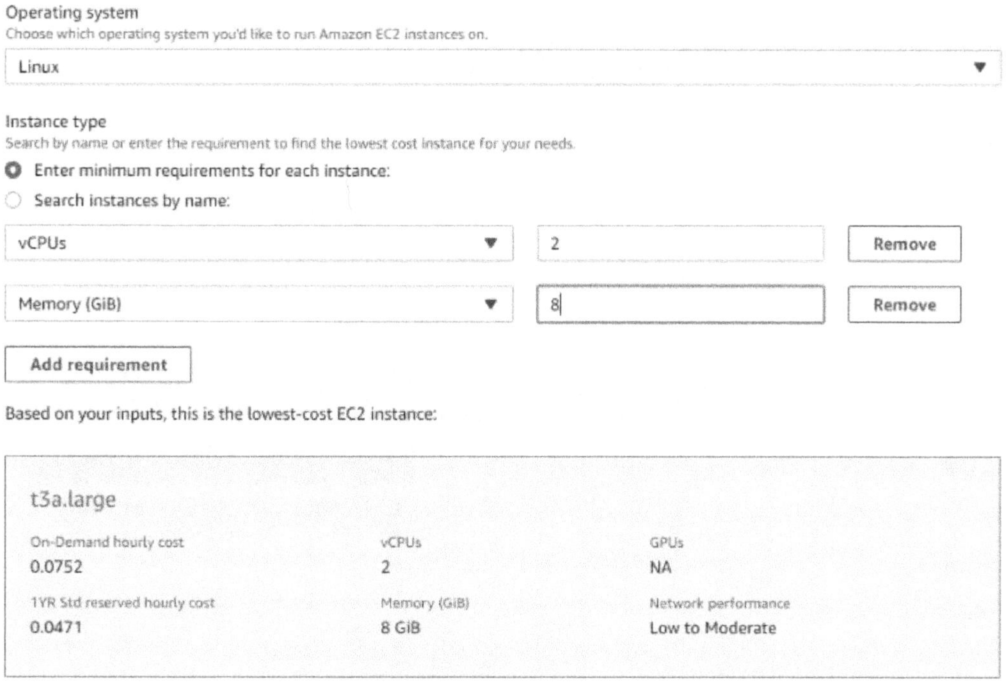

Figure 11.6 – Defining specifications for a VM in the AWS pricing calculator

The next decision to make is regarding the cloud strategy. AWS offers on-demand and reserved instances for 1 and 3 years, with the possibility of no, partial, or full up-front payments. With a relatively small VM such as our example, payment wouldn't become an issue, but also, AWS offers some huge instances of up to 64 vCPUs and up to 1 TB of memory, which would cost some serious money.

That's the reason for having guidelines and principles for provisioning. We don't want a developer being able just to *click* a very heavy machine with high costs, without knowing it or having validated a business case for using this machine; especially since the VM is only one of the components: storage and networking also need to be taken into consideration. Costs could easily rise to high levels.

It starts with the business and the use case. What will be the purpose of the environment? The purpose is defined by the business case. For example: if the business needs a tool to study maps geographic information systems, then software that views and works with maps would be needed. To host the maps and enable processing, the use case will define the need for machines with strong graphical power. Systems with **Graphics Processing Units** (**GPUs**) will fit best. In Azure, that would be the N-series; these machines have GPUs and are designed for that task. The equivalent in AWS is the G- and P-series, and in GCP, we can add NVIDIA Tesla GPUs to Compute Engine instances.

## Using the GCP instance pricing

GCP doesn't really differentiate from Azure and AWS. GCP has a full catalog of predefined instances that can deployed to a GCP project. The E2 instances are the standard machines, while the M-series is specially designed for heavy workloads with in-memory features, running up to and over 1 TB of memory. Details on the GCP catalog can be found on `https://cloud.google.com/compute/vm-instance-pricing`. And obviously, GCP has a calculator too. In the following screenshot, we've ordered a standard E2 instance with a free Linux operating system:

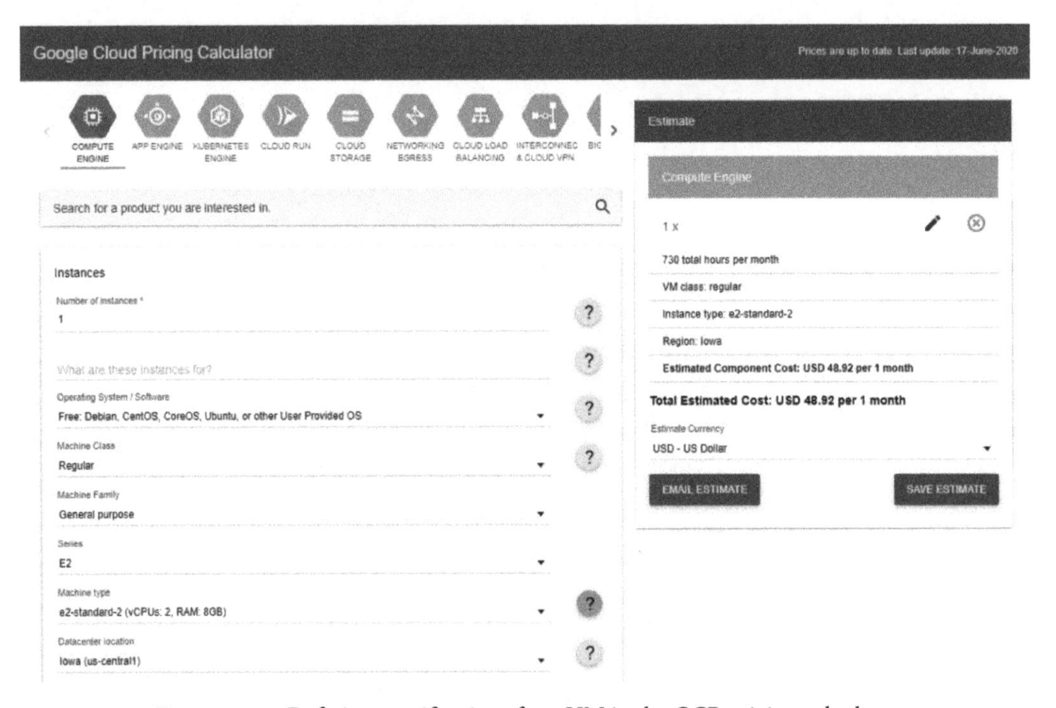


Figure 11.7 – Defining specifications for a VM in the GCP pricing calculator

The pricing calculator for GCP can be accessed at `https://cloud.google.com/products/calculator`.

So far, we have looked at the major cloud platforms and how to purchase and provision VMs to the cloud environments. The next question is: how do we define what is really needed and how do we make sure that we're only provisioning the things that we need, in order to stay in control of costs. That's what the next section is about.

## Design example for resource planning

In the architecture, we can define a principle for the type of VMs that are allowed for deployment. The following example is taken from a design document and contains the guidelines for the usage of VMs in an Azure production environment. In this case, the business case only foresees the use of development VMs and standard production VMs in Azure. Without the need for very heavy workloads, a maximum of 16 vCPUs is sufficient:

| VM Type | vCPU | RAM |
|---|---|---|
| Standard_A1_v2 | 1 | 2 |
| Standard_A2_v2 | 2 | 4 |
| Standard_A4_v2 | 4 | 8 |
| Standard_A8_v2 | 8 | 16 |
| Standard_A2m_v2 | 2 | 16 |
| Standard_A4m_v2 | 4 | 32 |
| Standard_A8m_v2 | 8 | 64 |
| Standard_DS2_v2 | 2 | 7 |
| Standard_DS3_v2 | 4 | 14 |
| Standard_DS4_v2 | 8 | 56 |
| Standard_DS5_v2 | 16 | 112 |

How do we make sure that only these types are actually deployed? The answer is through policies such as the following:

- In the case of Azure, the use of the ARM policy to restrict access to resources that aren't to be deployed in the environment or to limit the sizes of VMs that can be provisioned. This is besides the fact that in all cases, usage of naming and tagging should be enforced, as we will explore in the next chapter.

  In order to enforce that only certain types of resources can be deployed in Azure, we can create a JSON file that lists the exact specifications of the VMs that have been allowed for provisioning. That file is attached to a policy that next can be applied to a specific Azure subscription or even a resource group. The policy itself is relatively easy: it simply states that if someone issues a request to provision a VM that doesn't match the specifications of the machines that are allowed, then the request gets denied and the VM will not be provisioned.
- In AWS, we can use CodeDeploy. CodeDeploy specifies a workflow to deploy applications to AWS that utilize EX2 VMs. Provisioning the instances is part of the workflow in CodeDeploy. By specifying a deployment group, the type of instances can be provisioned.

  Tags can also be applied to these instances. To define the instances, we can work with CloudFormation and regular expressions. An expression contains a parameter, and in this case, this should be a parameter that specifies a certain instance type, `InstanceTypeParameter`. Parameters can be defined in JSON or YAML. AWS allows 60 parameters in one CloudFormation template.
- In Google, instance templates are created to define and enforce the use of specific VM types. To deploy multiple instances, we can add instance templates to a **Managed Instance Group** (**MIG**), but the instance template can also be used for individual instances.

In this section, we talked about VMs as the main type of resource in our cloud environments. One thing we haven't touched on so far is the provisioning of containers. All clouds will offer possibilities to run containers on VMs. The container will hold the application and the libraries, packed in a Docker image.

Next, we will create a VM with a container-optimized operating system. This is a requirement since we will need Docker runtime on our VM to start the container. However, this is not very efficient. If we want to run multiple containers on a VM, we need a container runtime environment, typically Kubernetes. All of the platforms provide Kubernetes runtime services that enable the deployment of containers.

# Controlling resource consumption using cost alerts

In the previous sections, we discussed how we can provision resources—VMs—to our cloud environments and learned why it's important that we have control over what resources teams or developers can deploy, mainly because we have to stay in control of costs. The cloud is agile and flexible, but it doesn't come for free.

How do we keep track of costs? All cloud providers have dashboards that show exactly how much resource consumption will cost. That's a reactive approach, which can be fine. But if we want to force teams and developers to stay within budgets, we can set credit caps on subscriptions and have alerts raised as soon the cap is reached. The different ways to set caps in Azure, AWS, and GCP are listed in the following overview:

- In Azure, we can set budgets and alerts. Both services are part of the Cost Management module in Azure. We can set budgets for specific services for a certain amount of time. Azure evaluates costs against the set budgets every 4 hours. We can also allow Azure to send email notifications as soon as budget limits are met.

  For this, we use cost alerts. Like budgets, these alerts can be defined through the Azure portal or with the Azure Consumption API. The latter enables programmatic access to retrieve data on consumption and generated costs. Since the API is available in various formats, such as Python and Node.js, it can integrate with service management tooling.

- AWS also offers the possibility to set budgets and generate cost alerts. Budgets are set in the AWS Budgets dashboard, which is accessed through the AWS console. We can create budgets for almost any timeframe and link them to a large variety of AWS services. Budget alerts are sent through email or by using Amazon's **Simple Notification Service** (**SNS**).

  To set cost or billing alerts, we can use the native monitoring service of AWS: CloudWatch. It calculates the costs several times per day, against the worldwide valid charges. In order to get alerts, we need to specify a threshold to the charged amount. As soon as this threshold is hit, the alarm will be triggered.

- And, of course, in GCP, we can set budgets and cost alerts too. Google offers Cloud Billing budgets. As in AWS, we set a threshold. Exceeding the threshold will trigger alerts, sending an email to every contact that has a billing role in GCP. That probably needs some explanation: a user in GCP can have a billing role, next to any other role that they have as an admin. In the Google console, it's specified in `roles/billing.admin` or `roles/billing.user`. Next to these users, we can customize the recipients of these alerts. For instance, we can add project managers so that they receive cost alerts for their projects directly from Cloud Billing.

Deploying resources to clouds means that we generate costs. An enterprise needs to be able to keep track of those costs. In this section, we provided tips and tools to enable cost management.

# Summary

In this chapter, we discussed various ways of how we can provision workloads to the different cloud platforms: Azure, AWS, and Google Cloud. It's recommended to decide what type of resources we plan to deploy before we actually start building our environment. We've seen that cloud providers offer a wide variety of resources—from simple, low-cost development VMs to heavy workloads with lots of memory—for use, such as in-memory databases. In order to stay in control of costs, it's wise to define what we really need and enforce it by policies that only allow those resources to be deployed. That's what is referred to as resource planning and should be part of the multi-cloud architecture.

We have also learned how we can set budgets and cost alerts in the cloud platforms. All major cloud providers allow us to set budgets on time and type of resources consumed. Next, we can set triggers as soon as budget thresholds are met and get notified by email when this happens.

It's important to remember to apply a naming convention and tagging to keep track of resources. In the next chapter, we will explore the naming and tagging best practices in the cloud platforms.

# Questions

1. If we plan to provision resources to an environment in Azure, what management layer makes sure that these resources are actually deployed?
2. A popular trend in on-premises private clouds is hardware that comprises compute, storage, and networking in one single stack. What do we call this type of hardware?
3. In all clouds, we can specify what type of resources we want to deploy, using policies or templates. What specific solution would you recommend in AWS?
4. Rate the following statement true or false: In order to receive cost alerts from GCP, you need to have the billing role.

# Further reading

- *VMware Cross-Cloud Architecture* by Ajit Pratap Kundan, Packt Publishing
- An article by Larry Dignan, ZDNet: `https://www.zdnet.com/article/cloud-cost-control-becoming-a-leading-issue-for-businesses/`
- Documentation on how to use ARM: `https://docs.microsoft.com/en-us/azure/azure-resource-manager/management/overview`
- Documentation about working with OpsWorks in AWS: `https://docs.aws.amazon.com/opsworks/latest/userguide/welcome_classic.html`
- Documentation about working with Deployment Manager in GCP: `https://cloud.google.com/deployment-manager/docs/`
- Documentation on cost control and billing in Azure: `https://docs.microsoft.com/nl-nl/azure/cost-management-billing/costs/cost-mgt-alerts-monitor-usage-spending`
- Documentation on cost control and billing in AWS: `https://docs.aws.amazon.com/AmazonCloudWatch/latest/monitoring/monitor_estimated_charges_with_cloudwatch.html`, documentation on cost and budget control in AWS
- Documentation on cost control and budgets in GCP: `https://cloud.google.com/billing/docs/how-to/budgets`, documentation on cost and budget control in GCP

# 12 Defining Naming Conventions and Tagging

Cost control starts with enabling the clear identification of resources and accountability for these resources. In multi-cloud environments, naming and tagging should be consistent across all utilized cloud platforms.

We will learn how we can define a consistent naming and tagging convention. Both naming and tagging are required to identify resources. A name is used to recognize resources and tags act as extra labels to specify the role and characteristics of a resource. We will see that there are differences between the major cloud providers when it comes to guidelines and restrictions on names and tags for resources. This chapter provides an overview of the main guidelines for the major platforms–AWS, Azure, and GCP. We will also learn that consistent naming and tagging is crucial for the billing process and for allocating the costs of cloud resources to the right cost center.

In this chapter, we're going to cover the following main topics:

- Creating a naming convention
- Creating a tagging convention
- Implementing naming and tagging
- Managing naming and tagging conventions

# Creating a naming convention

Let's assume that we will have a lot of resources deployed to our cloud environments. We need a way to identify these resources. This is what a naming convention does. The naming convention is part of our architecture. Of course, one way to identify resources such as virtual machines is by IP addresses, but with a lot of resources, this is not very convenient or even possible. A naming convention makes our lives a lot easier. Basically, it's just an agreement on how we want to identify resources. You can compare it with street names. In a small village, it might be sufficient to just give each house a number, but in a big city, street names make it easier to find a certain address.

The goal of a naming convention is to enable identification. Typically, the name of a resource also describes what the resource is or does. For example, the naming convention to specify a name for a VM might comprise the following information:

- Where the resource is deployed—for example, an Azure environment in the region West-US
- What the role of the resource is—for example, database, application server, or domain controller
- The type of resource (development, test, **quality assurance** (**QA**) or pre-prod, or production system)
- Who the owner of the resource is

So, if we have a production database server running SQL on a Windows operating system, hosted in the US West region of Azure, the name might be something like `DBSQLWIN-AZUSW_P`. But what if we have more SQL databases? Then we need to add a unique identifier. That can be a number or the name of an application to which the server belongs – in our example, `DBSQLWIN001-AZUSW_P`. Now the name tells us that this is the SQL database server number `001`, running on Windows, hosted in Azure West-US, and in production.

We would also need to specify who the owner of the resource is, typically expressed as an abbreviation that identifies the tenant. If company `XYZ` is the owner of the cloud tenant where the resources are hosted, then the naming convention would most likely start with `XYZ` followed by the rest: `XYZ_DBSQLWIN001-AZUSW_P`.

Unfortunately, it's not as easy as that. Major cloud providers Azure, AWS, and GCP all have specific demands for a naming convention. In our example, we have used 22 characters to specify the name for one resource, including the hyphens. Cloud providers differ in how they allow different numbers of characters and the use of special characters, such as hyphens. In the next sections, we will explore these standards as defined by the cloud providers.

## Naming convention standards in Azure

One important thing to remember is that we're only talking about databases and VMs when we discuss naming conventions. Since everything in the public cloud is software-defined—meaning that there is no physical device that we can identify—all assets or resource types that are used in the public cloud need to have a unique name. This includes networking, security assets such as gateways and firewalls, policies, and integration patterns such as APIs.

To make it a bit more complex, we're not completely free in how we define our naming convention. Azure prescribes a vast number of resource type prefixes.

Every resource group name needs to have the identification `rg-`, and every VNet must contain `vnet-` in the name. Every VM deployed in Azure is identified with `vm` and every SQL database with `SQL`. The list is extensive. A few things are up to us to define:

- The business unit—for example, `fin` for finance or the abbreviation of the company
- The subscription type—for example, `prod` or `prd` for production
- Application or service name
- Deployment environment—production, test, development, acceptance, staging, QA, or sandbox
- Region

Azure does provide guidance and recommendations to define naming standards for all resource types. Next, there are naming rules and restrictions that we need to apply. This is again a very extensive list.

Let's use the example of a VM. The prefix is -vm, so that needs to be included in the name. The scope of the VM is the resource group that it belongs to, so it needs to be clear in the name where the VM is hosted. Then we have to deal with a couple of restrictions. For a VM running on Windows, there is a limit of 15 characters. The following characters are forbidden: \/"'[]:|<>+=;,?*@&. Lastly, names can't begin with an underscore or end with a period or a hyphen.

A usable format would be <organization><deployment-environment><region><service><hostname>-vm. In the example used earlier, it would be xyz-p-usw-app-app001-vm. The organization is XYZ, the deployment environment is production (p), it is hosted in US-West, it's an application server for app001, and it's a VM, indicated by -vm, the prefix that Azure prescribes. In the *Further reading* section, you will find the references for naming and tagging in Azure.

## Naming convention standards in AWS

AWS takes VMs in EC2—the compute service of AWS—as a starting point to create a naming standard for resources, but they take a different approach than Azure. AWS connects the name to the **fully qualified domain name** (**FQDN**) of an instance. AWS assumes that a company already has a naming standard to identify servers, comprising the location, deployment type, role, application or service ID, and a unique identifier. AWS recommends associating this with the FQDN.

To use the previous example again, say application server 001 is in production for company XYZ but is now hosted in AWS. To identify this server, it's named p-app001. AWS now recommends assigning this name to the FQDN papp001.xyz.com. If we are running instances on-premises as well, it might be advisable to have something that indicates that this resource is in AWS or a specific AWS region—for instance, awspapp001.xyz.com.

Alternatively, a globally unique instance ID in AWS can be included in the name tag: i-06599a38675.xyz.com.

But how is that making our lives easier in identifying resources? Here's how:

- First of all, AWS assumes a very high level of automation, where we have as little human interference as possible. A script or API would be able to recognize the ID very quickly, so why not use the unique ID that AWS automatically assigns to a resource?
- Second, AWS has very extensive tagging possibilities, assigning metadata to resources in a lot of different ways. We will explore that in the section about tags. Tags are AWS' method to identify resources, rather than using names.

For that reason, AWS has a straightforward naming standard for other resources using dot notation. It contains only three fields:

- **Account name prefix**: For example, production (prod) or development (dev)
- **Resource name**: A free-form field that contains a logical name
- **Type suffix**: Indicates what type of resource it is—for example, security group or subnet

A security group for a web server in production would then get the following name: `prod.webserver.sg`, where `prod` is the account name, `webserver` the resource name, and `sg` the type suffix.

## Naming convention standards in GCP

The naming convention for GCP is very simple. For every resource in Compute Engine, the name has to be compliant with the following rules:

- Every name has a maximum of 63 characters.
- The following characters are allowed: `[a-z]([-a-z0-9]*[a-z0-9])?`.
- The first character must be a lowercase letter. All subsequent characters must be lowercase letters, digits, or hyphens. The last character can't be a hyphen.

There's one more restriction: GCP wants the naming convention to be compliant with RFC 1035 conventions. That probably needs some explanation. RFC 1035 is issued by the **Internet Engineering Task Force** (**IETF**) and describes the convention for domain names.

The reason for this is that name servers across the globe must be able to retrieve instances, no matter where they are hosted: whether in on-premises systems, in colocations, or on public clouds. RFC 1035 makes sure that instances are uniquely identifiable. Although only GCP mentions it explicitly, all providers should comply with this statement. For those who want to read the full document, it's published at `https://www.ietf.org/rfc/rfc1035.txt`.

In the *Further reading* section, you will find the references for naming and tagging in GCP.

# Creating a tagging convention

Tags are likely the most important attribute in terms of cost management and control in cloud environments. Naming conventions are much more focused on the identification of resources and are also crucial to the automation of cloud management. Tags are metadata that allow additional information on resources that can't be stored in a name. Tagging will help in understanding cost allocation, since we can use tags to categorize cloud resources.

All cloud providers offer extensive ways to apply tags to our resources. However, standard tags can be utilized across these different clouds. It's recommended to have tags for at least the following attributes:

- **Application**: Typically, a resource is part of an application or an application stack. To categorize resources—meaning VMs, storage, databases, and network components—that belong to one application or application stack, a tag should be added to identify to what stack or application a resource belongs.
- **Billing**: Especially large enterprises will have divisions, business units, or brands. These entities might have budgets or might be separate cost centers. Tags will ensure that resources are billed to specific budgets or the accounting cost centers.
- **Service class**: Tags can indicate what service level is applicable to resources. Are they managed 24/7, what is the patch schedule, and what is the backup scheme? Often enterprises have a tiered categorization for resources, such as gold, silver, and bronze. Gold is the highest level for production systems and may have disaster recovery solutions and uptime of 99.999%; silver and bronze would be for single systems with a much lower service level. A tag indicating gold, silver, or bronze will make clear what the service class is of that particular resource.
- **Compliance**: These tags indicate whether compliance rules apply. These can be industry compliance regulations, such as for healthcare or financial institutions, as well as internal compliance rules. These can be important in, for example, granting access to specific resources or the way data is securely stored.

Now that we have learned what the recommended parameters are for applying tags, we can look at how we can define tags in Azure, AWS, and GCP.

## Defining tags in Azure

All resources that can be deployed with **Azure Resource Manager** (**ARM**) can be tagged, but there are some restrictions to take into account.

Azure allows a maximum of 15 tags per resource with a length of 512 characters, strictly alphanumeric.

JSON strings can be used if more than 15 tags are needed. Azure recommends setting tags at the level of resource groups, because there are a limited number of tags. From the resource group, all the associated resources would be identifiable together, thus limiting tagging resources individually. Best practice for tagging in Azure includes the following:

- **Application taxonomy**: Indicator for the owner—for example, a specific business unit or DevOps team—of the resource group and the function of the application.
- **Environment type**: This indicates the purpose of the resource group—for example, test, development, or production.
- **Billing indicator**: This is the identifier for the cost center accountable for the costs that are generated with resources in this resource group.
- **End date of the project**: States when the project is ending; resources can be removed to save costs.

In the next section, we will look at tags in AWS.

## Defining tags in AWS

Of all the public clouds, AWS has the most extensive method of tagging resources. Resources can have 50 tags each, with a maximum length of 127 characters. Both alphanumeric, spaces, and the special characters `+ - = . _ : / @` can be used. On top of that, tags are case sensitive. But also, AWS has a few restrictions regarding tags.

Tags can primarily be used for resources that are deployed from the compute service of AWS–EC2. There are more services that can be tagged, but this doesn't comprise every service or resource that AWS offers.

More importantly, tags must be activated for cost allocation for these resources to show up in billing reports. There's a maximum of 500 tags that can be used for billing and cost management. So, the best practice is to first create user-defined tags using AWS' Tag Editor or through the API from the AWS console. Next, allocate these tags for billing and cost management through the console. Be aware that the console is not the same thing as the AWS portal. The management console is accessed through `https://console.aws.amazon.com/`; this is the console where we manage our environment in AWS.

With the possibility of having 50 tags per resource, it could easily be tempting to actually use them all. One of the best practices of AWS, however, is *less is more, start small*. Tags are reversible and can be removed, and new tags can be added—even in bulk—if needed. One exception: the `aws:` prefix can't be used or modified. It's reserved for AWS use only.

## Defining tags in GCP

Tagging is implemented differently in GCP. Google calls them labels as opposed to tags. The purpose of labels is the same—they are meant to group resources together easily.

Labels are pairs of keys and values. For example, say a key is `environment` and a value is `development`. The label, therefore, is `environment/development`. We need to include that in a script through the `gcloud` command line. It will look like this:

```
{
  "labels": {
    "environment": "development",
  … }
}
```

GCP allows 64 labels per resource, with a maximum of 63 characters for keys and values. There's also a restriction on the type of resources that can have labels. At the time of writing, labels are fully supported on VMs, images, disks, and storage buckets. Labels on forwarding rules, static external IP addresses, and VPN tunnels are in beta.

It's important to note that that GCP has network tags. These are not related to labels.

# Implementing naming and tagging

The successful implementation of a naming and tagging standard starts with a clear policy. Tags should be consistent and applied to all resources: VMs, storage, databases and network components, applications, and services. Remember that every resource in a cloud environment costs money. To have a complete overview of our cloud spending, we have to make sure that all resources are identified and tagged so that they appear in the billing. This means that every team deploying resources to cloud environments must be required to tag resources; even better, a policy should prevent—preferably in a fully automated way—resources without tags being deployed in the first place.

As a best practice, the following steps should be executed to implement a consistent naming and tagging convention:

- **Defining the policy**: This is part of the multi-cloud architecture. The naming and tagging policy need to be centrally defined so that it's consistent throughout every cloud environment to which we deploy. This will take time. Start with a policy following the recommendations and best practices of the clouds that the company will use, but the policy needs to be validated and agreed upon throughout the enterprise. Without the consent of stakeholders, naming and tagging might not be followed in the desired manner consistently.

- **Enforce the policy**: This doesn't sound nice, but it's an absolutely necessary step. Every team working in a company's cloud environment must adhere to the naming and tagging policy. Store the policy in a central place so that everyone has access to it. Don't make it too complicated: a wiki page with the proposed naming and tags can be stored on the intranet. Next, point the teams to this file. Often, teams are led by project managers or product owners; they should be alerted to use the policy.
- **Monitor the policy**: Especially at the beginning of projects, it's advised to check on a weekly basis whether naming and tagging is applied according to the policy. The reason to be strict in this is that naming and tagging are crucial for billing. We want a complete billing statement that shows all assets deployed in our clouds and be sure that costs are accounted for and allocated to the right cost center or budget. Without consistent naming and tagging, that's virtually impossible.
- **Automate**: The tagging process can be automated. As soon as the policy is accepted, it's strongly recommended to automate the tagging process. Automation can be triggering an alert as soon as resources get deployed without tags. A resource shutdown policy could also be automatically enforced when they don't have tags assigned. One step further would be full automation of the tagging process, where tags get automatically assigned as soon as resources are provisioned. This can be done from the CI/CD pipeline using native deployment tools from the cloud providers, or by using tooling for it.

  This tooling is often referred to as **cloud spend management** or **spend optimization**. Flexera is one example of this type of tooling. It uses policy-based automation to control spending over all major cloud providers and a wide variety of SaaS options. It also generates feedback on how to optimize costs, when resources are, for instance, no longer in use. One of the basic features is that it checks for tagging policies.

In the *Further reading* section, you will find URLs to documents explaining the implementation of tags and labels in Azure, AWS, and GCP.

# Managing naming and tagging conventions

Managing naming and tagging conventions is part of cloud governance. Once a convention is designed and confirmed by all stakeholders in the enterprise, it needs to be enforced. This means that an enterprise might want to deploy default tags on resources—as we have described in the previous sections—but also a policy that enables the termination of instances if they are not tagged or tagged correctly.

Regular reports must be published to verify that naming and tagging is applied as agreed and defined in the convention, but preferably this is automated.

Having said that, the naming and tagging convention will probably not be set in stone. There has to be flexibility in changing the convention when required. Think of a new service that is launched by a cloud provider and that an enterprise would like to use in future deployments, or an enterprise that acquires a new company with its own budgets or cost centers. In these cases, we will need to adapt the convention. The convention is part of our multi-cloud architecture and governance, and therefore change management is applicable.

A good practice is to review the convention at regular intervals. This can be done in an architecture review. Most companies have regular meetings or platforms such as an **architecture board** where architectural decisions are made. That's the place to decide whether changes to conventions are needed and how these changes should be applied. This is important since changing naming and tagging can have consequences for automation and for billing. Automation might not be able to identify resources or resources might not show up in billing reports anymore. Changes to a convention should therefore be considered very carefully.

# Summary

In this chapter, we have learned that names and tags are crucial to be able to identify our resources in public cloud environments. They are crucial to correct billing and to allocating costs to the appropriate budget or cost center. But they are also very important in terms of automation. We have learned that we can automate the naming and tagging process; however, it starts with a definition of the naming and tagging convention. After this chapter, you should have a good understanding of the different guidelines and restrictions for naming and tagging in AWS, Azure, and GCP.

Lastly, we've learned that as soon as a convention is agreed upon, we should apply it in a consistent way and that the convention itself should be part of the architecture. We've learned that updates to the naming convention should follow the change management control processes of the enterprise and be discussed by an architecture board or in an architectural board meeting/review.

The final step in cost management in multi-cloud is the billing itself. In the next chapter, we will learn how billing in public clouds works and how we can validate this.

# Questions

1. True or false: it's recommended to have the role of a resource indicated in the name of the resource.
2. AWS recommends connecting the name to the FQDN. What does FQDN stand for?
3. What are tags called in GCP?

# Further reading

You can refer to the following for more information on the topics covered in this chapter:

- Blog about applying best practices for tagging: `https://www.cryingcloud.com/2016/07/18/azure-resource-tagging-best-practices/`
- Documentation on applying naming and tagging in Azure: `https://docs.microsoft.com/en-us/azure/cloud-adoption-framework/ready/azure-best-practices/naming-and-tagging`
- Best practices for tagging resources in Azure: `https://docs.microsoft.com/en-us/azure/cloud-adoption-framework/ready/azure-best-practices/naming-and-tagging#metadata-tags`
- Best practices for tagging resources in AWS: `https://d1.awsstatic.com/whitepapers/aws-tagging-best-practices.pdf`
- Documentation on naming conventions in GCP: `https://cloud.google.com/compute/docs/naming-resources`
- Documentation on applying labels to resources in GCP: `https://cloud.google.com/compute/docs/labeling-resources`

# 13
# Validating and Managing Bills

Every month, a bill will arrive from different cloud providers. What are the different billing options? How do you validate the costs on the bill? And if you have deployments in more than one cloud, what are your options for having one centralized cost overview?

We will learn how to view and analyze costs in the consoles of Azure, AWS, and GCP. This chapter will show you how to define billing accounts and billing profiles so that specific roles in your organization can track their costs. We will also learn the importance of having a process in place to validate billing to ensure that all costs are tracked appropriately. In the last section, we will explore possibilities to consolidate billing in one centralized dashboard.

In this chapter, we're going to cover the following main topics:

- Exploring billing options and using cost dashboards
- Validating invoices
- Centralizing billing in multi-cloud

# Exploring billing options and using cost dashboards

It's very likely that a multi-cloud strategy will place several migrated systems into multiple different public clouds. With that, we are generating costs for pay-per-use instances and services, reserved instances for which companies have longer-term obligations, and, as explained in *Chapter 10, Managing Licenses*, also licenses. Invoices will arrive from different providers. How do we keep track of all that?

Let's have a look first at billing in the major cloud platforms being discussed in this book: Azure, AWS, and GCP. These platforms share the same billing approach: as soon as services are consumed on the platform, charges will begin to accrue to which the CSPs can send invoices. Typically, this is referred to as the billing account. We will be using the cost or billing dashboards from the clouds to view costs and invoices.

## Using cost management and billing in Azure

Azure billing has three types of billing:

- **Microsoft Online Services program**: Every user in Azure starts in this program. As soon as you sign in to Azure through the portal, you will get a billing account. This is also the case when you sign up for a free account. It's also needed for all pay-as-you-go services and for a subscription in Visual Studio, the Microsoft tool for development in cloud environments.
- **Enterprise Agreement**: An organization can sign an **Enterprise Agreement** (**EA**) with Microsoft to use Azure, which is valid across a lot of other products and services of Microsoft. An EA is a monetary commitment. An organization is entitled to extensive support from Microsoft, but it comes with contractual obligations such as a minimum spend.
- **Microsoft Customer Agreement**: If an organization signs up for Azure, in most cases a billing account will be issued for a Microsoft Customer Agreement. In some Azure regions, a Microsoft Customer Agreement can be issued if a free account is upgraded.

When a billing account is activated, a billing profile will be attached to it. This profile enables managing invoices and payments. Azure creates monthly invoices at the beginning of each month. Depending on the billing profile, the person who owns the account will see all costs associated with subscriptions and services in those subscriptions that are purchased under that specific account.

For example, if the billing profile is set to enterprise level, the billing account lists all costs that a company generates in Azure, in all subscriptions within the enterprise tenant. It's advised to define more billing profiles with specific invoice sections. This is done in the Azure portal under the **Cost Management + Billing** tab, as shown in the following screenshot:

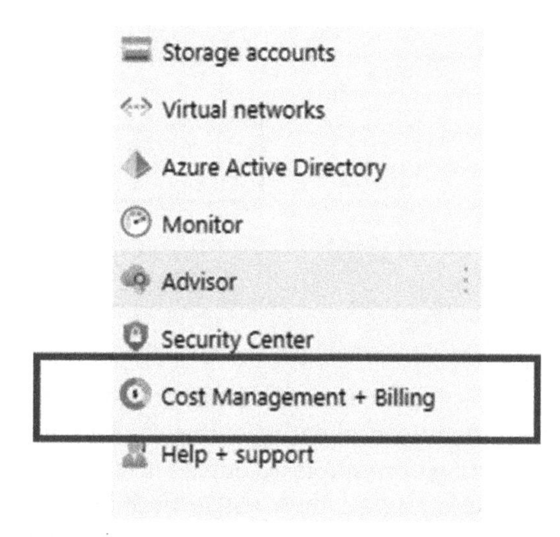


Figure 13.1 – The Cost Management + Billing tab in the Azure portal menu

It's true that the overall concept of cost management and billing is pretty much the same in the different clouds, but there are some differences in possible implementations for our own organization. Next, we will take a look at AWS and GCP.

# Using AWS Cost Management for billing

In AWS, the free tier is the typical entry point and provides a lot of services for us to use. Organizations will typically enter into a customer agreement with AWS. Be aware that if you sign up on behalf of a company, AWS considers you as the person with the legal authority to do so. Make sure that you are entitled to get into a commitment on behalf of your organization.

Similarly to the way Azure does, cost and billing management for AWS is viewed through its portal. It's under the **AWS Cost Management** menu item, as shown in the following screenshot:

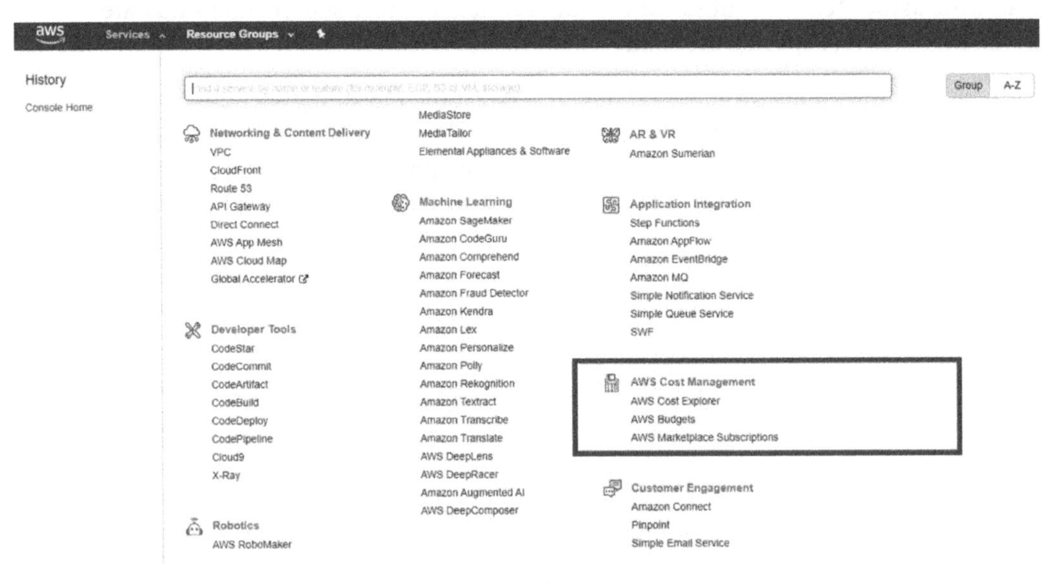


Figure 13.2 – Cost and billing in the AWS console menu

It's common in both AWS and Azure for an organization to have separate divisions of accounts. With AWS Organizations, consolidating billing can be activated. There's one account for the whole organization or multiple accounts reflecting the organizational structure of the company. In the latter case, there will be multiple accounts. These accounts can be grouped under one, consolidated master account to have an overview of all AWS costs generated.

In AWS Cost Management, we can analyze costs with Cost Explorer, get usage reports, and manage our payments. Billing preferences can be set, such as receiving billing alerts and invoices being emailed as PDFs. Payment preferences, such as paying through a credit card or bank account, can also be set in Cost Management. In Europe, **Single Euro Payments Area** (**SEPA**) is commonly used. In India, payments can be submitted through **Amazon Internet Services Private Limited** (**AISPL**).

## Using billing options in GCP

As soon as billing is activated in GCP, the portal will prompt the user to set a billing account, as shown in the following screenshot:

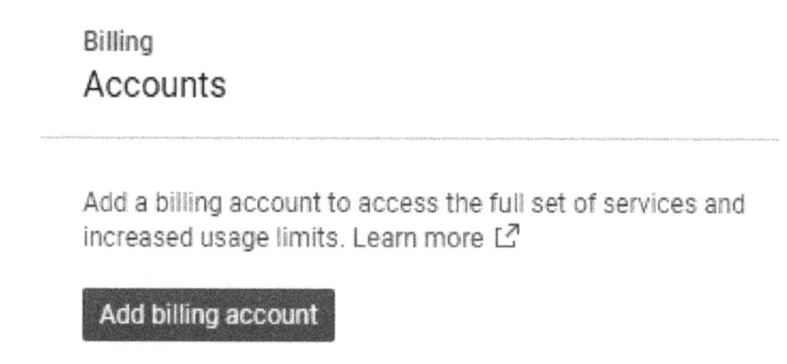


Figure 13.3 – Adding a billing account in GCP

In GCP, cloud billing accounts are always associated with projects, which are the equivalent of subscriptions in Azure and accounts in AWS. Like in Azure, the billing account is coupled with a Google payments profile. There are two types of billing account roles:

- **Billing account admin**: This is typically someone in the finance department. This account can view all costs, set budgets and billing alerts, and link or unlink projects.
- **Billing account user**: The only thing the user can do is link a project to a billing account and see the costs associated with that project. The user can't unlink the project, unlike the admin.

The payment profile contains information about the legal entity that is responsible for the accounts. It also stores information on tax obligations such as VAT, bank accounts, payment methods, and transaction information such as outstanding invoices. Only the billing account admin role can view and alter this information.

In the GCP Cloud Console, we can enable interactive billing reports where the views and reports on billing information can be customized. For example, cost breakdowns can be added per project or per service used in GCP. In the Cloud Console, this is all featured under **Billing** in the main menu, as shown in the following screenshot:

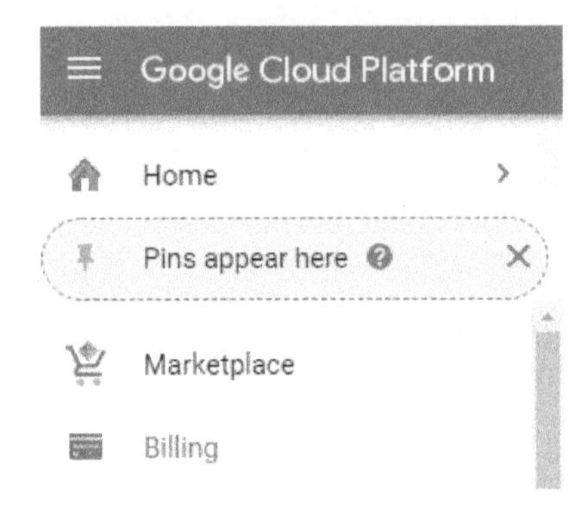


Figure 13.4 – The Billing tab in Google's Cloud Console

In this section, we have explored the various billing options in Azure, AWS, and GCP using the billing dashboard in these clouds. In the next section, we will learn how we can validate invoices.

# Validating invoices

Validating invoices has nothing to do with checking whether a cloud provider has charged us the correct amounts. Cloud providers have fully automated this process, so you may rest assured that if you or your company uses a resource in their cloud, it will show up in the bill. Validating invoices is about checking whether invoiced costs correspond with the forecasted usage of your company. Are you on budget or are you overspending? Are there resources on the bill that you aren't using anymore? And if so, why didn't you delete these resources?

Some key decisions will need to be made. These decisions are the same for all clouds covered:

- Will the organization use one or multiple billing accounts? If you want a project manager to be able to validate the costs for a specific project or in a particular environment, then he or she should be granted access to view these costs. As we have seen in the previous section, we can set these privileges granularly in roles and profiles that are attached to billing accounts.

- How will payments be processed? As discussed in the previous section, cloud providers offer various ways to process payments. Credit cards are popular, but most enterprises do their payments through invoiced billing and their respective bank accounts. The latter is strongly recommended for optimized cost control.

Next, we have to define the validation process. It might sound overdone, but the truth is that organizations tend to have significant overspending in public clouds—simply because they lack insights and control into the billing process and because they don't have accurate cost management in place.

A recommended approach comes in three steps:

1. **Project control**: A project manager, product owner, or Scrum Master should be aware of what costs are generated from a project. If a team works in Agile Scrum and uses Sprints, it is advised to validate deployed resources after each Sprint. Are the designed resources deployed and what other services are related to that? These overviews should match the costs that are allocated to the project.
2. **Architecture control**: The role of the architect is to verify that only resources that are agreed-upon artifacts are included. A simple example: if it is agreed that only VMs of a certain series may be used for deployment in production, then the architect should check that this requirement is met. The deployment of other resources could inflict higher costs.
3. **Finance and accounting**: Based on the checks by project management and architecture control, the finance department can be sure that resource deployment is done correctly and that costs can be accounted for. Finance now has the task of checking invoices on terms of payment conditions and contractual agreements.

This controlling process should be part of the overall governance of cloud environments, as it is part of the **Cloud Adoption Frameworks** (**CAFs**) of Azure, AWS, and GCP. On top of that, there's one overall crucial piece of advice: seek guidance from the account team or account manager of the respective clouds. They can advise exactly what the best options are for your company. They will also guide their customers in interacting with resellers or cloud service partners, for instance, in applying the appropriate discounts or in recommending what type of contract or deployment model would be best: pay as you go or reserved instances.

It's in the interest of Azure, AWS, and GCP that you get the best out of their clouds at the best possible rates without breaking the bank. Your success is their success.

# Centralizing billing in multi-cloud

In the previous sections, we discussed the various billing and cost management options that Azure, AWS, and GCP offer. However, we're talking multi-cloud, so we might have workloads in at least two different clouds. If we want to know what our costs are, we will need to log in to multiple consoles to find out what our invoice will look like at the end of the month. We can do some exports to get it all consolidated in one spreadsheet, but that won't solve a couple of challenges.

First of all, in terms of financial reporting, the invoicing period should be the same. For example, in terms of the consolidation of cloud services from different providers, the invoicing period should be from the first day of the month until the last day of the month, so the 30th or 31st (February being an exception). Some services are billed from the 1st until the 1st of the next month. It might not seem an issue for an engineer, but in financial accounting, it does make a difference.

Secondly, can all the services that we see in the different invoices be matched? Terminology in clouds does differ. Azure VMs are in B-, D- or DS-series, for instance. AWS has a completely different annotation: A1, T3a, or M6g. It makes consolidation complicated.

Can we make our lives a bit easier, by centralizing cost management for clouds, and have one single dashboard where we can see the total spending in multi-cloud? Yes, **Cloud Management Platforms (CMPs)** do this. However, there are only a couple of tools that really focus on centralized cost management. Flexera's Optima—formerly RightScale—(`https://www.flexera.com/products/spend-optimization/cloud-cost-management.html`) is such a tool. It collects costs from different clouds and presents these in one overall dashboard. Costs can be viewed per category, such as VMs or databases, but also in daily or monthly reports. Alternate tools are VMware's CloudHealth (`https://www.cloudhealthtech.com/`) and Fujitsu's Picco, which can aggregate costs from the major clouds, Azure, AWS, and GCP, in one single dashboard (`https://picco.cloud/`).

# Summary

This was the last chapter about financial operations in multi-cloud. We've discussed budgets and cost management, and in this chapter, we explored the billing options in the different clouds. We've learned that in all clouds, we need to have a billing account and an associated billing profile so that we view costs that are related to our projects or the whole enterprise. We've looked at the consoles of Azure, AWS, and GCP to find out where we can manage settings for billing and cost management in these clouds. After completion of this chapter, we should have an understanding of the billing process itself, but also of how can we validate costs. In the last section, we discovered that there are tools that can make our lives easier by providing one single dashboard where we can have a total overview of all our costs in the clouds.

The next part of this book will discuss security in multi-cloud, starting with defining security policies.

# Questions

1. What is the most common contract form for an enterprise in Azure?
2. What service would you use in AWS to analyze costs?
3. True or false: a billing account user can't unlink a project to a billing account in GCP.

# Further reading

Refer to the following links for more information on topics covered in this chapter:

- `https://docs.microsoft.com/en-us/azure/cost-management-billing/cost-management-billing-overview`: documentation on cost management and billing in Azure
- `https://docs.aws.amazon.com/awsaccountbilling/latest/aboutv2/billing-what-is.html`: documentation on billing in AWS
- `https://cloud.google.com/docs/enterprise/best-practices-for-enterprise-organizations#billing_and_management`: documentation on billing and cost management in GCP

# Section 4 – Security Control in Multi-Cloud with SecOps

Public clouds are likely to be the best secured platforms. However, they only provide you with tools. The responsibility to define and determine which security controls should be in place will always lie with the business. This chapter is about designing and implementing security controls using SecOps.

The following chapters will be covered in this section:

- *Chapter 14, Defining Security Policies*
- *Chapter 15, Implementing Identity and Access Management*
- *Chapter 16, Defining Security Policies for Data*
- *Chapter 17, Implementing and Integrating Security Monitoring*

# 14
# Defining Security Policies

Whatever we do in the cloud, it needs to be secure. Cloud providers only provide tools. You need to define how to use these tools. In order to determine what these tools should do, you need to think about what type of assets you want to protect and how you need to protect them. There are quite a number of security baselines; for example, the baseline as defined by the **Center for Internet Security** (**CIS**), which provides guidelines.

We will learn what a security framework is and why it's important as a starting point for security policies. We will discover what we need to protect in our cloud environments. Next, we will look at the globally adopted CIS benchmark for Azure, AWS, and GCP and learn how to implement CIS using the security suites of these platforms. Lastly, we will learn what the difference is between security governance and management.

In this chapter, we're going to cover the following main topics:

- Understanding security frameworks
- Learning how to define security policies
- Learning how to implement security policies using the CIS benchmark
- Managing security policies

# Understanding security policies

Let's start from our traditional, on-premises data center—a building traditionally used to host physical equipment that runs applications and stores data. The building is very likely secured by a fence and heavy, locked doors that can only be opened by authorized personnel. Access to the computer floors is also secured. There may be guards in the building or CCTV systems watching over equipment 24 hours a day. The next layer of defense is the access to the systems and data. Access to systems is strictly regulated: only authorized and certified engineers may access the systems. It's all common sense when it comes to running systems in a physical data center.

You would be surprised to see what happens if companies move these systems to cloud environments with **Infrastructure as a Service** (**IaaS**), **Platform as a Service** (**PaaS**), and **Software as a Service** (**SaaS**) solutions. For some reason, companies tend to think that by moving systems to the cloud, those systems are secured intrinsically, by default. That is not the case.

Platforms such as Azure, AWS, and GCP are probably the best secured platforms in the world. They have to be since they are hosting thousands of customers globally on them. But this doesn't mean that a company will not have to think about their own security policies anymore. The platforms provide a huge toolbox that enables the securing of workloads in the cloud, but what and how to protect these workloads is still completely up to the companies to implement themselves. We will need to establish and enforce our security policies in the cloud, think them through very carefully, and stick to them. That is what this chapter is about.

As with physical data centers, access needs to be regulated first by defining which identities are authorized to enter systems, and next, by determining what these entities are allowed to do in these systems. This is all part of identity and access management, a topic that we will cover in full in *Chapter 15, Designing Identity and Access Management*.

The foundation for security policies is the CIA principle:

- **Confidentiality**: Assets in the IT environment must be protected from unauthorized access.
- **Integrity**: Assets in the IT environment must be protected from changes that are not specified and unauthorized.
- **Availability**: Assets in the IT environment must be accessible for authorized users.

The security policy itself has nothing to do with technology. The policy merely defines the security principles and how these are safeguarded in the organization. The policy does not define what ports must be opened in a firewall or what type of firewall is required. The policy describes the requirement that assets belonging to a certain function in the enterprise must be protected at a certain level. For example, a business-critical functionality that is relying on a specific stack of applications needs to be available at all times and data loss must be zero. That will lead to an architectural design using mirrored systems, continuous backups, disaster recovery options, and a very strict authorization and authentication matrix for people who must be able to access these systems.

# Understanding security frameworks

Security policies and forthcoming principles do not stand on their own. Typically, they are defined by industry or public frameworks to which a company must adhere. There are two types of frameworks: mandatory industry frameworks and best practices.

Examples of industry frameworks are the **Health Insurance Portability and Accountability Act** (**HIPAA**) for health care and the **Payment Card Industry** (**PCI**) data security standard for financial institutions. These frameworks were created to protect consumers by setting standards to avoid personal data – health status or bank accounts – being compromised. The cloud architect must have a deep understanding of these frameworks since they define how systems must be designed.

Next to these industry frameworks, there are some overall security standards that come from best practices. Examples are the standards of the **International Organization of Standardization** (**ISO**) and the U.S. **National Institute of Standards and Technology** (**NIST**). Specific to the cloud, we have the framework of the CIS.

Cloud providers have adopted the CIS framework as a benchmark for their platforms, as the internationally accepted standard for cybersecurity. The reason is that CIS maps to the most important industry and overall security frameworks such as ISO, NIST, PCI, and HIPAA. The controls of CIS take the principles from these frameworks into account, but it doesn't mean that by implementing CIS controls, a company is automatically compliant to PCI or HIPAA. CIS controls need to be evaluated per company and sometimes per environment.

Basically, there are two levels of CIS controls:

1. Essential basic security requirements that will not impact the functionality of the workloads or service.
2. Recommended settings for environments that require greater security but may impact workloads or services through reduced functionality.

In summary, CIS provides a security framework based on best practices. These are translated into benchmarks that can be adopted for specific platforms and systems: Azure, AWS, and GCP, and the instances in those clouds using operating systems such as Windows Server or various Linux distributions. These benchmarks lead to settings in hardening.

CIS offers recommendations for the following:

- Identity and access management
- Storage accounts
- Database services
- Logging and monitoring
- Networking
- Virtual machines
- Application services

In the next section, we will learn how to define the baseline for security policies.

# Defining the baseline for security policies

It just takes a few mouse clicks to get a server up and running on any cloud platform. But in an enterprise that's migrating or creating systems in the cloud, there's a lot for an architect to think about – securing environments being the top priority. It is likely that IaaS, PaaS, and SaaS solutions will be used to build our environment. It could grow in complexity where a lack of visibility could lead to vulnerabilities. So, with every service enrolled in the cloud environment, we really need to consider how best to secure each service. Every service needs to be compliant with the security baseline and the policies defined in that baseline.

What are the steps for creating policies and the baseline?

1. **Check regulations**: Every company is subject to regulations. These can be legal regulations such as privacy laws or industry compliance standards. Make sure the regulations and compliance frameworks your company needs to adhere to are understood. Be sure to involve internal legal departments and auditors. This is the starting point in all cases.

   Also, check which security frameworks cloud providers have adopted. The major platforms – Azure, AWS, and GCP – are compliant with most of the leading compliance and security frameworks, but this may not be the case for smaller providers, for instance, specific SaaS solutions. Be aware that with SaaS, the provider controls the full stack: operating systems, hardware, network infrastructure, application upgrades, and patches. You have to be sure that this is done in a compliant way for your company.

2. **Restrict access**: This is what is often referred to as zero trust, although the term is even more related to network segmentation. But zero trust is also tightly connected to access management. We will have to design a clear **RBAC** model: **Role-Based Access Control**. Users have specific roles granting authorization to execute certain actions in cloud environments. If they don't have the appropriate role or the right authorization, they will not be able to execute actions other than the ones that have been explicitly assigned to that particular role. One term that is important in this context is least privilege: users only get the role and associated authorizations to perform the minimum number of actions that are really required for the daily job – and nothing more.

3. **Secure connections**: Cloud environments will be connected to the wide area network (WAN) of a company and to the outside world, the internet. The network is the route into cloud environments and must be very well secured. What connections are allowed, how are they monitored, what protocols are allowed, and are these connections encrypted? But also: how are environments in the cloud tenant segmented and how do systems in the tenant communicate with each other? Are direct connections between workloads in the cloud tenant allowed or does all traffic need to go through a centralized hub?

The security baseline should contain strict policies for all connectivity: direct connections, VPNs, in-transit encryption, traffic scanning, and network component monitoring. Again, we should think from the zero trust principle: network segmentation is crucial. The architecture must be designed in such a way that users can't simply hop from one segment of the environment to another. Segments must be contained and workloads inside the segments must be protected. A zero trust architecture typically has zones defined: for instance, a private zone where only inbound traffic is allowed or a public zone that has connections to the outside world. These zones are strictly separated from each other by means of a variety of security elements, firewalls, security groups, or access control lists.

4. **Protect the perimeter**: This is about protecting the outside of the cloud environment, the boundary. Typically, the boundary is where the connections terminate in the cloud environment. This can be a hub and that's where the gateways, proxy servers, and firewalls will be hosted. Typically, it also hosts the bastion host or jump server as a single point of entry where a user is allowed to gain access to the workloads in the environment.
5. **Protect the inside**: There will be workloads in our cloud: servers, applications, containers, and functions. Although there is boundary protection with gateways and firewalls, we must also protect our workloads, especially – but not limited to – the critical ones. These workloads must be hardened, reducing the vulnerability of systems with mandatorily applied security settings such as removing software components or disabling services that are not required to run on the system.
6. **Perform frequent audits**: This is a step that falls within managing security policies, which will be covered in the last section of this chapter. Security policies need to be constantly assessed. Hackers don't sit on their hands and will constantly think of ways to look for vulnerabilities. Therefore, it's necessary to continuously assess and audit policies and evaluate identified vulnerabilities. How critical are those vulnerabilities and what are the odds that our environments will get breached? Are we protected well enough? But also, how fast can action be taken if a vulnerability gets exploited and mitigate the consequences? This is not something that should be discussed once a month, but must be at the front of our minds at all times, for everyone developing or managing cloud environments.

We will need to define the scope of our security policies. One way to do that is by thinking in layers, derived from defense-in-depth as a common methodology in designing security architectures. Each layer comprises protective measures against specific threats. These layers are as follows:

- **Network layer**: As already stated in the previous section, the network is the entrance into our cloud environment. Networks need to be protected from unauthorized people getting in. Technologies to protect a network from threats are firewalls, **Intrusion Detection Systems** and **Intrusion Prevention Systems** (**IDSes/IPSes**), public key infrastructure, and network segmentation, preferably adhering to zero trust principles.
- **Platform layer**: Typically, this is the layer of the operating system. Systems should be fully patched with the latest fixes for (possible) vulnerabilities and hardened. Also, pay attention to ports that are opened on a system. Any port that is not required should be disabled.
- **Application layer**: This layer is not only about the application but also about middleware and APIs communicating directly with the application. Application code must be secured. Static code analysis can be very helpful and is strongly advised. Static program analysis is performed without actually executing software, validating the integrity of source code so that any attempt to change code or software parameters is detected.
- **Data layer**: This is the holy grail for hackers, the very target of almost every hacker. If a hacker succeeds to get through the first three layers – network, platform, and application – then the next layer is the data itself. We will extensively discuss data security in *Chapter 16, Defining Security Policies for Data*. All critical data should be encrypted, in transit and at rest.
- **Response layer**: This is the layer for all security monitoring, typically the layer for **Security Information and Event Management** systems (**SIEM**). This is the layer where all suspicious activity is captured, analyzed, and translated into triggers to execute mitigating actions.

Security policies must be defined and applied at each layer. Now, let's look at some best practices for security policies:

- **Access**: Only use named accounts to allow access to systems. Be extremely selective when granting global admin rights, implement role-based access, and use multi-factor authentication. In the next chapter, we will go into this subject in more detail.
- **Perimeter or boundary protection**: Implement firewalls or use the native firewalls from the cloud platforms. A recommended practice is to have the firewall set to "block all" as the default and then open up ports as per the requirements of a certain workload or functionality. Only have ports open when there's a validated reason.
- **Public Key Infrastructure (PKI)**: Public and private keys are used to verify the identity of a user before data is transferred. Breached passwords are still the number one root cause for compromised systems and data leaks. Therefore, it's recommended not to use passwords, but instead use keys, securely stored in a key vault. All major cloud providers offer PKI services and key vault solutions.
- **Logging and audit trail**: Be sure that you know what happens in your cloud environment, at all times. Even with the most rigid security policy, a company should never fully rely on security measures alone. Monitoring and an audit trail are highly recommended (or required, even) best practices.

Now it's time to discover how these policies should be implemented using the native security suites in Azure, AWS, and GCP.

# Implementing security policies

We have studied the compliance and security frameworks and we've defined our security baseline. Now we need to implement it in our cloud environments. In this section, we will explore implementations in the major clouds, using the native security platforms. Since CIS is widely and globally adopted as the baseline for security policies, all sections will explore specific settings that CIS benchmarks recommend for the different platforms. Links to the benchmarks are provided in the *Further reading* section of this chapter. CIS provides recommendations, but also documents how policies should be implemented.

For example, in GCP there is a recommendation to "ensure Cloud Audit Logging is configured properly across all services and all users from a project." CIS benchmarks also guide users to find where the setting needs to be configured and how; in this example, by going to audit logs at `https://console.cloud.google.com/iam-admin/audit` or by configuring it from the command line:

```
gcloud organizations get-iam-policy ORGANIZATION_ID
gcloud resource-manager folders get-iam-policy FOLDER_ID
gcloud projects get-iam-policy PROJECT_ID
```

The format in the CIS benchmarks is always the same, for all cloud platforms.

# Implementing security policies in Azure Security Center

Azure Security Center is a native service of Azure. In other words, you don't need to install or configure anything. From the Azure console, Security Center can be accessed immediately by simply enabling it. It then starts monitoring workloads that you have deployed in Azure: virtual machines, databases, storage accounts, networking components, and other Azure services.

However, policies will need to be configured in Security Center. CIS lists some recommendations specific to Azure Security Center. The most important one is to activate the standard pricing tier in Security Center: this enables threat detection for all networks and VMs in the Azure tenant. Every CIS recommendation to implement a policy comes with an explanation. In the case of enabling the standard pricing tier, the rationale is that it allows greater defense-in-depth, with threat detection provided by the **Microsoft Security Response Center** (**MSRC**).

Enabling the standard pricing tier and adjusting settings is done through the **Security Center** blade in the portal at `https://portal.azure.com/#home`, as shown in the following screenshot:

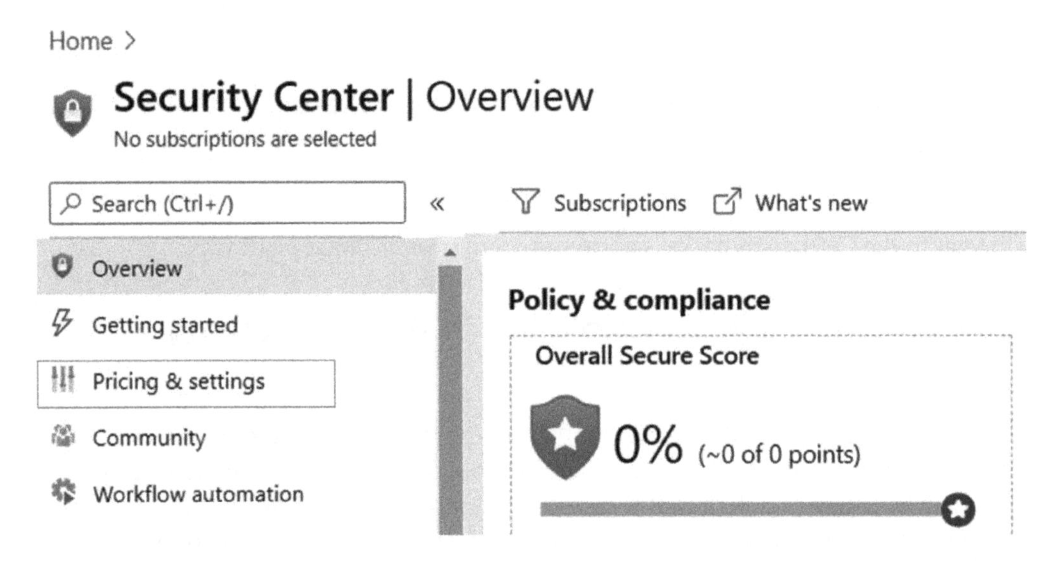


Figure 14.1 – Overview of the Security Center blade in the Azure portal

The next action is to enable the monitoring agent to actually collect the data and make sure that the default policy setting, **Monitor system updates**, is not set to **Disabled**. Enabling this setting retrieves a daily list of available security and critical updates from Microsoft, both for Windows systems and for systems that run Linux distributions. These are the basic configuration settings to get Security Center started.

The next step is to implement the security settings. In Security Center, enable settings for the following:

- Scanning vulnerabilities in operating systems
- Enforcing endpoint protection
- Monitoring disk encryption
- Monitoring network security groups
- Monitoring web application firewalls
- Monitoring next-generation firewalls
- Vulnerability assessment
- Monitoring blob storage encryption

- Monitoring **just-in-time** (**JIT**) network access
- Monitoring adaptive application whitelisting
- Monitoring SQL auditing
- Monitoring SQL encryption

Lastly, there are a few settings that enable communication in case of high-severity alerts, by sending email notifications or text messages.

> **Tip**
>
> Azure has something more than just Azure Security Center: Azure Sentinel, a native SIEM solution. Sentinel is an intelligent defense-in-depth solution, especially when activating the security framework of MITRE ATT&CK® in Sentinel. ATT&CK is a knowledge base that is constantly updated with the latest threats and known attack strategies. A group of developers under the name of BlueTeamLabs have published templates and code to implement ATT&CK in Sentinel. It's worthwhile taking a look at this at `https://github.com/BlueTeamLabs/sentinel-attack`.

# Implementing security policies in AWS Security Hub

AWS offers a single security dashboard with AWS Security Hub. The solution aggregates monitoring alerts from various security solutions, such as CloudWatch and CloudTrail, but also collects findings from Amazon GuardDuty, Amazon Inspector, Amazon Macie, AWS **Identity and Access Management** (**IAM**) Access Analyzer, and AWS Firewall Manager. CloudTrail, however, is the key element in Security Hub. CloudTrail constantly monitors the compliance of accounts that are used in the AWS environment. It also performs operational auditing and risk auditing, meaning it keeps track of all activity that is started from the console in your environment, enables analysis of changes to resources, and detects unusual activity. It's fair to say that CloudTrail is the engine underneath Security Hub.

Security Hub makes it easy to start monitoring all activity in your AWS environment. It's accessible from the AWS console, as shown in the following screenshot:

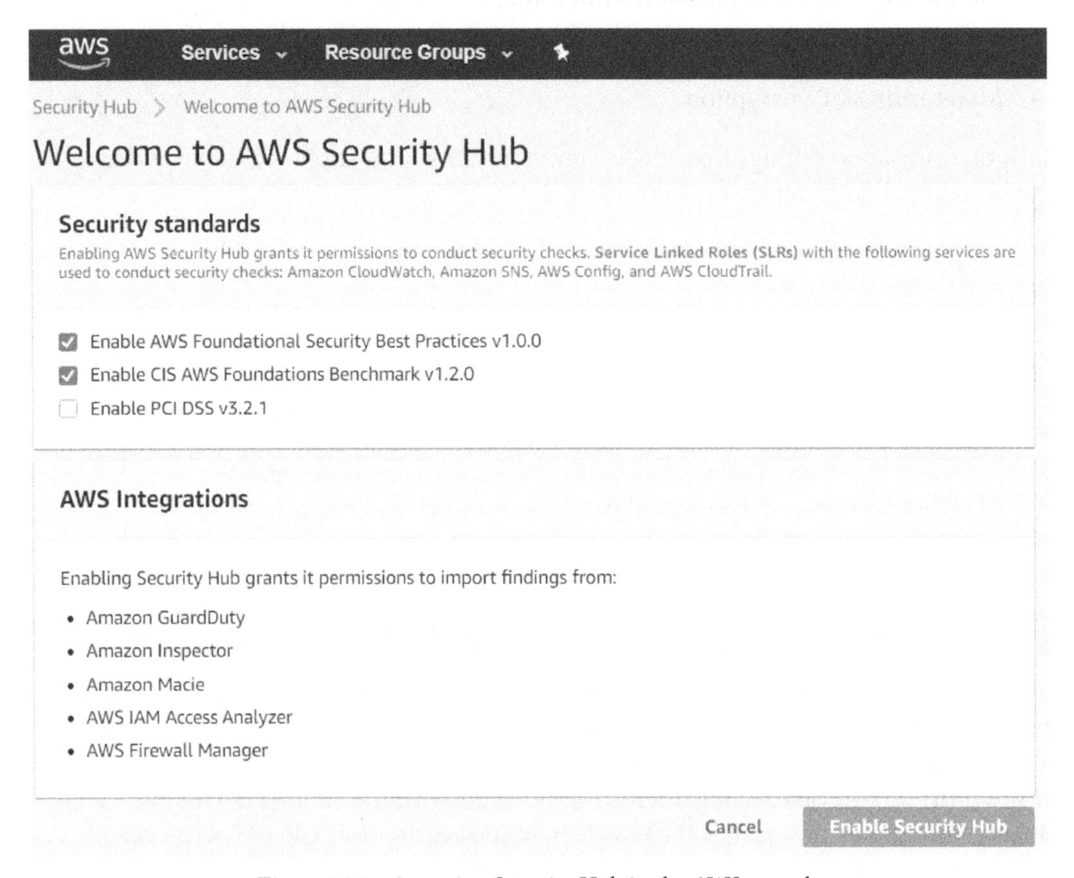


Figure 14.2 – Accessing Security Hub in the AWS console

There are a couple of things that need explaining in the preceding screenshot. The top part of the screen shows the security baselines that can be enrolled by default: **Enable AWS Foundational Security Best Practices v1.0.0** and **Enable CIS AWS Foundations Benchmark v1.2.0** have been ticked by default. The third one is the PCI DSS framework. **PCI DSS** stands for **Payment Card Industry Data Security Standard** and is specific to financial institutions.

In the lower part of the screen, we see all the integrations that Security Hub offers:

- **GuardDuty**: Amazon's solution for threat detection.
- **Inspector**: This tool assesses applications for exposure, vulnerabilities, and deviations from best practices valid for these applications.

- **Macie**: This solution monitors the data security and data privacy of your data stored in Amazon S3 storage.
- **IAM Access Analyzer**: This tool keeps track of accounts accessing environments in AWS and whether these accounts are still compliant with security policies.
- **Firewall Manager**: This tool enables centralized management of all firewalls in the AWS environment.

By clicking the **Enable Security Hub** button, the mentioned baselines with the named integrations will be enrolled.

The CIS baseline should definitively be implemented as the worldwide accepted standard for securing online environments. Specific to AWS, CIS includes the following recommendations for settings to control security policies:

- Ensure CloudTrail is enabled in all regions.
- Ensure CloudTrail log file validation is enabled.
- Ensure that an S3 (storage) bucket used to store CloudTrail logs is not publicly accessible.
- Ensure CloudTrail logs are integrated with CloudWatch logs.
- Ensure AWS Config is enabled in all regions.
- Ensure S3 bucket access logging is enabled on CloudTrail S3 bucket.
- Ensure CloudTrail logs are encrypted at rest using **KMS CMKs** (**Key Management Services – Customer Master Keys**).
- Ensure rotation for customer-created CMKs is enabled.
- Ensure **Virtual Private Cloud** (**VPC**) flow logging in all VPCs.

Obviously, these are not all the settings: these are the most important settings for getting the logging and monitoring of security policies right. In the *Further reading* section, we include links to the various CIS benchmarks for the major clouds.

## Implementing security policies in GCP Security Command Center

In GCP, we will have to work with Security Command Center. You can manage all security settings in Security Command Center and view the compliancy status from one dashboard. The concept is the same as AWS Security Hub – Security Command Center in GCP comprises a lot of different tools to manage security in GCP environments. In the GCP cloud console, we'll see **Security** in the main menu. Hovering over the **Security** subheading will pop up the products and tools that are addressed in **Security Command Center**, as shown in the following screenshot:

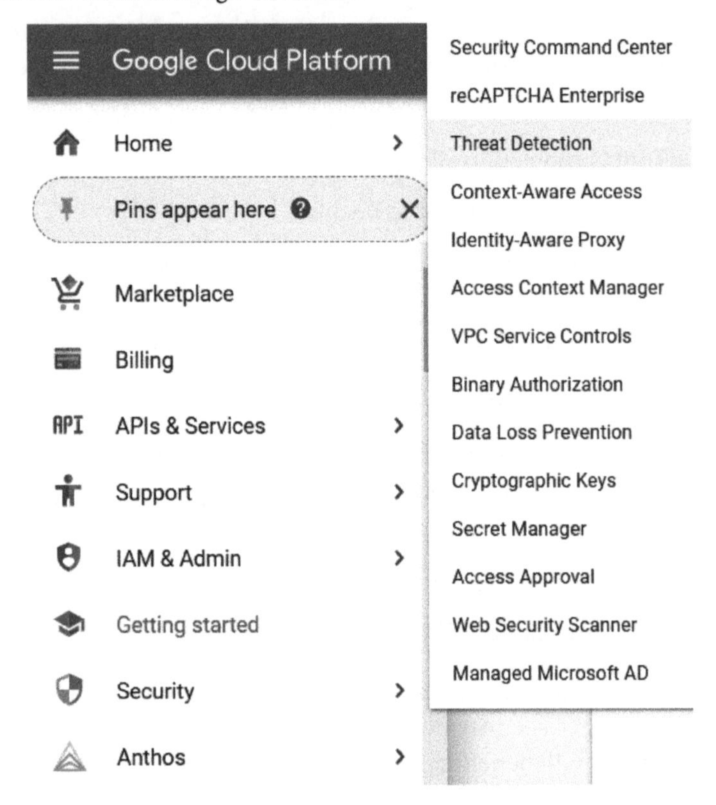


Figure 14.3 – Launching Security Command Center in the cloud console of GCP

Security Command Center does an inventory and discovery of all assets in the GCP environments and, next, starts monitoring them in terms of threat detection and prevention. One special feature that needs to be discussed here is Google Cloud Armor. Cloud Armor started as a defense layer to protect environments in GCP from **Distributed Denial of Services** (**DDoS**) and targeted web attacks. Cloud Armor has since been developed to a full security suite in GCP to protect applications using the functionality of **Web Application Firewalls** (**WAFs**).

Cloud Armor can be launched from the GCP console at `https://console.cloud.google.com/`. You won't find it under **Security Command Center**, but under **Network Security**, as shown in the following screenshot:

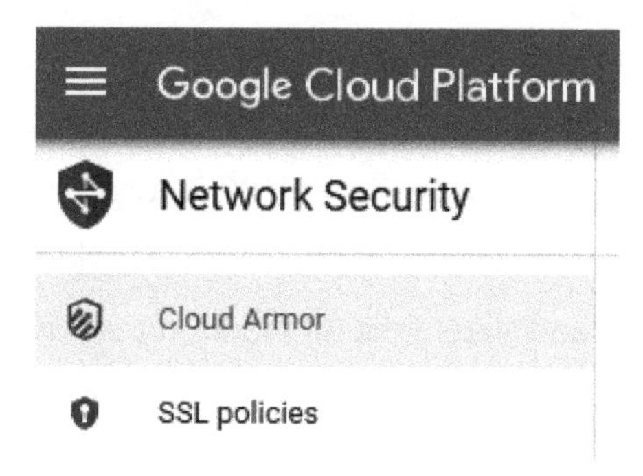


Figure 14.4 – Menu of Cloud Armor in GCP

We can specify security policies in Cloud Armor, but GCP already included a list of policies that can be evaluated. These preconfigured policies are based on **OWASP** CRS—the **Open Web Application Security Project**, a community that strives to find methodologies and practices to constantly improve the protection of online applications. **CRS** stands for **Core Rule Set**. Cloud Armor includes the top 10 OWASP threats in rule sets. The number one threat is the injection of hostile code in order to breach the application and get access to data. In *Chapter 16, Defining Security Policies for Data*, we will explore OWASP in more detail since this is all about securing applications and data.

However, OWASP does overlap with CIS, but OWASP merely identifies the threats, whereas CIS makes recommendations to avoid vulnerabilities and the chances of threats really being exploited. Misconfigured security, for example, is number 6 in the top 10 of OWASP. Insufficient logging and monitoring concludes the top 10. Both are heavily addressed in CIS.

The CIS 1.1.0 benchmark for GCP was released in March 2020. Specifically, for logging and monitoring, CIS recommends the following settings to audit security policies:

- Ensure Cloud Audit Logging is configured properly across all services and users in a project.
- Ensure sinks are configured for all log entries.

> **Note**
> A sink will export copies of all the log entries.

- Retention policies on log buckets must be configured using Bucket Lock.

- Ensure log metric filters and alerts exist for project ownership assignments and changes.
- Ensure log metric filters and alerts exist for audit configuration changes.
- Ensure log metric filters and alerts exist for custom role changes.
- Ensure log metric filters and alerts exist for VPC Network Firewall rule changes.
- Ensure log metric filters and alerts exist for VPC Network Route changes.
- Ensure log metric filters and alerts exist for VPC Network changes.
- Ensure log metric filters and alerts exist for cloud storage IAM permission changes.
- Ensure log metric filters and alerts exist for SQL instance configuration changes.

As with Azure and AWS, these are the settings to audit the security policies against the CIS benchmark. In the *Further reading* section, we included links to the various CIS benchmarks for the major clouds.

# Managing security policies

It doesn't stop with implementing security policies. We need to have governance in place to manage the policies. Governance is required on two levels:

1. The security policies themselves, auditing these to the compliancy frameworks that a business has to adhere to.
2. The technical implementation of the security policies, keeping the monitoring up to date, making sure that all assets are indeed tracked against the policies.

The first level is the domain of people concerned with the security governance in a business, typically, a **Chief Information Security Officer (CISO)** or **Chief Information Officer (CIO)**. They need to set directions for security policies and make sure that the business is compliant with the security strategy, industry, and company frameworks. The CISO or CIO is also responsible for assurance from internal and external auditing.

Level two is more about security management, concerning how to deal with security risks in the IT landscape, including the cloud environments. To make it simple: security governance is about making policies; security management is about (technically) implementing and enforcing policies. So, security engineers should worry about the management of security monitoring tools that were covered in this chapter. They will need to understand how to implement rule sets in Azure Security Center, AWS Security Hub, and Google Security Command Center. They will also need to know what to do in the event of an alert being raised in these systems, who should follow up, and what actions need to be taken. Those will be technical actions, such as isolating an environment when it's breached. The configuration of rules in the security suites is also in their hands.

However, the security policies themselves need to be defined from a higher level in the business. The CISO or CIO will hardly ever completely understand how to program the security console, but they will know what needs to be protected from a business perspective. Obviously, the strategic level of CISO/CIO can't do anything without input from the tactical level – the security architects and engineers. They will all have to work closely together.

# Summary

In this chapter, we discussed the basics of security frameworks as a starting point to define policies for cloud environments. We have learned that there are different frameworks and that it depends on the industry to determine the compliance requirements of a business. Next, we must decide which security controls to set to ensure that our cloud environments are compliant too.

One framework that is globally accepted and commonly used for clouds is CIS. For Azure, AWS, and GCP, we studied the CIS benchmarks. We learned that the CIS benchmarks for these cloud platforms greatly overlap, but also have specific settings that need to be implemented in the respective security suites – Azure Security Center, AWS Security Hub, and Google's Security Command Center.

In the last section, we learned the difference between security governance and security management, but also that one can't live without the other.

In the next chapter, we will dive into identity and access management, since that's where security typically starts: who is allowed to do what, how, and maybe even when in our cloud environments? In *Chapter 17, Using Security Monitoring and Management Tools*, we will further explore the use of the monitoring tools that we discussed briefly in this chapter.

# Questions

1. We've discussed the CIA principle. What does it stand for?
2. What are public and private keys used for in terms of PKI?
3. All major cloud platforms have adopted a certain security baseline. Name the framework that comprises this baseline.
4. True or false: the CIO should be concerned with security management.

# Further reading

You can refer to the following links for more information on the topics covered in this chapter:

- The CIS framework: `https://www.cisecurity.org/`
- The download page for CIS Benchmark for Azure: `https://azure.microsoft.com/en-us/resources/cis-microsoft-azure-foundations-security-benchmark/`
- The CIS baseline for AWS: `https://d0.awsstatic.com/whitepapers/compliance/AWS_CIS_Foundations_Benchmark.pdf`
- The CIS benchmark for GCP: `https://www.cisecurity.org/benchmark/google_cloud_computing_platform/`
- Link to the OWASP community pages: `https://owasp.org/www-project-top-ten/#:~:text=The%20OWASP%20Top%2010%20is%20the%20reference%20standard,software%20development%20culture%20focused%20on%20producing%20secure%20code`
- *Enterprise Cloud Security and Governance*, by Zeal Vora, Packt Publishing

# 15 Implementing Identity and Access Management

In *Chapter 4*, *Service Design for Multi-Cloud*, we discussed governance in multi-cloud. In that chapter, we learned that everything and everyone has an identity in the cloud. It is the core principle of identity and access management in cloud. In this chapter, we will learn how we can manage identities and control their behavior by granting them specific roles that allow them to perform only those activities that are related to the primary job of an administrator. We will see that **Role-Based Access Control** (**RBAC**) is very important to keep our cloud environments secure. We will learn about authenticating and authorizing identities, how to deal with least privileged accounts, what eligible accounts are, and why a central depository is needed. We will learn how we can federate with Active Directory from Azure, AWS, and Google Cloud.

After this chapter, you will have a good understanding of technologies such as federation, single sign-on, multi-factor authentication, privileged access management, and **Identity as a Service** (**IDaaS**).

In this chapter, we're going to cover the following main topics:

- Understanding identity and access management
- Using a central identity store with Active Directory
- Designing access management across multi-cloud
- Exploring Privileged Access Management (PAM)
- Enabling account federation in multi-cloud

# Understanding identity and access management

**Identity and access management** (**IAM**) is all about controlling access to IT systems that are critical to a business. A key element of IAM is **Role-Based Access Control**, **RBAC** for short. In an RBAC model, we define who is alleged to have access to systems, what their role is, and what they are allowed to do according to that role. An important principle of RBAC is **least privilege**, meaning that a system administrator will only get the rights assigned that are required to perform the job assigned. For example, a database administrator needs access to the database, but it's not very likely that they will need access to network switches too.

In this chapter, we will discuss concepts such as **single sign-on** (**SSO**), **multi-factor authentication** (MFA), and **Privileged Access Management** (**PAM**). Before we go into that, let's have a look at the basics of IAM. There are three layers that we have to consider in our architecture:

- **Managed identities**: In this book, we've written a number of times that in cloud environments, everything should be perceived as an identity. Identities must be known: users, systems, APIs – everything that communicates with components in your cloud environment and with people or systems in the outside world.
- **Managed roles**: Roles must be defined in our cloud environments and assigned to identities. This includes the process of adding, removing, and updating roles. This is not only valid for persons, but also for systems. A system is an identity and has a specific role: for instance, a domain controller or application server. Thus, system authorizations must be defined and access rights must be given to resources.

- **Managed access**: This is the definition of who and what are given appropriate levels of access. To use the example of the database administrator once more, a database administrator needs access to the database and not to a network switch. If the database resides in a specific virtual network within the cloud environment, the administrator may need access to that network as well. However, that access should be limited; it is only needed to get to the database. That must be defined in the role.

On all three layers, the principle of least privilege is valid and must be followed through to obtain maximum protection of (sensitive) data in systems. The following diagram shows the main principles and related services of IAM:

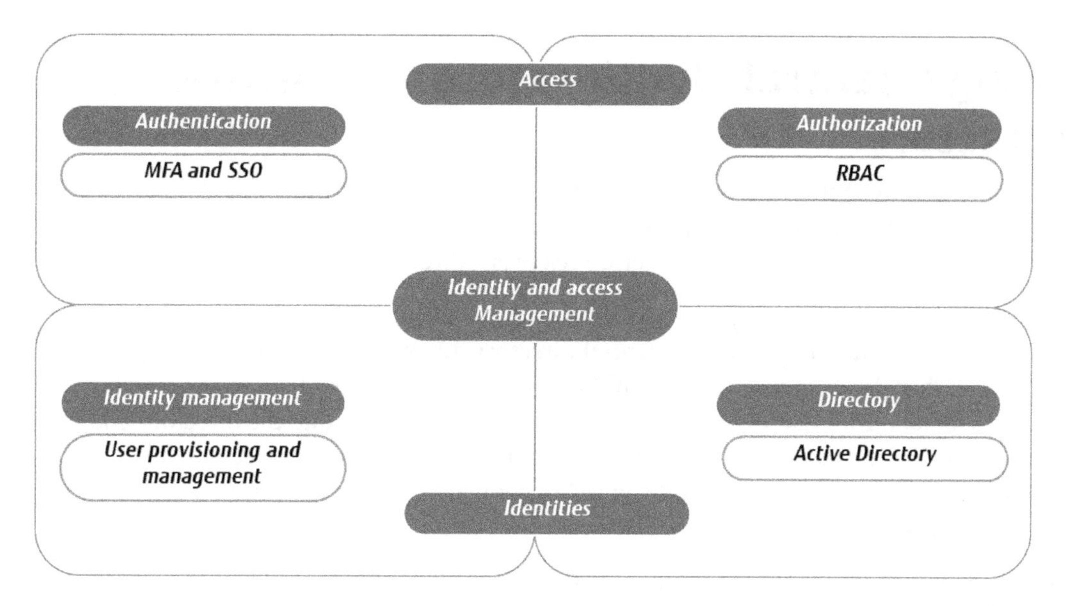


Figure 15.1 – Main principles of IAM

The next step is to define what an IAM system needs to do and what sort of tools it provides to control identities and access to our cloud systems.

Primarily, it needs to enable us to control identities. IAM should therefore contain a directory, basically a database that holds all identities. Typically, this directory contains the entities that will access the systems. Almost all enterprises use Active Directory (AD) as their central directory. AD uses objects. An object represents an entity and that can be a user or a computer. It also defines to which domain an object belongs.

Next, the IAM systems must be enabled to grant entities roles and the associated access. If a user is added and a role is assigned to that user, then the IAM system makes sure that access rights are provisioned to that user. Typically, roles and groups will be defined in the directory so that all that remains is to assign a user or object to that role or group. Access rights on the appropriate level are then automatically enabled. IAM should also facilitate a review process: only a few admins should have rights to add users to or remove users and objects from a directory. A user can request specific access, but they will always need a review and approval before rights are actually assigned. PAM and **Privileged Identity Management** (**PIM**) can be tools to define that process. We will explore these concepts in the next sections.

# Using a central identity store with Active Directory

Before we get into **Active Directory** (**AD**) itself, it's important to understand that it should definitively not be confused with Azure Active Directory. The latter is an authentication service in Azure, whereas Active Directory really is a directory.

Understanding AD is not easy, but basic knowledge is necessary when talking about IAM. An enterprise should only have one central directory. Identities should only be kept in one place. That also comes with a risk: if the directory gets breached, an attacker will have access to all identities that exist within the enterprise. It's crucial that the directory and the IAM system is very secure and that directory data is extremely well protected. This is an area where tools such as Saviynt and CyberArk come in: they add an extra security layer on top of IAM.

Both Saviynt and CyberArk offer solutions that are deployed on top of IAM, providing vaults and a way to secure access to systems, for instance, by hashing passwords in encrypted vaults so that users actually don't see passwords, but get them provided by the tools. These tools can also record sessions of logging into systems to enable maximum visibility of activity in an environment, often referred to as an audit trail.

Let's get back to the identity store and AD. The term is very much associated with Microsoft, as it was developed by that company for Windows domain networks. In the meantime, it has become a widely accepted term for the concept itself. AD comprises basically two major components, which are both relevant in cloud environments. The first component is the directory itself; the second component is the domain services.

Domain services comprise a domain controller that authorizes and authenticates objects – users and computers – in a network. That network can be in a public cloud. It can also be a standalone network, but more often, the internal network of the enterprise is extended to a cloud. Extended may not be the right word, though. The enterprise on-premises network and cloud network(s) are merely connected or – it's even better to say – we connect the domains.

To be able to do that, domain controllers are needed in the public cloud. The domain controller makes sure that a specific part of the public cloud is now within our domain. For all of this, AD Federation Services can be used to federate the domain in the cloud with the directory that enterprises already have, commonly on-premises. The following diagram shows **My Company X** with the AD on-premises. There is an environment in a public cloud as well. That environment federates with the on-premises AD:

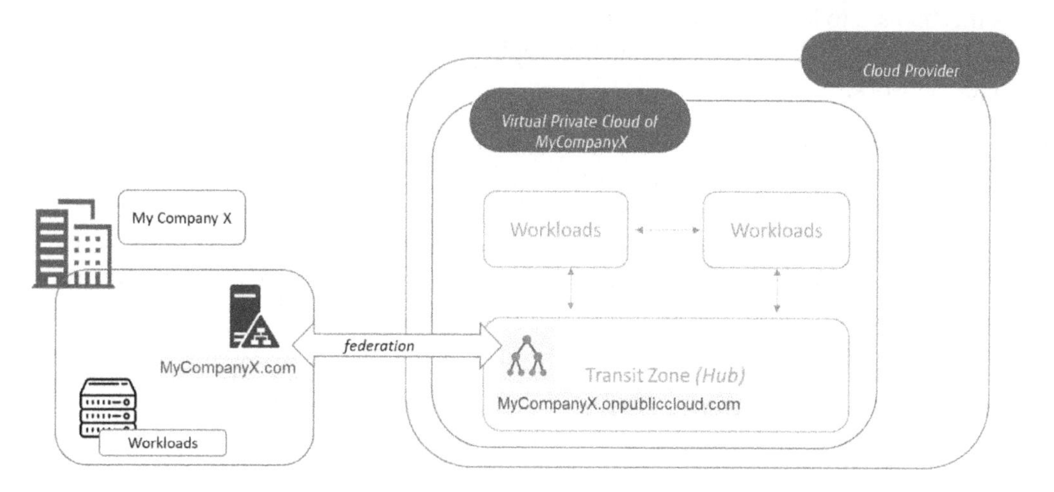


Figure 15.2 – Conceptual overview of AD federation

Microsoft AD uses **Lightweight Directory Access Protocol** (**LDAP**), Kerberos, and Domain Name Services for these services. LDAP enables authentication and storing data about objects and also applications. Kerberos is used to prove the identity of an object to another object that it communicates with. DNS enables the translation of IP addresses to domain names and vice versa.

This concludes the section about AD and how it's used as an identity store. The next section will explain how access to clouds is controlled.

# Designing access management across multi-cloud

In the previous section, we learned that we need to have federation with AD in our public cloud environment. The next question is: *how do we do that?* Azure uses **Azure Active Directory** (**AAD**). Just as a reminder: AAD is not the same as AD. AAD is an authentication service in Azure, using AD as the directory. Microsoft positions AAD as IDaaS, something that we will explore in more detail in the last section of this chapter, *Enabling account federation in multi-cloud*. The primary function of AAD is to synchronize identities to the cloud – Azure – using the existing AD. For the synchronization, it uses Azure AD Connect.

With AAD, enterprises will have a system that provides employees of these enterprises with a mechanism to log in and access resources on different platforms. That can be resources in Azure itself or resources such as applications hosted on systems in the corporate network.

But AAD also provides access to SaaS solutions such as Office365 and applications that can integrate with Azure. AAD makes sure that users only have to log in once using SSO. It's secured by MFA, meaning that when a user logs in by typing in a password, it is not enough. A second validation is needed to prove their identity. This can be a pin code through a text message or an authenticator app on a mobile device, but also a fingerprint. If the user is authenticated, access is granted to federated services.

The federation between the domains in the corporate network and the corporate domain in Azure cloud is done with **Active Directory Federation Services** (**ADFS**). In the cloud, a corporate cloud domain is situated on the domain of the public cloud itself. In Azure, that is defined by `onmicrosoft.com`: this domain name address signifies that an environment resides in Azure.

Now, if we have company X, which has its domain specified as `companyx.com` and it wants to have an environment in Azure, the domain in Azure would probably be `company.onmicrosoft.com`. Next, trust must be established between the corporate domain and the domain in Azure with ADFS. AD federation in Azure is shown in *Figure 15.2*.

The good news is that it works exactly the same in AWS and GCP. In AWS, ADFS can be enabled as a component of the AWS Federated Authentication service. With ADFS, a user is authenticated against the central identity store, AD. After authentication, ADFS returns an assertion – a statement – that permits the logging into AWS using AWS **Security Token Service** (**STS**). STS returns temporary credentials based on `AssumeRoleWithSAML`, which next allows access to the AWS Management Console of the enterprise environments in AWS. The following diagram shows the concept:

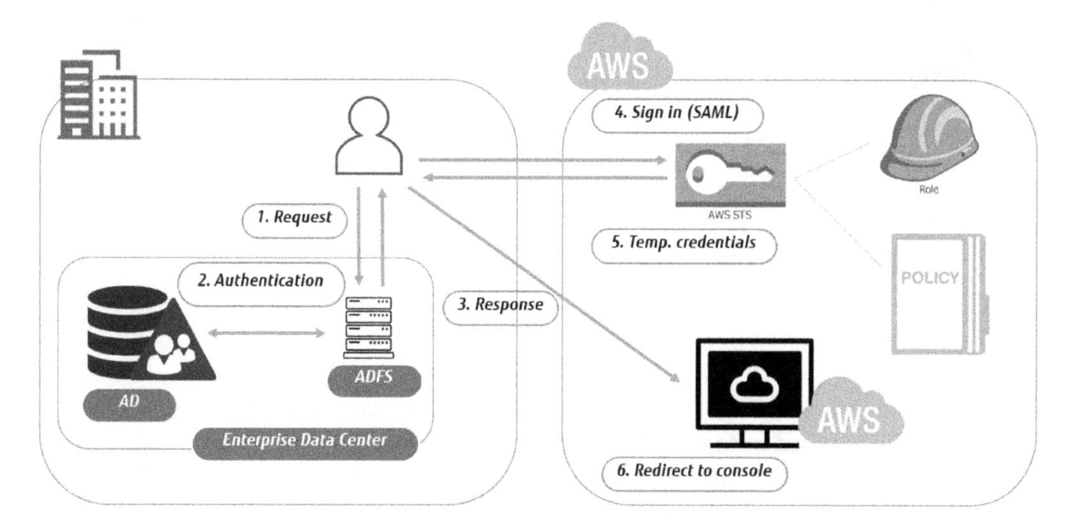


Figure 15.3 – Concept of AWS federated authentication

`AssumeRoleWithSAML` is something specific to AWS. This function in STS is providing a way to authenticate against the identity store with role-based AWS access. It uses **Security Assertion Markup Language** (**SAML**), an open standard for exchanging authentication and authorization data between parties, such as the identity store at a corporate level and the cloud provider. Yes, it's comparable to LDAP, but SAML is more commonly used in the cloud.

Also, GCP embraces SAML to do AD federation. At GCP, it starts with Google Cloud Identity, the service that GCP uses for IAM. But Google also understands that enterprises typically already have an identity store with AD. We can set up federation between GCP's Cloud Identity or G Suite and enable user provisioning from AD, including SSO. SSO is done through SAML.

For the actual federation, we use Google Cloud Directory Sync, a free service from Google. The concept is shown in the following diagram:

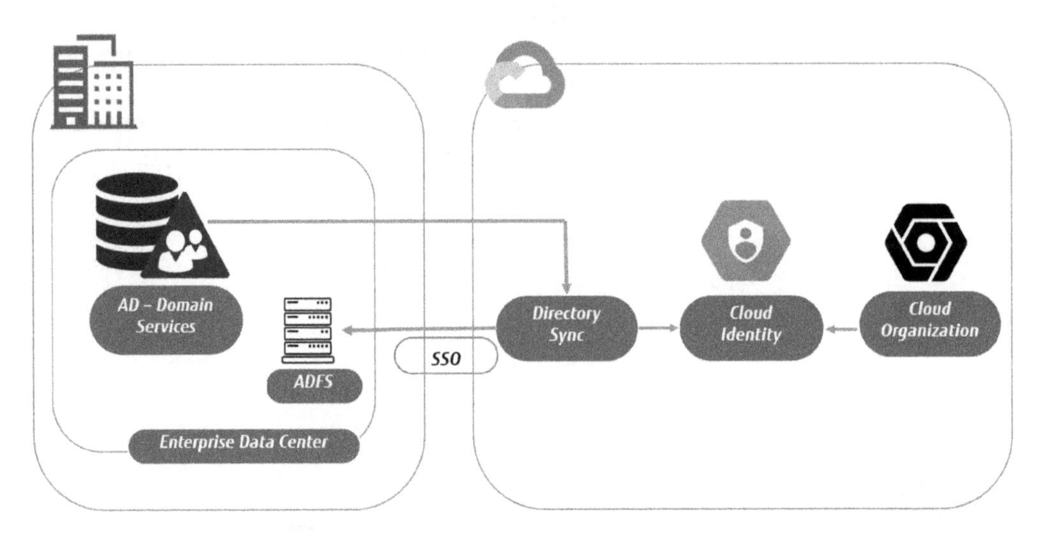


Figure 15.4 – Concept of Google Directory Sync

In all of these concepts, it's important to understand how the corporate AD is set up. This set up needs to be mapped to the IAM policies in the cloud platform. AD has a logical division with forests, trees, domains, and organizational units. Forests are the top-level segment of an AD and contain the root-level domain. Objects such as computers and users are grouped in domains. A group of domains forms a tree. Domains and trees within one forest trust each other.

In a public cloud, this division of forests, trees, and domains might not map by default to the structure that a public cloud has. Using GCP as an example, organizations are the container boundaries that hold the resources within GCP. Organizations contain all the projects that can be hierarchically subdivided into folders. These structures have to be mapped to the AD structure, otherwise federation will fail, leading to objects and users that can't authenticate nor have access to specific resources in cloud environments.

It's beyond the scope of this book to do a deep dive of AD, but in the *Further reading* section, we've listed literature that provides more in-depth insights.

# Exploring Privileged Access Management (PAM)

In previous sections, the principle of least privilege was introduced: users only get the minimum set of rights to the systems that they are authorized for/require. Least privilege works with non-privileged accounts or **least-privileged user accounts** (**LUA**). Typically, there are two types of LUA:

- Standard user accounts
- Guest user accounts

Both types of accounts are very limited in terms of user rights.

There are situations where these accounts simply aren't sufficient and inhibit people from trying to do their job. The user would then need elevated rights: rights that are temporarily assigned so that the user can continue with their work. An account with such elevated rights is called a **privileged account**. Examples of privileged accounts are the following:

- **Domain administrative accounts**: Accessing all resources in the domain
- **AD accounts**: Accessing AD with rights to, for example, add or remove identities
- **Application accounts**: Accessing applications and databases to run, for example, batch jobs or execute scripts

A special category would be the break glass accounts, sometimes referred to as emergency accounts. These are accounts that function as a last resort when users are completely locked out of an environment. The break glass account is an account that has access to all resources and has all the rights to literally unlock the environments again.

The issue with these accounts is that they form a much bigger risk than standard, non-privileged accounts. If privileged accounts get breached, a hacker can have control over critical systems and functions. PAM is a solution that mitigates these risks. In short, PAM makes sure that elevated rights can only be used by specified accounts for specific systems at a specified time and for specified reasons.

The principle behind this is called **just-in-time** and just enough administration. In this principle, an administrator can decide that specific users need certain privileges to perform tasks on systems. But these users will not get these privileges permanently; that would be a violation of the least privilege principle. These users will get eligible accounts, meaning that when a user needs to perform a certain task, the rights to do so will be elevated. To enable the eligible account, the user will need permission that expires after a pre-set time window.

So, the user requests permission to enable the elevated rights from the privileged account. Permission is granted for one, two, or the number of hours that are needed to perform the tasks. After the time has expired, the rights are automatically withdrawn.

## PAM on cloud platforms

How does this work on cloud platforms? PAM only works if the principle of least privilege is applied: what privileged accounts are needed, and what roles they will have. The cloud platforms all have an extensive role-based model that can be applied, enabling execution at a granular access level with separation of duties for resources.

Cloud providers work with only a few built-in general role types: roles that can do everything in the cloud tenant, roles that can do specific things in certain areas of the tenant, and roles that can only view things. In addition to those, there's often a role for the purpose of adding users and roles in the tenant. That's not sufficient for a role-based access model that requires more granularity. Cloud providers provide that and have roles specifically for network administrators, database administrators, or even very particular roles just for managing the backups of specific websites.

With a clear overview of our accounts and the roles that these accounts have, PAM can be configured in cloud environments. Azure offers PIM as their solution to identify and set eligible accounts. Be aware that this requires a premium license for AD in Azure. PIM sets eligible accounts, activates JIT, and configures MFA.

In AWS, PAM features are included in the IAM solution. Like Azure, AWS offers a role-based access model and the possibilities of having privileged accounts, using elevated rights, SSO, and MFA. The logic starts with requests being denied by default, except for the root account, which has full access. There must be an explicit `allow` in an identity or resource policy that overrides the default policy. If these policies exist and are validated, then access is allowed. AWS IAM checks every policy that is connected to the request.

As with many other services on their platform, AWS allows third parties to provide solutions on top of the native technology – in this case, AWS IAM. Both Saviynt and CyberArk are two vendors among the third parties that have developed PAM solutions for AWS.

Lastly, we will look at GCP. GCP offers cloud identities and, like the other clouds, a model for role-based access. One particular feature that needs mentioning here is Recommender. This feature provides usage recommendations to optimize GCP environments, but it also comprises tools to manage IAM in GCP. IAM Recommender automatically detects identities that may lead to security risks and can even remove unwanted access to resources. It uses smart access control.

From the Google Cloud console, the IAM page lists all accounts and the permissions that these accounts have. IAM Recommender displays the number of unused permissions over the past 90 days and will make recommendations, such as to replace the role with an account with a predefined role in Cloud Identity or to create a custom role with the appropriate rights. By doing so, we enforce least privilege in GCP.

# Enabling account federation in multi-cloud

We saw in *Chapter 2, Business Acceleration Using a Multi-Cloud Strategy*, that businesses are shifting more and more from software to services. Companies are looking more to adopt SaaS solutions. Typically, a user would have to log in to separate SaaS solutions, since these are provisioned from a service provider. The risk is that users create new passwords to log in to SaaS solutions. It's easy to lose control of who has access to what. This can be solved through SSO, but the directories of SaaS solutions or web applications need to be federated in that case.

In the field of account federation, Okta has become an increasingly popular IAM solution in recent years. To avoid confusion, it's not an alternative to AD. AD is typically the primary, central directory; Okta is a solution that utilizes AD and takes care of the federation to web applications using single sign-on (SSO). That's what Okta does: it enables IAM with SSO on top of AD.

This is also referred to as an IDaaS solution – a cloud-based service that enables cross-cloud authentication. This is a third-party solution that manages the identities of an enterprise and offers features such as MFA and SSO. These solutions will still need a central directory, though. IDaaS can federate with the existing AD or companies can use a central directory from the IDaaS provider. With the latter option, companies can achieve savings, since they won't be needing on-premises servers and software to host the directory themselves. The diagram shows the high-level concept of IDaaS, enabling authentication and SSO to different SaaS services from one directory:

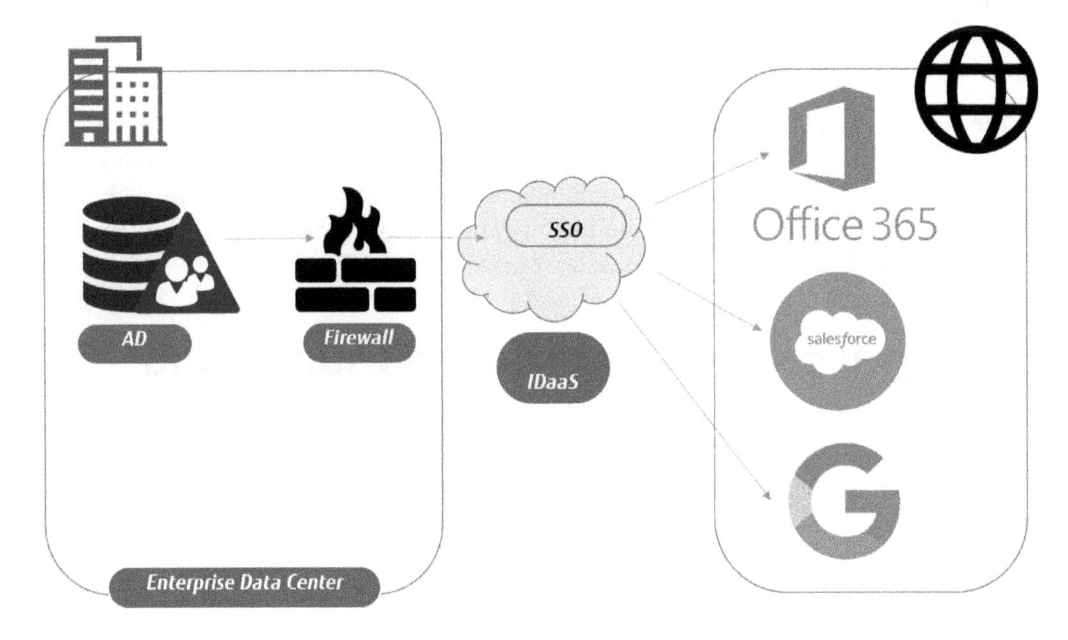


Figure 15.5 – High-level concept of IDaaS

To be clear, doing so will move all identities fully to the cloud. It's really a decision for the **Chief Information Security Officer** (**CISO**) or **Chief Information Officer** (**CIO**) to adopt this shift.

Enterprises will need federation using cloud solutions, though. Companies tend to have complex IT environments comprising on-premises systems, IaaS, PaaS, and SaaS. To be able to connect everything, as it were, all in one domain, federation is required. An IDaaS solution can be a valuable option to connect the existing AD to all these different solutions and enable secure access management to them.

# Summary

Security starts with IAM: making sure that we have control over who's accessing our environments and what they are allowed to do in systems. In this chapter, we have learned what identities are and that we need a central identity store. From this identity store, we have to federate between the different cloud solutions that an enterprise has. We have learned how we can set up federation and how IDaaS can be a good solution for this.

We've studied concepts of authorization and authentication in the major cloud platforms. An important concept is least privilege. After this chapter, you should be able to make a distinction between standard accounts and privileged accounts. Lastly, we have learned what benefits PAM can have in securing access to our clouds.

The reason to have our cloud environments maximally secured is to protect our data. We have studied identities, access management, and security policies to protect our infrastructure. In the next chapter, we will learn how we should define security policies to keep our data safe.

# Questions

1. In IAM, we have three layers that we must consider to identify identities. Can you name them?
2. Both AWS and GCP use a specific protocol for authentication. What's that protocol?
3. If a standard account isn't sufficient, we can "promote" users temporarily with another account that holds more rights. How do we name these accounts?

# Further reading

You can refer to *Mastering Active Directory*, by Dishan Francis, Packt Publishing, for more information on Active Directory.

# 16
# Defining Security Policies for Data

Data is an important asset of any company. Enterprises store their data more and more in multi-cloud. How do they secure data? All cloud platforms have technologies to encrypt data but differ on how they apply encryption and store and handle keys. But data will move from one cloud to another or to user devices, so data needs to be secured in transit, next to data at rest. This is done with encryption, using encryption keys. These keys need to be secured as well, preventing non-authorized users from accessing the keys and encrypted data.

Before we discuss data protection itself, we will briefly talk about data models and how we can classify data. We will explore the different storage solutions the major clouds offer. Next, we will learn how data can be protected by defining policies for **data loss prevention** (**DLP**), information labeling to control access, and using encryption.

In this chapter, we're going to cover the following main topics:

- Storing data in multi-cloud concepts
- Exploring storage solutions
- Understanding data encryption
- Securing access, encryption, and storage keys
- Securing raw data for big data modeling

# Storing data in multi-cloud concepts

If you ask a **chief information officer** (**CIO**) what the most important asset of the business is, the answer will be very likely be *data*. The data architecture is therefore a critical part of the entire business and IT architecture. It's probably also the hardest part in business architecture. In this section, we will briefly discuss the generic principles of data architecture and how this drives data security in the cloud.

Data architecture consists of three layers – or data architecture processes – in enterprise architecture:

- **Conceptual**: A conceptual model describes the relation between business entities. Both products and customers can be entities. A conceptual model connects these two entities: there's a relationship between a product and the customer. That relationship can be a sale: the business selling a product to a customer. Conceptual data models describe the dependencies between business processes and the entities that are related to these processes.
- **Logical**: The logical model holds more detail than the conceptual model. An enterprise will likely have more than one customer and more than one product. The conceptual model only tells us that there is a relation between the entity customer and the entity product. The next step would be to define the relation between a specific customer and product. Customers can be segregated by adding, for instance, a customer number. The conceptual model only holds the structure; the logical model adds information about the customer entity, such that customer X has a specific relation with product Y within the entity product.
- **Physical**: Neither conceptual nor logical models say anything about the real implementation of a data model in a database. The physical layer holds the blueprint for a specific database, including the architecture for location, data storage, or database technology.

The following diagram shows the relationship between conceptual data modeling and the actual data – data requirements are set on a business level, leading to technical requirements on the storage of the data and eventually the data entry itself:

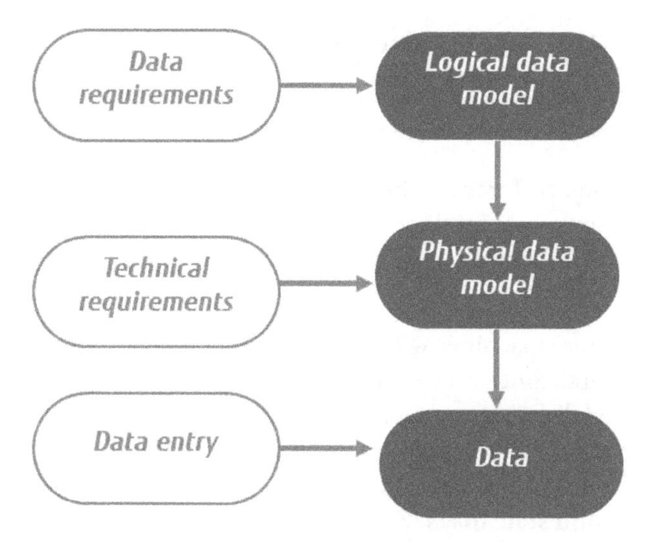


Figure 16.1 – Concept of data modeling

Data modeling is about structuring data. It doesn't say anything about the data types or data security, for that matter. Those are the next steps.

Each data type needs to be supported by a data model. Each data type drives the choice for the technology used to store and access data. Common data types are integers (numeric), strings, characters, and Booleans. The latter might be better known as true/false statements since a Boolean can only have two values. Alongside these, there are abstract types, such as stacks (a data structure where the last entered data is put on top of the stack), lists (countable sequences), and hashes (associative mappings of values).

Data types are not related to the content of data itself. A numeric type doesn't say whether data is confidential or public. So, after the model and the definition of data types, there's also data classification. The most common labels for classification are public, confidential, sensitive, and personal data. For example, personal data needs to be highly secured. There are national and international rules and laws forcing organizations to protect personal data at the highest possible level, meaning that no one should be able to access this data without reasons justified by legal authorities. This data will be stored in strings, arrays, and records and will likely have a lot of connections to other data sources.

An architect will have to think about security on different layers to protect the data, including the data itself, the database where the data is stored, and the infrastructure that hosts the database. If the data model is well-architected, there will be a good overview of what the dependencies and relationships are between data sources.

# Exploring storage technologies

Aside from data modeling and data types, it's also important to consider the storage technologies themselves. All cloud platforms offer services for the following:

- **Object storage**: Object storage is the most used storage type in the cloud – we can use it for applications, content distribution, archiving, and big data. In Azure, we can use Blob; in AWS, **Simple Storage Services** (**S3**); and GCP simply calls it Cloud Storage.
- **Virtual disks**: Virtual machines will either be comprised of a virtual disk of block storage or ephemeral. Since every component in the cloud is virtualized and defined as code, the virtual disk is also a separate component that must be specified and configured. There are a lot of choices, but the key differentiators are the required performance of a disk. For I/O-intensive read/write operations to disks, it is advisable to use **solid state disks** (**SSD**). Azure offers managed disks and AWS has **Elastic Block Store** (**EBS**). GCP offers SSD persistent disks – the VMs access these disks as if they were physically attached to the VM.
- **Shared files**: To organize data in logical folders that can be shared for usage, filesystems are created. The cloud platforms offer separate services for filesystems – in Azure, it's simply called Files; in AWS, **Elastic File System** (**EFS**); and in GCP, the service is called Filestore. GCP does suggest using persistent disks as the most common option.
- **Archiving**: The final storage tier is archiving. For archiving, high-performance SSDs are not required. To lower storage costs, the platforms offer specific solutions to store data that is not frequently accessed but that needs to be stored for a longer period of time, referred to as a retention period. Be aware that the storage costs might be low but the cost of retrieving data from archive vaults will typically be higher than in other storage solutions. In Azure, there's a storage archive access tier, where AWS offers S3 Glacier and Glacier Deep Archive. In GCP, there are Nearline, Coldline, and Archive – basically different tiers of archive storage.

The following diagram shows the relationship between the data owner, the actual storage of data in different solutions, and the data user:

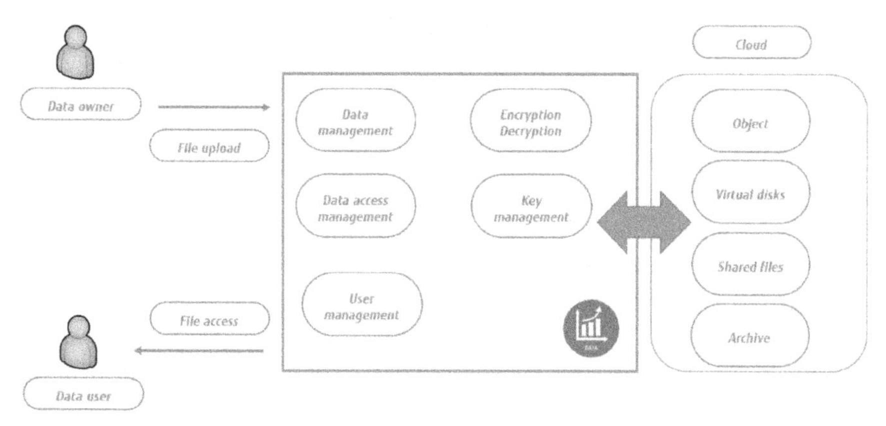


Figure 16.2 – Conceptualized data model showing the relation between the data owner, data usage, and the data user

All mentioned solutions are ways to store data in cloud environments. In the next section, the principles of data protection are discussed.

# Understanding data protection in the cloud

In a more traditional data center setup, an enterprise would probably have physical machines hosting the databases of a business. Over the last two decades, we've seen a tremendous growth in data, up to the point where it has almost become impossible to store this data in on-premises environments – something that is often referred to as big data. That's where public clouds entered the market.

With storing data in external cloud environments, businesses were confronted with new challenges to protect this data. First of all, the data was no longer in on-premises systems but in systems that were all handled by third-party companies. This means that data security has become a shared responsibility – the cloud provider needs to offer tools and technologies to be able to protect the data on their systems, but the companies themselves still need to define what data they need to protect and to what extent. It's still largely the responsibility of the enterprise to adhere to compliance standards, laws, and other regulations.

There's more to consider about data than its current or live state. An enterprise should be equally concerned about historical data that is archived. Too often, data protection is limited to live data in systems, but should also focus on archived data. Security policies for data must include live and historical data. In the architecture, there must be a mapping of data classification and there must be policies in place for **data loss prevention (DLP)**.

Data classification enables companies to apply labels to data. DLP prevents sensitive data from being transferred outside an organization. For that, it uses business rules and data classification. DLP software prevents classified data from being accessed and transferred outside the organization. To set these rules, data is usually grouped, based on the classification. Next, definitions of how data may be accessed and by whom are established. This is particularly important for data that can be accessed through APIs, for instance, by applications that connect to business environments. Business data in a **customer relationship management** (**CRM**) system might be accessed by an application that is also used for the sales staff of a company, but the company wouldn't want the data to be accessed by Twitter. A company needs to prevent business data from being leaked to other platforms and users than those authorized.

To establish a policy for data protection, companies need to execute a **data protection impact analysis** (**DPIA**). In a DPIA, an enterprise assesses what data it has, what the purpose of that data is, and what the risk is when the data is breached. The outcome of the DPIA will determine how data is handled, whom or what should be able to access it, and how it must be protected. This can be translated into DLP policies. The following table shows an example of a very simple DLP matrix. It shows that business data may be accessed by a business application, but not from an email client. Communication with social media – in this example, Twitter – is blocked in all cases. In a full matrix, this needs to be detailed:

| | Data Source | | |
|---|---|---|---|
| Connection | | | |
| | Business Data | Email | Twitter |
| | | | |
| Business Application | Allowed | Denied | Blocked |
| | | | |
| Email | Denied | Allowed | Blocked |
| | | | |
| Twitter | Blocked | Blocked | n/a |

Labeling and DLP are about policies: they define what must be protected and to what extent. The next consideration is the technologies to protect the data – the how.

# Understanding data encryption

One of the first, if not *the* first, encryption devices to be created was the Enigma machine. It was invented in the 1920s and was mostly known for its usage in World War II to encrypt messages. The British scientist Alan Turing and his team managed to crack the encryption code after 6 months of hard work.

The encryption that Enigma used in those days was very advanced. The principle is still the same – we translate data into something that can't be read without knowing how the data was translated. To be able to read the data, we need a way to decipher or decrypt the data. There are two ways to encrypt data – asymmetric, or public key, and symmetric. In the next section, we will briefly explain these encryption technologies, before diving into the services that the leading cloud providers offer in terms of securing data.

Encryption uses an encryption algorithm and an encryption key – symmetric or asymmetric. With symmetric, the same key is used for both encrypting and decrypting. The problem with that is that the entity that encrypts a file needs to send the key to the recipient of the file so it can be decrypted. The key needs to be transferred. Since enterprises use a lot of (different types of) data, there will be a massive quantity of keys. The distribution of keys needs to be managed well and be absolutely secure.

An alternative is asymmetric encryption, which uses a private and a public key. In this case, the company only needs to protect the private key, since the public key is commonly available.

Both encryption methods are used. A lot of financial and governmental institutions use **AES**, the **Advanced Encryption Standard**. AES works with data blocks. The encryption of these blocks is performed in rounds. In each round, a unique code is included in the key. The length of the key eventually determines how strong the encryption is. That length can be 128-, 192-, or 256-bit. Recent studies have proven that AES-256 is even quantum-ready. The diagram shows the principle of AES-encryption:

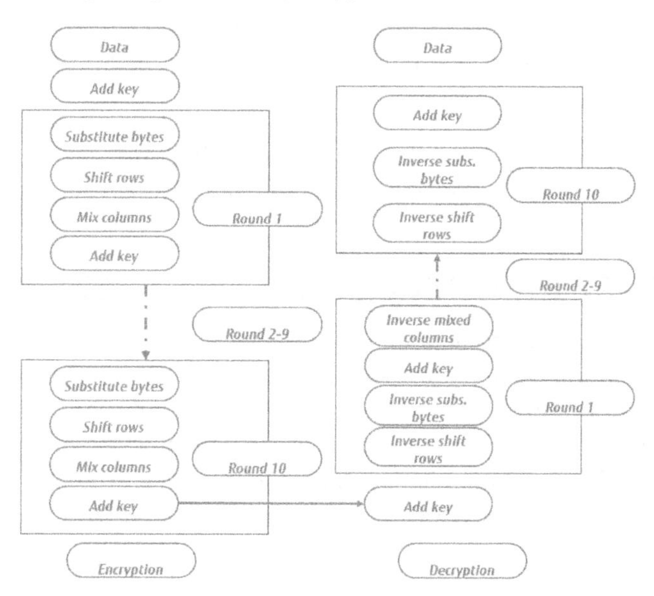


Figure 16.3 – Simple representation of AES encryption principle

**RSA**, named after its inventors, **Rivest, Shamir, and Adleman**, is the most popular asymmetric encryption method. With RSA, the data is treated as one big number that is encrypted with a specific mathematical sequence called **integer factorization**. In RSA, the encryption key is public; decryption is done with a highly secured private key. The principle of RSA encryption is shown in the following diagram:

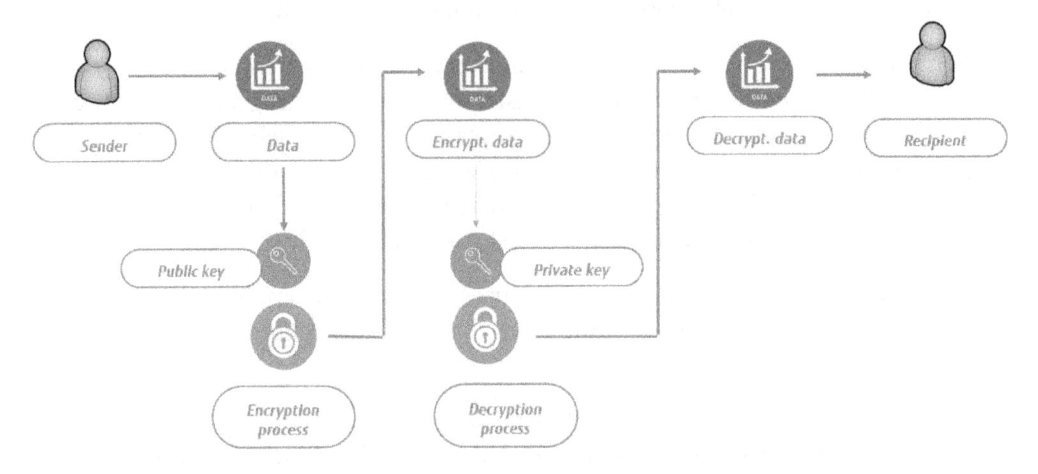


Figure 16.4 – Concept of RSA encryption

Both in AES and RSA, the length of the keys is crucial. Even today, the most common way to execute an attack on systems and retrieve data is by brute force, where the attacker will fire random keys on a system until one of the keys matches. With high-performance computers or computer networks executing the attack, the chance of success is still quite high. So, companies have to think about protecting the data itself, but also protecting the keys used to encrypt data.

In the next section, we will explore the different solutions in public clouds for storage and secure keys, and finally, draw our plan and create the data security principles.

# Securing access, encryption, and storage keys

The cloud platforms provide customers with technology and tools to protect their assets, including the most important one – data. At the time of writing, there's a lot of debate about who's actually responsible for protecting data, but generally, the company that is the legal owner of the data has to make sure that it's compliant with (international) laws and standards. In the UK, companies have to adhere to the Data Protection Act and in the European Union, all companies have to be compliant with the **General Data Protection Regulation** (**GDPR**).

Both the Data Protection Act and GDPR deal with privacy. International standards ISO/IEC 27001:2013 and ISO/IEC 27002:2013 are security frameworks that cover data protection. These standards determine that all data must have an owner, so that it's clear who's responsible for protecting the data. In short, the company that stores data on a cloud platform still owns that data and is therefore responsible for data protection.

To secure data on cloud platforms, companies have to focus on two aspects:

- Encryption
- Access, using authentication and authorization

These are just the security concerns. Enterprises also need to be able to ensure the reliability. They need to be sure that, for instance, keys are kept in another place other than the data itself and that even if a key vault is not accessible for technical reasons, there's still a way to access the data in a secure way. An engineer can't simply drive to the data center with a disk or a USB device to retrieve the data. How do Azure, AWS, and GCP take care of this? We will explore this in the next section.

## Using encryption and keys in Azure

In Azure, the user writes data to blob storage. The storage is protected with a storage key that is automatically generated. The storage keys are kept in a key vault, outside the subnet where the storage is itself. But the key vault does more than just storing the keys. It also regenerates keys periodically by rotation, providing **shared access signature** (**SAS**) tokens to access the storage account. The concept is shown in the following diagram:

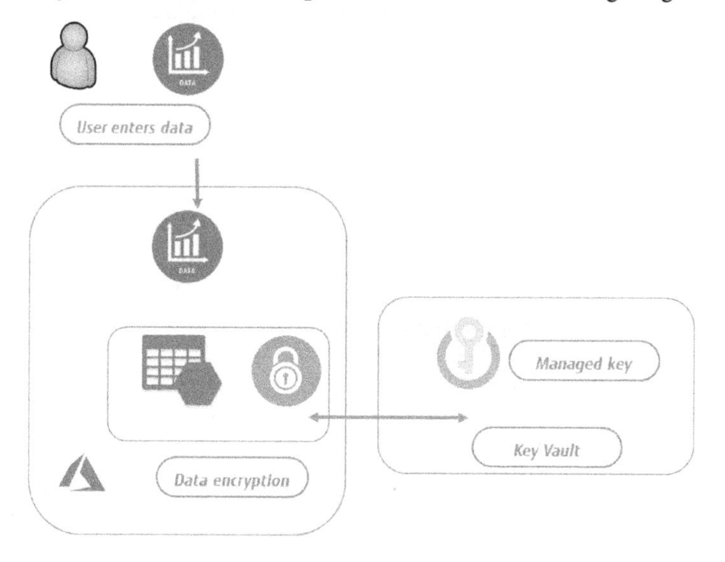


Figure 16.5 – Concept of Azure Key Vault

The key vault is highly recommended by Microsoft Azure for managing encryption keys. Encryption is a complex domain in Azure, since Microsoft offers a wide variety of encryption services in Azure. Disks in Azure can be encrypted using BitLocker or DM-Crypt for Linux systems. With Azure, **Storage Service Encryption** (**SSE**) data can automatically be encrypted before it's stored in blob. SSE uses AES-256. For Azure SQL databases, Azure offers encryption for data at rest with **Transparent Data Encryption** (**TDE**), which also uses AES-256 and **Triple Data Encryption Standard** (**3DES**).

## Using encryption and keys in AWS

Like Azure, AWS has a key vault solution, called **Key Management Service** (**KMS**). The principles are also very similar, mainly using server-side encryption. Server-side means that the cloud provider is requested to encrypt the data before it's stored on a solution within that cloud platform. Data is decrypted when a user retrieves the data. The other option is client-side, where the customer takes care of the encryption process before data is stored.

The storage solution in AWS is S3. If a customer uses server-side encryption in S3, AWS provides S3-managed keys (SSE-S3). These are the unique **data encryption keys** (**DEKs**) that are encrypted themselves with a master key, the **key encryption key** (**KEK**). The master key is constantly regenerated. For encryption, AWS uses AES-256.

AWS offers some additional services with **customer master keys** (**CMKs**). These keys are also managed in KMS, providing an audit trail to see who has used the key and when. Lastly, there's the option to use **customer-provided keys** (**SSE-C**), where the customer manages the key themselves. The concept of KMS using the CMK in AWS is shown in the following diagram:

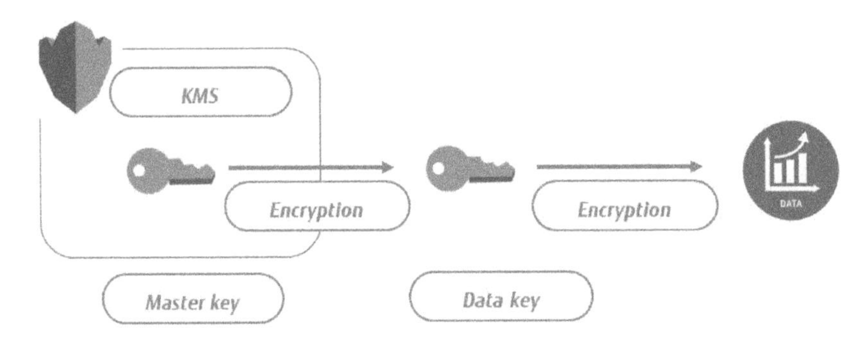


Figure 16.6 – Concept of storing CMKs in AWS KMS

Both Azure and AWS have automated a lot in terms of encryption. They use different names for the key services, but the main principles are quite similar. That counts for GCP too, which is discussed in the next section.

## Using encryption and keys in GCP

In GCP, all data that is stored in Cloud Storage is encrypted by default. Just like Azure and AWS, GCP offers options to manage keys. These can be supplied and managed by Google or by the customer. Keys are stored in **Cloud Key Management Service**. If the customer chooses to supply and/or manage keys themselves, these will act as an added layer on top of the standard encryption that GCP provides. That is also valid in the case of client-side encryption – the data is sent to GCP in an encrypted format, but still GCP will execute its own encryption process, as with server-side encryption. GCP Cloud Storage encrypts data with AES-256.

The encryption process itself is similar to AWS and Azure and uses DEKs and KEKs. When a customer uploads data to GCP, the data is divided into chunks. Each of these chunks is encrypted with a DEK. These DEKs are sent to the KMS where a master key is generated. The concept is shown in the following diagram:

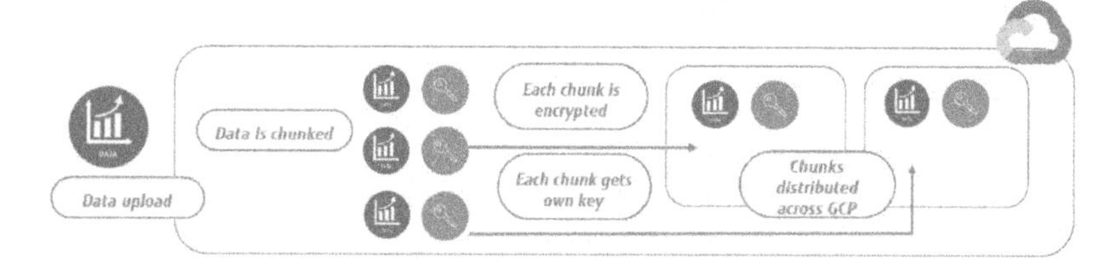


Figure 16.7 – Concept of data encryption in GCP

So far, we have been looking at data itself, the storage of data, the encryption of that data, and securing access to data. One of the tasks of an architect is to translate this into principles. This is a task that needs to be performed together with the CIO or the **chief information security officer** (**CISO**). The minimal principles to be set are as follows:

- Encrypt all data in transit (end-to-end).
- Encrypt all business-critical or sensitive data at rest.
- Apply DLP and have a matrix that shows clearly what critical and sensitive data is and to what extent it needs to be protected.

In the *Further reading* section, some good articles are listed on encryption in the cloud and best practices for securing data.

Finally, develop use cases and test the data protection scenarios. After creating the data model, defining the DLP matrix, and applying the data protection controls, an organization has to test whether a user can create and upload data and what other authorized users can do with that data – read, modify, or delete. That does not only apply to users, but also to data usage in other systems and applications. Data integration tests are therefore also a must.

Data policies and encryption are important, but one thing should not be neglected: encryption does not protect companies from misplaced **identity and access management** (**IAM**) credentials. Thinking that data is fully protected because it's encrypted and stored safely gives a false sense of security. Security really starts with authentication and authorization.

# Securing raw data for big data modeling

One of the big advantages of the public cloud is the huge capacity that these platforms offer. Together with the increasing popularity of public clouds, the industry saw another major development in the possibilities to gather and analyze vast amounts of data, without the need to build an infrastructure themselves in on-premises data centers to host the data. With public clouds, companies can have enormous data lakes at their disposal. Data analysts program their analytical models to these data lakes. This is what is referred to as big data. Big data modeling is about four Vs:

- **Volume**: The quantity of data
- **Variety**: The different types of data
- **Veracity**: The quality of data
- **Velocity**: The speed of processing data

Data analysts often add a fifth V to these four, and that's value. Big data gets value when data is analyzed and processed in such a way that it actually means something. The four-V model is shown in the following diagram:

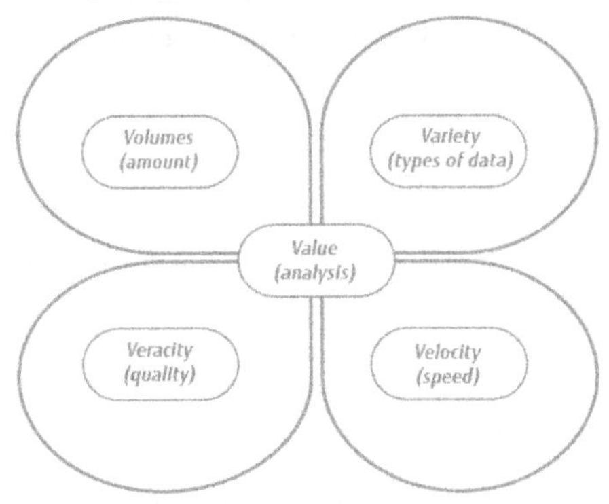


Figure 16.8 – The four Vs of big data

Processing and enriching the data is something that is done in the data modeling stage. Cloud providers offer a variety of solutions for data mining and data analytics – Data Factory in Azure, Redshift in AWS, and BigQuery in GCP. These solutions require a different view on data security.

As with all data, the encryption of data at rest is required and in almost every case is enabled by default on any big data platform or data warehouse solution that is scalable up to petabytes. Examples are Azure Data Lake, AWS Redshift, and Google's BigQuery. These solutions are designed to hold any kind of unstructured data in one single repository.

To use Azure Data Lake as an example, as soon as the user sets up an account in Data Lake, Azure encryption is turned on and the keys are managed by Azure, although there's an option for companies to manage keys themselves. In Data Lake, the user will have three different keys – the Master Encryption Key, the Data Encryption Key, and the Block Encryption Key. The latter is necessary since data in Data Lake is divided into blocks.

Whenever data traverses from its origin or rest state to another, we talk about data in transit. The most common technology to protect data in transit is by using the **Transport Layer Security** (**TLS**) protocol. TLS provides strong authentication, but also technology that detects when data is modified during transmission or intercepted. TLS1.2 or higher is the recommended standard.

AWS Redshift works in clusters to store data. These clusters can be encrypted so that all data created by users in tables is encrypted. This data can be extracted to SQL database clients. In that case, data in transit is encrypted using **Secure Sockets Layer** (**SSL**). Finally, the Redshift cluster will sit in a **virtual private cloud** (**VPC**) in AWS – access to the environment is controlled at the VPC level.

Google's BigQuery is a fully managed service, yet users have a ton of choices for how to treat data in BigQuery. The service comprises over 100 predefined detectors to scan and identify data. Next, GCP offers a variety of tools to execute DLP policies, such as data masking and the pseudonymization of data. Scanning data in BigQuery is easy through the GCP cloud console. This is also the place where the user can enable the DLP API. As with all data in GCP, it will be encrypted upon entry by default. BigQuery doesn't check whether data is already encrypted, it runs the encryption process at all times.

# Summary

This chapter was about securing and protecting data in cloud environments. We have learned that when moving data from on-premises systems to the cloud, companies have to set specific controls to protect their data. The owner of the data remains responsible for protecting the data; that doesn't shift to the cloud provider.

We have learned that companies need to think first about data protection policies. What data needs to be protected? Which laws and international frameworks are applicable to be compliant? A best practice is to start thinking about the data model and then draw a matrix, showing what the policy should be for critical and sensitive data. We've also studied the principles of DLP using data classification and labeling.

This chapter also explored the different options a company has to store data in cloud environments and how we can protect data from a technological point of view. After finishing this chapter, you should have a good understanding of how encryption works and how Azure, AWS, and GCP treat data and the encryption of data. Lastly, we've looked at the big data solutions on the cloud platforms and how raw data is protected.

The next chapter is the final one about security operations in multi-cloud. The cloud providers offer native security monitoring solutions, but how can enterprises monitor security in multi-cloud? The next chapter will discuss **Security Information and Event Management** (**SIEM**) in multi-cloud.

# Questions

1. To define the risk of data loss, businesses are advised to conduct an assessment. Please name this assessment methodology.
2. In this chapter, we've studied encryption. Please name two encryption technologies that are commonly used in cloud environments.
3. What's the service in AWS to manage encryption keys?
4. In Azure, companies keep keys in Azure Key Vault. False or true: a key vault is hosted in the same subnet as the storage itself.

# Further reading

You can refer to the following links for more information on the topics covered in this chapter:

- Information about the management of storage keys in Azure: `https://docs.microsoft.com/en-us/azure/key-vault/secrets/overview-storage-keys`
- Encryption overview in Azure: `https://docs.microsoft.com/en-us/azure/security/fundamentals/encryption-overview`
- Data protection in AWS: `https://docs.aws.amazon.com/AmazonS3/latest/dev/UsingEncryption.html`
- Encryption options in GCP: `https://cloud.google.com/storage/docs/encryption`
- Blog by Kenneth Hui on Cloud Architect Musings about encryption in Azure, AWS, and GCP: `https://cloudarchitectmusings.com/2018/03/09/data-encryption-in-the-cloud-part-4-aws-azure-and-google-cloud/`

# 17
# Implementing and Integrating Security Monitoring

Enterprises go multi-cloud and use cloud services from different cloud providers. These solutions will be secured, but enterprises want an integrated view on the security status on all of their platforms and solutions. This is what solutions such as **Security Information and Event Management** (**SIEM**) and **Security Orchestration, Automation, and Response** (**SOAR**) do.

In this chapter, we will learn why these systems are a necessity in multi-cloud. First, we will discuss the differences between the various systems, and then we will explore the various solutions that are available on the market today. The big question we're going to answer in this chapter is *how do we make a choice and, more importantly, how do we implement these complicated solutions?*

We're going to cover the following main topics in this chapter:

- Understanding SIEM and SOAR
- Setting up the requirements for integrated security
- Exploring multi-cloud monitoring suites

# Understanding SIEM and SOAR

All cloud providers offer native services for security monitoring, such as Azure Security Center, AWS Security Hub, and Security Command Center in Google Cloud. However, companies are going multi-cloud using **Infrastructure-as-a-Service** (**IaaS**), **Platform-as-a-Service** (**PaaS**), and **Software-as-a-Service** (**SaaS**) from different providers. Enterprises want an integrated view of their security in all these solutions. If an enterprise is truly multi-cloud, it will need an integrated security solution with SIEM and SOAR.

Next, the enterprise needs a unit that is able to handle and analyze all the data coming from SIEM and SOAR systems and trigger the appropriate actions in case of security events. Most enterprises have a **Security Operations Center** (**SOC**) to take care of this. In this section, we will explain what the differences are between SIEM and SOAR, why an enterprise needs these systems in multi-cloud, and what the role of the SOC is.

## Differentiating SIEM and SOAR

Let's start with SIEM. Imagine that workloads – systems and applications – are deployed in Azure and AWS, and the enterprise also uses a number of SaaS services, such as Microsoft Office 365 and Salesforce. All these environments are protected with firewalls in both Azure and AWS, along with on-premises data centers. Traffic is routed through virtual network devices, routing tables, and load balancers. The enterprise might also have implemented intrusion detection and prevention to protect systems in the public clouds and on-premises data centers. All these security systems will produce a vast amount of information on the security status of the enterprise environments.

SIEM systems collect, aggregate, and analyze this information to identify possible threats. Since it collects data from all environments, it's able to correlate the data and recognize patterns that might hint toward attacks. For this, SIEM uses machine learning and specific analytics software. It recognizes abnormal behavior in systems with anomaly detection. A simple example is if user A logs in from an office in London at 9.00 AM and again logs in at 9.30 AM from Singapore, a SIEM system would know that this is impossible and will raise an event or alert. The architecture of a SIEM system is shown in the following diagram:

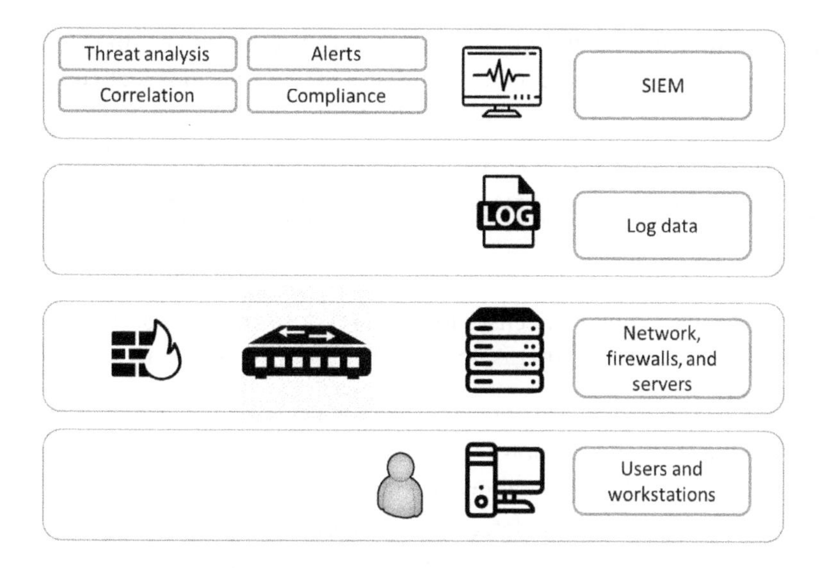


Figure 17.1 – The conceptualized architecture of a SIEM system

SOAR goes beyond SIEM. Like a SIEM system, SOAR collects and analyzes data that it gathers from a lot of different sources, such as the public cloud environments. But the added value of SOAR is in orchestration and automation. In SOAR systems, companies can define automated responses to events, using playbooks that integrate with security solutions in the platforms. If a SOAR system detects a threat in a system, it can immediately remediate it by taking actions such as closing communication ports, blocking IP addresses, or putting systems into quarantine. It does that fully automated, including logging and raising tickets to service management systems. This gives security professionals time to investigate the actual threat, without needing to worry about remediation first. That task is fixed preemptively from them by SOAR.

## The role of SOC

Since the world is moving to digital, companies are increasingly threatened by digital threats. It also seems that hackers are always one step ahead of the companies themselves in protecting their digital assets. It takes a lot of skills to keep up and counter these attacks. Therefore, enterprises rely more and more on specialized groups where security expertise is bundled: the SOC. Enterprises can have these in-house or outsourced to specialized companies.

The SOC is responsible for monitoring and analyzing the security state of an enterprise on a 24/7 basis. A team of security engineers will use different technology solutions, including SIEM and SOAR, to detect, assess, and respond as quickly as possible to security incidents.

In the next section, we will explain how an enterprise can set up a SOC. In the last section of this chapter, we will explore some major SIEM and SOAR solutions that companies can use to protect their systems in multi-cloud environments.

# Setting up the requirements for integrated security

Before a company gets into buying licenses for all sorts of security tools, security architects will need to gather requirements. That is done by the following four stages that a security team needs to cover:

1. **Detect**: Most of the security tools focus on detecting vulnerabilities and actual attacks or attempts to breach systems. Some examples are endpoint protection, such as virus scanners and malware detection, and **Network Traffic Analyzers** (**NTA**). In multi-cloud, architects need to make sure that detecting systems can operate on all platforms and preferably send information to one integrated dashboard.
2. **Analyze**: This is the next phase. Detection systems will send a lot of data, including false positives. Ideally, security monitoring does a first analysis of events, checking them against known patterns and behavior of systems and users. This is the first filter. The second phase in the analysis is prioritization, which is done by skilled security staff. They have access to knowledge base repositories of providers and security authorities. They have the information that enables them to give priority to potential threats, based on relevant context. Remember one thing: where there's smoke, there's usually a fire. The question is how big the fire is.
3. **Respond**: After a threat is detected and prioritized, the security team needs to respond. First of all, they need to make sure that the attack is stopped and exploited vulnerabilities are identified. The next step is remediation: preventing systems from enacting (further) damage or data breaching. The final step in response is recovery – restoring systems and making sure that the data is safe. Be sure that processes for following up security events are crystal clear. Who needs to be informed, who's mandated to take decisions, and what is the escalation path?

4. **Prevent**: SIEM and SOAR systems can do a lot in detecting, analyzing, and responding to security events. However, security starts with preventing vulnerabilities from being exploited in the first place. Security teams need to have continuous visibility on all the platforms that the enterprise uses and must have access to security reports, assessments, and threat detection scans from the providers. It's also essential that recommendations from Azure, AWS, GCP, VMware, or any other provider are followed up. These providers issue security updates on a regular basis and give recommendations to improve the state of security of environments that are deployed on their platforms. These recommendations should be followed.

In January 2020, market analyst Gartner issued a report (available on `https://swimlane.com/resources/access-selecting-soc-tools-gartner/`), which stated that by 2024, 80 percent of all SOCs will have invested in tools using artificial intelligence and machine learning. In that same report, Gartner analysts concluded that these investments will not necessarily bring down the amount team security teams have to spend on investigating security events. So, what would be wise investments in terms of security tools and systems?

First, leverage what providers already have. Azure, AWS, and GCP all have security suites that gather a lot of information on the health and integrity of systems. In almost all cases, it's a matter of ticking the box to enable these security systems, although security engineers will have to set a baseline to which the tools monitor the systems. This was discussed in *Chapter 14, Defining Security Policies*.

# Implementing the security model

A lot of companies already have a multi-cloud setup. For example, they use AWS to host websites and have Office 365 from Microsoft, a SaaS solution. In AWS, security teams will work with AWS Inspector and GuardDuty and for monitoring security. In Office 365, they might use **Microsoft Defender and Advanced Threat Protection** (**MDATP**). The challenge for security teams is to have an integrated vision on the full IT environment. How do companies get there?

- **Define a target operating model**: What does the entire environment look like and who's responsible for all or some of it? Companies must have a clear demarcation model on roles and responsibilities in the management of cloud platforms, services, and systems. The target operating model describes the landscape of components and the owner of these components. Security is an overall component for which the security officer is responsible.

- **Define workflows and escalation procedures**: This defines the workflow when security events occur. What is the procedure in the case of high-priority events, medium-rated events, and low-risk events? When a high-priority event is detected, it should be raised to the security officer. The security officer decides who needs to be informed and what actions must be taken. These are operational tasks. They may report to the **Chief Security Officer** (**CSO**) or the **Chief Information and Security Officer** (**CISO**). The CSO or CISO is responsible for strategic security decisions.
- **Analyze the capabilities of security tools that are already in place**: Evaluate the tools that are in place already. What do these tools cover? How are APIs configured and can they communicate with overlaying systems? What are the default baselines that these tools use?
- **Gap analysis**: There will always be blind spots. A common example in batch jobs is are these monitored as well from a security perspective? What happens when jobs are stopped? Is communication between systems then halted and is the integrity of systems still safeguarded? In cloud-native environments, companies should also have a good understanding of how containers and serverless solutions are monitored. Not all monitoring tools can handle these native environments yet.
- **Make a strategic plan**: This is what the CSO or CISO must be concerned with. The first question that must be covered in a strategic plan is the maturity goal of the enterprise. The next question is what the major security concerns are for the enterprise: what are the biggest risks and threats? Hint: it is not always about the loss of money. Reputational damage goes far beyond revenue loss when systems are breached. Finally, the company must be able to identify whether existing tools, processes, and expertise are sufficient and what needs to be done to get to the desired maturity goal.

The following diagram shows a maturity model for security:

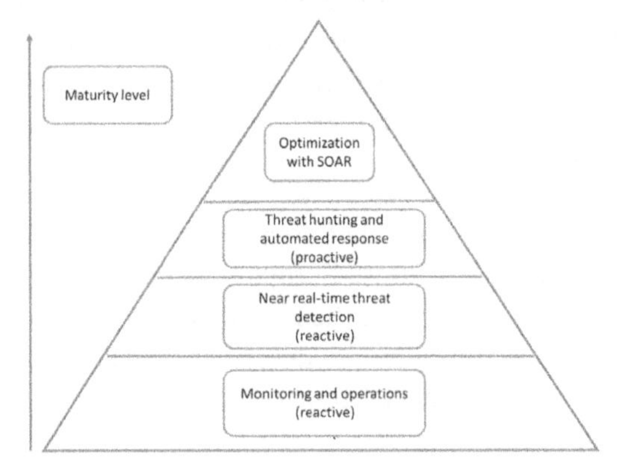


Figure 17.2 – Security maturity model, from reactive monitoring to proactive threat hunting

It's strongly advised to set up a security team or SOC. It's not realistic to have one or two security engineers to watch over multi-cloud environments. The difficult part is how to get there. The best practice is to plan the setup in three stages:

- **Stage 1 – get visibility for the business**: In this stage, we gather the security policies and align the security processes between business and IT.
- **Stage 2 – integrate IT security operations with business security**: This is the stage where security operations enable security monitoring and onboard the security baselines – as defined with the business in stage 1 – in the monitoring systems. Part of this stage is also the risk assessment on the platforms. It's recommended to do an assessment on the security baselines of the cloud providers and analyze whether these baselines concur with the security principles of the enterprise.
- **Stage 3 – optimize**: This is the stage where the true integrated view is created, using one dashboard that covers the entire security state of the IT landscape.

The stages are shown in the following diagram:

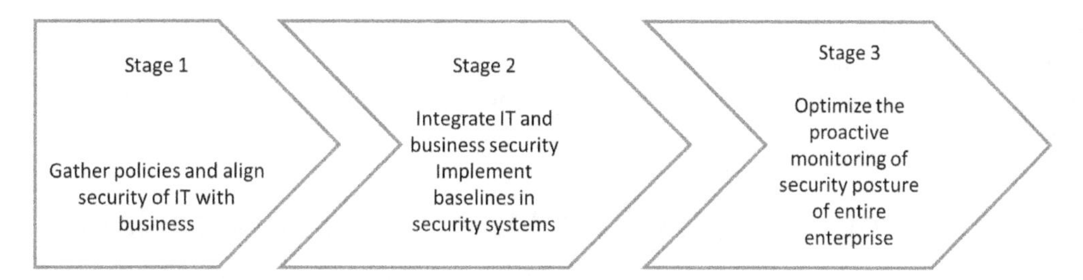


Figure 17.3 – Three stages of security onboarding

Integrated security means that a company has a clear model of processes, tools, and expertise. In multi-cloud, this also means that cloud providers are part of these processes, tools, and certainly expertise. The security architect will have the task of getting this defined, designed, and modeled. SIEM and SOAR tools can help to get an integrated view of the entire security state – or posture – of an enterprise. In the next section, we will discuss popular solutions for this in multi-cloud.

# Exploring multi-cloud monitoring suites

Companies have a wide variety of choices when they're looking for a SIEM solution. In the next sections, some popular solutions are discussed.

## Exploring SIEM solutions from Splunk, LogRythm, and Rapid7

Each year, market analyst Gartner publishes a list of leading solutions in different IT domains. For a number of years, Splunk, LogRythm, and Rapid7 have been named as leading products for SIEM by Gartner. These solutions can work with all major cloud providers using REST APIs. **REST** stands for **REpresentational State Transfer**.

A REST API is a programmable interface that connects to the service in the cloud and enables that data from that service to be captured and sent to an application. In this case, the SIEM suite uses an API to get security data such as alerts from the cloud and transfers it to the dashboard of the SIEM solution. Splunk, LogRythm, and Rapid7 have APIs for Azure and AWS. Splunk and LogRythm integrate with Azure Monitoring using **Azure Log Integration** (**AzLog**). In AWS, these tools work with AWS Config, CloudTrail, and CloudWatch to collect data.

Splunk also offers integration with GCP. Rapid7 was already available from the marketplaces in Azure and AWS but did not have an API for Google Cloud. Since a growing number of enterprises are expanding cloud services in all major clouds, Rapid7 acknowledged that a multi-cloud security solution needed to integrate with GCP too. For that reason, they acquired DivvyCloud in spring 2020, a multi-cloud security and compliancy tool.

## Implementing SecOps with VMware and ServiceNow

Over the last 5 years, the market for enterprise IT has seen an enormous growth in security monitoring tools, including companies that didn't have security as their main focus, but invested heavily in developing or acquiring security products. It's a logical move when you realizes how fast cybercrime is growing. Good examples of companies that made big investments in security are VMware and ServiceNow.

VMware transformed itself from a company that virtualized server environments into a company that can perform a central role in managing multi-cloud. In 2019, it introduced Intrinsic Security, which consists of several products, including VMware Secure State. Secure State, or CloudHealth, as it was originally called, is a SOAR system. It analyzes misconfigurations of systems and threats, and detects changes that are applied to systems. It calculates the security risk of these systems and is able to automate remediating actions when systems are at risk. In order to do so, security engineers need to load baselines into Secure State to which the tool measures compliance of systems. Secure State is multi-cloud and can be used as a single tool on top of Azure, AWS, GCP, and hybrid platforms that hold both public and private clouds. The latter does not necessarily have to be built with VMware, but can also run, for example, Hyper-V or OpenStack.

In ServiceNow, enterprises can configure the same functionality using SecOps and **Governance, Risk, and Compliance** (**GRC**). GRC can be seen as the repository that holds the security policies and compliance baselines of an enterprise. Next, GRC continuously monitors the compliance of systems, analyzes the business impact of risks, and collects audit data. SecOps is the SOAR module of the ServiceNow suite; it continuously monitors the security posture of the entire IT environment and can automatically mitigate security issues, based on security incident response scenarios that are defined as workflows in SecOps.

A workflow can, for example, be that a system is suspended when SecOps detects that software has not been checked for patches in more than 3 months. If the enterprise has a compliance rule that states that software needs to be checked for patches at least once every 3 months, an automated workflow could trigger the action to suspend the use of the software.

## Introducing cloud-native SIEM with Azure Sentinel

One final product that is reviewed here is Azure Sentinel, the native SIEM and SOAR solution for Azure. Sentinel does what all SIEM and SOAR solutions do: collect data, check it against compliancy baselines that have been defined in Azure, and respond to threats and vulnerabilities with automated workflows. It also uses artificial intelligence to detect and analyze possible attacks, by learning the behavior of systems and users. With Sentinel, Microsoft has a very extensive suite of security solutions in the cloud with MDATP, Cloud App security, and Azure Security Center. Although Sentinel is based in Azure, enterprises can also connect AWS CloudTrail to Sentinel. At the time of writing, an integration with GCP is not available.

This list of tools and suites is not exhaustive. Enterprise architects and security specialists should together start with gathering requirements from the business, define the needed security level of systems against compliance frameworks, agree to the security processes between business and IT, and then decide what sort of security tools would best fit the requirements. SIEM and SOAR solutions are complex. These solutions can add a lot of value to safeguard the security posture of the IT environment, but need careful consideration and evaluation of the business case.

# Summary

Enterprises use a wide and growing variety of cloud solutions. Cloud platforms, systems, software, and data need to be protected from threats and attacks. Likely, a company will also have a variety of security solutions. To create one integrated view of the security of the entire IT environment, companies will have to implement security tooling that enables this single point of view. In this chapter, we looked at SIEM and SOAR systems, tools that can collect data from many different sources and analyze this data against security baselines. Ideally, these tools can also trigger automated responses to threats, after calculating the risks and the business impact.

The functionality and differences between SIEM and SOAR have been explained. After this chapter, you should have a good understanding of how these systems can integrate with cloud platforms.

In the last section of this chapter, leading SIEM and SOAR solutions were discussed. The chapter concludes this section of our book about security operations, or SecOps. There are two more *ops*-concepts that must be discussed: DevOps and AIOps (operations using artificial intelligence). The next chapters will be about DevOps and AIOps.

# Questions

1. What is a SOC?
2. What is a common technology to integrate SIEM and SOAR systems into cloud platforms?
3. Monitoring and operations are the first level in the security maturity model. Rate the following statement true or false: the reason for this is that monitoring and operations are reactive.

# Further reading

*Enterprise Cloud Security and Governance*, by Zeal Vora, Packt Publishing

# Section 5 – Structured Development on Multi-Cloud Environments with DevOps

We are building a multi-cloud foundation – or landing zone – for a reason. We are building it to build and host applications. So, we are trying to reach our end goal: the app and how we optimize our landing zone for that app.

The following chapters will be covered in this section:

- *Chapter 18, Designing and Implementing CI/CD Pipelines*
- *Chapter 19, Introducing AIOps in Multi-Cloud*
- *Chapter 20, Introducing Site Reliability Engineering in Multi-Cloud*

# 18
# Designing and Implementing CI/CD Pipelines

The typical reason why most enterprises adopt the cloud is to accelerate application development. Applications are constantly evaluated and changed to add new features. Since everything is codified in the cloud, these new features need to be tested on the infrastructure of the target cloud. The final step in the life cycle of applications is the actual deployment of applications to the cloud and the handover to operations so that developers have their hands free to develop new features again, based on business requirements.

To speed up this process, organizations work in DevOps cycles, using release trains with continuous development and the possibility to test, debug, and deploy code multiple times per week, or even per day, so that these applications are constantly improved. Consistency is crucial: the source code needs to be under strict version control. That is what CI/CD pipelines are for: continuous integration and continuous delivery and deployment.

We will study the principles of DevOps, how CI/CD pipelines work with push and pull mechanisms, and how pipelines are designed so that they fit multi-cloud environments. Also, tooling for DevOps and CI/CD is discussed.

In this chapter, we're going to cover the following main topics:

- Understanding CI/CD and pipelines
- Using push and pull principles in CI/CD
- Designing the multi-cloud pipeline
- Exploring tooling for CI/CD

# Understanding CI/CD and pipelines

Before we get into the principles of CI/CD and pipelines, we need to have a good understanding of DevOps. There are a lot of views on DevOps, but this book sticks to the definition and principles as defined by the **DevOps Agile Skills Association** (**DASA**). They define a DevOps framework based on six principles:

- **Customer-centric action**: Develop an application with the customer in mind – what do they need and what does the customer expect in terms of functionality? This is also the goal of another concept, domain-driven design, which contains good practices for designing.
- **Create with the end in mind**: How will the application look when it's completely finished?
- **End-to-end responsibility**: Teams need to be motivated and enabled to take responsibility from the start to the finish of the application life cycle. This results in mottos such as *you build it, you run it* and *you break it, you fix it*. One more to add is *you destroy it, you rebuild it better*.
- **Cross-functional autonomous teams**: Teams need to be able and allowed to make decisions themselves in the development process.
- **Continuous improvement**: This must the goal – to constantly improve the application.
- **Automate as much as possible**: The only way to really gain speed in delivery and deployment is by automating as much as possible. Automation also limits the occurrence of failures, such as misconfigurations.

DevOps has been described in the literature as *culture*, a new way of working. It's a new way of thinking about developing and operating IT systems based on the idea of a feedback loop. Since cloud platforms are code-based, engineers can apply changes to systems relatively easily. Systems are code, and code can be changed, as long as changes are applied in a structured and highly controlled way. That's the purpose of CI/CD pipelines.

**Continuous Integration** (**CI**) is built on the principle of a shared repository, where code is frequently updated and shared across teams that work in the cloud environments. CI allows developers to work together on the same code at the same time. The changes in the code are directly integrated and ready to be fully tested in different test environments.

**Continuous Delivery or Deployment** (**CD**) focuses on the automated transfer of software to test environments. The ultimate goal of CD is to bring software to production in a fully automated way. Various tests are performed automatically. After deployment, developers immediately receive feedback on the functionality of the code.

CI/CD enables the DevOps cycle. Combined with CI/CD, all responsibilities, from planning to management, lie with the team, and changes can reach the customer much faster through an automated and robust development process. The following diagram shows the DevOps cycle with CI/CD:

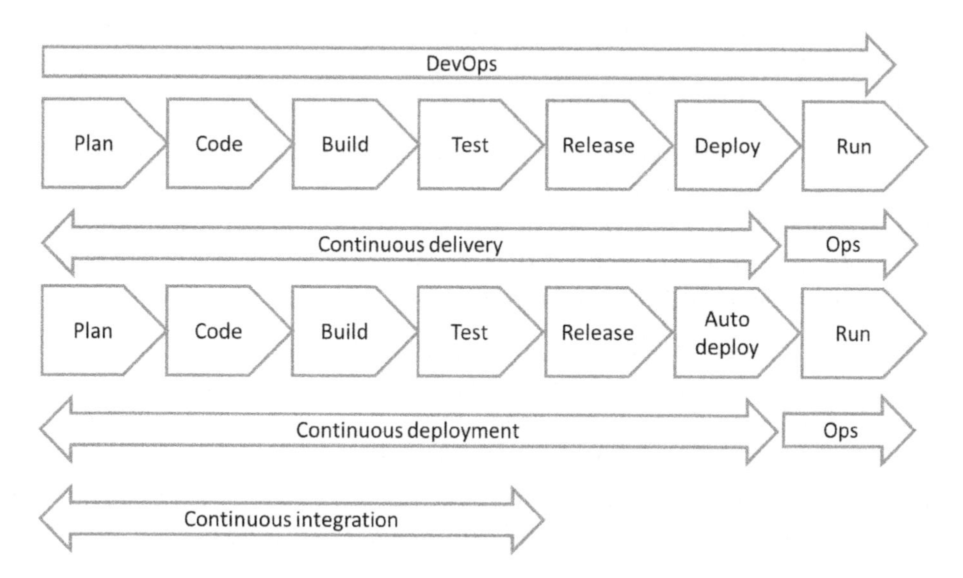


Figure 18.1 – DevOps cycle with CI/CD

In the next section, we will study how to get started with CI/CD.

# Getting started with CI/CD

CI/CD is widely adopted by enterprises, but a lot of projects fail. This section explains how enterprises can successfully implement CI/CD and how they can avoid pitfalls. The major takeaway should be that an implementation starts with consistency. That counts for cloud implementations as well as for CI/CD.

With CI, development teams can change code as often as they want, leading to the continuous improvement of systems. Enterprises will have multiple development teams, working in multi-cloud environments, which makes it necessary to have one way of working. Fully automated processes in CI/CD pipelines can help keep environments consistent. CI/CD and DevOps are, however, not about tools. They're about culture and *sticking to processes.*

To get to a successful implementation of DevOps, an organization is advised to follow these steps:

1. Implementing an effective CI/CD pipeline begins with all stakeholders implementing DevOps processes. One of the key principles in DevOps is autonomous teams that take end-to-end responsibility. It's imperative that the teams are given the authority to make decisions and act on them. Typically, DevOps teams are agile, working in short sprints of 2 to a maximum of 3 weeks. If that time is wasted on getting approval for every single detail in the development process, the team will never get to finish anything in time.
2. Choose the CI/CD system. There are a lot of tools on the market that facilitate CI/CD. Jenkins is a popular one, but a lot of companies that work in Azure choose to work in Azure DevOps. Involve the people who have to work daily with the system and enable them to take a *test drive*. Then, make a decision and ensure all teams work in that system. Again, it's about consistency.
3. It's advised to do a proof of concept. An important element of CI/CD is the automation of testing, so the first step is to create an automated process pipeline. Enterprises often already have quality and test plans, possibly laid down in a **Generic Test Agreement** (**GTA**). This describes what and how tests must be executed before systems are pushed to production. This is a good starting point, but in DevOps, organizations work with a **Definition of Done** (**DoD**).

   The DoD describes the conditions and the acceptance criteria a system must meet before it's deployed to production. The DoD is the standard of quality for the end product, the application, or IT system that needs to be delivered. In DevOps, teams work with user stories. An example of a user story is: as a responsible business owner for an online retail store, I want to have multiple payment methods so that more customers can buy our products online. This sets requirements for the development of applications and systems. The DoD is met when the user story is fulfilled, meaning that unit testing is done, the code has been reviewed, acceptance criteria are signed off, and all functional and technical tests have been passed.

The following diagram shows the concept of implementing a build and release pipeline with various test stages. The code is developed in the build pipeline and then sent to a release pipeline where the code is configured and released for production. During the release stages, the full build is tested in a test or **Quality and Assurance Environment** (**Q&A**). In Q&A, the build is accepted and released for deployment into production:

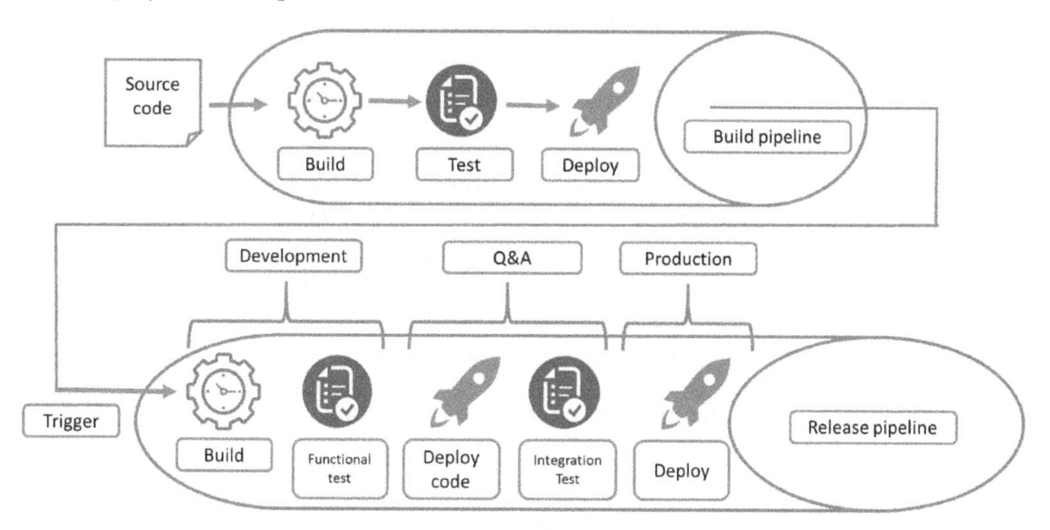


Figure 18.2 – Conceptual diagram of a build and release pipeline

4. Automate as much as possible, as one of the principles of DevOps. This means that enterprises will have to adopt working in code, including **Infrastructure as Code** (**IaC**). In CI/CD, teams work from one repository, and this means that the application code and the infrastructure code is in the same repository, so that all teams can access it whenever they need to.

If all these steps are followed through, an organization can start working in DevOps teams using CI/CD. In the next sections, CI/CD is explained in more detail, starting with version control, and then discussing the functionality of commits, push and pull mechanisms in the pipeline.

## Working under version control

By working from one code repository with different teams, version control becomes crucial in CI/CD. Git and Subversion are popular version control systems that enable teams to organize their files that form the source code, test scripts, deployment scripts, and configuration scripts used for applications and infrastructure components. Everything is code, which means that systems consist of a number of code packages: the code for the VM, code for how the VM should be configured based on policies, and the application code itself. A version control system also enables teams to retrieve the historical state of systems, in case a deployment fails or systems are compromised and need to be rebuilt.

Version control systems keep track of changes to files that are stored in the repository. In DevOps, these changes are commonly referred to as commits, something that we'll discuss further in the next section, *Using push and pull principles in CI/CD*, forking and merging code. A commit comprises the code change itself and metadata, holding information on who made the change and the rationale behind the code change. This ensures that code is kept consistent and with that, repeatable and predictable. It also means that teams are forced to document everything in the repository and bring it under version control.

This list contains many of the items that need to be under version control:

- Application code
- API scripts and references (what is the API for?)
- Infrastructure components such as VMs, network devices, storage, images for operating systems, DNS files, and firewall configuration rules
- Infrastructure configuration packages
- Cloud configuration templates, such as AWS CloudFormation, **Desired State Configuration** (**DSC**) in Azure, and Terraform files
- Code definitions for containers, such as Docker files
- Container orchestration scripts, such as Kubernetes and Docker Swarm
- Test scripts

Once companies have implemented this, they need to maintain it. This is not a one-time exercise. Teams should confirm that version control is applied to application code, systems configuration, and automation scripts that are used in the CI/CD pipeline. Only if this is applied and used in a consistent way will enterprises be able to deploy new applications and systems rapidly, yet securely and reliably.

# Using push and pull principles in CI/CD

CI/CD pipelines work with branches, although other terms can be used for this. The master branch is sometimes referred to as a mainline or, when teams work in GCP, as a trunk. The most important principle to remember is that a development team has one master branch or mainline. Next, there are two ways of pushing new code to that master branch. These two methods are described in the following sections.

## Pushing the code directly to the master

In this method, the developers work directly in the master code; they change small pieces of the code and merge these directly back into the master branch. Pushing code back to the master is called a **commit**. These commits are done several times per day, or at least as soon as possible. Working in this way ensures that releases can be done very frequently, as opposed to working in code forks that result in separate or feature branches, which are described in the second method. The following diagram shows the way of working with a direct push to a master branch:

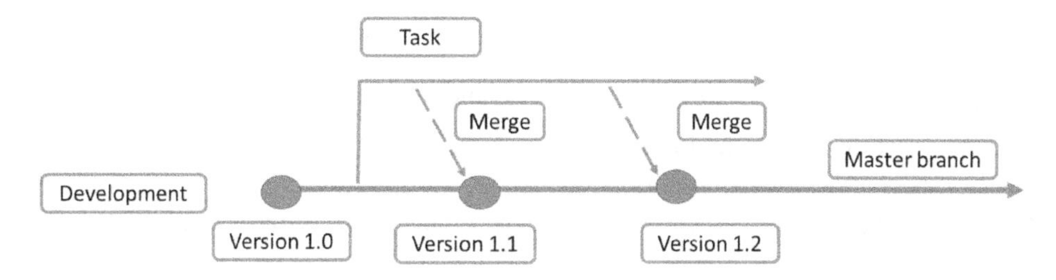


Figure 18.3 – Developers merging code directly to the master branch

The idea behind CI is that companies get rid of long, complex integrations. Developers work in small batches of the code that they frequently commit to the master. The big advantage is that developers immediately see whether the change is done correctly, with the possibility to revert the change without having a huge impact on the master as a whole. This is DevOps – the developers are responsible for the build, the commit, and the result: you break it, you fix it. Automated tests that are executed after the code commit are crucial to ensure that systems keep running without failures.

## Pushing code to forks of the master

In this method, teams copy code from the master and create a separate or feature branch. This is also referred to as forking: developers create a feature branch by taking a copy from the source code, the master. They do their development on this forked code. In GCP, this is not trunk-based development, or better said: this is referred to as feature-driven development.

This method is often used for major developments, creating new features. Developers can work in isolation on the forked code, and when they're done, commit the code back to the master, where the new features or new builds are merged with the master. The downside is that this can lead to complex integrations. This can't be done on a frequent basis, but takes intensive testing before the merging takes place. The following diagram shows the way of working with feature branches:

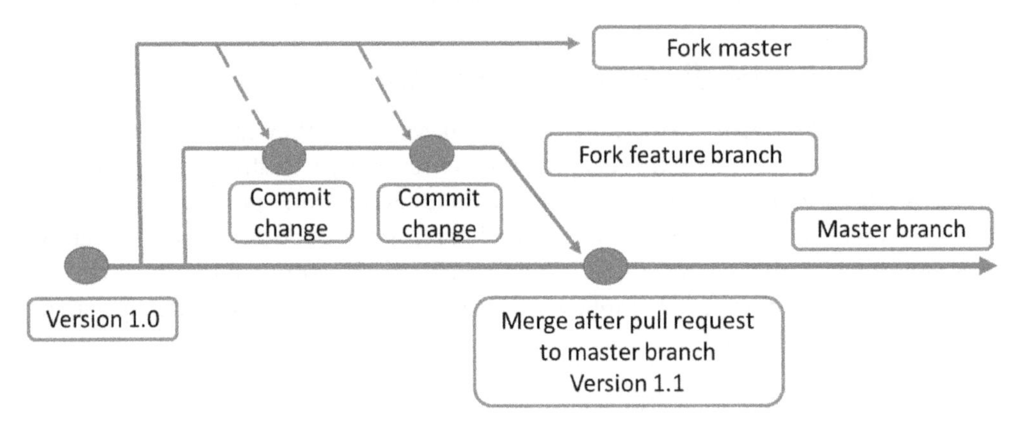


Figure 18.4 – Developers working in a feature branch before merging to the master

In both methods, code gets pushed to the repository in, for example, GitHub. As soon as a developer has committed their code, they will do a pull request. This is the stage where the new, changed code is reviewed before the changes are actually merged into the master branch.

# Best practices while working with CI/CD

There are a few best practices to remember when working with CI/CD. One of the biggest pitfalls is that code reviews are too extensive, meaning that developers have to get approval from different stakeholders before they can push the code to production. This will cost a lot of time and effectively slow down the DevOps process. Companies that adopt DevOps should have two principles implemented:

- The four-eyes principle: Have code reviewed while programming. By working in developer pairs, where the second developer reviews the code of the first developer. This is also referred to as Extreme Programming. Peer review is another method: here, the author of the code reviews and at least one other developer, typically at the end of the development process.
- Running automated test scripts is most important. These scripts must be executed before code is actually committed to the master branch to make sure that systems keep functioning after the code commit.

If these two principles are followed, then extensive reviews and approval processes are not required – at least when developers work in small batches of the master. When creating new features and builds where developers work in a forked copy of the source or feature branch, a more intensive review process is advisable.

# Designing the multi-cloud pipeline

The development of code for applications can be cloud-agnostic, meaning that it doesn't matter to which cloud the code is pushed: the functionality of the code remains the same. However, a lot of developers will discover that it does matter and that's it not that simple to develop in a truly multi-cloud fashion. For the DevOps process itself, it probably doesn't matter on which platform the code lands, but it does matter as soon as teams push code into production. Then there are platform specifics that need to be taken into consideration.

In multi-cloud, developers also work from one repository, but during deployment, platform-specific configuration is added and tested. This is the staging phase. AWS, Azure, and GCP all have their specific provisioning features that need to be tested with the application code. In the staging phase, the code package is merged with infrastructure configuration for provisioning to a target cloud platform and is tested.

There are a few steps that developers have to take to make it successful. First of all, the DevOps way of working should be consistent, regardless of the platform where applications will eventually land. A company might want to run applications in Azure, AWS, GCP or even on-premises, but the way application code is written in DevOps cycles should be the same. Each of these platforms will have specific features to run the code, but that's a matter of configuration. Staging is meant to find out whether the whole package is ready for release to production.

In *Chapter 8, Defining Automation Tools and Processes*, we already learned that developers need to think in layers: they need to abstract the application layer from the resources in infrastructure and the configuration layer. That's the only way to get to a consistent way of application development with CI/CD. One other challenge that developers need to tackle in multi-cloud environments is the high rate of changes in the various cloud platforms. DevOps tools must be able to adapt to these changes in deployment, but without having to constantly change the application code itself.

Developers, however, need to have a good understanding of the target platforms and their specifics. It also makes sense to study the best practices in DevOps in these platforms and the recommended tooling: this will be discussed in more detail in the *Exploring tooling for CI/CD* section of this chapter about tooling for CI/CD. Most common tools are cloud-agnostic, meaning that they can work with different clouds, leveraging the native APIs.

So, the ground rules for the successful implementation of DevOps are as follows:

- One repository
- One framework or *way of working*
- A unified toolset that can target multi-cloud environments

In terms of one framework, SAFe by Scaled Agile should be mentioned. **SAFe** stands for **Scaled Agile Framework**, and it's used by a lot of enterprises as the foundation of DevOps. One of the key assets of SAFe is the Agile Release Train.

The Agile Release Train is built around the principle of the standardization of application development and the release management of code. This is done by automating everything:

- Build by automating the process of compiling the code
- Automated test of units, acceptance, performance, and load
- Continuous integration, automated by running integration tests and releasing units that can be deployed to production
- Continuous deployment, by automated deployments to different environments of the version-controlled code
- Additional automation tools for configuration, provisioning, security by design, code review, audit trail, logging, and management

This supports the application life cycle management, the continuous improvement, and release of the application code. Details and courseware on SAFe can be found at `https://www.scaledagileframework.com/DevOps/`.

# Exploring tooling for CI/CD

The tooling landscape for CI/CD and DevOps is massive and changes almost every month. A good overview is provided by Digital.ai at `https://digital.ai/periodic-table-of-DevOps-tools`; Digital.ai maintains and publishes the Periodic Table of DevOps. It's based on the format of the periodic table of elements, but contains an overview of various tools to execute DevOps in cloud environments. It also explains how to build a pipeline diagram using the tools that are selected from the periodic table.

There's no right or wrong answer in choosing the toolset, as long as it fits the need of the enterprise and people are trained in the usage of the tools. In this section, the native CI/CD tooling in the major clouds are discussed: Azure DevOps, AWS CodePipeline and CloudFormation, and Google Cloud Build.

## Working with Azure DevOps

Azure DevOps enables teams to build and deploy applications; it caters for the full development cycle. Azure DevOps contains the following:

- **Boards**: This is the planning tool in Azure DevOps and supports scheduling with Kanban and Scrum. Kanban works with cards, moving tasks through stages, while Scrum works with short sprints to accomplish tasks.
- **Repos**: This is the repository in Azure DevOps for version control, based on Git or **Team Foundation Version Control** (**TFVC**). The term Team Foundation still refers back to the original name of Azure DevOps: Visual Studio **Team Foundation Server** (**TFS**).
- **Pipelines**: This is the CI/CD functionality in Azure DevOps, which supports the build and releases of code to cloud environments. It integrates with **Repos** and can execute scheduled tasks from **Boards**.
- **Test Plans**: This allows teams to configure test scripts, manually and automated.
- **Artifacts**: This feature allows developers to share code packages for various sources and integrate these into pipelines or other CI/CD tooling. **Artifacts** supports Maven, **Node Packet Manager** (**NPM**, for Node.js and JSON), and NuGet packages.

The following screenshot shows the main menu of Azure DevOps with a project defined as Scrum that divides the work items in backlog items and sprints:

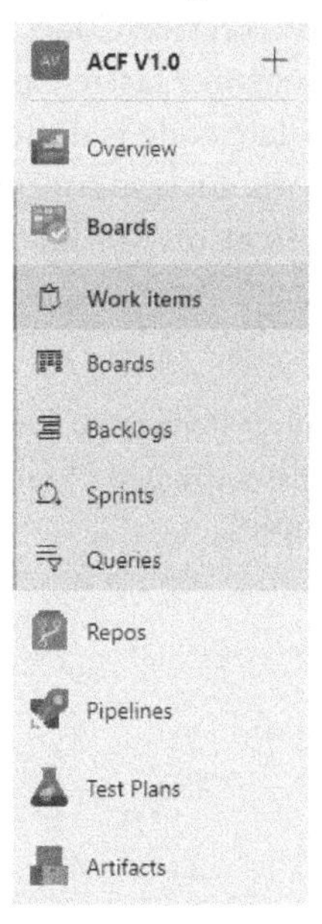


Figure 18.5 – Main menu of Azure DevOps

When a team starts in Azure DevOps, the first thing to do is to define a project and assign project members. Next, the project manager or product owner defines the development methodology. Depending on that choice, DevOps presents the possibilities to define work items, such as features, backlog items and tasks, and a board to plan the execution of these items. A work item or product can be a piece of code that may be deployed; in DevOps, this can be automated with Azure Pipelines, which after review actually deploys the code to the target cloud environment.

Developers can use Azure DevOps for AWS too, using the AWS Toolkit for Azure DevOps. The toolkit even accepts the use of AWS CloudFormation templates to provision and update AWS resources within Azure DevOps. In the *Further reading* section, a link to the documentation has been added.

## Working with AWS CodePipeline

AWS CodePipeline is the CI/CD tool for AWS and offers development teams a tool to deploy applications and infrastructure resources. CodePipeline provides the following:

- **Workflow modeling**: You could see this as the planning tool in CodePipeline. Workflow modeling defines the different stages for the release of code: build, test, and deploy. Teams can create tasks that need to be executed in the different stages.
- **Integrations**: As any CI/CD tool, CodePipeline works with version control for the source code. With Integrations, developers can use various sources, such as GitHub, but also the native AWS service CodeCommit (the default in the main menu of CodePipeline), Amazon **Elastic Container Registry** (**ECR**), and Amazon S3. Provisioning and update code is done with AWS CloudFormation. AWS Integrations can do a lot more, such as continuous delivery to serverless applications with **Serverless Application Model** (**SAM**) and automating triggers with AWS Lambda functions to test whether application code has been deployed successfully.
- **Plugins**: It looks like AWS mainly uses its own tools, but developers absolutely have freedom of tools. AWS Plugins allow the use of GitHub for version control and Jenkins for deployment, for example.

The following screenshot shows the main menu of CodePipeline:

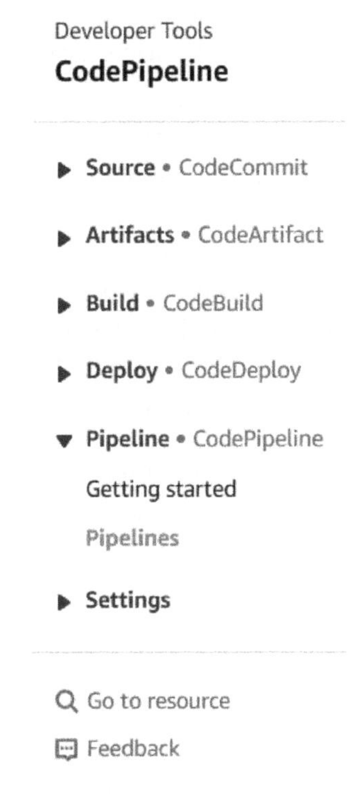


Figure 18.6 – The main menu of AWS CodePipeline

As shown in the screenshot, creating a pipeline from the CodePipeline main menu will start by pulling code from a repository that sits in CodeCommit. The pipeline itself is built in CodeBuild and deployed in CodeDeploy.

Be aware that Artifacts is not the same as it is in Azure. In AWS, Artifacts uses a S3 artifacts bucket where CodePipeline stores the files to execute actions in the pipeline.

## Working with Google Cloud Build

The CI/CD tool in GCP is Cloud Build. The main functions in Cloud Build are as follows:

- **Cloud Source Repositories**: These are private Git repositories that are hosted on GCP. This is where the pipeline workflow starts: developers can store, access, and pull code from this repository using Cloud Build and Cloud Pub/Sub. Creating a repository can be done through the GCP UI portal or Google Cloud Shell with the `gcloud source repos create` command. After the creation of the repository, developers can start pushing code to it with the `git add`, `git commit`, and `git push` commands from the `gcloud` console.

- **Artifact Registry**: This is basically the same service as Artifacts in Azure DevOps. It allows the creation and management of repositories that hold Maven and NPM packages. In GCP, **Artifact Registry** is also used to create repositories for Docker container images.
- **Cloud Build**: This is the engine of the CI/CD functionality in GCP. In Cloud Build, developers define the pipelines. It imports source code from Cloud Source Repositories, but can also pull code from other sources, such as GitHub. Cloud Build tests and deploys the code to the targeted GCP infrastructure. Cloud Build integrates with a lot of different solutions – for example, with Jenkins and the open source tool Spinnaker for automated testing and continuous delivery. These solutions can also be used to work with the **Google Kubernetes Engine** (**GKE**) to enable CI/CD on container platforms running Kubernetes.

The following screenshot shows the menu of Cloud Build:

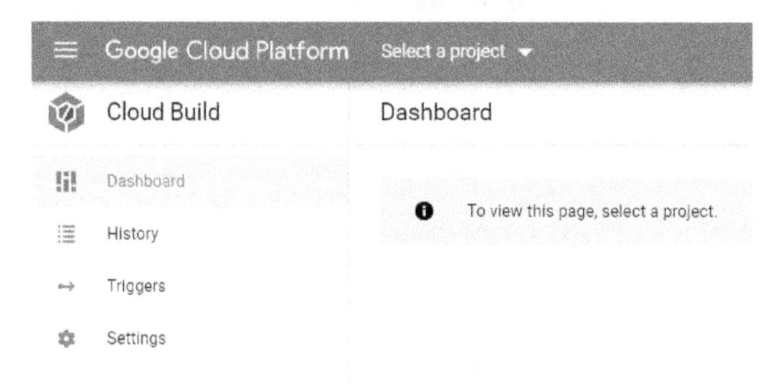


Figure 18.7 – Introduction screen to start with Cloud Build in the GCP console

The main menu is very lean, as shown in the preceding screenshot. Only when a project is defined and started can developers start using Cloud Build to create the code repository. That service is available from the console, as shown in the following screenshot:

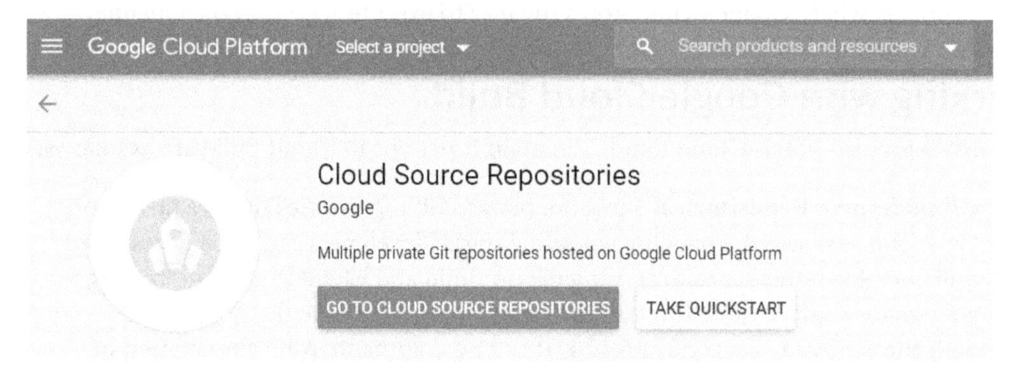


Figure 18.8 – Starting a repository in GCP's Cloud Source Repositories

In this section, the native CI/CD toolsets of Azure, AWS, and GCP have been discussed. At the beginning of the section, it was mentioned that there are a lot of tools available to developers for developing, storing, testing, and deploying code. The main principles of CI/CD are the same, but there are differences in the way that these tools deploy code and especially how they test and validate code in an automated way. The tools discussed - Azure DevOps, AWS CodePipeline, and GCP Cloud Build - may cover a lot of functionality already, but typically, additional tools are required. In the *Further reading* section, some suggestions are provided for study material to help in choosing the right tools.

# Summary

After completing this chapter, you should have a good understanding of the DevOps way of working and the use of CI/CD pipelines in cloud environments. Everything is code in cloud, from the application to the infrastructure and the configuration. Code needs to be stored in a central repository and brought under version control. That's where the CI/CD pipeline starts. Next, the DevOps team defines the phases of the pipeline, typically build, test, and deploy. Actions in these phases are automated as much as possible.

We discussed the push and pull principles in CI/CD pipelines using master and feature branches, describing the different methodologies to push and commit code to branches. If teams work consistently from one repository and with a unified way of working, they can deploy code to different clouds. Teams also need tooling: the last section provided an overview of the native CI/CD tooling in Azure, AWS, and GCP, working with Azure DevOps, AWS CodePipeline, and Cloud Build in GCP.

In the next chapter, the final concept for operations will be discussed: AIOps.

# Questions

1. Systems must meet the acceptance criteria before it's signed off as ready. In DevOps, a specific term is used for this sign off - what is that term?
2. What is a commonly used framework for working in DevOps structures?
3. Azure DevOps has a specific tool for agile planning, such as Kanban or Scrum. What is this tool called?
4. Rate the following statement true or false: Artifact Registry in Google Cloud Build also supports Docker images.

# Further reading

You can refer to the following links for more information on the topics covered in this chapter:

- **DevOps Agile Skills Association** (**DASA**): `https://www.DevOpsagileskills.org/`
- Documentation on Azure DevOps: `https://docs.microsoft.com/en-us/azure/DevOps/get-started/?view=azure-DevOps`
- Information on integrating Azure DevOps with AWS: `https://aws.amazon.com/vsts/`
- Documentation on AWS CodePipeline: `https://aws.amazon.com/codepipeline/`
- Documentation on Google Cloud Build: `https://cloud.google.com/docs/ci-cd/`
- *Hands-On DevOps for Architects*, by Bob Aiello, Packt Publishing

# 19
# Introducing AIOps in Multi-Cloud

**AIOps** stands for **Artificial Intelligence for Operations**, but what does it really mean? AIOps is still a rather new concept but can help to optimize your multi-cloud platform. It analyzes the health and behavior of workloads end-to-end – that is, right from the application's code all the way down to the underlying infrastructure. AIOps tooling will help in discovering issues, thereby providing advice for optimization. The best part is that good AIOps tools do this cross-platform since they operate from the perspective of the application and even the business chain.

This chapter is an introduction to the concept of AIOps. The components of AIOps will be discussed, including data analytics, automation, and **Machine Learning** (**ML**). After completing this chapter, you will have a good understanding of how AIOps can help in optimizing cloud environments and how enterprises can get started with implementing AIOps. The chapter concludes with a brief overview of some market-leading tools in this space.

In this chapter, we're going to cover the following main topics:

- Understanding the concept of AIOps
- Optimizing cloud environments using AIOps
- Exploring AIOps tools for multi-cloud

# Understanding the concept of AIOps

AIOps combines analytics of big data and ML to automatically investigate and remediate incidents that occur in the IT environment. AIOps systems learn how to correlate incidents between the various components in the environment by continuously analyzing all logging sources and the performance of assets within the entire IT landscape of an enterprise. They learn what the dependencies are inside and outside of IT systems.

Especially in the world of multi-cloud, where enterprises have systems in various clouds and still on-premises, gaining visibility over the full landscape is not easy. How would an engineer tell that the bad performance of a website that hosts its frontend in a specific cloud is caused by a bad query in a database that runs from a data lake in a different cloud?

AIOps requires highly sophisticated systems, comprising the following components:

- **Data analytics**: The system gathers data from various sources containing log files, system metrics, monitoring data, and also data from systems outside the actual IT environment, such as posts on forums and social media. A peak of incidents logged into the systems of the service desk may also be a source. AIOps systems will aggregate the data, look for trends and patterns, and compare these to known models. This way, AIOps is able to determine issues quickly and accurately.
- **ML**: AIOps uses algorithms. In the beginning, it will have a baseline that represents the normal behavior of systems, applications, and users. Applications and the usage of data and systems might change over time. AIOps will constantly evaluate these new patterns and learn from them, teaching itself what the new normal behavior is and what events will create alerts. From the algorithm, AIOps will prioritize events and alerts and start remediating actions.
- **Automation**: This is the heart of AIOps. If the system detects issues, unexpected changes, or abnormalities in behavior, it will prioritize and start remediation. It can only do that when the system is highly automated. From the analytics output and the algorithm, AIOps systems can determine what the best solution is to solve an issue. If a system runs out of memory because of peak usage, it can automatically increase the size of memory. Some AIOps systems may even be capable of predicting the peak usage and already start increasing the memory before the actual usage occurs, without any human intervention. Be aware that cloud engineers will have to allow this automated scaling in the cloud systems themselves.

- **Visualization**: Although AIOps is fully automated and self-learning, engineers would want to have visibility of the system and its actions. For this, AIOps offers real-time dashboards and extensive ways of creating reports that will help in improving the architecture of systems. That's the only thing AIOps will not do: it will not change the architecture. Enterprises will still need cloud architects for that. The next section discusses how AIOps can help in improving cloud environments.

AIOps is a good extension of DevOps, where enterprises automate the delivery, deployment, and operations of systems. With AIOps, they can automate operations. Is there something after AIOps? Yes, it's called **NoOps**, or **No IT Operations**, where all operational activities are fully automated. The idea here is that teams can completely concentrate on development. All daily management routines on IT systems are taken over by automated systems, such as system updates, bug fixing, scaling, and security operations. Although it's called NoOps, engineers will still be needed to set up the systems and implement the operation's baseline.

# Optimizing cloud environments using AIOps

The two major benefits of AIOps are first, the speed and accuracy in detecting anomalies and responding to them without human intervention. Second, AIOps can be used for capacity optimization. Most cloud providers offer some form of scale-out/-up mechanism driven by metrics, already available natively within the platform. AIOps can optimize this scaling since it knows what thresholds are required to do this, whereas the cloud provider requires engineers to define and hardcode it. Since the system is learning, it can help in predicting when and what resources are needed. The following diagram shows the evaluation of operations, from descriptive to prescriptive. Most monitoring tools are descriptive, whereas AIOps is predictive:

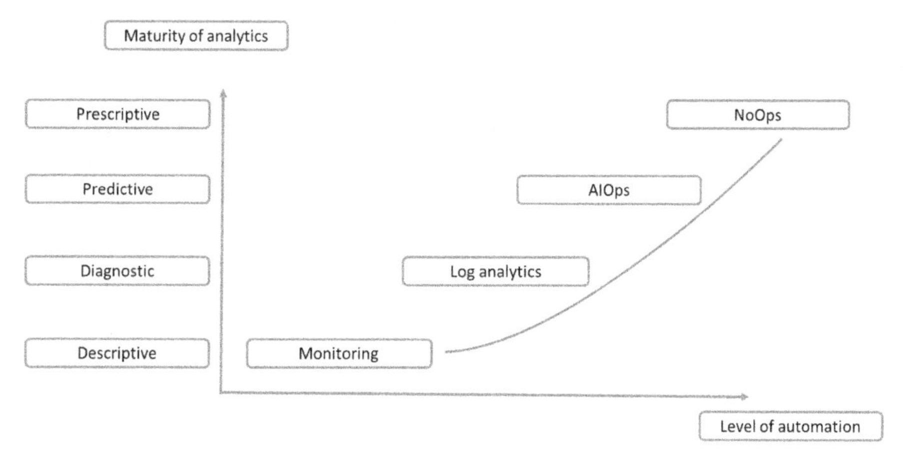


Figure 19.1 – Evolution of monitoring to AIOps

Monitoring simply registers what's happening. With log analytics, companies can set a diagnosis of events and take remediation actions based on the outcomes of these analyses This is all reactive, whereas AIOps is proactive and predictive. By analyzing data, it can predict the impact of changes. The last step is systems that are prescriptive, being able to tell what should happen and already prepare systems for events, fully automated. Some very sophisticated AIOps systems can already do that, but generally, market analysts see this as the domain of NoOps.

Enterprises are discovering AIOps because it helps them in optimizing the IT infrastructure. But how do companies start with AIOps? The following guidelines are recommended to successfully implement an AIOps strategy:

- **AIOps systems are learning systems**: Enterprises will have to learn to work and interpret analysis from these systems as well to get the best out of it. So, don't try to get the entire IT environment under AIOps in one go, but start with a small pilot and iterate from there.
- **Data is essential in AIOps**: This should not only be data that comes from IT systems, but also business data. After all, the great benefit of AIOps is that it can take actions that are based on business data. If AIOps knows that certain products sell better at specific times of the year – which is business-driven data – it can take actions to optimize IT systems for that peak period. Also, if it turns out that systems are not used as expected, AIOps will be able to analyze the usage and correlate it with other events. In that way, AIOps can be a fantastic source for the business in becoming a truly data-driven organization. Businesses, therefore, absolutely need to be involved in the implementation of AIOps.
- **Most important in a successful implementation is to standardize**: Throughout this book, it has been stressed that multi-cloud environments need to be implemented in a consistent way, meaning that infrastructure must be defined as infrastructure and configuration as code so that it can be deployed in a consistent manner to various cloud platforms. The code must be centrally managed from one repository, as much as possible. This will ensure that AIOps systems will learn quickly how systems look and how they should behave so that anomalies can be detected quickly.

Next, how does AIOps help in optimizing IT environments? As explained in the *Understanding the concept of AIOps* section, AIOps can best be seen as an extension to DevOps: it helps development in optimizing systems. The key is in testing. In the previous chapter, the principles of CI/CD were discussed. An important phase in CI/CD is testing. Typically, developers test against the functionality of one application first with unit testing and then integration with other applications or systems. The problem is that developers can't test everything; for instance, they can't test against scenarios where system components in an IT chain change. These can be changes that theoretically might not have a major impact, but in real life do or even trigger completely unexpected behavior.

AIOps can help in testing against real-life scenarios and take much more into consideration in terms of testing. AIOps will know what systems would be impacted when changes are applied to a certain system and also vice versa: what systems will respond to changes in terms of performance and stability. These can be systems that are hosted in different clouds or platforms; they can be part of the application chain.

This problem of the coexistence of applications and systems that disproportionately consume resources is referred to as noisy neighbor. AIOps will identify the neighbors, warn them of upcoming changes, and even take proactive measures to avoid the applications and systems from running into trouble. This goes beyond the unit and integration tests that are triggered by a CI/CD pipeline.

Today's environments in multi-cloud are complex, with servers and services running in various clouds. Systems are connected over network backbones of different cloud platforms, routing data over the enterprise's gateways, yet continuously checking whether users and systems are still compliant against applied security frameworks. There's a good chance something is missed when distributing applications across these environments.

AIOps can be used to improve the overall architecture. Architects will have much better insight into the environment and all the connections between applications and systems; this includes not only servers but also network and security devices. Next, AIOps will help in the distribution of applications across platforms and the scaling of infrastructure without impacting the neighbors, even if the neighbors are sitting on a different platform.

## Exploring AIOps tools for multi-cloud

The market for AIOps is in its infancy, although market analysts expect that use of AIOps will grow from around the current 5 percent to 30 percent of big enterprises in 2023 (refer to `https://www.gartner.com/smarterwithgartner/how-to-get-started-with-aiops/`). This explains why a lot of leading IT companies are investing heavily in AIOps. Manufacturers include big names such as IBM, Splunk, VMware, Moogsoft, Dynatrace, BMC, and ServiceNow. But there are a lot more tools that are certainly worthwhile to have a look at, such as DataDog, ExtraHop, FixStream, Grok, and StackState, just to name a few.

How does an enterprise choose the right tool? When an enterprise is working in multi-cloud, it needs AIOps that can handle multi-cloud. These are AIOps platforms that have APIs to the major cloud providers and can integrate with the monitoring solutions of these providers and third-party tools that enterprises have in the cloud environments. An example of such a platform is Splunk Enterprise, which collects, correlates, and analyzes data from IT infrastructure, applications, and security systems.

In essence, all of these tools work in layers. The layers are depicted in the following diagram:

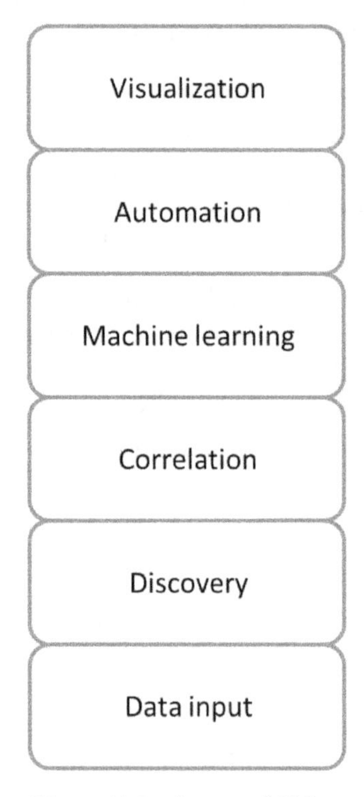


Figure 19.2 – Layers of AIOps

Most AIOps systems combine a set of tools in the different layers into an AIOps platform that can handle the various aspects of AIOps.

Splunk is one of the platforms that have a wide variety of products that can support development and operations in an enterprise. The suite contains the following products, among others:

- Splunk Cloud to manage infrastructure in any cloud.
- Splunk User Behavior Analytics to detect threats and anomalies in behavior using ML.
- Splunk Phantom for cross-platform security orchestration and automating specific solutions, such as Splunk Insights for AWS Cloud Monitoring. The latter is a solution that offers tools to migrate mission-critical workloads to AWS, monitor them, gain insights into costs, and keep track of security and compliance.

All these solutions come together in Splunk Enterprise.

Comparable solutions are ServiceNow, Dynatrace, and StackState, the latter being recognized by market analysts as a platform that will grow significantly in the coming years and might become one of the market leaders, according to a Gartner report, shown here: `https://www.gartner.com/en/documents/3971186` (be aware that a login is required to download reports from Gartner). ServiceNow has the Now Platform, connecting various solutions to get visibility of all IT systems in any environment to detect issues, automate workflows and responses, and manage security. Dynatrace works with Davis, the AI solution of Dynatrace. StackState follows the **4T** model – **time**, **topology**, **telemetry**, and **tracing**. It actually visualizes changes in the full, cross-cloud environment so that operators can time travel and spot where changes have occurred. To do that, the systems correlate infrastructure data from all layers, such as applications, databases, servers, operating systems, and traffic routing through network and security devices.

Key in all these solutions is that they auto-discover any changes in environments in real time, and can predict the impact on any other component in the IT environment before events actually occur, also from changes that are planned from CI/CD pipelines.

AIOps helps enterprises in becoming data-driven organizations. From the first chapter of this book, the message has been that IT – and IT architecture – is driven by business decisions. But business itself is driven by data: how fast does a market develop, where are the customers, what are the demands of these customers, and how can IT prepare for these demands? The agility to adapt to market changes is key in IT and that's exactly what cloud environments are for – that is, cloud systems can adapt quickly to changes. It becomes even faster when data drives the changes directly, without human interference. Data drives every decision.

That's the promise of AIOps. An organization that adopts the principle of becoming a data-driven enterprise must have access to vast amounts of data from a lot of different sources, inside and outside IT. It needs to embrace automation. But above all, it needs to trust and rely on sophisticated technology with data analytics, AI, and ML. That's a true paradigm shift for a lot of companies. It will only succeed when it's done in small steps. The good news is that companies already have a lot of business and IT data available that they can feed into AI and ML algorithms. So, they can get started.

# Summary

AIOps is the new kid on the block. These are complex systems that help organizations in detecting changes and anomalies in their IT environments and already predict what impact these events might have on other components within their environments. AIOps systems can even predict this from planned changes coming from DevOps systems such as CI/CD pipelines. To be able to do that, AIOps makes use of big data analysis: it has access to a lot of different data sources, inside and outside IT environments. This data is analyzed and fed into algorithms: this is where **AI** comes in, and ML. AIOps systems learn so that they can actually predict future events.

AIOps are complex systems that require vast investments from vendors and thus from companies that want to start working with AIOps. However, most organizations want to become more and more data-driven, meaning that data is driving all decisions. This makes a company more agile and faster in responding to market changes.

After completing this chapter, you should have a good understanding of the benefits as well as the complexity of AIOps. You should also be able to name a few of the market leaders in the field of AIOps. At the end of the day, it's all about being able to respond quickly to changes, but with minimum risk and keeping IT systems running at all times. That is what the final chapter of this book is about: site reliability engineering.

# Questions

1. AIOps correlates data from a lot of different systems, including IT systems that are not directly in the delivery chain of an application, but might be impacted by changes to that chain. What are these systems called in terms of AIOps definitions?
2. Name at least two vendors of AIOps systems, recognized as such by market analysts.
3. AIOps works in layers. Rate the following statement true or false: most AIOps systems have separate solutions for the layers that are combined in an AIOps platform.
4. In terms of the level of automation, would you rate NoOps before or after AIOps?

# Further reading

You can refer to the blog and video on AIOps at `https://searchitoperations.techtarget.com/feature/Just-what-can-AI-in-IT-operations-accomplish`.

# 20
# Introducing Site Reliability Engineering in Multi-Cloud

This book has dealt with designing, implementing, and controlling a multi-cloud platform. That said, we have built that for a reason—to host applications. Applications cannot live without infrastructure, and infrastructure is useless without apps. Controlling an environment means controlling applications and infrastructure. Google has the answer: **Site Reliability Engineering** (**SRE**). SRE incorporates aspects of software engineering and applies them to infrastructure and operations problems.

How would that work in multi-cloud? After completing this chapter, you will have a good understanding of the concept behind SRE. You will learn that SRE is driven by risk analysis that determines the **service-level objective** (**SLO**). Next, the monitoring of the SLO is discussed, since reliability is something that can be measured, and for that, teams need observability. In the last section, the implementation of SRE is studied, including a brief introduction to the main principles of SRE.

In this chapter, we're going to cover the following main topics:

- Understanding the concept of SRE
- Working with risk analysis in SRE
- Applying monitoring principles in SRE
- Applying principles of SRE to multi-cloud – building and operating distributed systems

# Understanding the concept of SRE

Originally, SRE was meant for mission-critical systems, but overall, it can be used to drive the DevOps process in a more efficient way. The goal is to enable developers to deploy infrastructure quickly and without errors. To achieve this, the deployment is fully automated. In this way of working, operators will not be swamped with requests to constantly onboard and manage more systems.

The original description of SRE as invented by Google is well over 400 pages long. In the *Further reading* section, a good book is listed to have a real deep dive into SRE. This chapter is merely an introduction.

Key terms in SRE are **service-level indicators** (**SLI**), SLO, and the error budget, the number of failures that lead to the unavailability of a system. The terms are explained in more detail in the next paragraphs.

SLI and SLO differ from **SLA**, the **service-level agreement**. The SLA is an agreement between the supplier of a service and the end user of that service. SLAs comprise of **key performance indicators** (**KPIs**), typically indicators about the uptime of systems. For example, an SLA may contain an uptime – or **mean time to failure** (**MTTF**) – of 99.9% for a system. It means that the system may be unavailable to the end user for 44 minutes per month, often called downtime. Even the most reliable systems will suffer from failure every now and then, and then KPIs such as **mean time to repair or recovery** (**MTTR**) become important: the average time needed to fix an issue in systems.

Fixing problems can become a large part of the work that operation teams do: in SRE, this is referred to as toil. Explained simply, toil is manual reactive tasks that keep teams away from other proactive tasks and eventually slow down development. SRE is built on the principle that SRE teams have to spend up to 50 percent of their time improving systems, which means that toil has to be reduced as much as possible so that teams can spend as much time as possible developing.

To enable this, SRE teams set targets, defined in SLIs and SLOs:

- **SLO**: In SRE, this is defined as *how good a system should be*. The SLO is more specific than an SLA, which comprises a lot of different KPIs. One could also state that the SLA comprises a number of SLOs. However, an SLO is an agreement between the developers in the SRE team and the product owner of the service, whereas an SLA is an agreement between the service supplier and the end user.

  The SLO is a target value. For example, the web frontend should be able to handle 100 requests per minute. Don't make it too complex in the beginning. By setting this SLO, the team already has a number of challenges to be able to meet this target, since it will not only involve the frontend but also the throughput on, for instance, network and involved databases. In other words, by setting this one target, architects and developers will have a lot of work to do to reach that target.
- **SLI**: SLOs are measured by SLIs. In SRE, there are a couple of indicators that are really important: request latency, system throughput, availability, and the error rate. These are the key SLIs. Request latency measures the time before a system returns a response. System throughput is the number of requests per second or minute. Availability is the amount of time a system is usable to the end user. The error rate is the percentage of the total number of requests and the number of requests that are successfully returned.
- **Error budget**: This is probably the most important term in SRE. The SLO also defines the error budget. The budget starts at 100 and is calculated by deducting the SLO. For example, if we have an SLO that says that the availability of a system is 99.9%, then the error budget is 100 - 99.9 = -0.1. This is where the SRE teams have to apply changes without impacting the SLO. It forces developers in the SRE team to either limit the number of changes and releases, or to test and automate as much as possible to avoid the disruption of the system and overspending the error budget.

  Remember that SRE is about reducing toil in operations. SRE teams are DevOps teams and they have to make sure that they can spend more time in Dev than in Ops. That starts with the architecture of systems: are these systems fault-tolerant, meaning that systems will still continue to run even if one or more components fail? There might be a reduction in throughput or an increase in latency, but systems should still be available and usable.

To detect failures or performance degradation, monitoring is extremely important in SRE. But before teams get to monitoring, building, and operating with SRE, architects need to define the SLO and SLI. This is done through risk analysis, to be discussed in the next section.

# Working with risk analysis in SRE

The basis of SRE is that reliability is something that you can design as part of the architecture of applications and systems. Next to that, reliability is also something that one can measure. According to SRE, reliability is a measurable quality, and that quality can be influenced by design decisions. Engineers can take measures to decrease the detection, response, and repair time, and they can develop systems in such a way that changes can be executed safely without causing any downtime. Architects can design fault-tolerant systems; engineers can develop these.

The major issue is it all comes at a cost, and whether systems really need to be fault-tolerant is a business decision, based on a business case. Already in *Chapter 1*, *Introduction to Multi-Cloud*, we've learned that business cases are driven by risks. Let's go over risk management one more time.

The basic rule is that *risk = probability x impact*. Enterprises use risk management to determine the business value of implementing measures that limit either the probability and/or the impact – or, to put it in SRE terminology: risk management is used to determine the value of reliability engineering. Risk management is also used to prioritize reliability measures in the product backlogs of SRE teams. That is done by following the risk matrix, sometimes referred to as PRACT:

- **Prevent**: The risk is avoided completely.
- **Reduce**: The impact or likeliness of the risk occurring is reduced.
- **Accept**: The consequences of the risk are accepted.
- **Contingency**: The measures are planned and executed when the risk occurs.
- **Transfer**: The consequences of the risk are transferred, for instance, to an insurance company.

If the impact of failure is great, it might be worthwhile looking at a strategy that prevents the risk. This will drive the SLO, how good a system should be. In this case, the availability might be set to 99.99%, leaving only 0.01% for the error budget. This has consequences for the architecture of the system, after all, the risk rating only allows 52 minutes of downtime per year. The diagram shows how business risks drive SLOs in SRE:

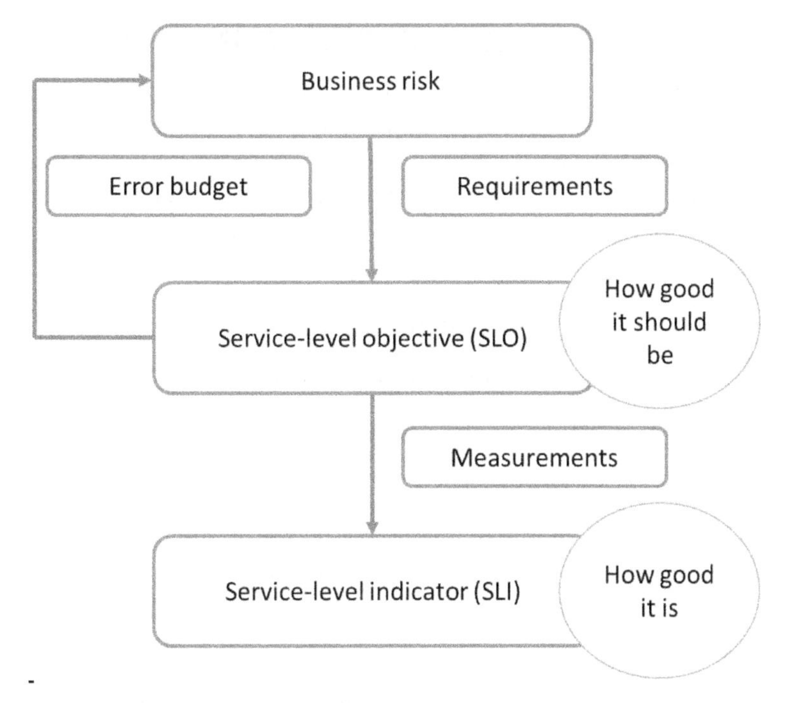


Figure 20.1 – The concepts of SLO and SLI

The error budget is used to control the risks and make decisions that don't compromise the SLOs. To calculate the impact on the SLO, the following items have to be taken into consideration:

- **Time to detect (TTD)**: The time taken to detect an issue in software or a system.
- **Time to resolve (TTR)**: The time taken to resolve or repair the issue.
- **Frequency/year**: The frequency of errors per year.
- **Users**: The number of users that are impacted by the error.
- **Bad/year**: The number of minutes per year that a system is not usable, or the "bad minutes" per year.

An example will make things clearer. A team deploys bad code to an application. It takes 15 minutes to detect that the application is not performing well with this code and another 15 minutes to resolve the issue by executing a rollback. It's estimated that this will happen at least once every 2 weeks, so 24 times per year. It will impact 25% of the user population. This will lead to a number of bad minutes per year. If this is higher than the error budget, then the team needs to take measures to reduce the risk. If the SRE team doesn't do that, it will lead to a lot of work in operations. Engineers will have to spend more time fixing problems.

# Applying monitoring principles in SRE

Reliability is a measurable quality. To be able to measure the quality of the systems and their reliability, teams need real-time information on the status of these systems. As mentioned in the previous section, the TTD is a crucial driver in calculating risk and subsequently determining the SLO. Observability is therefore critical in SRE. However, SRE stands with the principle that monitoring needs to be as simple as possible. It uses the four golden signals:

- **Latency**: The time that a system needs to return a response.
- **Traffic**: The amount of traffic that is placed on the system.
- **Errors**: The number of requests placed on a system that fail completely or partially.
- **Saturation**: The utilization of the maximum load that a system can handle.

Based on these signals, monitoring rules are defined. As the starting point in SRE is avoiding too much work for operations or toil, the monitoring rules follow the same philosophy. Monitoring should not lead to a tsunami of alerts. The basic rules are as follows:

- The rule must detect a condition that is urgent, actionable, and visible to the user. The condition would not be detected without the rule.
- Can the team ignore the alert that is triggered by the rule? What would happen if the alert is ignored?
- If the alert can't be ignored, then how can teams action the alert? For example, if a majority of users are affected by the condition, then the alert can't be ignored, and action must be taken.
- Are there short-term workarounds to improve the condition? This doesn't mean that SRE promotes short-term workarounds, but it does promote actions that ensure that systems are available and usable, even when an error occurs. Remember that SRE is about making systems reliable. And also remember, there's nothing as permanent as a temporary workaround (the origin of this lies in this poem: `https://www.poetryfoundation.org/poetrymagazine/poems/55235/after-a-greek-proverb`). Architects and engineers really should avoid accepting workarounds as solutions.
- Are teams allowed to take action the alert?
- Can actions on alerts be automated in a safe manner?

All monitoring rules in SRE must adhere to these principles. In short, monitoring in SRE is about making a good distinction between signals that require action and noise. Monitoring should only do two things in theory: define what is broken in a system and, next, determine why it is broken, getting to a root cause. Most monitoring systems focus on what is broken, the symptoms. It requires more sophisticated monitoring to correlate data and get to the cause of an error.

Especially in multi-cloud environments, the error of a system can find its cause in a system that is hosted on a different platform. Since this is already complex in itself, monitoring rules should be designed in such a way that teams are only alerted when the thresholds of the four golden signals are compromised, making systems unavailable to users.

# Applying principles of SRE to multi-cloud – building and operating distributed systems

This book exists because a majority of enterprises are moving or developing systems in cloud environments. One reason to do this can be cost efficiency, but the main reason is likely because companies benefit from the agility and speed that the cloud offers. That is driven by customers: their demands are getting higher. Customers and users want more functionality in applications and above all, demand stability in applications. They perceive IT as water from the tap: it's always there. Companies have to make big efforts in making systems reliable, yet able to develop quickly.

Today's enterprises are in a constant transformation mode. This also means a big change for operations. To put it simply, they have to keep up with the speed of change. Traditional operations can't handle this. There has to be a seamless collaboration between developers and operations, DevOps.

But just putting development and operations together in one room isn't enough. It requires specific skills and tools to make it work. That's why Google invented SRE: it's based on the idea that developers define how operations should work. SRE focuses on operations; better said: it focuses on creating solutions to reduce operational issues. By doing this, SRE teams create reliable systems in cloud environments.

There are a couple of important rules to SRE to enable this:

- **Automate everything**: Automation leads to consistency, but automation also enables scaling. This requires a very well thought out architecture. Automation enables issues to be fixed faster since it only has to be fixed in one place: the code. Automation makes sure that the proper code is distributed over all systems involved. With large distributed systems spanning various cloud platforms, this would take days to do manually. SRE was invented by Google, which already had massive services running from cloud services – services that consumers were relying on, such as Gmail. Without automation, these services never would have been as stable as they are today. Without automation, operations would simply be drowned by manual tasks.
- **Eliminate toil**: This is a specific term used in SRE and might be a bit difficult to understand. It's not just work that teams would rather not do; it's every piece of work that keeps teams away from developing. Toil is manual work, repetitive, and can be automated. But toil is also work that doesn't add value to the product: it's interruptive and slows down the development of services that add value. SRE has a rule for toil: an SRE team should not spend more than 50% of their work on toil. The rationale behind that is that toil can easily consume up to 100% of a team's time.

  How does SRE deal with that? This is where the error budget is important again. If the SRE team needs to spend more than half its time on operations and toil, the error budget is likely exceeded. This calls for engineering, typically meaning that systems need to be refactored by the product team that is responsible for the system. Refactoring aims to improve the design and often also to reduce complexity. The following diagram shows the concept of eliminating toil in SRE

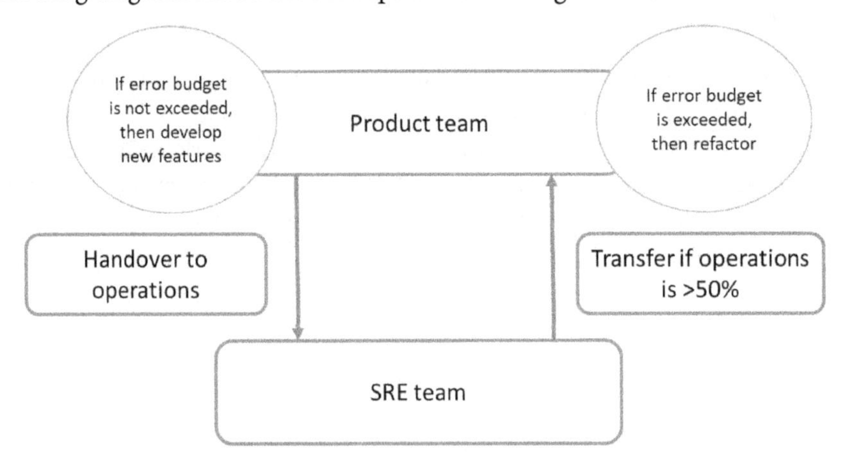


Figure 20.2 – Concept of eliminating toil

- **Keep it simple**: Simplicity is a key principle in SRE. Software needs to be simple as a prerequisite to be a stable and reliable system. As a consequence, SRE teams have a strong mandate to push back against product teams when systems are getting too complex. This is often caused by the fact that code for new features is added, but old code is not removed. Code needs to be simple and clean, the use of APIs should be limited and, if used, APIs should be as simple as possible. SRE lives by the golden rule of less is more.
- **Release engineering**: To keep systems stable and reliable, while changes to developments are applied constantly and at high speed, companies need a rock-solid release process. Google added release engineers to their teams, specialists that are experts in source code management, software compiling, packaging, configuration builds, and automation. In *Chapter 18, Designing and Implementing CI/CD Pipelines*, the principle of branches was discussed. SRE works with the principle of checking in code not directly to a master branch but through feature branches.

  Testing is, as in any pipeline, a crucial gate in the release process. Here, another term is introduced that is more or less specific to SRE: the canary test. It refers to the tests that were used in the coal mines to detect whether shafts contained toxic gasses. To determine this, a canary would be sent into the shaft of the mine. If the canary came back alive, it was meant to be safe for miners to go in.

  In SRE, the canary test refers to a subset of servers or services where new code is implemented. These servers are then left for an incubation period. If the servers run fine after this period, all other servers get the new code. If the canary servers fail, then these servers are rolled back to the last known healthy state.

  > **Important note**
  >
  > Testing is done against the key values of SRE, that is, latency, traffic, errors, and saturation.

- **Postmortem analysis**: Of course, SRE doesn't mean that mistakes will not happen at all anymore. Multi-cloud environments with distributed systems in different clouds will eventually fail. Systems are getting more complex, mainly because of increasing demands by their users. New features are applied at an ever-increasing speed. Systems are getting more and more intertwined, so they're bound to encounter issues every now and then because of a deployment mistake, bugs, hardware failure – remember also that in cloud environments, there is some hardware involved – or, indeed, security breaches.

In SRE, these issues are opportunities to improve systems and software. As soon as an issue has been solved, a postmortem analysis is conducted. It's important to know that these postmortem analyses are blameless. Google itself even talks about a postmortem culture or even a philosophy. Teams register the issue, fix it, document the root causes, and implement the lesson learned. All without finger-pointing, all to grab the opportunity to make systems more resilient.

SRE is about constantly learning. It's about learning by failure and learning by doing. If there's one message that one should remember after completing this book that is multi-cloud architecture and governance is also about learning. Azure, AWS, Google, VMware, and all the other platforms that have been discussed will change constantly. It also means that an organization has to change. That's not a one-time exercise. It's a constant transformation.

# Summary

Systems are getting more complex for many reasons: customers constantly demand more functionality in applications. At the same time, systems need to be available 24/7 without interruption. Cloud platforms are very suitable to facilitate development at high speed, but how do teams ensure reliability, especially with systems that are truly multi-cloud and distributed across different platforms? Google's answer to these questions is **Site Reliability Engineering** (**SRE**).

The most important principles of SRE have been discussed in this chapter. You should have an understanding of the methodology, based on determining the SLO, measuring the SLI, and working with error budgets. You've learned that these parameters are driven by business risk analysis. We also studied monitoring in SRE and learned how to set monitoring principles. In the last section, some important guidelines of SRE were introduced, covering automated systems, eliminating toil, simplicity, release engineering, and the postmortem analysis.

The final conclusion of the chapter and this book is *learn by doing and learn by failure*. The world of multi-cloud is changing rapidly and thus companies will see themselves as being in a constant transformation mode.

# Questions

1. Risk analysis is important in SRE. What are the five risk strategies, often referred to as PRACT?
2. SRE mentions four golden signals in applying monitoring rules. Latency and traffic are two of them. Name the remaining two.
3. SRE has a specific term for manual work that is often repetitive and should be avoided. What's that term?
4. Postmortem analysis is a key principle in SRE. True or false: Postmortem analysis is about finding the root cause and finding out who's to blame for the error.

# Further reading

For more information on SRE, you can refer to *Practical Site Reliability Engineering* by Pethuru Raj, Packt Publishing.

# Assessments

## Chapter 1

1. Latency
2. Storage
3. Software components, not a hardware appliance. Running GKE as a container platform

## Chapter 2

1. KPIs
2. Mission and vision
3. Rebuild, refactor, repurchase, rearchitect, retire, retain
4. VM to container

## Chapter 3

1. Virtual private gateway
2. ExpressRoute
3. VMware NSX
4. Private link

## Chapter 4

1. Yes
2. Yes
3. Active Directory

# Chapter 5

1. Systems of intelligence
2. Business vision
3. True

# Chapter 6

1. Accounts and security
2. Hub and spoke
3. Shared services account
4. The policy of least privilege

# Chapter 7

1. Recovery Point Objective and Recovery Time Objective
2. Debugger
3. True

# Chapter 8

1. Resources
2. Chef Automate and Puppet Enterprise
3. True

# Chapter 9

1. True
2. Azure Lighthouse and AWS Control Tower
3. Pro-active
4. Kubernetes – cross-cloud

# Chapter 10

1. Limited agreement
2. Software asset management
3. Enterprise enrollment and creating departments

# Chapter 11

1. ARM
2. HCI
3. CodeDeploy
4. True

# Chapter 12

1. True
2. Fully Qualified Domain Name
3. Labels

# Chapter 13

1. EA
2. Cost Explorer
3. True

# Chapter 14

1. Confidentiality, integrity, and availability
2. Public and private keys are used to verify the identity of a user before data is transferred
3. CIS
4. False

# Chapter 15

1. Managed identities, managed roles, managed access
2. SAML
3. Eligible accounts

# Chapter 16

1. **Data protection impact analysis** (DPIA)
2. RSA and AES
3. KMS
4. False

# Chapter 17

1. Security operations center
2. REST API
3. True

# Chapter 18

1. DoD
2. SAFe
3. Boards
4. True

# Chapter 19

1. Noisy neighbors
2. Splunk, Dynatrace, DataDog, StackState
3. True
4. After

# Chapter 20

1. Prevent, reduce, accept, contingency, transfer
2. Errors and saturation
3. Toil
4. False – the postmortem is blameless

# Other Books You May Enjoy

If you enjoyed this book, you may be interested in these other books by Packt:

**Hands-On Kubernetes on Azure – Second Edition**

Nills Franssens, Shivakumar Gopalakrishnan, and Gunther Lenz

ISBN: 978-1-80020-967-1

- Plan, configure, and run containerized applications in production
- Use Docker to build apps in containers and deploy them on Kubernetes
- Improve the configuration and deployment of apps on the Azure Cloud
- Store your container images securely with Azure Container Registry
- Install complex Kubernetes applications using Helm
- Integrate Kubernetes with multiple Azure PaaS services, such as databases, Event Hubs and Functions

**Azure for Architects – Third Edition**

Ritesh Modi, Jack Lee, and Rithin Skaria

ISBN: 978-1-83921-586-5

- Understand the components of the Azure cloud platform
- Use cloud design patterns
- Use enterprise security guidelines for your Azure deployment
- Design and implement serverless and integration solutions
- Build efficient data solutions on Azure
- Understand container services on Azure

# Leave a review - let other readers know what you think

Please share your thoughts on this book with others by leaving a review on the site that you bought it from. If you purchased the book from Amazon, please leave us an honest review on this book's Amazon page. This is vital so that other potential readers can see and use your unbiased opinion to make purchasing decisions, we can understand what our customers think about our products, and our authors can see your feedback on the title that they have worked with Packt to create. It will only take a few minutes of your time, but is valuable to other potential customers, our authors, and Packt. Thank you!

# Index

## A

# B

## C

## D



## E

# F



# G

## K



## L



## M

## N

## O



## P

## Q



## R

# S

# T

## U



## V



## W

Lightning Source UK Ltd.
Milton Keynes UK
UKHW051342311022
411392UK00021B/405

9 781800 203198